BLUE PENCILS &
HIDDEN HANDS

BLUE PENCILS & HIDDEN HANDS
Women Editing Periodicals, 1830–1910

EDITED BY Sharon M. Harris
WITH Ellen Gruber Garvey

Northeastern University Press
Boston

NORTHEASTERN UNIVERSITY PRESS

Copyright 2004 by Sharon M. Harris

All rights reserved. Except for the quotation of short passages for the purposes of criticism and review, no part of this book may be reproduced in any form or by any means, electronic or mechanical, including photocopying, recording, or any information storage and retrieval system now known or to be invented, without written permission of the publisher.

Library of Congress Cataloging-in-Publication Data

Blue pencils & hidden hands : women editing periodicals, 1830–1910 / edited by Sharon M. Harris with Ellen Gruber Garvey.
p. cm.
Includes bibliographical references and index.
ISBN 1-55553-613-1 (alk. paper)
1. Women's periodicals, American—History—19th century. 2. Women's periodicals, American—History—20th century. 3. Women periodical editors—United States—Biography. 4. American periodicals—History—19th century. 5. American periodicals—History—20th century. I. title: Blue pencils and hidden hands. II. Harris, Sharon M. III. Garvey, Ellen Gruber.
PN4879 .B56 2004
051'.082'09034—dc22   2003026144

Designed by Christopher Kuntze

Composed in Scala text with Penumbra display by Coghill Composition, in Richmond, Virginia. Printed and bound by Integrated Book Technology, in Troy, New York. The paper is acid-free.

MANUFACTURED IN THE UNITED STATES OF AMERICA
08 07 06 05 04   5 4 3 2 1

For my beloved mother
BETTY JANE SPERBER HARRIS
1921–1999

CONTENTS

Acknowledgments   ix

Foreword | ELLEN GRUBER GARVEY   xi

Introduction | SHARON M. HARRIS   xxv

PART I APPRENTICESHIP

Editing *The Jabberwock*: A Formative Experience for
Nineteenth-Century Girls | LUCILLE M. SCHULTZ   3
    Excerpt from *The Jabberwock*   19

Literary and Commercial Aspects of Women's Editions
of Newspapers, 1894–1896 | ANN MAUGER COLBERT   20
    Excerpt from *The Nashville American*   36

PART II EDITING AS IMPETUS

"Her Object Is Good": Ann S. Stephens and *Portland Magazine* |
JENNIFER BLANCHARD   41
    Excerpts from *Portland Magazine*   58

"Where Women May Speak for Themselves": Miriam Frank Leslie's
"Ladies' Conversazione" | LINDA FROST   60
    Excerpts from *Frank Leslie's Chimney Corner*   75

Frances Wright of the *Free Enquirer*: Woman Editor
in a Man's World | CAROLYN KARCHER   80
    Excerpt from the *Free Enquirer*   96

Lucy Stone and *The Woman's Journal* | KATHARINE RODIER   99
    Excerpt from *The Woman's Journal*   121

Eyes in the Text: Marianna Burgess and *The Indian Helper* |
JACQUELINE FEAR-SEGAL   123
    Excerpt from *The Indian Helper*   144

Pauline E. Hopkins as Editor and Journalist: An African American
Story of Success and Failure | HANNA WALLINGER   146
    Excerpt from *Colored American Magazine*   170

"Yours for the Indian Cause": Gertrude Bonnin's Activist Editing
at *The American Indian Magazine*, 1915–1919 | JAMES H. COX   173
    Excerpts from *The American Indian Magazine*   198

PART III CAREER EDITORS

Antebellum Lady Editors and the Language of Authority |
STEVEN FINK   205
    Excerpt from *Ladies' Magazine*   222

Subtle Subversion: Mary Louise Booth and *Harper's Bazar*
(1867–1889) | PAULA BERNAT BENNETT   225
    Excerpts from *Harper's Bazar*   244

"It has served the truth without fear and without favor": Kate
Field and *Kate Field's Washington* | GARY SCHARNHORST   248
    Excerpt from *Kate Field's Washington*   261

Notes on Contributors   265

Index   269

ACKNOWLEDGMENTS

Special thanks to our editors, Elizabeth Swayze and Robert Gormley. Sincere appreciation also for the instructive evaluations from the two anonymous readers; their thoughtful input has benefited the project as well.

FOREWORD

ELLEN GRUBER GARVEY

MAGAZINES were the United States' dominant mass medium from the late nineteenth to the mid-twentieth century. They helped create a national culture of literature through the sharing of information and perspectives and promulgated and compartmentalized American literature. About 60 percent of Americans were regular magazine readers from the 1920s through the 1960s, following the explosive growth of magazine readership in the 1890s. Women edited an unknown percentage of the thousands of magazines published in the United States in the nineteenth and twentieth centuries.

Women editors were most in evidence in domestic, children's, and fashion magazines. Successful women's magazines such as *Godey's Lady's Book* (1830–1898, edited 1837–1877 by Sarah Josepha Hale) had large readerships; *Godey's* circulation reached 150,000 as early as the 1860s. Men and children read women's magazines too; sailors exchanged bundles of *Godey's* when their ships met at sea, and soldiers asked for other women's magazines. The label "ladies" reassured readers that the work would be concerned with matters of the home and would not be improper or controversial. Yet recent researchers find that some of the work editors did on domestic, children's, and fashion magazines was surprisingly at odds with conventional ideology about women's roles.

The work of many women editors in both the commercial and noncommercial magazine field has remained largely invisible, in spite of the fact that the project of "recovering" women authors that began in the 1970s has extended to identifying women editors. The prominence of writers, often male, associated with some of the magazines women edited has overshadowed the women's work, and the collaborative nature of editorial work itself has made the contributions of individuals harder to uncover and their editorial work, harder to write about. New scholarship on this, however, has sought new angles from which to recover these women's work.

Women's editorship underwent twists and contradictions in the nineteenth and early twentieth centuries, as recent scholarly writing in this field has shown. In general, we tend to hear most about editorial work when there is a famous author involved—most often as part of the trajectory of the writer's rise through discovery by a fortunate editor. In a few cases, editorship is a sideline of a writer's career, often seen as detracting from his or her superior calling of writing—William Dean Howells's editorship of the *Atlantic Monthly*, Theodore Dreiser on *The Delineator*. Willa Cather's work at *McClure's* and Harriet Beecher Stowe's at *Hearth and Home* also fit this category, and so editing briefly enters the spotlight in their biographies. We see their editorships as a detour on the way to something else. Willa Cather was a capable and talented editor at *McClure's*, helping to steer the course of that magazine. Among her other accomplishments, she prompted one writer, who later became a successful playwright, to try her hand at drama. But Cather's readers are grateful that she took seriously Sarah Orne Jewett's opinion that her writing was "being hindered by such incessant, important, responsible work as you have now" and left her editing job (Lee 69, 79).

The work of the magazine editor in general was varied and demanding and could well interfere with a writer's concentration. It included large, well-defined duties like soliciting or selecting the work for the issue, and myriad small tasks. Editors act as crucial gatekeepers, admitting or excluding materials, and as generators of community, inviting readers to see themselves as gathered around the magazine. The community of readers resembles an "imagined community" in the sense Benedict Anderson uses the term for both readership and nation. They will "never know most of their fellow-members, meet them, or even hear of them, yet in the minds of each lives the image of their communion" (6). But membership in these imagined readerly communities was often active and contested.

Editors convene the community of readers buying and reading the magazine and occasionally visible in its pages. Scholars are increasingly exploring these communities. Sarah Robbins, for example, finds real communities of writers and readers corresponding with one another in the principal nineteenth-century Presbyterian missionary magazine, using its letters columns and reports as a network to follow one another's movements from their missions in different countries. Linda Frost's recent research on Miriam Squier Leslie ("Mrs. Frank Leslie") shows readers essentially collaborating to create the magazine. As founder and editor of the family magazine *Frank Leslie's Chimney Corner* from 1865 to 1885, Miriam Leslie orchestrated correspondence into conversation, and set up letters as replies to one another. It is not known if the letters were actually written by readers or by the editor herself. Still, Miriam Leslie's 1865 column establishes the sense that the readers are grouped together in the "Ladies' Conversazione." It allowed readers to participate in an imagined community that closely approximated a real one (Frost).

Editors also act as gatekeepers. In this role women are both assigned attributes of power and are belittled. Editors' power to choose the contents of the magazine and reject other submissions is acknowledged, but writers and scholarly researchers have generally assumed a sharp split between higher gatekeeping functions and seemingly less powerful roles, sometimes classified as housekeeping of sorts. Recent research and reports from editors themselves, however, establish that even the more mundane and less visible tasks guard the gates: Copyediting, for example, has a gatekeeping element in that a published article with faulty spelling will be interpreted by readers as an authorial and institutional failing and will be taken as a sign of other weaknesses of judgment and intellect, calling into question the editors' ability to select material, while clean, error-free copy will help the publication be taken seriously. Copyediting is essential, therefore, to the commodification of authors for the readers' consumption. The readers' approval in turn creates and maintains the magazine's market value. Women's supposed special attraction to detail work has sometimes marked copyediting and proofreading as jobs particularly suited to women, who have then been seen either as nurturers saving authors from their mistakes or as grim punishers of error.

A more minor function, but one that scholars writing casually about magazines tend to foreground, was the writing of editorials, columns with such titles as "From the Editor's Table." While these are highly visible and can be essential statements of the editor's vision, writing them was rarely an editor's main work. Nor is an editorial the only site in the magazine where an editor addresses the readers. In many nineteenth-century instances, editors wrote other material in their magazines under various pseudonyms. In rare cases, as with Charlotte Perkins Gilman's magazine *The Forerunner* (1909–1916), they even wrote the whole magazine themselves.

Women have edited many types of magazines, from scientific journals to trade magazines to high-circulation popular magazines to small-press literary magazines with minuscule circulations. Patricia Okker, in *Our Sister Editors*, mapped the field of the midnineteenth century. Her invaluable appendix listing over 700 nineteenth-century women editors has itself now instigated research into some of them. Those 700 nineteenth-century women editors were heavily concentrated in women's and children's periodicals, though magazines in both categories were read by a larger audience than the names imply.

What was the position of these women's and children's magazines? Editors in these traditional women's ghettos were considered thoroughly respectable—enough so that the U.S. government named World War II Liberty ships Mary Mapes Dodge of the children's magazine *St. Nicholas* and Sarah Josepha Hale of *Godey's Lady's Book*. We may know of fashion magazine editors through the lens of the film *Funny Face* (1957), in which intellect is explicitly set in opposition to fashion, and the glamor-radiating woman editor announces that she will brainwash all the women of America—"no, make that women *everywhere*"—to wear nothing but pink. But reexamination of women's work in such arenas reveals that it was not a stifled, antipolitical field that they settled for, but often had tremendous potential, which they developed. Two scholars recently researching editors of the fashion monthly *Harper's Bazar*, Paula Bennett writing about Mary Louise Booth in the nineteenth century, and June Howard about Elizabeth Jordan in the early twentieth, found that both editors took advantage of the fashion magazine's mandate to be up to date to promote unconventional political ideas as well as the latest trends in fashion.

Women edited some of the midnineteenth-century children's magazines that Lesley Ginsberg has examined. She found editors had coded political messages in their choice of animal stories: abolitionist children's periodicals told stories of animals trapped and chained and demonstrated that a good child's duty was to free them, while in proslavery Southern children's magazines, animals were pathetically in need of helpful care (Ginsberg).

Careers for Women

The title "editor," or the even more genteel "editress," could cover demanding, authoritative, and grueling work. In an 1857 novel by Eliza Ann Woodruff Hopkins (sometimes classified as an autobiography), for example, the narrator is a destitute woman supporting her children. She takes a job assisting the "editress" of the *Ladies' Budget* and complains of working "morning till evening, writing, reading manuscripts, reviewing books, reading proofs" from 8 A.M. to 5 or 6 P.M. and then in her boarding house until 11 P.M. (E.A.W.H.[Hopkins] 337). Women in such positions were routinely paid less than men. The title "editress" implies a diminutive and genteel form of professionalism, and points to the transitional place such women occupied in the public imagination.

Editorial work itself occupied an interesting transitional role for late-nineteenth-century middle-class unmarried women, who were beginning to find it possible to work for wages without losing class standing and who were beginning to think of embarking on careers rather than simply taking up work for money when other sources of support failed. Because many people believed that editing was simply an extension of reading, and perhaps because women had long been associated with fiction reading, editorial work seemed a fitting occupation in which middle-class women could establish themselves. Moreover, into the 1890s, magazine editing had a reputation as a gentleman's profession. Cultured male editors of the elite magazines waited for stories and articles to drop in "over the transom," evaluated the work that came in, and made up their magazines from it. But as Christopher Wilson has shown, that model changed even for the genteel magazines by the late 1890s, as new, aggressive magazines shifted to actively soliciting articles and stories and then competitively publicizing their contents and authors. Work on commercial magazines moved more overtly into the commercial hustle and bustle of business (Wilson).

This period of transition for magazines coincided with shifts in women's expectations of careers. For middle-class women, the gentlemanly aura of magazine editing evidently seemed congruent with sheltered, ladylike work, or at least women were charged with mistakenly seeing it that way. Magazine careers, regardless of the magazine's content, attracted middle-class women. The work seemed genteel and cultured; many women thought working on a commercial magazine would be an ideal use for a liberal arts college education in the first half of the twentieth century. By 1906, one guide to careers for women, written by Anna Steese Sausser Richardson, an editor herself (and later the women's editor of *McClure's* and the associate editor of *Women's Home Companion*), was bent on disabusing middle-class women of their fantasies about magazine work:

> Women have hazy ideas, often grave misconceptions, concerning proof reading and all work for their sex offered by publishing concerns. For some inexplicable reason, the average out-of-town woman imagines that every branch of work connected with the publication of books or magazines is extremely lady-like and elegant. . . . They picture women employees at home, turning out in leisurely fashion the 'work' which is finally shipped by messenger, mail or express to the few poor unfortunates who must remain at the 'shop' and keep the wheels spinning round. . . . Fully half the girls who have led a life of leisure, after leaving boarding school or a fashionable finishing school, and who meet with sudden financial reverses, think they would succeed best as assistant editors. (Richardson 195–96)

Richardson quotes a representative sample letter from an applicant:

> "I have always read the best literature and kept up in current magazines. I write a good hand, and I never grow tired of books. I understand that all editors have assistants who read things for them." . . . Generally the writer adds that she "understands the editorial hours are short and editorial offices elegant and refined."

In the midst of her general book on careers for women, Richardson thus speaks tartly from her role as a magazine worker herself, addressing her book's advice seekers, who are also presumably magazine readers. As I will discuss further below, career books like Richardson's construct and demolish supposedly typical aspiring editors fresh from school as grotesquely naive. These texts suggest that perhaps the magazines had been *too* successful in creating their imagined community of readers: readers now thought of their participation in that community as on a par with the editors' and considered magazine reading essentially identical to editing.

Becoming an Editor

These fierce attacks on the naiveté of such aspirations beg the question of how *anyone* became an editor. Male editors, publishers, and advertising workers of the nineteenth century often wrote about their childhood experiences creating a homemade amateur newspaper on a hand press and using the hand press for job printing, setting their feet on the path of publishing. The act becomes a standard trope in biographies and memoirs of Cyrus Curtis, publisher of *Ladies Home Journal*, advertising man Ernest Elmo Calkins, *Smart Set* and *American Mercury* editor H. L. Mencken, and others (Bok 15–19; Calkins 93–95). Magazine and newspaper advertisements for hand presses were specifically aimed at boys, promoting the notion that only boys' careers could start off this way.

In 1897, a woman job printer, A. Florence Grant of Boston, noted the resulting discrepancy. She explains: "A business woman of today has received her business education in a much shorter time than a man. He is trained from early youth to his career, while the girl is usually overtaken by circumstances and has to learn through experience many things which the boy has been taught" (quoted in Willard 409).

Some girls, however, did take up work that developed into career training. Lucille Schultz's investigation of *The Jabberwock*, a turn-of-the-century newspaper from Boston Girls' Latin High School, begun by the schoolgirls themselves, found several of its former editorial workers in positions of some prominence as writers and editors. Their work on *The Jabberwock* is of interest both as a process itself and because it trained girls for later periodical work.

Girls in other schools—particularly coed institutions—may not have had the same opportunities. One 1916 girls' career book (which elsewhere patronizingly explains that in periodical work, the "editors, the reporters, and the men who rewrite stories, must be able to work under the pressure in a way that is beyond the power of most women") sets readers the "practical exercise" at the end of the chapter to "write a brief for an article on why girls are not as active in conducting the high school periodicals as the boys" (Weaver 172, 175). The assignment leaves current researchers tantalized and frustrated: What answers did the girls turn in for this assignment?

What obstacles were they aware of and how would they have articulated that awareness? Did any rip up the assignment and take over the school paper?

Some girls did become involved in magazine creation in childhood, however. Although the iconic hand press features less often in women's accounts, we do find girls working on amateur newspapers, sometimes handwritten, as in L. M. Montgomery's semiautobiographical novel *The Golden Road* (1910), in which a family of teenagers creates a handwritten paper in the 1880s or '90s. The young people carefully create departments parallel to those in magazines they read and then write partly in parody of them. In the twentieth century, Letty Cottin Pogrebin, founding editor of *Ms*, reports that she wrote and illustrated a monthly magazine at age nine, ran it off on a hectograph, and sold it to friends and family for three cents a copy. Incidentally, she learned an important business lesson when the subscription revenues were entirely devoured by the postage, also three cents a copy (Seal A15).

Even after magazine work's attraction was no longer its gentility, it still seemed different from ordinary business: not simply a job taken to earn money, but—even in commercial magazines—cultured work that would bring a woman into contact with exciting currents of the time. It was particularly attractive to the growing numbers of women graduating from college. Literature was a popular field of study among middle-class college women, and the question "what can one do with a B.A. in English?" was sometimes answered by pointing to publishing. A 1926 career book by a Vassar English professor, for example, investigating the vocations taken up by graduates of his school who had taken composition courses, found publishing and publishing-related work the largest field (Johnson 8). Such a connection was made more explicit when magazines like *Mademoiselle* brought in college girls to work as junior editors on a special issue. The narrator of Sylvia Plath's *The Bell Jar* (1963) works for a month as college guest editor at a women's magazine, where the editorial content is literally sickening: a feast of crab salad displayed for the magazine's readers in its pages flattens the staff with food poisoning.

Even if women liberal arts graduates thought a career on a commercial magazine was the ideal berth for them, many actual magazine employees were more skeptical about whether a liberal arts degree was such a useful qualification for the work. Staff and executives in related media occupations, such as advertising, voiced similar anxiety: were middle-class or college-educated people too distant from the lives and tastes of their readers? *Good Housekeeping* editor James Eaton Tower, writing in a 1910 career guide, expresses a particular anxiety about educated women editors. He joins with Edward Bok of the *Ladies' Home Journal* and other male editors of women's magazines in expressing the need to stake out a special place for male editors of women's magazines, and he does so by claiming that men are categorically superior in this work and assuming that women's real place on a women's magazine is as a kind of consultant:

> A magazine addressed to the mass of women is like a department store, with its manifold branches of trade. Here come in play the instinct and judgment of the daughter of Eve, unspoiled by education—or, rather, over-education. The editors are very like the department store buyers, compelled to get what the rank and file of women want. . . . We editors want representative young women as our co-workers. The right training whether in college or in the newspaper harness, or in both, should make them representative. Plans, ideas, articles, must often be "tried on" a person or persons near at hand . . . those who come nearest to representing the rank and file are the safest guides. (Tower 252–53)

Although women editors would surely have disagreed with Tower's assertion that men made better editors because "the male mind . . . [is] better able to keep the whole field in view," Ida Verdon, managing editor of *Cosmopolitan*, does seem to agree with Tower about the need for editors to be more representative. She is one of several writers who recommends that the aspiring editor work first as a reporter, not just to develop writing ability, but to broaden perspective, mix with different people, develop an understanding of the tastes of ordinary people, and become more "alert and sensitive to the problems of our day. This will be invaluable in your editorial work" (Verdon 134). (*Cosmopolitan* was not then a women's magazine, but a Hearst-owned general interest magazine publishing much popular fiction.)

Although we have seen that work on school periodicals could lead to editorial careers, in this 1928 career guide, Verdon's mock interview of a hypothetical applicant ridicules "an ambitious college graduate" for her limited experience and her belief that her background editing *The Red Robin* at college qualifies her for professional magazine work. *The Red Robin* will be of little use, says Verdon. Instead, Miss White will need stenography, because "we have a small staff and each one must be able to jump in in any emergency. You will find that you will never grow too important to be able to dispense with making a hasty stenographic note in a critical moment" (Verdon 133). Despite the usual connection between the liberal arts college degree and magazine editing, Verdon's nudging of the eager university graduate toward a "business course" in stenography or bookkeeping suggests that her entire education has been misguided, since in U.S. high schools of this period, bookkeeping and stenography were mainstays of a separate commercial track for those not planning on college.

Noncommercial Magazines

Noncommercial magazines were not at all genteel, and glamour was hardly an attraction. Traditionally, political magazines have been examined only in relation to the movements from which they grew. Current scholarship examines them within the history of magazines. Grouping them this way—with those other publications that arrive every month—reveals a new set of connections and contrasts. Craig Monk's study of the early twentieth-century anarchist publication *Mother Earth*, edited by Emma Goldman, reports that although this magazine was bent on agitation, it had in its daily operations problems similar to other "little" magazines. There were also differences: though nearly every other little magazine was forced to publish irregularly at some period, Goldman published *Mother Earth* for twelve years without interruption. Focusing on *Mother Earth*'s position as a magazine foregrounds the community-building work of magazines in general: like many other publishers, Goldman continued to send the magazine to delinquent subscribers. Unlike advertising-dependent publishers who might inflate their subscription list to gain advertising revenues, she gained no profit from this. But when a publisher charges people to belong to a magazine's virtual community and wants them to remain a part of it, the magazine must keep sending issues in hopes of keeping readers in the community so that they will feel sufficiently responsible toward it to contribute. Of course, if money is not the motive but spreading ideas is, then a publisher may prefer to keep sending the magazine out to nonrenewing subscribers, at least to imagine that it is communicating with a readership. The publisher or editor's work of imagining a community into being emerges from the shadows.

Editing a magazine has sometimes been compared to teaching, the preeminent acceptable profession for unmarried nineteenth-century women. But Goldman—like Lucy Stone, Victoria Woodhull, Charlotte Perkins Gilman, and other women editors whose work was primarily in service of a cause—also shared an unwomanly vocation as a public speaker. Stone (for woman suffrage) and Woodhull and Gilman (separately, for various women's rights topics) were among these speaker-editors. The two undertakings were similar. Notwithstanding recent discoveries of the political agendas of fashion and children's magazines, public speaking by crusader-editors highlights the differences between editors of fashion and children's magazines and those of overtly political magazines. Public speaking remained a daring activity for middle-class women even into the twentieth century, and most women editors of commercial magazines avoided it.

Editorial and speech writing share certain characteristics: both are timely, topical, and perhaps less likely to paralyze with the expectation of something more polished or complex. Uses of the podium and the editorial role may be similar. A work for publication may have been given as a speech first, with responses shaping the written version, while feedback from the community of readers may have helped develop a speech. Magazines in this context functioned as a souvenir of the speech, as well as an extension of it, introducing the reader to ideas not discussed in the speech itself. Goldman, for example, sold *Mother Earth* at her talks and rallies. *Mother Earth* allowed Goldman to communicate her ideas more widely, helped by the fact that it staked out a temporal presence like other magazines and could be counted on to appear regularly. It gave daily newspapers serious journalistic copy about anarchism that went beyond bomb-throwing stereotypes.

The surprising numbers of women who started or ran some of the important literary magazines of the twentieth century were attracted not by glamour but by the opportunity to develop and create publication venues for new authors and ideas. Editors such as Margaret Anderson and Jane Heap of the *Little Review* and Harriet Monroe and Alice Corbin Henderson of *Poetry* were largely self-taught, and they invented a new kind of magazine as they went along. Anderson proclaimed, "I began *The Little Review* because I wanted an intelligent life," and proceeded to publish James Joyce, Gertrude Stein, Ernest Hemingway, Sherwood Anderson, and works on gay themes—at the cost of having several issues seized and destroyed for obscenity by the post office (M. Anderson 3). Monroe also made an original and distinctive mark on (and with) her magazine, publishing William Carlos Williams, Wallace Stevens, Vachel Lindsay, and the works of Native American and Hispanic American poets. Yet scholarly accounts of the *Little Review* and *Poetry* have often paid less attention to the actual editors than to Ezra Pound's role as a kind of outside consultant, weighing in from Europe with suggestions of writers.

It is not accidental that these are such sharply gendered examples. The desire to find the single actor, big name, or hero obscures the deeply collaborative nature of writing and editing. Unlike researchers and commentators who have treated editing as a solitary enterprise, new scholarship about magazines now looks beyond the star stories of Pound, Joyce, and Anderson to explore the communities that created the journals. Jane Marek in her *Women Editing Modernism* moved the spotlight not just to women editors, but to the working relationships among them. Lynn Keller and Cristanne Miller note that because many of the modernist women editors of the 1920s "including masthead editors like [Marianne] Moore downplayed their own influence and direction, [they] encouraged their male collaborators or employees to take credit for joint work, or didn't protest when joint work was interpreted as 'his' (with her 'help'), it is still difficult to sort out precisely what roles various women played in the collaborative editing" (Keller and Miller).

New Territory to Be Explored

Researchers studying both commercial and noncommercial magazine publishing have often assumed a binary division between a powerful gatekeeping acquisitions and editorial shaping role—selecting articles, discovering and nurturing authors, and writing editorials—and a subordinate role involving copyediting, correspondence, page makeup, the enforcement of deadlines, and, as Verdon put it, "taking a hasty stenographic note." But as Verdon's 1928 essay affirms, the reality was far more murky, with the two overlapping considerably, especially on smaller magazines. And yet researchers have rarely explored the role of tasks like copyediting on the magazine.

One important strain of feminist literary scholarship beginning in the 1970s sought out and reinterpreted hidden work of forgotten or unknown women authors. Such recovery work is still in process for editors. When 1970s recovery work noticed editors, it assumed that women editors were of interest because they were anomalous—either as heroic pioneers, as *Godey's* Sarah Josepha Hale was for a time believed to be, or as radicals such as *Mother Earth's* Emma Goldman, or exponents of free love such as Victoria Woodhull and Tennessee Clafin, editors and publishers of *Woodhull & Clafin's Weekly* (1870–1876), whose articles precipitated the Beecher-Tilton adultery scandal. In this paradigm the women editors worth examining were the ones working on the overtly feminist or anarchist or working-class magazines. Of course that idea entailed blinders.

While the 1970s burgeoning of women's historiography spurred interest in the lives of the women working in the mills of Lowell, Massachusetts, and therefore, in *The Lowell Offering* magazine they produced there in the 1840s, feminist historians generally found the magazine disappointing. It seemed clothed in gentility and piety, "stilted and conventional" and lacking clarion cries of working-class solidarity or something that might seem closer to workers' authentic voices. But the reexamination of nineteenth-century women's writing that has gone on since, the reexploration of such disparaged forms as sentimental fiction, and the discovery of stances that nineteenth-century readers customarily took in their reading have allowed scholars to reconsider that material (Alves).

The past two decades of work on American women's traditions in reading and writing allow us to read over a century and a half of American magazines edited by women with fresh eyes. Recent work on the print culture and publishing history is allowing us to go beyond seeing magazines as containers for literature to see new aspects—the magazines' role in creating communities, their relationships with one another, and their commercial importance. And new research on women editing periodicals is allowing us to examine and reexamine questions about magazines as a genre: about their creation, about the communities surrounding them, about how women, who might have been excluded from other kinds of careers, created and ran them.

Works Cited

Alves, Susan. "Lowell's Female Factory Workers, Poetic Voice and the Periodical." In *The Only Efficient Instrument: American Women Writers and the Periodical, 1837–1916*, ed. Aleta Feinsod Cane and Susan Alves. Iowa City: University of Iowa Press, 2001.

Anderson, Benedict. *Imagined Communities: Reflections on the Origin and Spread of Nationalism*. London: Verso, 1991.

Anderson, Margaret. "Editorial." *The Little Review* 12 (May 1929): 3.

Bok, Edward. *A Man from Maine*. New York: Scribner's, 1923.

Calkins, Earnest Elmo. *"Louder Please!": The Autobiography of a Deaf Man*. Boston: Atlantic Monthly Press, 1924.

Cane, Aleta Feinsod, and Susan Alves, eds. *The Only Efficient Instrument: American Women Writers and the Periodical, 1837–1916*. Iowa City: University of Iowa Press, 2001.

Frost, Linda. "'Where Women May Speak for Themselves': Miriam Frank Leslie's 'Ladies' Conversazione.'" Paper presented at American Literature Association Conference, Long Beach, Calif., May 2000.

Ginsberg, Lesley. "Babies, Beasts, and Bondage: Slavery and the Question of Citizenship in Antebellum American Children's Literature." In *The American Child: A Cultural Studies Reader*, ed. Carol Singley and Caroline Levander. New Brunswick, N.J.: Rutgers University Press, 2003.

H., E.A.W. [Eliza Ann Woodruff Hopkins]. *Ella Lincoln, or, Western Prairie Life*. Boston: J. French, 1857.

Howard, June. *Publishing the Family*. Durham: Duke University Press, 2001.

Johnson, Burges. *Earning a Living by the Pen: Vocational Opportunities for Young Women*. Poughkeepsie, N.Y.: Vassar College Bureau of Publication, 1926.

Keller, Lynn, and Cristanne Miller. "Gender and Avant-Garde Editing: Comparing the 1920s with the 1990s" *How2*, I: 2, http://www.scc.rutgers.edu/however/vi_2_1999/current/readings/keller-miller.html (26 October 2003), archived at Rutgers' Scholarly Communication Center, 1999.

Lee, Hermione. *Willa Cather: Double Lives*. New York: Vintage, 1989.

Marek, Jane. *Women Editing Modernism: "Little" Magazines and Literary History*. Lexington: University Press of Kentucky, 1995.

Monk, Craig. "Emma Goldman, *Mother Earth* and the Little Magazine Impulse in Modern America." In *The Only Efficient Instrument: American Women Writers and the Periodical, 1837–1916*, ed. Aleta Feinsod Cane and Susan Alves. Iowa City: University of Iowa Press, 2001.

Montgomery, L. M. *The Golden Road*. 1910. Rept., New York: Bantam, 1989.

Okker, Patricia. *Our Sister Editors: Sarah J. Hale and the Tradition of Nineteenth-Century Women Editors*. Athens: University of Georgia Press, 1995.

Penny, Virginia. *The Employments of Women: A Cyclopaedia of Woman's Work*. Boston: Walker, Wise, 1863.

Plath, Sylvia. *The Bell Jar*. New York: Harper, 1963.

Richardson, Anna Steese Sausser. "Proofreading and Work in Publishing Houses." In *The Girl Who Earns Her Own Living*. New York: B. W. Dodgem, 1909.

Robbins, Sarah. "Woman's Work for Woman: Gendered Print Culture in American Mission Movement Narratives." In *Women in Print: Essays on the Print Culture of American Women from the Nineteenth and Twentieth Centuries*, ed. James Danky and Wayne Wiegand. Madison: University of Wisconsin Press, forthcoming 2004.

Schultz, Lucille. "Editing the *Jabberwock*: A Formative Experience for 19th Century Girls." Paper presented at the Society for the Study of American Women Writers conference, San Antonio, 2001.

Seal, Kathy. "Too Much Homework, Too Little Play." *New York Times*, 3 September 2001.

Tower, James Eaton. "Educated Women in Magazine Work." In *Vocations for the Trained Woman: Opportunities Other Than Teaching*, ed. Agnes F. Perkins. Boston: Women's Educational and Industrial Union, 1910.

Verdon, Ida . "Editing." In *An Outline of Careers for Woman*, ed. Doris E. Fleischman. Garden City, N.Y.: Doubleday, Doran, 1928.

Weaver, E. W. *Profitable Vocations for Girls*. New York: A. S. Barnes, 1916.

Willard, Frances Elizabeth, et al. *Occupations for Women: A Book of Practical Suggestions for the Material Advancement, the Mental and Physical Development, and the Moral and Spiritual Uplift of Women*. New York: Success, 1897.

Wilson, Christopher. *The Labor of Words: Literary Professionalism in the Progressive Era*. Athens: University of Georgia Press, 1985.

INTRODUCTION

Women Editors in the Nineteenth Century

RECOGNIZING women in the nineteenth century as editors has been an important aspect of late-twentieth-century scholarship on women's writings and cultural influences. Even when a woman edited a conservative periodical, she cast doubts on constructions of women's limited roles in society by the very act of being an editor. Though the amount of power vested in an editor varied from magazine to magazine and depended equally on the woman's own conceptualization of her role within the publishing establishment, there was no question that editing a periodical moved a woman into the realm of public commentator, of laborer outside the domestic arena, and of someone who wielded power in her own right. The woman editor's role was always one of public performance; some, such as Sarah Josepha Hale, chose to represent themselves as arbiters of conventional womanhood while others, such as Frances Wright, explicitly sought to counter the ideals of feminine conventionality. Wright broached topics considered unfeminine and voiced her opinions in a style at odds with the expounded ideals of female propriety. In both instances, editorial practices by women shifted the landscape of nineteenth-century U.S. women's roles in the publishing world.

Blue Pencils and Hidden Hands offers an extensive view of that changing landscape. Examining the work of editors of regional and national periodicals, the essays in *Blue Pencils and Hidden Hands* extend the work of earlier scholars, as outlined in Ellen Gruber Garvey's Foreword, by exploring the various roles within editing in which women engaged, from apprentices to influential editors. Their perspectives ranged widely due to age, experience, opportunity, race, and their own ambitions. The periodicals studied in this collection are widely different in their sense of audience. Newspapers, even special women's editions, sought a mass audience across several classes. Magazines often were more focused, though nonetheless interested in wide circulation. Although disparate, the radically political *Free Enquirer* and the fashion-oriented *Harper's Bazar* each sought a specific audience not only attuned to particular cultural and political ideals but equally so to a particular range of advertisers for their audience. More diverse in scope were periodicals for newly emerging audiences. The *Colored American Magazine*, for example, recognized its role in bringing to its audience of primarily African Americans who were advancing in education and economic status "the higher culture of Religion, Literature, Science, Music, and Art." Equally diverse were the attitudes toward editing that individual women brought to their experience as editors. This collection broadly examines three types of editorial practices—the apprentice, the women for whom editing was an impetus to other kinds of literary or activist endeavors, and the women for whom editing was their primary work.

Apprentice Editors

Apprenticeship was an important means for girls and women to learn about the nuts-and-bolts realities of publishing, about the challenges involved in producing a respectable periodical, and about the negotiations with authors that were necessary to bring to fruition the quality of writing and ideas that an editor envisioned for her magazine or newspaper. In this section of *Blue Pencils and Hidden Hands*, apprenticeship is viewed through two distinct avenues. In Lucille M. Schultz's "Editing *The Jabberwock*," we see the ways in which young schoolgirls were exposed to the demands of publishing a school newspaper. Several of the early editors of *The Jabberwock* continued their careers in publishing as adults. But it was not only schoolgirls who had opportunities to do apprentice work in the field. As Ann Mauger Colbert observes, some women gained similar experience by editing a special issue. Such apprentice work raises important distinctions between editors who were amateurs and those who were professionals. When feminists of the 1970s began to study women editors—then considered rare figures in publishing—Ann Douglas asserted that women in the antebellum period "were professionals masquerading as amateurs" (85). While a few women of the period may still be viewed in that manner, *Blue Pencils and Hidden Hands* suggests how much that sense of the woman editor changed by the end of the nineteenth century. Yet for women who *were* amateurs but who published a periodical's special issue, the roles of amateur and professional were blurred in ways that bring together important dialogues about apprenticeship, professionalization, and the masquerade necessitated by gender restrictions in the long nineteenth century. Schultz's and Colbert's essays also lead us into the next section of the collection: women editors who used editing as a bridge to a literary career or to political and social activism.

Editorship as a Bridge

Some of the women examined in Part II were one-time magazine editors who gained valuable experience in that role but were interested in other forms of communication as well. Other editors would explore other kinds of literary work but would always keep a hand in editing. As Jennifer Blanchard argues, Ann S. Stephens used her initial foray into editing *Portland Magazine* to establish her cultural authority as both editor and author, thus launching what would remain dual careers for herself throughout her publishing life.

For some women editors, editorial work was a means of self-expression. Among this group of editors, contributions to the periodical were not limited to the traditional sense of editing—shaping the overall scope of a periodical and determining what articles and literary contributions were to appear in its pages. Instead, following in the footsteps of Margaret Fuller, editors such as Ann Stephens, Pauline Hopkins, and Kate Field were significant (or, in Field's case, the sole) contributors to their magazines as well as editors. Hopkins, for instance, wrote not only editorials but also essays, biographies, short stories, and serialized novels for *Colored American Magazine*, helping to establish the quality of its literary sections as well as edit them.

For other women editors, the editorial role allowed them to create a sense of communication—or "conversations"—with and among readers. Periodicals were extremely important to women and girls of all ages as places for exchanges of ideas throughout the decades of the nineteenth century. The young editors of *The Jabberwock* recognized this point; they published a column open to writers of other school newspapers, and they inspired additional contributors by encouraging them to write about the exchanged material. The young readers themselves recognized that such writing was preparatory for speaking on public issues. The idea of sharing experiences and ideas was a comfortable formula of intimacy and education for women, who had a long history of exchanging letters among female schoolmates and friends throughout their lives, an exchange that often included sharing letters with other family members.[1] Educational practices, such as teachers' reviewing students' letters to their parents,[2] and the more public exchange of ideas such as Margaret Fuller's much-copied "Conversations" and, later in the century, the emphasis on exchanging ideas in the women's club movements, made the idea of exchanges or conversations among readers and/or with the editor an important marketing tool for periodicals largely aimed at a female audience. The idea of conversations was continued by editors such as Miriam Leslie who, as Linda Frost details, recognized this conversational exchange was especially important for women who were part of the increasingly mobile populace or who lived in remote areas; their domestic isolation was eased by the print version of a conversation with like-minded women. The transference from oral to printed conversation would have been true even of women in the new urban apartment or row-house environment; where neighbors were often strangers, the conversational nature of periodical exchanges filled a familial or neighborly gap. As important as editor/audience conversations were, they did not carry the threat of being silenced that came with the more overt political proclamations of women editors. Frances Wright and Pauline Hopkins, for instance, both paid a high price—the loss of their editorial positions—for their refusals to compromise their political and moral values in print. This risk was enhanced when an editor chose, like Hopkins, to create a historical record. Then as now, history not only reflected the author's views of the past but, perhaps most powerfully, it helped determine for the future which individuals and which ideologies would be valued. Women in the United States had a long record of history writing,[3] but that record made entering into contemporary political and moral history making no less treacherous for women.

Both self-expression and the creation of a space for exchanges present a form of performance on the part of the editor. In the former, the editor is authoritative, seeking openly to shape opinions; in the latter, the editor presents herself as interested in communal exchanges. Though in the latter role she may be no less interested in shaping opinions, she does so more subtly. Often it was important to the success of the periodical for the editor to be identified or at least to be identified as a female. Even young Abbie Brown knew the importance of this aspect of an editorial persona for her readers at a girls' school. Though she often referred to herself in the third person, she clearly marked herself as female.

In a few instances, an editor wielded a devastating brand of power, as in the case of Marianna Burgess. As Jacqueline Fear-Segal argues, Burgess's sense of racial superiority and power over the children for whom she was writing led to an extraordinary covertness and an overpowering sense of control in the lives of her readers. Creating an omnipotent male persona as editor marked her performance as the most extreme among the editors examined in this collection—but that very extremism also gave her extraordinary power. In other instances, presenting the female editorial voice as one of cultural authority was as much a necessity in shaping the editor's sense of her new role as it was for the reader's benefit. As Jennifer Blanchard notes, Ann Stephens's first published story coincided with her debut as an editor. An astute marketer of her magazine, Stephens was equally good at promoting her own image as a cultural authority. Her assertions that her own productions were gaining important recognition and that she moved in key publishing circles was as much performance for her readers as it was a beginning of her own public recognition beyond the literary and publishing circles of Portland, Maine. For Lucy Stone, a reverse process was enacted. Stone was already well known in the United States and beyond for her lectures against slavery and in favor of women's rights. Her reputation as a firebrand created specific expectations when she helped found and edit *The Woman's Journal*. It was not just editors who were engaged in performance via the publishing industry. For many women readers, contributors, and correspondents with editors, the periodical was a vehicle through which they could try out evolving identities, learn to maintain certain aspects of propriety but also to expand the boundaries of women's increasingly diverse roles in U.S. society.

But performance is a complex system that sometimes aligns and sometimes fractures the many strands of identity involved in the act of taking on a particular role or persona. Where does one's "real" identity stop or bleed into the performed identity? Perhaps nowhere are the complexities of editorial identity, performance, and self so carefully negotiated as in the case of Zitkala-Ša, who moved not only between identities of writer and editor but also across often conflicted lines of Native and non-Native cultures, as James Cox astutely demonstrates in his essay on Zitkala-Ša's editing of *The American Indian Magazine*. Marianna Burgess's persona of the Man-on-the-band-stand is fascinating for its bizarre portraiture of a white woman who finds power and control in a system that means to invest such attributes in white males only. But for all the fascination in Burgess's play with identity, her primary goal is supremacy over Native American children, to control the identity formation of the Other. Ultimately, far more compelling is the struggle for alliance and identity that Zitkala-Ša undertakes to live as a Native woman who mediates between cultures and ideologies. That both women were involved in the Carlisle school only accentuates those differences.

One aspect of identity development that may have surprised some early women editors was the necessity of becoming a businesswoman and facing the financial side of publishing. Few women editors came to publishing with the astute business skills of Mary Louise Booth, but these skills were an essential part of their education as editors. As Steven Fink argues, in the antebellum period the commercial side of business was suppressed in magazines in order to maintain "the masquerade of separate spheres" and of gentility itself. But the realities of the marketplace were altogether different. As Ann Mauger Colbert observes in her study of editors of special women's editions of newspapers, these women were engaged in an "increasingly market-driven world where fundraising and journalism met" (21). Certainly women writers were aware of the financial side of writing,[4] but editors were often required to look at a much broader perspective—the cost of attracting first-rate contributors, and also of advertising revenues, the profitability of their endeavor, and many other facets of the financial realities of preparing a periodical for distribution. If, as Ellen Garvey has astutely put it, the adman was in the parlor, he was also always in the thoughts of the woman editor. Founding a periodical, as many of these editors did, was a costly and tenuous project; even successful magazines and newspapers faced constant production and financial pressures. As Katharine Rodier notes, Lucy Stone described *The Woman's Journal* as "a big baby which never grew up, and always had to be fed" (105). This was especially true for a weekly publication such as Stone's.

If editorship required women to become immersed in the marketplace, it was worth the change in status for these women to have the opportunity to help shape public opinion. As Part II of this collection demonstrates, women editors used the power of their positions to address women's rights issues, but they also had many other, often related political agendas in mind. Some of those causes, already overtly on the national stage, were openly discussed—suffrage, work outside the home, antislavery. But other issues, less acceptable in the national debates of the period, were represented in women's periodicals. Not the least of these was domestic violence. Just as recently recovered nineteenth-century novels, such as Lillie Devereux Blake's *Fettered for Life* (1874), reveal that domestic violence may have been a topic of greater discussion than previously understood, so too does the study of periodicals, especially those edited by women, expand our understanding of the diversity of the topics entering the public domain in the nineteenth century. The process of exposing a range of attitudes was not, of course, without risks. Some periodicals, including Stone's *The Woman's Journal*, became embroiled in publishing opposing opinions on such controversial topics as Lady Byron and the Beecher-Tilton affair. Unlike the genteel "conversations" of other periodicals, *The Woman's Journal, Woodhull & Claflin's Weekly,* and other periodicals that engaged (and helped create) national controversies offered editors, contributors, and often readers the opportunity to engage in heated debate. As controversial—and sometimes biased—as these debates may have been, they were significant contributions toward the reassessment of women's roles in society and their ability to shape pubic opinion.

Race and class issues became increasingly important in periodical literature edited by women. Fanny Wright made both topics central to her editorial work on the *Free Enquirer*. Wright, like Stephens, understood the potential of self-promotion, albeit in far more aggressive terms. Stephens's carefully placed comments about her association with the major literary circles of her region pale against the "clamorous crowd" Wright asserted was awaiting each weekly printing of her periodical. Integral to self-representation for Wright was her vision of egalitarianism in all aspects of U.S. life, and her editorials—like her activism—demand a reconceptualization of class and race matters in America in order to enact the ideal of egalitarianism.

Pauline Hopkins and Zitkala-Ša engaged racial issues but from a perspective of communal exchange. They were editors and writers in a period of extraordinary change in race matters. The African American press flourished in the last decades of the nineteenth century. By 1891, the African American publishing industry had developed to such a degree that it warranted a full-length study, *The Afro-American Press and Its Editors*, which included a section titled "Women in Journalism." Several major black newspapers of the period (including the *Boston Advocate*, the *Washington Bee*, and the *Cleveland Gazette*) were important outlets for women journalists. The *Repository of Religion and Literature and of Science and the Arts*, founded by the African Methodist Episcopal Church in 1858, continued to be a major source for women writers, as did the *Woman's Era*, founded in 1894 by members of the National Federation of Afro-American Women. The emergence of the *Colored American Magazine* in 1900 gave writers significant new opportunities, including Hopkins's position as columnist for the women's section of the journal. Native American women also presented voices of resistance and alternative social visions in this era. In their literary productions, issues of race reflect the other side of the westward movement, which included the 1877 forced march of the Poncas from the Dakota Territory to Indian Territory and the General Allotment Act of 1887, which eliminated Native American rights to own tribal lands collectively. Both as a resistance to such oppression and as an outlet for their creative talents, Native Americans began publishing essays, short fiction, and poetry in periodicals. Two Cherokee sisters, Myrta Eddleman Sams and Ora V. Eddleman Reed, were instrumental in establishing the Native American press by the founding and editing of *Twin Territories: The Indian Magazine of Oklahoma* at the turn of the century.

Both Hopkins and Zitkala-Ša were political activists first and editors second, as a means of extending their activist ideals. Neither found such expression—even in periodicals designed to address race-specific audiences—an easy path to pursue. Each had to negotiate between assimilation, uplift, and resistance to ideologies within their own communities as well as the United States at large. Paternalistic males often thwarted their efforts, and each woman had to struggle with an earlier editor or a publisher who sought greater accommodation to conservative beliefs and institutions than they themselves preferred. Balancing a desire to maintain cultural traditions and to negotiate a changing, increasingly multiethnic world was a challenge of immense proportions.

While both Hopkins and Zitkala-Ša employ reform discourse, they are often writing to quite different elements of their respective communities. The primary audience for the *Colored American Magazine* was middle- to upper-class readers. Little attention was focused on the working- and lower-middle classes in the magazine. Zitkala-Ša, however, faced an audience of distinctly more varied economic status, and, unique to the editors in this collection, she extended her ideas to a global context. Recognizing—even promoting—the class distinctions of one's audience was central to the focus of many periodical editors. The majority of periodicals sought an educated, middle-class, largely female audience. A few, however, such as *Harper's Bazar*, made their mark by aiming for a more elite audience. *The American Indian Magazine* may have had one of the most class-diverse audiences among these periodicals. The need to understand her audience and yet always seek to increase subscriptions often stretched the editor's creative and commercial talents to their limits.

Career Editors

The final section of *Blue Pencils and Hidden Hands* examines editors for whom editing was their primary role in the publishing field. Steven Fink offers an overview of women editors in the antebellum period—what we might term the class period in women's editing of periodicals in the United States—and the important inroads they made in the profession. Their inroads would be followed and reshaped by subsequent women editors. Not the least of these important inroads were confronting the economics of the marketplace and challenging separate-sphere ideologies that privileged gentility over the hard labor of the publishing industry.

While early women's magazines such as *Godey's* and *Peterson's* attended to fashion, it was done largely on a pragmatic, even patriotic plane—patterns for the homemaker-seamstress—though illustrations of the latest European fashions were also included. But these early periodicals in no way rivaled the likes of *Harper's Bazar*, a magazine created for *haute couture*. As Paula Bernat Bennett demonstrates, however, under Mary Louise Booth's editorial direction, high fashion was framed in *Harper's Bazar* by equally trend-setting texts that supported advancements in the women's rights movement. As Zitkala-Ša negotiated between making radical demands for her race and assimilating into white culture, Booth also sought to influence without going to extremes. Less complicated than Zitkala-Ša's diasporic role, Booth's position represents a more common struggle for women of all races: to engage the political while seeming to remain within the realms of family and propriety. From such disparate perspectives, women editors had, ironically, to balance a range of compromises in order to retain their power.

If Booth subtly advanced "gender modernity" (Bennet 226), Kate Field lived that modernity broadly. By beginning her career as an essayist and then journalist, Field followed a long tradition of women who combined careers as author and journalist. Certainly Margaret Fuller is the best-known figure in this tradition, but closer to Field's example would have been predecessors such as Grace Greenwood and Gail Hamilton, both of whom made journalism a major part of their lives in Washington, D.C. Yet Field combined the role of journalist with that of editor of her own periodical.[5] Like Wright, Hopkins, and Zitkala-Ša, Field never separated her ardent political activism from her vision as an editor—and she made that connection the major focus of her life.

The Primary Texts

Perhaps nothing so clearly demonstrates the diversity of women's editorships and the content of their periodicals as the selections from their publications that are included in this volume. Issues highlighted in the Foreword and this Introduction are evident in these selections—and many other aspects of editorial positioning become evident.

The negotiation of one's identity as a female editor is evidenced in Abbie Brown's sketch for *The Jabberwock*, "Going to School." The first editor described in the sketch is a dejected man, worrying about the financial aspects of editing. Yet the final image is of the schoolgirl editor—the observer apart from the more carefree boys and girls of her neighborhood. She is struggling for her dignity in the slippery streets on a stormy day—a perfect metaphor for the young female's understanding that as an editor she is moving into an unknown, often treacherous, but exciting public arena. Just how "slippery" taking the role of editor-in-chief may be is reiterated in Elizabeth Gilman's comic description of her friend's editing of a special women's edition of a newspaper. Balancing democracy and autocracy in the workplace is only part of her vision. Equally important is the subtle way in which the woman editor's emphasis on fashion veils what is, in fact, a political discussion. Thus the "amateur" woman editor's work interestingly parallels that of the high-fashion magazine editor, Mary Louise Booth at *Harper's Bazar*.

Editorials, especially those in first issues, offer a delicate balance between asserting the importance of a periodical (necessary to attract new readers) and asking for indulgence while the magazine finds it legs, as it were. Ann Stephens is especially overt in her claims for *Portland Magazine* and her own sense of a precarious undertaking. Such initial editorials are not unlike the apologia so often included in prefaces of early woman-authored books. Miriam Leslie is representative of the assertive women who feel compelled to balance that trait with the requisite feminine modesty. *Frank Leslie's Chimney Corner* may be intended for the whole family to read by the fireside, but it is described as an emerging "institution" with more than two hundred contributors already at hand. For all of the domestic imagery of the fireside, this magazine is clearly a force with which to reckon. A modest balance between domesticity and the workplace is the most common representation of the editor, however, as depicted in "Our Office" from *The Woman's Journal*. In virtually all of the initiating editorials, a claim is made for the necessity of a new periodical because of what Sarah Josepha Hale termed "this age of innovation"—that is, a moment of cultural change that supports the necessity of new voices in the world of magazine and newspaper publication.

A few periodicals, however, are conceived with a confrontational voice in mind. The 29 October 1828 editorial in Frances Wright's *Free Enquirer*, for example, takes on religious conventions. Wright's style is clearly asserted—it will be anything but "orthodox." Zitkala-Ša also demands "[f]rank discussions," arguing that they are necessary to alleviate the "suppressed emotions of the American Indian" (198). Like Pauline Hopkins and Frances Wright, Zitkala-Ša is tackling historical wrongs, insisting they be publicly exposed and challenged. Thus her rewriting of the Powhatan incident in the July–September 1918 issue of *The American Indian Magazine* not only puts into practice the ideal of frank discussions but challenges the ethnocentric representations of Native peoples by white writers.

Rather surprisingly, didacticism is rare among these texts. Miriam Burgess co-opts didacticism—common in children's literature, a category which *The Indian Helper* fits to some extent—does so out of covert racist ideologies. The seemingly trivial comparison of weeds and flowers in "The Story of a Peach Tree" in fact exemplifies the Carlisle Indian School's insistence on white supremacy and assimilation of Native peoples into the dominant culture.

Editorials and announcements could also be used in positive ways, of course. The publishers' announcement, including a letter from a South African reader, in the May–June 1903 edition of the *Colored American Magazine* works as a vehicle for highlighting the talents of their literary editor, Pauline Hopkins, and for an overtly race-oriented magazine (unlike the magazines for a white, middle-class audience in which race is assumed) to make connections with periodicals in South Africa. The reprinted letter highlights the connections of black peoples of the earth and posits the *Colored American Magazine* as a global force in publishing.

If *Colored American Magazine* and *The American Indian Magazine* are invested in both righting and writing history, *Kate Field's Washington* joins them in understanding the importance of history in the making. By interviewing Susan B. Anthony—"this Nineteenth Century Sibyl"—as she prepares for the 1895 Women's Council, Field takes the convention of the conversation in women's periodicals to another level: that of overt intervention in political practices. By combining hagiography with inquiry, Field captures the editor's power to shape public opinion even as she writes about another woman's long history of that very practice.

Conclusion

Perhaps the most important aspect of studying women editors and the periodicals they produced is understanding how women wielded the editorial pen to influence public opinion. In a century in which women increasingly became a part of the public arena—as teachers, factory workers, writers, lecturers, reporters, shopgirls, physicians, lawyers, scientists, and activists for innumerable reform movements—the woman editor of a periodical became an integral part of the redefinition of women's roles in U.S. culture. *Blue Pencils and Hidden Hands* offers students and scholars a broad exposure to women's editorship and, hopefully, to the field of periodical literature as an immense arena for further study of nineteenth-century literature and culture.

Notes

1. See Joan Hedrick's "Parlor Literature" for a good example of how letters were integrated into family reading practices.

2. Sarah Pierce, founder of the renowned Litchfield Female Academy, used this practice. Such practices were common in the late eighteenth and early nineteenth centuries. For a discussion of this aspect of women's education, see Sharon M. Harris's *American Women Writers to 1800*, especially the selection from Anna Green Winslow's letterbook (51–53).

3. See Nina Baym's *American Women Writers and the Work of History, 1790–1860*, and Sharon M. Harris's *Women's Historical Narratives in Early America*.

4. A study of almost any nineteenth-century woman writer reveals, however, her involvement in negotiating what she would be paid per word or per article, when serialized stories would be published in book form, and other economic aspects of publishing. The most extensive representation of this awareness of marketplace realities was *A Battle of the Books* (1870), written by Gail Hamilton.

5. Greenwood also edited a children's magazine for a few years, but her editorship did not reflect the extent of the political activism Field undertook in her editorial role.

Works Cited

Baym, Nina. *American Women Writers and the Work of History, 1790–1860.* New Brunswick, N.J.: Rutgers University Press, 1995.

Blake, Lillie Devereux. *Fettered for Life.* 1874. Rept., Grace Farrell. New York: Feminist Press, 1996.

Douglas, Ann. *The Feminization of American Culture.* New York: Knopf, 1977.

Garvey, Ellen Gruber. *The Adman in the Parlor: Magazines and the Gendering of Consumer Culture, 1880s to 1910s.* New York: Oxford University Press, 1996.

Hamilton, Gail [Mary Abigail Dodge]. *The Battle of the Books.* Cambridge, Mass.: Riverside Press, 1870.

Harris, Sharon M. *American Women Writers to 1800.* New York: Oxford University Press, 1996.

———. *Women's Historical Narratives in Early America.* New York: Penguin, 2003.

Hedrick, Joan D. "Parlor Literature: Harriet Beecher Stowe and the Question of 'Great Women Artists.'" *Signs* 17.2 (Winter 1992): 275–303.

PART I
APPRENTICESHIP

Editing *The Jabberwock*: A Formative Experience for Nineteenth-Century Girls

LUCILLE M. SCHULTZ

IN February 1888, a student in an algebra class at Boston's Girls' Latin School scribbled a note to the girl sitting next to her that read, "Let's have a class paper." According to Mabel Hay Barrows, a friend of the note-passers who later became an associate editor of *The Nation*, that note was the beginning of *The Jabberwock*, the student newspaper published by the students at Girls' Latin (*The Jabberwock* March 1928, 31).[1] *The Jabberwock* was one of more than seventy-five student newspapers (a conservative estimate) published by private schools or prestigious public schools in the nineteenth century. It is one of the few whose run was uninterrupted (and continues to the present day), and it was, in the nineteenth century, one of a small number of papers from a school for girls.

Abbie Farwell Brown, one of the first editors of the paper, is credited with suggesting that she and her friends name the paper *The Jabberwock*, a word they knew from Lewis Carroll's poem "Jabberwocky" in *Through the Looking Glass* (see Appendix for the Carroll poem as it appears on page 1 of the first issue of the school paper in February 1888). Abbie and her colleagues wrote to Carroll in London and received this reply dated February 6, 1888:

> Mr. Lewis Carroll has much pleasure in giving to the Editresses of the proposed magazine permission to use the title they wish for. He finds that the Anglo-Saxon word 'wocer' or 'wocor' signifies 'offspring' or 'fruit.' Taking 'jabber' in its ordinary acceptation of 'excited and voluble discussion,' this would give the meaning of 'the result of much excited discussion.' . . . Mr. Carroll wishes all success to the forthcoming magazine. (March 1888, 1)

The Jabberwock thus became a site for "much excited discussion" among the girls who worked for it, who wrote for it, who edited it. The four-page monthly paper, over the years growing to eight pages, even to sixteen, routinely included editorials, short articles on school news, letters to the editor, poems, jokes, short fiction, an exchange column with writers of other school papers, an occasional prize-winning composition, and, of course, advertisements from local shopkeepers and booksellers. Predictably, topics for writing included life at school; summer travels; childhood recollections;

accounts of holiday celebrations, both in and out of school; and rhapsodies about past or future vacations.

Student Writing in the Nineteenth Century: An Historical Framework

A sea change in composition instruction occurred in nineteenth-century schools. At the century's beginning, originality as we understand that concept was not highly valued in school. More highly prized was students' ability to demonstrate that they were learning the received wisdom of their culture and tradition. So a popular composition lesson at century's beginning included a teacher's reading an essay to students, perhaps an essay about a Greek or Roman myth; asking students to remember as much as they could; and then asking them to write an essay based on what they remembered (see John Walker's *The Teacher's Assistant in English Composition*, England, 1801; Carlisle, Pa., 1808). Another common pedagogy asked young students to write an essay about an abstract concept, such as "adversity" or "ardour of mind" or "clemency" (see, for example, Richard Green Parker's widely used *Progressive Exercises in English Composition*, 1832).

As the century progressed, the ideas of European philosophers and reform educators such as John Amos Comenius, Moravian preacher and educator; John Locke, British philosopher; Jean Jacques Rousseau, Swiss-French philosopher, political theorist, and, according to some, the father of romantic sensibility; and Johann Heinrich Pestalozzi, Swiss education reformer who believed that children learned from objects, not from abstract concepts, spread to the United States under the umbrella of "Enlightenment thinking" or "romanticism" and affected pedagogy in this country in several ways: The understanding of the child changed from that of a depraved being ever in need of correction to that of a benevolent being, innocent and pure. Nineteenth-century American reform educators such as Horace Mann and Henry Barnard began to call for school-based educational practices that emphasized the senses, experience, and the concrete. Perhaps most significantly, teachers began writing a new genre of textbook, one geared not to the child as miniature adult, but to the child and the child's way of learning.

In 1839, John Frost (a graduate of Harvard in 1822 who won the Bowdoin prize for original dissertations, the same prize that Ralph Waldo Emerson had won in 1821) published a landmark composition book for beginners called *Easy Exercises in Composition* while he was teaching at Philadelphia's Central High School, the second-oldest public high school in the United States, still in existence today. In his book, Frost broke with long-standing practice: he asked students to write original texts—descriptions or narratives—based on illustrations of objects or animals, of home scenes, of school scenes. And he asked students to include their own experience as part of their text. The writing prompt that accompanies a picture of children relaxing with a book and their pet dog reads, "Pleasure of spending holiday in a garden. Describe your own idea of a pleasant summer holiday" (24). It is in assignments like this that we see the beginnings of the democratization of writing instruction: for the first time in our country's history, students were invited to use knowledge from their home lives in a school composition; what they knew from their immediate experience was valued at school.[2]

In addition to their school-based writing, controlled largely by teachers and textbooks, nineteenth-century school-age students had two avenues for extracurricular writing at home. Students learned to write letters to distant friends and family members, and especially after the Civil War, were taught to write short business letters, often grounded in trade or commerce. Students might write to a shop, for example, to order a pair of gloves, or to a shipping agent to inquire about the cost of delivery for a particular item. Also home-based—that is, the writing was not a school assignment—was the writing students did in a memoir or journal or commonplace book, widely used writing avenues for children of privileged families. Today, this writing serves as a powerful informant about the lives of children in the nineteenth century; Harvey J. Graff, for example, relies heavily on archived examples of these kinds of children's writing in his study *Conflicting Paths: Growing Up in America*.

The second extracurricular site for school-age children to write—and to begin to learn to edit—was the school newspaper. Public high schools did not flourish in the United States until well after the Civil War. Prior to that, children who attended school after the elementary years were, for the most part, at an academy or other form of private school. It is in these schools that I see the first examples of a student literary magazine or of a student newspaper. Students at Boston Latin School (founded in 1635, a school for boys of privilege whose graduates include Samuel Adams, John Hancock, and Cotton Mather) published their *Literary Journal* in 1829; this is the first student publication from a school that I can document.

After the war and by the last decades of the century, many student newspapers flourished, so many that when the students of St. Mark's School in Southborough, Massachusetts, published the first issue of *The Vindex* (February 1877), they wrote that since a student paper was a "prominent feature" of large schools, they, too, were inaugurating a paper at their school. By 1911, Willard Bleyer, assistant professor of journalism at the University of Wisconsin, could write in *The High School Course in English* that "the possibility [for fourth year students] of making practical application of their ability to write in preparing orations and debates, reporting for local newspapers, or editing the school publications" made the last year of high school composition instruction more attractive than earlier composition courses (50).

Composition books did not, however, routinely offer advice to students about writing for a school paper; an exception is W. W. Davis, who advises students about writing for a school paper in his 1864 *Composition Writing: A Practical Guide* (see especially page 47). As Katherine Adams explains, training in journalism *qua* journalism was not part of the high school curriculum for most of the nineteenth century (*A History* 99–122). The consensus among historians of journalism education is that courses in high school journalism most often came into being only after the students had been publishing a newspaper or yearbook, and that the earliest examples of high school journalism courses often appeared in what we would think of as vocational high schools. These were geared toward teaching students the mechanisms of typesetting and printing.

In the early twentieth century, both the number of student publications and the number of schools teaching journalism courses experienced a growth spurt. Frederick Gruber and Thomas Bayard Beatty report that secondary schools in the United States experimented with student publications since Colonial times, but that such publications flourished after 1915 (183). In a 1925 essay, "Journalism in the High School," Grant Milnor Hyde reports that his textbook on high school journalism was being used in 200 high schools and that the 800 members of the five-year-old Central Interscholastic Press Association had entered 250 newspapers, 50 magazines, and 200 annuals in an annual publication contest (1–2).[3] It is important to note that "journalism" would not have been a course offering in a school like Girls' Latin, where the emphasis was on preparing students for college, not for the world of work; the girls editing the paper would have done so on their own initiative.

While a few histories of individual school publications have been written (Greg Lawless on the *Harvard Crimson*, for example), histories of composition instruction have paid almost no attention to these newspapers and periodicals; standard works on the history of newspapers/magazines do not address student publications, and I have not been able to locate a bibliography of school-sponsored student publications or a history of nineteenth-century student publications.[4] Both of these areas suggest rich possibilities for further study.

Founding, Editing, and Writing for The Jabberwock

It is particularly noteworthy that at a time in U.S. history when public writing or editing possibilities for women were limited, and even more limited for girls, a group of girls in a small school decided themselves not only to start a newspaper but also to assume the responsibility for soliciting the subscriptions and advertising that would allow its financial success as well as for its writing and editing. Perhaps even more noteworthy is the fact that the girls undertook the publication of *The Jabberwock* without any academic training in journalism; the newspaper itself became the girls' journalism classroom. It would thus be easy to dismiss the writing in nineteenth-century student newspapers as "unimportant" (and no doubt some of it was) or as juvenilia, texts written by youth that are immature in style, thought, and/or development and therefore not worthy of regard other than as they predict or contrast with the writer's mature work.[5]

Here, though, I want to argue for the value of the writing and editing that appeared in these publications on different grounds. I suggest that *The Jabberwock*, a student-run school paper, offered late-nineteenth- and early-twentieth-century girls the opportunity to write about writing and what it meant to be a writer, a forum for shaping school opinion and engaging with other writers and thus for anticipating the adult role of public citizen, and a site from which to launch a career as a published, even acclaimed, writer or editor. In a word, *The Jabberwock* provided a site where a girl might experience herself as a writer in a public forum of students, faculty, and friends of the school; I look at the first twenty years of the newspaper, with particular attention to the earliest issues.

Writing About Writing. Nineteenth-century student periodicals often struggled financially. Editors pleaded with students to subscribe or, if they had subscribed, to pay their bill, and students wrote of their dislike of soliciting advertisers to help offset their costs. Mabel Hay Barrows Mussey, recalling the first days of editing *The Jabberwock* from a distance of some thirty years, wrote:

> Financial terror was our heaviest burden. How often it seemed that the next issue must be our last! We had a healthy fear of debt and paid our way as we went. As we were not of the generation that lisps Publicity in the kindergarten, we had few ideas on building up circulation. We were, in fact, so modest, that any family friend who paid his fifty-cent subscription was regarded as a public benefactor. (March 1928, 31)

But the papers also struggled for contributors. As the writers of many nineteenth-century composition textbooks wrote in their prefaces, students often found composing school-sponsored texts difficult or unpleasant. So it is probably more surprising that some girls wanted to create a student newspaper than that the editor's desk did not overflow with contributions.

It's this need for contributions that inspired some of the writing about writing in *The Jabberwock*. The simplest expression of this occurs in a space called "Editorial Notes," a miscellany of comments from the editors. In March 1888, the editors wrote, "Do send more contributions, girls. Do not be afraid of the editorial waste-basket. We have not bought one yet" (2). In April 1888, an editorial note read, "*The Jabberwock* for this month makes its appearance later than usual, on account of vacation. Ten days of freedom seems to have been too much for some of our correspondents, as they either wholly neglected to send notes or sent them too late" (1). More elaborately, in the lead editorial in May 1890, Abbie Farwell Brown wished her subscribers well for the upcoming vacation, and as part of that wish, she had a number of suggestions for how her colleagues might be productive during their summer if they did not want to spend all their time reading Xenophon or Horace; they might, she suggested, grow and then press flowers, collect and study the rocks they found in their summer travels, or they might, in her words, "write a little every week,—just a little, but enough to result in some nice article to be sent in to us next fall?" She goes on to say, "You can't think what a satisfaction it is to see some nice sheets of manuscript all ready for the press on our desk when we come back to school. . . . [This next fall, we hope] to see a great pile reaching up to the ceiling, so that all we shall have to do will be to sit down and make up the paper, and be glad we *are* editors" (1).

At the end of that summer, another editorial appeared, again on the first page. This time, though, the editors were consoling girls about pieces that they, the editors, had rejected:

> Whenever we have to 'return with thanks' any of the girls' articles, we always feel sorry, and do it as gently as we know how. Sometimes the articles are very good, and worthy of being printed, but are not suited to *The Jabberwock*. Instead of being angry with the editors, we advise such contributors to send the rejected article elsewhere. . . . If the other girls only knew how many things the editors write which are rejected in the end. Often have we spent an evening on an article, and then found, by broad daylight and the atmosphere of school, that it would not do. . . . And yet we must keep on writing. We remember how, before we were put on the staff of this paper, we had articles repeatedly refused. If we had been discouraged at the beginning, we never should have been elected to our present position. (September 1890, 1)

The power of the chunks of text I quote here goes beyond, I would suggest, simple statements asking for contributions and reminding colleagues to be brave in the face of rejection. The power, I would suggest, is that these young women writers, while not articulating a composing process the way a textbook would, are nonetheless demonstrating that they have internalized, whether from experience and/or from textbooks and teachers, the principles of writing. That is, they are authorizing themselves to remind others what they have learned about writing: to write about the familiar, to write in stages, to write for a particular audience and purpose, and to write on, even in the face of rejection. Perhaps most importantly, they are authorizing themselves to do the work of editors, accepting and rejecting work as it meets or fails to meet the selection criteria for a particular publication context.

Shaping Public Opinion. A second way in which writing for *The Jabberwock* was a formative experience for the young writers/editors is that it allowed them a public platform from which they might express their views. A small example of this occurred in "Exchanges," a column that appeared not only in the Girls' Latin School paper, but in most nineteenth-century student newspapers. Common practice among the editors of school papers was to exchange copies with colleagues in other schools, and then to comment, in their own paper, on an issue of another school's paper. Student editors thus learned to read with a critical eye, praising what they liked, critiquing what they didn't like. So, for example, in the early issues of 1889, *The Jabberwock* editors wrote:

> In the *Academe* are many reports of clubs and societies. We wish we understood them. (January 1889, 6)

> The December *Cue* contains a thrilling story, which caused one of our editors to have a nightmare after reading it. The January number seems to be overrun with cats. (January 1889, 6)

> The *Stray Shot* has a very good composition on "Boys," written from a little girl's stand-point. It reminds us of a composition we once read on girls, written by a boy, published by Mark Twain. (February 1889, 6)

And here are two examples from the December 1912 issue, students now addressing their colleagues in other schools more directly, even using the pronoun "you":

> *Hackettstonian*, Hackettstown, N.J.: You show great originality in your October number. The article "How the Faculty Spent the Summer," is very novel and interesting. We think the plan of editing the paper every other month, and thereby having a larger and better number, an excellent one. (13–14)

> *The Key*, Battle Creek, Mich.: You have a well-edited paper with an excellent literary department. The editorial, "Advice to the Freshmen," is very good.

We agree with you that one should get into the habit of writing for the school paper. (14)

An elaborated example of this preparation for the adult role of "citizen who speaks out on public issues" occurs in March 1888, one of the earliest issues of the periodical. In their editorial, the writers argue on behalf of a gymnasium for their school. Following the protocol for a classical argument, the writers articulate what they perceive to be the history of the problem, state their proposal, give their reasons, anticipate objections, and deploy both ethos and pathos to sway both students and faculty. Here is a portion of their statement of the problem:

> Very often one hears a girl asking her teacher to excuse her from some recitation 'on account of a bad headache.' With a proper amount of exercise, these girls would soon lose the tired-feeling and aching heads of which so many complain. To be sure, a slight attempt is made in that direction in the calisthenics; but what good do three minutes of these simple exercises or a march around the class-room do to girls in tight sleeves and heavy dresses? Some of them cannot lift their arms above their heads: most of them do not try to. They have no interest whatever in these exercises, which are sometimes wrongly called gymnastics. Impeded by the weight of their skirts, they march heavily up and down the aisles to the dull and uninspiring strains of the piano. (March 1888, 1)

To construct their argument, the writers rely on the importance of exercise for a girl's health. Anticipating the objection that working out in a gym is too strenuous for a girl's health, they counter that when a trainer works with the girls, "They are carefully helped along, until, from being able to have one weight on the chest pulleys, they have four; from vaulting a low bar to a high" (1).

As far as I can tell, a gymnasium was not built at that time. The girls did succeed, though, in winning for themselves a flannel blouse and full skirt for their exercise program. In my reading, less important than their not persuading the authorities to build a gym and more important than the addition of what we would call "gym clothes" to their wardrobe is that these girls were constructing an argument in a public forum and thus acquiring experience that would prepare them for life in a larger public arena as adult women.

Launching a Career. Finally, *The Jabberwock* served as a hands-on training ground as well as first publication venue for those girls who would have careers as writers or editors. As part of this analysis, I offer brief biographical data for several girls who became professional writers; I do this to suggest the richness and the accomplishments of their professional lives and also, and more importantly, to suggest the formative value of their early work on their school paper.

To celebrate the fiftieth anniversary of the school, the 1928 editors of *The Jabberwock* published a special edition that included reminiscences by alumnae. In that anniversary issue, Mabel Hay Barrows Mussey (1873–1931), credited with facilitating a writers' group at Girls' Latin known as the Scribblers, wrote that from her work on *The Jabberwock*, she learned "not only the craft of editing, the fun of writing, the providing of ways and means, the benefit of association . . . but in the process of 'getting things up' (as we called the organizing), we touched drama, music, handicrafts, dancing, and wholesome social life" (31). She also explains what I don't see recorded anywhere else: how the girls learned to edit the paper. I quote her words at some length here because they capture not only a piece of *The Jabberwock*'s history but also the fondness with which she recalls her work editing the paper. She writes,

> It was a pioneer enterprise, for there was no one in the school to bid us follow any trail, to advise this, or warn against that. My Father and Mother, experienced and sympathetic editors, were already ready to give advice and encouragement when needed, and from them we had our first lessons in copy revision, proof reading, and making up the paper, as well as helpful suggestions on all our enterprises. But they remembered that the paper was ours and we must do its work ourselves. In the same way, Mr. Tetlow [the headmaster] and our teachers helped [us] by keeping their hands off, so that we never dreamed of such a thing as censorship. (March 1928, 31)[6]

Mabel Hay Barrows Mussey worked as an associate editor for *The Nation* from July 26, 1919, to March 27, 1920, reporting that "the editorial equipment" she gained from *The Jabberwock* stood her in good stead. Mussey also wrote for *The Nation*. In the December 13, 1919, issue, for example, she has a long review entitled "Books for Children" in which she suggests that adults, "Instead of investing in the latest war-tank, or the giraffe descendant of the teddy bear" (778), might give a child a book as a holiday gift. She organizes her review for different readers (books for families, books for boys, books for girls), and she includes a number of categories, including, for example, fairy tales, animal stories, nature stories, classic children's stories, and books of rhyme for her audience. Throughout her commentary, she celebrates authors, titles, and illustrators she admires and criticizes those she doesn't like. She is particularly appreciative of Edward Frentz's *Uncle Zeb and His Friends*, of stories about Native Americans, and of Maurice Day's illustrations wherever they appear, and she is particularly critical of H. Irving Hantock's *Uncle Sam's Boys Smash the Germans*.

Abbie Farwell Brown (1875–1927) was the first editor of the paper and the student who wrote to ask Lewis Carroll if the girls might trade on the title of his poem in the name of their paper.[7] When she published her first book, she wrote, "It is all the Jabberwock's fault that I wrote any book at all. For in four years' care of you, I acquired a taste for scribbling, which is rarely cured and which has broken out at last in this awful way" (quoted in *The Jabberwock*, March 1928, 10). I look here at excerpts of two pieces she published in the school paper because they suggest the writing skills she was learning in school as well as her growing understanding of the role of editor, both of which would serve her in her professional life.

In the first issue of *The Jabberwock* (February 1888), Brown published a short humorous essay entitled "Only a Piece of Ice." The essay begins with an encomium to ice: "The bliss of a cool glass of lemonade in a parching July noontide, a melting, sweet nectar called 'ice-cream,' the winter's delight of the skater as he skims over the frozen surface of the pond, and the rapture of the tobogganer must each and all be foregone without this one element,—ice!" And the essay ends with a reversal: the writer falls on a piece of ice, chides the ice as "eliding, treacherous, false, and fleeting," and laments, "Ah, never more shall those lofty feelings be inspired in this trusting heart! All the vain, deluding fancies concerning ice are forever vanished" (2). In these few sentences, as throughout the essay, the writer's work bears the mark of a classical education and suggests a facility with language: she uses schemes (parallel structure, repetition, periodic sentences, for example) and tropes (metaphor and hyperbole, for example), which would have been part of language study in a girls' preparatory school.

In a later piece of writing, editor Brown crafts an essay she calls "Going to School," a humorous classification of the people she meets on her way to school (see page 19 for the entire text, an example of the kind of informal writing that appeared in the paper). While she is writing about the other, that is, she is classifying people from different walks of life, she focuses on people whose lives are affiliated with school: the primary school child creeping like snail, the boys en route to Boys' Latin, the girls en route to high school, the teacher, the college student.

While readers might comment on this writing in a number of ways, I offer these observations: Brown authorizes herself to write with humor about the Boys' Latin student; that is, from the anxious expression on the boy's face, she can't tell if he is worried about the Harvard examinations or the football prize. She authorizes herself to write about her own role as an editor; that is, she sends out pity to the editor she meets, but she is no doubt projecting her own feelings as editor, her own dejected look and wrinkled forehead when she learns she's short on text or ads. Finally, she authorizes herself to write with humor about her demeanor as editor; on an icy day when the sidewalks are a glare of ice, she asks, "How can [an editor's] dignity be suitably maintained when she has a bag of heavy books under one arm and an umbrella and roll of manuscript under the other? Sad it is to see her try to look calm and unruffled under these trying circumstances, for she does not always succeed" (January 1889, 1).

Even in this very short piece, we see the writer deploy a number of writing strategies: she uses a classification scheme as her organizing principle; she relies on observation; she uses a particularized, local scene; she uses humor easily; she constructs a chatty voice; she demonstrates her familiarity with the "All the World's a Stage" speech from *As You Like It* when she writes, "There is the small boy of the primary school 'creeping like snail' toward the Temple of Learning", and she incorporates her own experience into a text. This and similar pieces were among Brown's first published writing. The National Union Catalogue has entries for more than twenty published books by Abbie Farwell Brown, and her poems appeared in more than twenty periodicals, including *The Atlantic, Harper's, Radcliffe Quarterly*, and *Life*.

In her reminiscence for *The Jabberwock*, Theodora Kimball Hubbard (1887–1935), editor of *The Jabberwock* in 1904, detailed the editorial skills she learned during her years at Girls' Latin: "I can state in all seriousness that my real editorial work did begin there. I learned the mysteries of galley proof and dummies and the extraordinary conspicuousness of typographical errors,—how strange old friendly words look when spelled 'Nuatre', or 'momey', or 'Grlis', or 'Ltani', or 'Shocol'" (March 1928, 23). Hubbard went on to say that above all, she learned three invaluable disciplines from her work on *The Jabberwock*. She names them as "accuracy"; "the priority sense" (that is, given all the demands on one's time, even a pleasant task like writing for the 'Jab'—"must be placed in its proper order among the multifarious tasks that crowd around"); and "the ability to organize our own program," the careful planning, that is, "that makes magazines come out on time" (23).

Hubbard's first job was as editorial writer for the New England Historic Genealogical Society in Boston; she also worked as librarian in Harvard's school of landscape architecture for more than a decade. For the most part, though, she had a distinguished career writing and editing materials related to landscape architecture and city planning. With her husband, Henry Vincent Hubbard, she edited the journal *Landscape Architecture* and founded and edited the journal *City Planning*. And with Frederick Law Olmsted, Jr., she edited the papers of Frederick Law Olmsted, Sr., including a volume on Central Park. She was a member of numerous professional organizations and from 1928 to 1933 served as a trustee of Simmons College, her college alma mater.

Finally, a fourth example of a *Jabberwock* editor who published her first work in that publication and achieved lifelong success as a writer and/or editor is Louise Bogan (1897–1970). The honors of this acclaimed modernist poet, who continues to be studied and read today, included a Guggenheim Fellowship, a place as Fellow in American Letters at the Library of Congress, the Harriet Monroe Award from the University of Chicago, and awards from the Academy of American Poets and the National Endowment for the Arts. While Bogan did not contribute to the school's anniversary issue, she wrote in her autobiography, "I went to the Girls' Latin School in the autumn of 1910, at the age of thirteen, for five most fruitful years. I began to write verse from about fourteen on. The life-saving process then began. By the age of 18 I had a thick pile of manuscript, in a drawer in the dining room—and had learned every essential of my trade" (*Journey Around My Room* 50). An associate editor of *The Jabberwock*, Bogan had signed pieces in the paper that included editorials and short fiction. It is also in *The Jabberwock* that she published her first poetry and thus took the first step on her journey to becoming the poetry editor of *The New Yorker*, a position from which she would influence the canon of American poetry for almost four decades. Her volumes of poetry include *Body of This Death* (1923), *Dark Summer* (1929), and *Sleeping Fury* (1937). She also published several collections of her poems; the final and most complete is *The Blue Estuaries: Poems 1923–1968* (1968).

Conclusion

Even by the second half of the nineteenth century, when common schools were well established, public high schools were beginning to sink their roots, and normal schools were growing in number, not all children had an equal opportunity to attend school. Most white children attended school for the early grades. But pointing to a class differential, Stuart Blumin uses census data to show that in Philadelphia in 1860, while most children of nonmanual workers were still in school at age fifteen, children from working-class homes were not (190). Carl Kaestle reports that in the nineteenth-century United States, only a "small minority of teenagers attended secondary school of any kind" (121), and we know that those who did were primarily boys. He also writes that at the time of the Civil War, blacks in the North had "separate and unequal" school opportunities, black schools were not affected by early public school reform, and American Indians and Hispanic Americans struggled for educational opportunities (179–80).

It is important to remember, therefore, that the girls who attended Girls' Latin at the end of the nineteenth century were a small and privileged group whose families believed in and could afford a classical education for their daughters. In 1878, the year of the school's founding, twenty-six girls were enrolled; in 1888, the year of the founding of *The Jabberwock*, the number had risen to 160. In school, girls wrote compositions and exams; out of school, they wrote letters and journals. A school newspaper was a liminal space, a space that was neither as heavily determined as classroom-assigned writing nor as free as home writing. It is also important to remember that not all the students who wrote for *The Jabberwock* went on to careers as editors or writers, and not all the texts they produced for the paper was writing we would admire.

But in spite of the limitation that a paper like *The Jabberwock* does not represent all the voices of nineteenth-century children, or the limitation that the voices do not engage complex social issues (I don't, for example, see references to the Great War in the issues of the paper that occurred during the time of the United States' entry into the war), the paper provides an important window on nineteenth-century student writing and editing, a window through which we can see that what might have seemed like a modest school girls' effort was in fact identity-forming: editing a periodical (in this case a monthly school paper) gave the young women of Girls' Latin School the opportunity to experience themselves as writers and editors in a public forum. This work, in turn—work that began with a note passed in an algebra class—gives us the opportunity to interrogate one of the many formation processes of young women editors and writers at the end of the nineteenth century. Mary Mapes Dodge, editor of *St. Nicholas* from 1873 to 1905, wrote that she viewed her magazine as a "pleasure ground" for children. I would suggest that *The Jabberwock* was also a "pleasure ground," a source of joy and camaraderie to both readers and writers; in addition, however, the school paper was a significant training ground for those high school–age girls who would go on to careers as writers and editors of national and international acclaim.

From *The Jabberwock*, February 1888

For the benefit of those who do not know from what source we derive our name, we print the whole of Mr. Carroll's interesting poem in "Through the Looking Glass":

> 'Twas brillig, and the slithy toves
>   Did gyre and gimble in the wabe;
> All mimsy were the borogoves,
>   And the mome raths outgrabe.
>
> "Beware the Jabberwock, my son!
>   The jaws that bite, the claws that scratch.
> Beware the Jubjub bird, and shun
>   The frumious Bandersnatch."

> He took his vorpal sword in hand:
>   Long time the manxome foe he sought,—
> So rested he by the Tumtum tree,
>   And stood awhile in thought.
>
> And, as in uffish thought he stood,
>   The Jabberwock, with eyes of flame,
> Came whifling through the tulgey wood,
>   And burbled as it came!
>
> One, two! one, two! And through and through
>   The vorpal blade went snickersnack!
> He left it dead, and with its head
>   He went galumphing back.
>
> "And hast thou slain the Jabberwock?
>   Come to my arms, my beamish boy!
> O frabjous day! Callooh! Callay!"
>   He chortled in his joy.
>
> 'Twas brillig, and the slithy toves
>   Did gyre and gimble in the wabe;
> All mimsy were the borogoves,
>   And the mome raths outgrabe. (February 1988, 1)

Notes

1. In November 1877, when petitions to open the all-male Boston Latin School to girls failed, a group of supporters persuaded the Boston School Committee to open a separate school for girls. These supporters included Mr. William Claflin, Dr. and Mrs. William F. Warren, Professor and Mrs. Borden P. Bowne, Mrs. Emily Talbot, Miss Florence M. Cushing, Miss M. Richards, Mr. J. W. Howe, Mr. Carroll D. Wright, Mrs. Mary A. Livermore, Mrs. Alice Freeman, Mrs. Elizabeth Stuart Phelps, Mrs. James T. Fields, Rev. James Freeman Clarke, Mr. John D. Runkle, and Mr. Robert D. Smith (*The Jabberwock*, March 1928, 9). Girls' Latin opened in 1878 with thirty-seven pupils, one teacher, and a headmaster. Today, the school is known as Boston Latin Academy. For current information on the school, as well as its history, see http://boston.k12.ma.us//BLA/ (2 November 2003).

2. For a fuller account of school-based writing, see my *The Young Composers: Composition's Beginnings in Nineteenth-Century Schools*; for a study of college writing, see John Brereton's *The Origins of Composition Studies in the American College, 1875–1925*; and for a study of women writing in college, see Katherine H. Adams's *A Group of Their Own: College Writing Courses and American Women Writers, 1880–1940*.

3. Other early-twentieth-century authors who write about high school journalism include Carl Miller in *High-School Reporting and Editing* (1929), George Wells and Wayde McCalister in *Student Publications* (1930), and B. J. R. Stolper in *A Newspaper Unit for Schools* (1937). See especially the bibliography in Riverda Harding Jordan's *Extra-Classroom Activities* (1928). For a brief history of journalism instruction at the college level, see O'Dell's *The History of Journalism Education in the United States* (1935).

4. A partial list of school papers ("listed as being unusually good") appears in Harrington and Harrington's 1927 *The Newspaper Club* (352–54). Most of the papers listed here, however, are from the Midwest, and conspicuously absent are papers from schools in the East, which were established considerably earlier than those in this list.

Harvard's Gutman Library has in its Public School Reports (EducR) collection the largest archive of student newspapers that I know of. In some cases, it holds a long run of the papers, in others, just a few issues. At Gutman, I have read sample issues and longer runs of student publications from approximately fifty nineteenth-century schools located in the eastern part of the United States. I extend particular thanks to Marylene Altieri, special collections librarian/archivist at Gutman, for her help in accessing these school publications; to Marsha Bradeen, librarian at Boston Latin Academy, for her help with locating particular issues; and to Katherine Adams, the Audrey and William Hutchinson Professor of English at Loyola University, for help with sources on the history of the teaching of journalism. At the University of Cincinnati, librarian Mark Kovacic in the Reference and Research Services Department provided invaluable help with locating the year of death for Mabel Hay Barrows Mussey; many biographical sources that I checked simply use a question mark for her year of death.

5. The word "juvenalia" is often used (by booksellers and Web sites) to refer to the immature writing of an author; the correct word, though, is "juvenilia." ("Juvenalian" refers to work resembling that of the first-century Roman poet Juvenal.)

6. Mabel Barrows Mussey's father, Samuel June Barrows, was editor of the *Christian Register* from 1880 to 1896; Mussey's mother, Isabel Chapin Barrows, worked closely with Samuel Barrows on the periodical. Mussey's husband, Henry Raymond Mussey, served as managing editor of *The Nation* from 1918 to 1920 and 1929 to 1930.

While there may have been no overt censorship, school papers, then as now, were monitored by faculty, and if indeed no articles were censored, I would suggest it was because a good deal of self-censorship was exercised.

7. In an article about Brown in *Notable American Women, 1607–1950*, Jo Ann Abraham Reiss notes that Abbie Farwell Brown's mother occasionally contributed to the *Youth's Companion* and that Abbie herself sent contributions to *St. Nicholas*, many of which were illustrated by her sister, "Ann Underhill."

Works Cited

Adams, Katherine H. *A History of Professional Writing Instruction in American Colleges.* Dallas: Southern Methodist University Press, 1993.

———. *College Writing Courses and American Women Writers, 1880–1940.* Albany: SUNY Press, 2001.

Bleyer, Willard G. *The High School Course in English.* 4th ed. Madison: University of Wisconsin Press, 1911.

Blumin, Stuart M. *The Emergence of the Middle Class.* Cambridge: Cambridge University Press, 1989.

Bogan, Louise. *Journey around My Room.* Ed. Ruth Limmer. New York: Viking, 1980.

Brereton, John, ed. *The Origins of Composition Studies in the American College, 1875–1925.* Pittsburgh: University of Pittsburgh Press, 1995.

Davis, W. W. *Composition Writing, A Practical Guide.* Chicago: George and C. W. Sherwood, 1864.

Frost, John. *Easy Exercises in Composition.* 2d ed. Philadephia: W. Marshall, 1839.

Graff, Harvey J. *Conflicting Paths: Growing Up in America.* Cambridge, Mass.: Harvard University Press, 1995.

Greer, Jane, ed. *Girls and Literacy in America.* Santa Barbara: ABC-CLLO, 2003.

Gruber, Frederick C., and Thomas Bayard Beatty. *Secondary School Activities.* New York: McGraw-Hill, 1954.

Harrington, Harry, and Evaline Harrington. *The Newspaper Club.* Boston: D. C. Heath, 1927.

Hyde, Grant M. "Journalism in High School." *Journalism Quarterly* 2.1 (1925): 1–9.

The Jabberwock. Girls' Latin School/Boston Latin Academy. February 1888– .

Jordan, Riverda Harding. *Extra-Classroom Activities.* New York: Thomas Crowell, 1928.

Kaestle, Carl F. *Pillars of the Republic: Common Schools and American Society, 1780–1860.* New York: Hill and Wang, 1983.

Lawless, Greg, ed. *Harvard Crimson Anthology: 100 Years at Harvard.* Boston: Houghton Mifflin, 1980.

Miller, Carl G. *High-School Reporting and Editing.* New York: McGraw-Hill, 1929.

O'Dell, De Forest. *The History of Journalism Education in the United States.* New York: Teachers College Press, 1935.

Parker, Richard Green. *Progressive Exercises in English Composition.* Boston: Lincoln and Edmands, 1832.

Schultz, Lucille M. *The Young Composers: Composition's Beginnings in Nineteenth-Century Schools.* Carbondale: Southern Illinois University Press, 1999.

Stolper, B. J. R. *A Newspaper Unit for Schools.* New York: Teachers College Press, 1937.

Walker, John. *The Teacher's Assistant in English Composition.* 1801. Carlisle, Pa.: G. Kline, 1808.

Wells, George C., and Wayde H. McCalister. *Student Publications.* New York: A.S. Barnes, 1930.

"Going to School"
The Jabberwock, January 1889

Many people does the editor meet as she pursues her daily way to school. As she walks the classic streets of the Hub, she encounters the people of the great city thronging to their daily occupations: and she mentally classifies them, as they pass.

There is the small boy of the primary school, "creeping like snail" toward the Temple of Learning. There is the High School boy striding along with a dignified mien, his brain intent upon drill and visions of an officer's sword. Then the B.L.S. student, his mind bent on the Harvard examinations or the foot-ball prize—we cannot tell which by the anxious expression on his noble brow. Then the girls of the High School, in groups of three and four, chatting gayly on all subjects, from the last symphony to "Annie's new jacket" and "Sadie's *dear* little pug dog!"

Occasionally, we meet an editor, whose dejected look and wrinkled forehead furnish the conviction that he is a page short, or that there are not "ads" enough for the next copy. He has our sincerest pity.

Then there is the business man, who ambles placidly down the avenue on the way to his office. There is the teacher, with his arms full of books and examination papers; the college student, looking wise and absent-minded; the street-laborer, with his dinner-pail; the omnipresent hand-organ man; and many, many others, passing one by one.

It is a great sport to watch the expressions on the faces of the people on the different days, corresponding to the weather. How dreary and tired and draggled they all look on a rainy day! How miserable the world seems, and how discouraged its inhabitants! Every school-boy looks as if his lessons were not well prepared to-day. But on a sunny day how smiling everyone is,—how good-natured and self-satisfied and happy in the consciousness of well-learned lessons! Yet there is considerable fun to be had out of nearly every kind of weather, if one would but try. How queer the girls all look, bundled up so completely in their gossamers, with an umbrella almost hiding them! And what fun it is to see two stout old gentlemen bump into one another, and struggle to extricate their entangled umbrellas! A snow-storm is great fun, too,—that is, as well as we can remember. But an icy day! An editor is out of her element on a slippery day, when the sidewalks are one glare of ice. How can her dignity be suitably maintained when she has a bag of heavy books under one arm and an umbrella and roll of manuscript under the other? Sad it is to see her try to look calm and unruffled under these trying circumstances, for she does not always succeed. —A.F.B.

Literary and Commercial Aspects of Women's Editions of Newspapers, 1894–1896

ANN MAUGER COLBERT

ANNE of Green Gables, who is trying to break into freelance writing, faces a professional dilemma: Shall she sell her writing to promote a particular brand of baking powder or will she ignore this possible source of income and prestige, and keep her fiction "pure" and free of the taint of profit motives? Her quandary—or a version of it, at least—had been faced earlier by women from around the country involved in the editing of special issues of newspapers called women's editions. Anne, an ambitious new woman with a desire to make a good impression on editors and readers, believes that baking-soda advertisements masquerading as fiction are practically immoral. Accordingly, she is facing an impediment to success that mirrored the one faced by many would-be writers trying to earn a living as a writer by pleasing a mass audience accustomed to having their reading matter underwritten by advertising.

While Anne Shirley tried to remain true to an ideal of writing as a higher calling to art, many of the amateur[1] journalists involved in publishing women's editions of newspapers had no such scruples. Indeed, journalism itself was a model of free (but profitable) enterprise. In fact, when criticism was made of the front page of the woman-published *Indianapolis Sentinel* because it was "nothing but an ad," the novice journalists did not react at all. This lack of reaction probably told the tale as well as anything: profits (albeit for philanthropy) were the *point* of their efforts, as we shall see.

Anne Shirley had only begun her development as a writer when she faced her challenge to the profit motive, and she stands in contrast to Helen Sherwood, the capable woman who takes over the Plattville newspaper when its editor is roughed up by night riders in Booth Tarkington's *The Gentleman from Indiana*. In Helen's case, the problems are related to issues of power, not money, but her abilities are strong and she is drawn sympathetically. Both Helen and Anne are can-do characters who might indeed have been modeled on their authors' lives, and both present fictional pictures that are probably accurate depictions of women beginning their careers. Maud Montgomery, Anne's author, was a working journalist who—like her heroine—was trying to build a reputation at the time baking-powder contests offered money to beginning writers[2] willing to use their talents to promote products. Similarly, Helen's character appears to have been based on Booth Tarkington's sister Haute. In addition to being the force behind his earliest publishing success, she was one of the editors of the *Indianapolis Sentinel* women's edition, the same paper that had used a bicycle ad on its front page.[3] While that group of women clearly had no profit-art dilemma, their paper had been criticized by a rival editor for turning the entire front page over to a bicycle company. Whatever concerns Haute Tarkington and the other women might have had privately, their clear public decision was that profits (in this case, $7,000) would probably be worth any public criticism they might receive.[4]

It might seem strange to mix images of fictional women in a discussion of real nineteenth-century community newspapers, women community leaders, and their philanthropic projects. But the fact that women were given control of one issue of a local paper for charity *seems* fictional to anyone who has worked on a daily newspaper. And the images of Anne Shirley and Helen Sherwood are credible portraits of women at the end of the nineteenth century; in fact, to a modern mind they are more credible than the *real* women involved with publishing one issue of a mainstream newspaper for charity purposes. Imagine these journalists entering the San Francisco *Examiner* office to publish their newspaper.[5] There, the novice editors discovered a maid available for their every need, new mirrors in a freshly designed women's powder room, and congratulatory telegrams from New York journalist Nellie Bly and editor Jeannette L. Gilder, Wild Bill Hickok, the vacationing owner William Randolph Hearst, and other contemporary celebrities. So while these preliminary remarks may seem whimsical in the extreme, the issue of what were the extents of women's possibilities in the power structure of a community provokes new examinations, new evidence, and new answers when women's editions of newspapers are consulted.[6]

Power can be money, of course, and the women involved in publishing women's editions were fully aware of their access to an elite lifestyle and to the power in their communities. They were also good philanthropists and were largely interested in charities that benefited women.[7] While the charitable beneficiaries will be mentioned, my goal here is to discuss this increasingly market-driven world where fundraising and journalism met. I also hope to introduce a few of the thousands of women involved in what was eventually called a fad by publishers' organizations.

The phenomenon appears to have begun in Rockford, Illinois. There, an editor challenged "women not associated with journalism" to put out an issue of the paper,[8] and there, as in newspaper offices around the country, women appeared to take similar challenges in stride. The editions grew more elaborate as the fad expanded; ten months after the first women's edition in Rockford, the women of Cleveland produced a lavish number with silk wrappers. Indeed, before moving ahead, it is necessary to define, more adequately, the phenomenon called women's editions of newspapers.

Although today it seems incomprehensible that groups of local women writers and club women took over local newspapers for a day, community women—novices at journalism, for the most part—did in fact invade hundreds[9] of newsrooms throughout the country to publish one special issue for charity.[10] For the women, the object was fundraising, although it is clear that for some participants and would-be writers, the women's editions offered career building tips from professionals such as Elizabeth Jordan[11] and opportunities for publishing, illustrated by the inclusion of short fiction pieces such as that written by Elizabeth Gilmer about editing a women's edition.[12] Literature was the goal for many, and many newspapers—especially those from the South—had a tradition of being an outlet for creative writing.[13] A difference in the way the staffs of the women's editions saw their work can be seen by the numbers of staff listings related to literature: A "literary department" appeared in Atlanta, in Jamestown, New York, and in Charlotte, North Carolina, while in San Francisco, a literary supplement was published. A "literary club" editor was listed in New Albany, Indiana, and the title of "literary editor" appeared in many of the women's editions, including those from Milwaukee, Memphis, Chicago, and Charleston. Literary staffs were also commonly listed, and these staff positions would suggest that women saw the role of journalism as including the literary side. Perhaps these opportunities also might have served as ways for novices to get much-needed exposure and experience.

While the women worked to benefit charitable organizations and themselves, for the newspapers, the primary object appears to have been the building of good will between the community elite and the press. Charles Kennedy, an editor of the *Cleveland Plain Dealer* and author of a history of Cleveland, noted that the publication of the women's edition there did much "to stimulate the work of womankind in the community" and stressed that the women's work was both serious and tied to profit-making. "To make it financially effective," he explained, the women's edition had to be five or six times larger than the regular issue: "A score or more dummy pages with headings such as 'Financial and Commercial,' 'Railroads,' 'Steel and Iron,' 'Retail Merchants' were prepared by the artists and . . . solicitation of advertisements carefully laid out . . . at three times the regular *Plain Dealer* advertising scale!"[14] He noted that the women made a net profit of

$5,300 to apply to the Friendly Inn, a local charity for women. But, in addition, the whole experience brought a world of good public relations to the door of the *Plain Dealer*. As Kennedy explained, the women's edition "enlisted the warm support of all Cleveland, furnished a fund of excitement in society circles, and incidentally, introduced the morning *Plain Dealer* into many homes where it had never been welcome" (97).

Newspaper histories from Memphis, Milwaukee, and Chicago indicate the same positive outcome for their editions, though only Cleveland's Kennedy goes so far as to point out that the women's edition served a clear public relations and marketing function for the newspaper itself. In Rockford, Illinois, where the first of these special editions was published, the publisher reportedly challenged the women with the notion, but in most places the women reportedly asked permission—sometimes repeatedly—for a day's chance to take over the local paper. That indeed is what happened in Milwaukee, where the publisher did not agree at first. He finally "demurred," and the reason given for his acquiescence, as reported by an historian of the paper, was that his wife was involved (Conrad and Wilsons).

Whatever the rationale for publishers' permissions, the women used their foray into publishing to form firm links of communication and marketing with other women's groups around the country.[15] As one advance item in the *Cincinnati Tribune* put it, the women had messages "pouring in ... from every state in the Union.... Orders have come in from California, Connecticut, West Virginia and all over the South and from New York. The orders are usually for 100 copies ... and indicate a growing interest in the forthcoming issue."[16] In most communities, rival papers forgot their differing politics and points of view and furnished support for the women's efforts. Congratulations and warm supportive statements appeared for days, sometimes weeks. Typical is a notice that appeared in the *New Orleans States* on February 2 in support of the women from nearby Monroe: "Our enterprising and able Monroe contemporary, the Daily Evening News has just issued a special edition ... and it is highly creditable to the journalistic ability of the ladies, ... and strange to say, the local department is in every sense complete."[17]

Even professional and trade publications offered gallant (if sometimes patronizing) comments about the women's journalistic endeavors. Many of the editions are mentioned in *Fourth Estate*, a prominent trade publication for newspaper editors and publishers, in which comments of congratulations evolve into announcements that the talented women of such-and-so community had recently published a very creditable women's edition. In July, the trade paper even ran a picture of the three primary editors of the

Springfield Union, from Springfield, Massachusetts. These same women were congratulated warmly by a rival editor on page one of the *Springfield Republican*: "Our merchants have had an example of how earnestly women will work for charity, and meantime, the literary end of the women's paper had not been neglected." Continuing, the article notes that the editor, a Mrs. Newell, occupied herself "with dignity." The women, the report continues, were on the lookout for fake calls and they "weren't caught by the stories of a remarkable prize fight and of a fearful and wonder [sic] accident to an electric car way up on the Hill."[18]

The one exception to a general sense of good will from rivals and other professionals appeared in Cincinnati, where the *Cincinnati Tribune* published several articles and a page one cartoon mocking and criticizing the *Commercial Gazette* and women of that city who were publishing a women's edition. To illustrate, a cartoon shows an old woman labeled *CG* throwing wash water on the young women putting out the women's edition. One obvious reading of this image is that the *Commercial Gazette*'s criticisms are a result of jealousy (and the *Tribune* quickly says as much).[19] Cincinnati was the source for the critique of the Waverly Bicycle ad in Indianapolis, so clearly the Cincinnati *Commercial Gazette* was looking for ways to be critical of the women's efforts.

Although the focus of this discussion is the women's editions published from 1894 to 1896, the period of time the phenomenon reached "fad" proportions, special issues of newspapers had previously been put out by women for charitable concerns. These were not special issues of regular papers. Indeed, these were publications *only* put out for raising money for some charitable enterprise. The first such effort appears to have been one organized by famous magazine editor Sarah Josepha Hale in 1840. Hale's career has been discussed elsewhere and her masked feminism is described lucidly by Patricia Okker.[20] In addition to her career work as editor of *Godey's Ladies Book*, Hale worked for charity. Her promotion of Bunker Hill, in Charlestown, Massachusetts, as an important historic site resulted in the publishing of the *Monument*, a periodical issued to encourage and support fundraising efforts.

This early model of a philanthropic newspaper was followed by papers published during the sanitary fairs of the Civil War. Various community women (working with well-known writers such as Julia Ward Howe) were involved in these efforts, which gave women practical experience in newspaper work. Called sanitary fair newspapers, these publications were issued from fairs in Baltimore, Boston, Chicago, New York City, Philadelphia, and Saint Louis, as well as in Albany and Brooklyn, New York; Portland, Maine; Springfield and Westfield, Massachusetts; and Wheeling, West Virginia

(Kantor and Kantor 294).[21] Yet later, expositions such as those celebrating the 1876 centennial in Philadelphia and state centennials a few years later also published women-run newspapers. The Philadelphia effort is of particular note here because of its stated editorial policy to provide women who needed careers with practical experience in journalism. Their efforts resulted in a daily newspaper called *New Century* (also called *New Century for Women*). These clear antecedents of success show that what the women did from 1894 to 1896 was not completely revolutionary, but their involvement of mainstream newspapers in women-sponsored benevolent activities was indeed something new.

What was most new, from a perspective of more than a century later, was the fadlike spread of the phenomenon. The editors listed in a staff listing for a women's edition tended to mirror the host paper's organizational structure—editor-in-chief, managing editor, news editor, telegraph editor—and in addition to this typical journalistic lineup were editors of poetry and of literature. Some cities had pioneer editors, history editors, Confederacy editors, even sporting and turf editors, and a number of women's editions had children's page editors. Some listings were whimsical and witty—a hotel and fires editor was listed in Memphis, and in many papers, humorous columns called "To the Gentlemen" appeared on "men's pages." (These clearly were critical of the contents of women's pages, criticism that was unheeded by publishers until the 1960s, when women reporters refused to work on what had become "society pages.") A parody of women's editions themselves was also published in the Nashville paper.

The importance of the fundraising aspect of the editions for many of the community women is clear from some of the staff listings. In addition to editors and "editresses," we see "treasurer" and "cashier." These positions were enumerated on the editorial page listings along with the "city desk" or "copy reader" or the "literary department editors" mentioned earlier. Their inclusion suggests much about the way the women thought about their work. It might be argued that these women—part of a group known to eschew personal publicity in the newspapers—found themselves able to cross the lines of what might be considered impropriety because they were engaged in fundraising for some worthy cause. Typical was the San Francisco *Examiner*, published on Christmas Day, 1894, for the benefit of the Children's Hospital. One of the early efforts, the women received behind-the-scenes guidance from Annie Laurie (pen name of Winifred Sweet), a reporter who had spent several weeks providing publicity about "Little Jim," a victim of poverty and of some incurable disease. School children sent pennies to the Little Jim Fund and columns of names appeared day after day, as the crusade wound toward its optimistic end. Like the publisher from Cleveland, William Randolph Hearst of the *Examiner* must have been fully aware of the public relations gained by these gestures, because Annie Laurie was one of his most popular writers (Beasley and Gibbons 118).

Certainly attitudes and issues about what constituted appropriate behavior for serious writers were illustrated by Maud Montgomery, who takes Anne a step further than just considering the ethics of publishing advertisements masked as literary items. Anne was to receive a contest prize for the best story using Rollings Baking Powder, but unfortunately, she herself had not entered her story in the competition. Instead, a friend had changed a few details, then mailed the story entry in Anne's name. As the friend explains the additions and alterations later, "You know where Averil makes the cake? Well, I just stated that she used the Rollings Reliable . . . we will never using any baking powder except Rollings Reliable" (114). We have been given some hints that something will probably happen when Anne herself—a hardworking would-be writer—reacts to the idea of baking powder writing contests with "I'd never dream of competing for it. I think it would be perfectly disgraceful to write a story to advertise a baking powder. It would be almost as bad as Judson Parker's patent medicine fence" (113). Obviously, then, when Anne's doctored story wins the baking powder company's prize, she is less than pleased. She sees her friend's interference as ruining her art: "I feel as if I were disgraced forever. What do you think a mother would feel if she found her child tattooed over with a baking powder advertisement? I feel just the same. I loved my poor little story, and I wrote it out of the best that was in me" (115).

Anne's doctored story of true love enhanced by Rollings is similar to "A Bride's Triumph," which appears on page 10 of the women's edition of the *Milwaukee Journal* of February 22, 1895. Two columns long and illustrated with three engravings, the piece presents a moral related to good cooking (and happy marriages, presumably): "Soda and cream of tartar, my child? Are you so behind the times as that? Not a dust of either, simply Royal Baking Powder. If you put your stuff together right and put one teaspoonful of Royal Baking Powder in, it can't fail."[22]

In Lafayette, Indiana, a different kind of reference to Royal appears in the poem "A Ballade of Sad Biscuits." Written by Evaleen Stein, known throughout her home state for art and children's books, the doggerel begins: "A dole, and dolor, an I wailing woe!/ Hark! Hark! whilst our heavy hearts make moan./ Cut down in the flour of our blameless dough,/heavy and hard as a paving stone!? Nor rise our cries for ourselves alone,/But for saddened flapjacks of every land,/For bilious biscuits of every zone,/We were not raised with the Royal brand!" The poem, worth continuing, goes on:

It leavened us not! Alas, no, no!
By perfidious powders blasted, prone
Low in our ovens we sink, and so
The wrecks of innumerous pies lie strown!
In the name of sense why must we groan,
We were not raised with the Royal brand.
. . . .
In the bold, bad powders made from bone!
O, the U.S. chemists have plainly shown
Their skim milk of tartar, chalk and sand.
And through fumes of ammonia our griefs intone
We were not raised with the Royal brand!

   Envoy.
What profit that goodly seeds were sown,
And the wheat grew green on every hand,
That our flours from golden meads were mown,
We were not raised with the Royal brand!

Clearly, the women's editions at one point became part of a sophisticated marketing phenomenon more interesting than an advertising campaign. A bit of doggerel that appeared in the *Knightstown Sun* of Knightstown, Indiana, makes the point: "Week before last, I remember the date/ Two of us took Main Street/to agitate a Woman's Edition of the Knightstown Sun/ and get advertising by the pound or ton."[23]

The editions are magazine-like in their contents; an understanding of them would be enhanced by reading Ellen Garvey. She asserts that nineteenth-century magazines—and I would add women's editions of newspapers—were texts embedded within the world of commerce and the worlds of their readers. "Read this way," she explains, "magazines no longer appear to be the site of a war between commerce and culture, in which literary or editorial interests are separate from and in conflict with advertising and commerce." According to Garvey, readers of stories were like shoppers in department stores, moving freely from fiction and stories to images that invite the reader to imagine a happy family meal with Quaker oatmeal or some other brand of breakfast food (4).

Magazines were changing as well, as journalism historian Carolyn Kitch recently noted in her study. She looks at the images of women in the *Ladies Home Journal* during the 1890s in an effort to examine the beginnings of some visual stereotypes in American mass media. In a chapter entitled "From True Woman to New Woman" she looks at images of corseted women who were nevertheless symbolically transitional because they depicted women both inside and outside the house. Like our women's editions, these periodicals illustrate the close relationships between women, ties also apparent by looking at the contributors to the women's editions (Kitch 17–36).

The newspapers, of course, saw the successes of advertisers in women's magazines[24] and at the same time were recreating themselves from politically supported tools to self-supporting publishing ventures. As we've seen in the Cleveland example, readership possibility, then loyalty, among female readers would certainly have been a goal for any publisher. Joseph Pulitzer receives the credit for providing one of the earliest efforts to woo women readers. In a chapter called "A Newspaper for Women," biographer George Juergens discusses the *New York World*'s pioneer efforts to shed a masculine orientation. Pulitzer's marketing talents clearly map a successful plan, as he did not win a female following solely by discoursing on subjects of general interest: Pulitzer "knew that it is the business of popular journalism to persuade groups of people that the newspaper contains material specifically for them" (Juergens 45). Pulitzer's contributions to journalism history and sensationalism, even his potential as a study in marketing, are beyond the scope of this chapter, except to note that he served as a model for others, including Hearst (Juergens 45).

Once women were established in publishers' minds as a significant group of newspaper readers (and the company that manufactured Royal was clearly a pioneer in assisting that process), and once the newspaper was established as a product serving multiple markets, the problem for publishers was what marketers and advertisers have called "brand loyalty." The problem in environments in which many newspapers were published was how to develop and sustain reader loyalty, how to develop a formula that would offer variety, that would appeal to new businesses with enough merchandise to advertise, that would, in the process, please multiple members of a family. As *Fourth Estate*, a publishers' trade association periodical, put it in 1895, women are important to this process because a woman's choice of a newspaper will be the family's paper.

In 1895, the year that women's editions reached their peak, *Fourth Estate* devoted several columns to discussing the successful, bold advertising of Royal Baking Powder. Of particular interest to the discussion was the use of a bold graphic design, a reversed image of a woman's hand holding a Royal can with the slogan "Absolutely Pure." According to the writer for the publishers' organ, Royal Baking Powder's advertising was the particular interest and concern of its inventor, Joseph C. Hoagland, a former druggist who had invented baking powder.[25]

As the women's editions illustrate, Royal positioned itself with both women and progressive politics through its advertising. It must have moved quickly to create the appropriate contacts and advertising plates, for the first really big women's editions were published in December of 1894 in San Francisco, Minneapolis, and Denver. (Smaller communities had tried the novice approach to newspapering first in Rockford, Illinois, and shortly thereafter in Grand Rapids, Michigan, and South Bend, Indiana.) The previously cited story about baking powder and romance from the *Milwaukee Journal* appeared in February. A few months later, in Orange, New Jersey, on page 9 of the women's edition of the *Orange Chronicle*, a beautiful half-page advertisement with a hand holding the baking powder can (the same as that in *Fourth Estate* mentioned earlier) appears in white on a black box printed on top of what appear to be ten handwritten letters testifying to the superior quality of Royal Baking Powder. These names do not match those of the women who worked on the paper and could be fictitious testimonials used for the visual appeal of the "handwritten" testimonial letters.

What is significant is that two months later, a similar half-page ad appears in the nearby Montclair, New Jersey, women's edition with the names of the women who *were* involved with the paper. Instead of signatures, however, a note appears that suggests yet another evolutionary step for the Royal campaign: "A fine engraving plate designed for this page failed to arrive in time for publication and the managers substitute therefor the present page and add thereto the personal endorsement of the Editors and Staff of the Woman's Edition—an endorsement they can conscientiously give without reservation." Was the engraving plate similar to that which appeared in Orange or was this one with "real" names and facsimiles of signatures?

A gradual evolution can be seen throughout the women's edition fad; an evolution in advertising can be seen as well. The progression shows movement from small regular Royal ads featuring their typical "Absolutely Pure" slogan to full-page testimonial ads with the signatures of the women involved in the edition. Other variations would include the combination of one-column ads illustrated by signatures and brief testimonials, as throughout the *Nashville American* women's edition on May 9, 1895.

During 1895, the primary year of this special publishing fad, Royal Baking Powder was not just appearing in women's editions of newspapers. The company had caused some controversy with its use of what newspapers call "reading notices" (and these circumstances may explain an absence of Royal advertising in later women's editions). Reading notices were not like the fiction story that Montgomery writes about or that appeared in the *Mil-*

waukee Journal but instead are items that masquerade as news, as in the magazine item mentioned earlier. Sometimes they are blatant criticisms of other brands: "A Baking Powder to Avoid," reads the headline of one such item. Measuring six inches, the "story" concerns the inferiority of cheap baking powders, especially those containing alum. "Alum baking powders are rank poison to many constitutions," says the item,[26] typical for the times. These reading notices were later discredited by publishers and the credit for some of that impetus is given by journalism historian Sally Foreman Griffith to William Allen White, the publisher of *Emporia Gazette*, who was also a correspondent for *McClure's* and probably the most famous of the small town Progressives (95). She also provides some evidence of the hassle publishers must have felt in dealing with the Royal and quotes a letter White wrote the company: "Send us a check for anything *you* think is reasonable, and let us saw this matter off, and for heavens sake don't ever write to us again" (90).

What the actual relationship between the women's editions and Royal Baking Powder was remains to be determined. Clearly, many of the papers printed advertising that became increasingly sophisticated as time went on, and clearly the Royal Baking Powder company was active in creating a tie between the papers and the women. That the readers of the women's editions would be a natural target market for Royal is clear. That Royal was a major advertiser for community papers throughout the country is also clear. Whether Royal initiated the idea of women's editions at some papers or whether the company simply made itself available to community groups remains unanswered.

What is also evident is that the women themselves (and the organizations they represented) were involved in networking through publicity that appeared in the various women's editions throughout the country. They were also part of the network of women supporting women during efforts to enter the various literary professions.[27] Issues of the papers were ordered by other women's clubs and items from the editions were later reprinted in papers in other cities. The complete chronology of the women's editions, from what appears to be the first, in Rockford, Illinois, to the larger city editions with ties to Progressivism and municipal reform, needs to be established.

As seen throughout this discussion, these newspapers offer much for the future researcher. They show an evolution that illustrates sophisticated communication as well as the simple development of a fad in publishing. Among good samples of communication are those of the women themselves, the publishers, and the advertisers—especially the efforts of Royal Baking Powder to tap into a timely women's publishing phenomenon.

Some of the women's fundraising ties to churches (especially in small towns) are also of particular interest and illustrate much about sectarian communication during the late nineteenth century. Also of interest are the contributors to the papers; some are famous women journalists like Ida Tarbell and Ida B. Wells; others are famous fiction writers. Much useful cultural research could be done in these editions, because they provide a discrete picture into a women's world we frequently only generalize or muse about. Finally, these special newspapers provide an interesting example of an intersection between mainstream journalism and women's organized exercises in community power. With their fabulous full-page signature ads, their famous contributors[28] and "signature" notes, their men's pages[29] and fundraising goals, women's editions are certainly more important than the ephemera they appear to be at first glance.

As shown, women's editions gave women throughout the country an opportunity to share with each other municipal housekeeping progress and goals, they made money for charitable enterprises, and they gave publishers a chance to develop newspaper loyalty among the so-called new women. To the modern researcher, they offer pictures of the ambiguous relationship between advertising/marketing, literary publishing, and newspaper work, and they also give a picture of the development of an important ad campaign for one of the experts in marketing to women—Royal Baking Powder. Most importantly, I believe, the women's editions of newspapers provide us, more than a century later, with a window into a world in which women, even married women from small towns, exercised considerably more power than we might have predicted.

Notes

1. I am using the word "amateur" because it seems the appropriate one. There is no evidence in these editions to suggest that the women involved in these projects were regularly contributing to the papers as amateurs, however. And there is no evidence to suggest that the participants were members of amateur journalism press associations, which seemed to be populated by young people. Some of the women's editions participants were professionals, a few may have been regularly published amateurs, but the majority appear to be women who were involved in community philanthropic endeavors and treated this foray into publishing as just one more effort at fundraising.

2. It is interesting to speculate about these baking-powder ads in the light of the idea that most successful ad campaigns are said to offer fantasies based on wish-fulfillment. If, as others have suggested, women in the late nineteenth century saw professional writing as the path toward independence, then pairing that idea with the matrimonial goal believed to be women's *real* secret fantasy was indeed a clever basis for a successful marketing campaign.

3. Most biographies of Tarkington tell the story of Haute Tarkington Jameson's visit to a New York publisher on her rejected brother's behalf. James Woodress describes Mrs. Jameson's encounter with S. S. McClure as one in which she *bullies* him into reading something

by her brother and then promises to see that he receives a manuscript about a crusading small-town Hoosier newspaper editor (see Woodress's introduction to Susanah Mayberry, *My Amiable Uncle*, 6–7).

4. And they were ridiculed by one gentleman from a Cincinnati newspaper, if contemporary clips can be believed.

5. Two days before the San Francisco *Examiner*'s women's edition was printed, an article mentioned the Empress of the Dailies, a reference to the newspaper's self-promotional tag, "The Emperor of the Dailies." In that article, a reference to "society ladies" as being the workforce behind the paper makes the distinction between journalists and women editors clear. Nevertheless, several professional women journalists were involved with the paper. The article says, "Of course, most of the ladies came to the editorial council with but a vague idea of their real duties and privileges. The position and rights of each desk were explained, first generally to the council and then specially to each individual member of the council." (See "The Empress of the Dailies," San Francisco *Examiner*, 23 December 1894: 17.)

6. Marsha Wedell uses the edition published in Memphis by the *Commercial-Appeal* on Valentine's Day as a source of information about many of the subjects discussed in her study of elite women and reform work in Tennessee. See Wedell, *Elite Women and the Reform Impulse in Memphis, 1875–1915*. Another in women's history who has cited women's editions of newspapers is award-winning historian Suzanne Lebsock. See, in particular, a series of essays by her for the Virginia Women's Cultural History Project in *"A Share of Honour": Virginia Women 1600–1945*.

7. Among the charitable objects of the women's editions were a women's building in Albion, Michigan; a YMCA women's auxiliary in Charlotte, North Carolina; the DAR building fund in Danbury, Connecticut; a kindergarten in Muncie, Indiana; a maternity home for indigent women in Minneapolis, Minnesota; and the Central Friendly Inn, a home for women in Cleveland, Ohio. Many other objects for the fundraising were libraries, hospitals, and homes for children, as well as the women's building at the Cotton States Exposition.

8. See Julie Snively, "Extra! Extra!" This "bet" was also mentioned by contemporaries and by the women themselves in "A New Idea in Journalism," *The Morning Star*, 24 March 1894: 1. Snively's article quotes the great niece of Belle Keith, one of the editors, as saying she isn't surprised that the women would take the challenge, that they were well-educated and were encouraged to be extraordinary.

9. While this might seem like an exaggerated figure, I think it is not. I have identified more than 100, and in each state in which I've been able to do extensive research, I've found at least 10 more.

10. I have introduced basic aspects of these newspapers elsewhere. See Ann Mauger Colbert, "Philanthropy in the Newsroom."

11. Typical of the articles that were obviously solicited for the women's editions are a couple concerning Elizabeth Jordan, a successful journalist who later was known as an "author." Jordan began freelancing for the *St. Paul Globe* and *Chicago Tribune* and then went to the New York *World*. Her early career path was obviously of interest to readers of the women's editions who wished to know how to build a journalism career and open doors to a broader literary world. In the *Milwaukee Journal*, she writes of her life in New York City and of her early career path; in the Columbia, South Carolina, *State*, a profile of Jordan offers similar information and is clearly written to aid the would-be journalist/writer.

12. Elizabeth M. Gilmer's amusing piece about a fictional women's edition in Kamchatka might well be a piece that helped launch her writing career. The date given for her beginning employment is late 1894, but her first position at the *New Orleans Picayune* was more secretarial than editorial, according to her biographers, Harnett Kane with Ella Bentley Arthur in *Dear Dorothy Dix*. Gilmer's article in the *Nashville American* women's edition is entitled "A Woman's Experience as a Newspaper Editor" (9 May 1895: 35). Like Jordan, Gilmer becomes successful and respected after beginning with modest freelancing efforts for newspapers. The date of her contribution would suggest that her humorous piece might have been one

of her early articles, perhaps one that led to her eventual successful career as one of William Randolph Hearst's famous sob sisters.

13. See Joan Wylie Hall, "Louisiana Writers of the Postbellum South," 203–4.

14. Charles Kennedy, *Fifty Years of Cleveland 1875–1925*, 96–102. Kennedy asserted that the women's edition there resulted in the paper being welcomed into homes where it wasn't normally read.

15. In San Francisco, an article put it this way: "In two days the first big daily newspaper ever managed by women will be published. In a week that paper will be on sale in every city in America. In two weeks every newspaper in Europe will have had a comment . . . and in three weeks the whole thing will have gone the way of all journalism and be a part of the past." San Francisco *Examiner*, 23 December 1894, 17.

16. "All Will Read It," *Cincinnati Tribune*, 30 November 1895, 1, 9.

17. "The Ladies' Newspaper," *New Orleans States*, 7 February 1895, 4.

18. "Women on Duty as Editors," *Springfield Republican*, 19 May 1895, 1.

19. "Behold the C.G.'s Revenge!" *Cincinnati Tribune*, 29 November 1895, 1.

20. Patricia Okker, in *Our Sister Editors*, offers a broad picture of women in publishing and the model given by Sarah Hale. See also Ruth E. Finley, *The Lady of Godey's*, 70–81. This picture of charitable work is given in an earlier biography of Hale that describes efforts at conducting a fair and related publishing for fundraising efforts.

21. Sanitary fair newspapers were published in Albany, New York; Baltimore; Boston; Brooklyn, New York; Chicago; Cincinnati; Cleveland; Philadelphia; Portland, Maine; Poughkeepsie, New York; Saint Louis; Westfield, Massachusetts; and Wheeling, West Virginia.

22. Whether such pieces were written by marketing account managers or by competing authors, the story illustrates another aspect of Royal Baking Powder company's marketing plan. And according to business historians such as James D. Norris in *Advertising and the Transformation of American Society, 1865–1920*, Royal's efforts were always part of some larger marketing plan.

23. Mrs. J. D. Maple, "Our Experience," *Knightstown Sun*, 4 April 1894, 2.

24. Linda Lawson has discussed the use of reading notices in her work, as does Sally Foreman Griffith in her biography of William Allen White. I might add here that long before there were concerns about Royal's advertising policies, a two-column Royal plate began to appear in *Demorest's Monthly Magazine*. In March 1880, for example, there appears a story that seems to be a news notice about alum and its negative effects on bread. Then on the next page, an ad for Royal touts the fact that Royal is pure, alum-free, baking powder. "Absolutely Pure" becomes the slogan for the company for years.

25. After success in Fort Wayne and in northeastern Indiana, Hoagland and his partner Thomas M. Biddle moved to Chicago in 1875. Royal Baking Powder's success was not the formula, a common mix of cream of tartar and baking soda, but its bold marketing, discussed throughout this chapter.

26. In regular issues of newspapers in the 1890s, the Royal Baking Powder ad appears on the editorial page, suggesting women were regular readers of opinion pages. Royal ads frequently appear on front pages, as well. It is interesting to observe this same placement of ads by competitors. Dr. Price's Cream Baking Powder is one of the frequent ones and is often paired with the Royal ads.

27. Maurine Beasley calls for a broader conceptualization of women and their relationship to and involvement in journalism in "Women's History in American Journalism," *Journalism Studies* 2, No. 2 (2001): 207–20. Similarly, Jayne E. Marek in *Women Editing Modernism* examines the importance of supportive relationships between women in the publishing world of the little literary magazines.

28. Those who appear in more than one of the papers I have collected so far include Susan B. Anthony, Mrs. Ira Barnett, Lillie Devereux Blake, Nellie Peters Black, Alice Stone Blackwell, M. E. M. Davis, Florence Doulliard, Margaret W. Farrand, Kate Field, Mary Jameson Judah, Marion Harland, Mrs. W. A. Hemphill, Ellen M. Henrotin, Julia Ward Howe,

Mrs. Frank Leslie, Olive Thorne Miller, Louise Chandler Moulton, Bertha Honore Palmer, Sarah S. Pratt, Margaret Sangster, May Wright Sewall, May French Sheldon, Emma Speed, Charlotte Perkins Stetson (later Gilman), Susan (Mrs. Lew) Wallace, and Ella Wheeler Wilcox. Clearly the majority of those who appeared in more than one paper are literary figures, and one of them, Julia Ward Howe, was later to write in her autobiography that the eventual outcome of women's editions was probably to wear out those asked to contribute regularly.

29. Many of the women's editions had pages that were obviously parodies of the standard women's pages, which were growing in popularity in the 1890s and were probably a result of increased advertising directed at women (although Royal itself typically advertised on the editorial page). In Chicago, for example, a typical man's page is called "Men's Corner" and includes a poem called "The Good Old-Fashioned Man" with a final stanza reading "And if he beat her that was part/Of the wise domestic plan./There's nothing wins a woman's heart/Like the good old-fashioned man." Taken out of context, the poem might seem to be advocating domestic violence, but the women were clearly trying to make fun of an "old-fashioned" practice. The page also includes clearer efforts at humor: "Advice to the New Man" and "A Man's Complexion," for example. See *Chicago Evening Journal*, 1 November 1895, 11.

Works Cited

Beasley, Maurine H. "Women's History in American Journalism." *Journalism Studies* 2.2 (2001): 207–20.

Beasley, Maurine H., and Sheila J. Gibbons. *Taking Their Place: A Documentary History of Women and Journalism*. Washington, D.C.: American University Press, 1993.

Colbert, Ann Mauger. "Philanthropy in the Newsroom: Women's Editions of Newspapers, 1894–1896." *Journalism History* 22 (Autumn 1996): 90–99.

Conrad, Will C., Kathleen Wilson, and Dale Wilson. *The Milwaukee Journal: The First Eighty Years*. Madison: University of Wisconsin Press, 1964.

"The Empress of the Dailies." San Francisco *Examiner*, 23 December 1894, 17.

Finley, Ruth E. *The Lady of Godey's: Sarah Josepha Hale*. Philadelphia: Lippincott, 1951.

Garvey, Ellen Gruber. *The Adman in the Parlor: Magazines and the Gendering of Consumer Culture, 1880s to 1910s*. New York: Oxford University Press, 1996.

Griffith, Sally Foreman. *Home Town News: William Allen White and the Emporia Gazette*. New York: Oxford University Press, 1989.

Hall, Joan Wylie. "Louisiana Writers of the Postbellum South." *The History of Southern Women's Literature*. Ed. Carolyn Perry and Mary Louise Weaks. Baton Rouge: Louisiana State University Press, 2002. 203–4.

Juergens, George. *Joseph Pulitzer and the New York World*. Princeton, N.J.: Princeton University Press, 1966.

Kane, Harnett, with Ella Bentley Arthur. *Dear Dorothy Dix: The Story of a Compassionate Woman*. Garden City, N.Y.: Doubleday, 1952.

Kantor, Alvin Robert, and Marjorie Sered Kantor. *Sanitary Fairs, A Philatelic and Historical Study of Civil War Benevolences*. Glencoe, Ill.: Amos Philatelics, dba Scott Publishing, 1992.

Kennedy, Charles. *Fifty Years of Cleveland, 1875–1925*. Cleveland: Wiedenthal, 1925.

Kitch, Carolyn. *The Girl on the Magazine Cover: The Origins of Visual Stereotypes in American Mass Media*. Chapel Hill: University of North Carolina Press, 2001.

Marek, Jayne E. *Women Editing Modernism: "Little" Magazines & Literary History*. Lexington: University Press of Kentucky, 1995.

Mayberry, Susanah. *My Amiable Uncle: Recollections about Booth Tarkington*. West Lafayette, Ind.: Purdue University Press, 1983.

Montgomery, L. M. (Maud). *Anne of the Island*. New York: Bantam Books, 1987.

Norris, James D. *Advertising and the Transformation of American Society, 1865–1920*. Westport, Conn.: Greenwood Press, 1990.
Okker, Patricia. *Our Sister Editors: Sarah J. Hale and the Tradition of Nineteenth-Century American Women Editors*. Athens: University of Georgia Press, 1995.
Snively, Julie. "Extra! Extra!" *Rockford* (Illinois) *Register Star*, 9 March 1993, 1C, 4C.
Tarkington, Booth. *The Gentleman from Indiana*. New York: Doubleday and McClure, 1899.
Virginia Women's Cultural History Project. *"A Share of Honour": Virginia Women 1600–1945*. Richmond: Virginia Women's Cultural History Project, 1985.
Wedell, Marsha. *Elite Women and the Reform Impulse in Memphis, 1875–1915*. Knoxville: University of Tennessee Press, 1991.

"A Woman's Experience as a Newspaper Editor"
The Woman's Edition, *The Nashville American*, 9 May 1894

When I heard there was to be a woman's edition of the Kamschatka Herald, and that my friend, Elise Horton, had been appointed its editor-in-chief, the selection struck me at once as admirable. Elise, I knew, never read anything in the papers except the fashion notes and the society column. She could, therefore, bring to the subject a mind absolutely unbiased by previous knowledge or experience and was quite as likely to take one side as the other, or both sides at once, of the great public questions of the day.

From time to time I saw in the daily papers that the woman's edition was making great progress, and so when I called on Elise the other day, I was not surprised to find her library table piled high with mountains of copy and stacks of proof sheets. I dropped into a low chair and gazed regretfully at a paste pot which occupied the place where, at that hour of the day, I was accustomed to see the cheering tea service.

"Pray don't let me interrupt you," I said. "I've only come to see you edit. How do you like it?"

"It's just simply delicious," replied Elise with a smile that showed her dimples. "I don't mind telling you in confidence that we are going to get out the best paper ever published in Kamschatka; perhaps I shouldn't say that, as we are running a borrowed paper, owned by men, but you know what sort of paper men get out."

I assented.

"So inaccurate," complained Elise. I assented again.

"Why, not long ago they described me as going to a ball in a gown that was C in front and V in the back."

"Shocking ignorance," I agreed.

"Men's papers," went on Elise, "are just full of murders and politics and wars and things like that. Now, we are going to leave most of that out. We have got some splendid articles to go in place of that tiresome stuff. One on 'How to Sit Down in a Stiff Skirt With Organ Folds in the Back,' that is one of the most interesting and thoughtful things I ever read. Then there is another on 'Whether Sleeves Should Droop . . .'"

"Did you have any difficulty," I interrupted, "in making up your staff?"

"No-o," she replied airily, "you see the difficulty was principally about me—the editor-in-chief. Most of the ladies said that as it was a Democratic paper there wasn't any necessity of having an editor-in-chief, that what Democracy meant was that everybody was just the same and there wasn't any head to it."

"When one remembers the last Congress, it certainly seems like it," I murmured.

"Well, that was simply nonsense," Elise replied, "so they made me editor-in-chief and I appointed the rest—a literary editor, you know, and a reform editor, and so on. Yes, and a lot of pretty girls for reporters—half from the Whist Club and half from the church societies, for we intend to have all the news. Everything went along finely until I got to the telegraph editor, and not a single woman would take that. Every one said it just scared her to death to get a telegram and nothing on earth would induce her to open one. Fancy not recognizing whom one's telegrams are from by the hand-writing!" "Fancy!" I repeated with a smile. "May I ask," I continued, "what position you take on the silver question?"

"We are down on that," replied Elise emphatically; "we oppose the coinage of any more silver—it is just utterly impossible to handle silver money with light colored gloves on without ruining them. Why I have often ruined a $3.50 pair of gloves with 10 cents' worth of car fare. What we want is nice, clean paper money and plenty of it."

"Oh, we have a settled financial policy."

"That's a scoop, certainly," I said, "on most of the men's papers. As a general thing, they haven't found out yet where they are on the subject."

"Really," continued Elise, "I think we are getting along beautifully with the paper. There has only been one hitch in the arrangement so far. The Poetical editor has broken down—nervous prostration, the doctor says, brought on by the amount of spring poetry."

"I know it," I interrupted, "good moral sentiment, but rickety meter, all about 'Singing Birds' and 'Lowing Herds' and 'April Showers' and 'Fairy Bowers.'"

"Why you must have seen it, and we thought we were keeping everything such a secret," exclaimed Elise. I shook my head. "Any way," she went on, "you have no idea of the amount of poetical talent there is in the community, and that this woman's edition has brought out. People you would never have thought it of."

"No one is above suspicion in these days," I responded gloomily. "And they all say," she continued—ignoring my remark—"that they just dashed off these few lines on the spur of the moment. Why—they might be great poets like Tennyson or James Whitcomb Riley, if they had a mind to."

"The spelling of a great deal of it," I said meditatively, "reminds you of Riley dialect."

"After all," said Elise, leaning back in her chair, "it isn't all fun to edit a newspaper. The other day an old man came in here begging me to suppress some dreadful story about his daughter. She'd got in the police courts and he was afraid it would be put in the papers. His poor old hand shook like a leaf and his voice broke—'her mother died when she was a baby,' he said, 'and she never had no chance and she never meant no harm,' and she was all he had in the world."

"And there was a woman—her wretch of a husband was in prison, justly enough I dare say, but she sat there in that chair so pitiful and worn and cried—that stifled kind of a sob you know that goes through one like a knife—and wouldn't the woman's edition appeal for mercy for him. It was just awful. Do real editors—men—have to go through that?"

I rose to go. "Yes," I said, "sad or gay the newspaper voices the cry of the world." —ELIZABETH M. GILMER.

PART II
EDITING AS IMPETUS

"Her Object Is Good":
Ann S. Stephens and *Portland Magazine*

JENNIFER BLANCHARD

ON October 3, 1834, the *Portland Advertiser* of Portland, Maine, ran a small article about the arrival of a new literary magazine in the city. Wedged between stories about the upcoming elections in New Hampshire and New York, the short notice announced that the first edition of *Portland Magazine* had been found "deserving of favorable notice" and would need only "the fostering care of the public to be worthy of the highest praise." The notice also commented that the plan of the editor looked "excellent" and that "enough appears in the present number from the editorial pen to warrant the belief that that department will be respectably managed." Finally, the notice remarks that the magazine "certainly promises more fairly than did Mrs. Hale's Ladies Magazine at its commencement.... There is no reason, why a work of the kind, *at half the price*, commanding equal talent in its support, should not flourish as successfully in Portland as in Boston."

The editor and creator of *Portland Magazine*, Ann S. Stephens, could not have written a better advertisement for the publication herself. Stephens, a twenty-four-year-old woman whose passion for literature was equaled only by her passion for notoriety, must have read this notice in the *Advertiser* with great satisfaction. Her first real literary effort was also the first wholly literary publication in Portland and, notably, the first publication of any kind in that city to be edited by a woman. Not only had it been well received, it had even been portrayed as a worthy competitor of Sarah Josepha Hale's more established and popular *Ladies' Magazine*. Though the article does not name Stephens outright, she wielded the lauded "editorial pen" and could comfortably claim the *Advertiser*'s praise for herself.

Ann Stephens is not a particularly well-known figure in America's literary history, though she was an enormously successful editor and writer of periodical literature throughout the nineteenth century, and is generally named as the first American dime novelist. When she is discussed at all, Stephens is usually recognized for authorship of the first Beadle dime novel, a frontier adventure titled *Malaeska* (1860), or for her editorial work on such magazines as *Peterson's*, *Graham's*, and the *Ladies' Companion*. But with her first project, *Portland Magazine*, Stephens began to develop not only her literary craft but her literary personality: the themes she would pursue in her stories and poems; the tone of moral and cultural guidance she would adhere to throughout her career; and, most importantly, her assumption of cultural authority, as enacted in her stories, poems, and editorial notes.

For Stephens, cultural authority was a tangible quantity, a desirable goal measured in critical plaudits and publications sold. Her assertive positioning of herself as a voice of authority is not subtle—from *Portland Magazine* onward her works are littered with dropped names and casual (but concerted) references to her own importance. Stephens was an intelligent woman and a keen observer of the social climate, and even her most obvious expressions of self-satisfaction are couched in a characteristically nineteenth-century rhetoric of modesty and self-effacement. Stephens knew the social and literary terrain of her time and negotiated cultural constructs and mores for her own use. She thrived in her environment even as she found ways to challenge its conditions and create a new place for herself within it.

Stephens's first published story, "The Tradesman's Daughter," appeared in Portland's *Jeffersonian* weekly in early October 1834. That same month marked the debut of *Portland Magazine*, in which Stephens assumed the voice of cultural authority that she would maintain throughout her career. Stephens negotiated and asserted this authority in the pages of *Portland Magazine*, in the stories and verse she and other literary luminaries contributed, and in her own editorial notes. The rhetoric she employed in these notes established her authority as a woman—as an educated and genteel woman, that is. In her fiction and in her notes, Stephens relied upon her status as a member of the "well-educated, well-connected" cultural elite Jane Tompkins refers to in her study of late-eighteenth- and early-nineteenth-century literature. Stephens belonged to the group of men and women who "controlled New England's cultural life [and] thought of themselves as spiritually and culturally suited to raise the level of popular taste and to civilize and refine the impulses of the multitude" (Tompkins 25). Marked by a singular moral and cultural code, issues of class and gender underscore many of Stephens's addresses to readers and, together with a consciousness of Portland as the magazine's cultural location, form the basis of her asserted cultural authority. Stephens was keenly aware of herself and her position, and used her status both to cater to and to shape a literary elite in early-nineteenth-century Portland.

Though many of the details of Ann Sophia Winterbotham Stephens's early years have been lost to time or obscured by romantic recollection, we do know that she was born in Humphreysville, Connecticut, in 1810 to parents who had only recently emigrated from England. Her father, John, was a manufacturer who had been recruited to manage and become a partner at one of the new American woolen mills. Ann's mother, also named Ann, was a sickly woman, and died when Ann Sophia was just a baby. Shortly after the death of his first wife, John Winterbotham married her sister Rachel, who became the only mother Ann ever really knew. The Winterbothams were a successful, well-respected family in their community, and Ann had every advantage offered to a girl of her era and class. She attended a school for girls in Humphreysville when she was very young, and later went to a finishing school in nearby New Britain. Ann learned sewing, needlepoint, and painting, but also excelled in reading and writing. In an oft-quoted and telling remark, Stephens, at the height of her popularity, recalled that "long before I knew what authorship was, I had made up my mind to write stories and make books" (qtd. in Thompson 11). With this statement, Stephens successfully characterizes herself as a born storyteller with a sense of mission in the world of letters and reveals her talent as a master of self-creation. It positions her as helpless in the face of destiny—ever since she was a child, she had known that she *must write.*

When she was about twenty years old, Ann Sophia Winterbotham met a young merchant from Plymouth, Massachusetts, named Edward Stephens, and the two were soon married. In 1831, the Stephenses moved to Portland, Maine, where Edward worked as a dealer in West Indian goods, while Ann began to write stories. Ann's ambitions were not limited to writing, however, and in 1834 *Portland Magazine* debuted, with Ann listed as editor and her husband Edward as publisher.

Portland was a fairly vibrant and cultured city in the 1830s, with, in the words of Lawrence Buell, "a lively theater, two Congregational ministers of some literary note; two rival newspapers receptive to local literary talent . . . and a knot of young professionals who liked to write" (29). During the 1830s, Portland already supported three major publications, all of which published limited selections of fiction, poetry, and essays. The city had numerous booksellers and publishers and access to the latest literary works. It also had a library, the complete holdings of which—3,500 volumes—Ann Stephens is reputed to have read. Despite its thriving and competitive seaport, Portland felt its inferior status vis-à-vis Boston, and was, in the 1830s, trying hard to assert and cultivate its cultural worth. It was ready for a venture like *Portland Magazine.*

One of Ann Stephens's most cunning decisions was to ingratiate herself with one of Portland's favorite sons, John Neal. Described by Van Wyck Brooks as "a shopkeeper, clerk, teacher of drawing and fencing, auctioneer, merchant, editor, lawyer, journalist," the notorious and versatile Neal had published his own weekly, the *Yankee*, in the late 1820s, and was probably the best known of Portland's literary men in the 1830s. In his 1874 memoirs of life in Portland, Neal recalled how a young, attractive woman came into his offices one day, asking for his opinion on a story she had written. As Neal recollected, this was Ann Stephens's first effort at writing, and he was pleased to tell the young lady that she "wrote with great ease, and great earnestness, and from the heart." Neal worked with Stephens on her stories, and probably helped her make contacts at the magazines where those stories were first published. Without name or wealth to recommend her, but endorsed by Neal as "a woman of great original genius, with poetry in her blood, patient, industrious, and full of impassioned enthusiasm," Stephens managed to get her publication off the ground and into the hands of Portland's literary audience (Neal 69).

Ann Stephens's first major literary project relied on its content and the reputation of its editor to attract readers from the outset. The first issue of *Portland Magazine* was, like all those that would follow, a slight volume of about thirty pages, constituted primarily of stories and poems by Stephens herself, with titles such as "The Polish Boy," "Romance and Reality," and "My Natal Bowers." "The Polish Boy" actually became a widely published and well-known piece of literature, memorized by decades worth of schoolchildren. In addition to Stephens's own works, the magazine included an essay by John Neal on phrenology.

The first issue begins with Stephens's address to readers, in which she outlines the magazine's mission and constructs a role for herself as the director of this literary endeavor. She adopts a tone of modesty and self-effacement, but this rhetoric actually allows her to assert her own authority. Offering *Portland Magazine* to "the Ladies of Maine," Stephens concedes the daunting nature of her project:

> The editor is fully aware of all that can be said in opposition to the present undertaking. She knows that days and nights of application and anxiety will be but a small part of the task she has imposed on herself. With no hopes of fame or personal distinction does she step into the field of literature. Well she knows that what could be attained through the medium of a magazine would be far outbalanced by the sacrifice of private ease and personal comfort; yet knowing this, she still undertakes her task, certain that her object is good, and feeling resolved to do her duty to her subscribers so far as her powers will admit.

Stephens's language is steeped in nineteenth-century ideals of gender and class. She depicts herself as a martyr to the literary cause, sacrificing herself for the greater good of the "Ladies of Maine," but she might as well be describing the selfless travails of a new mother: devoted to her responsibility, embracing the hardship as well as the glory that surely lie ahead. Of course, Stephens betrays her own obvious hope for that glory in her assertion that she undertakes this project with no hopes of fame or personal distinction. This modest rhetoric is a strategy often employed by female writers of the nineteenth century, and here helps Stephens align herself with her subscribers, many of whom were probably relatively genteel ladies with literary interests—or aspirations—of their own. She associates herself with these ladies later in the address, when she states that "the privilege of deep research is man's right. . . . But poetry, fiction, and the lighter branches of the sciences are woman's appropriate sphere, as much as the flower garden, the drawing room, and the nursery." Literature, then, takes its place in Ann Stephens's world alongside other "domestic" pursuits.

By making this connection, Stephens both aligns herself with the women whom she views as her audience—those women who have the time for flower gardens and reading, even as they raise their children—and addresses those who might criticize a woman taking such an active role in the publishing world. As Paola Gemme writes in her profile of Ann Stephens, the editor "argued for the perfect compatibility of the nineteenth-century ideal of True Womanhood and authorship. Not only was writing an 'honorable,' 'dignified' profession for women, it was one that would not interfere with their responsibilities as mothers and wives" (48).[1] Other female writers and editors of the nineteenth century, including Sarah Josepha Hale, Lydia Maria Child, and Harriet Beecher Stowe, made similar connections between domesticity and authorship. Because she has, in this passage, differentiated between her own work and the "deeper" work of men, Stephens has articulated her own cultural sphere and her authority within it.

Stephens builds upon the *Portland Advertiser*'s praise for her magazine by referencing Hale in her own editorial address, relying on her readers' familiarity with Hale and her *Ladies' Magazine*. She writes, "The Ladies' Magazine, of Boston, has succeeded well in a city where it has been surrounded by competitors which the proud spirit of man might have yielded to, yet does the Magazine flourish there, in the center of our literary emporium; and from the commencement until now, the American Ladies' Magazine has been edited by a woman." If Hale can succeed in the great literary center that is Boston, Stephens seems to say, I will certainly triumph in Portland, where there is no real competition for a publication of this kind. Making reference to Hale without mentioning her by name, and employing what Patricia Okker names "the sisterly editorial voice," Stephens connects herself with the 1830s model of female editorship (7). Her allusions to Hale and Boston mark her as a woman of some experience, and as a woman familiar with the literary landscape. These references also speak to the early-nineteenth-century cultural competition between Portland and Boston, and none too subtly goad Portland readers into subscribing to *Portland Magazine*, since it is, ostensibly, a virtual counterpart to Boston's respected and respectable *Ladies' Magazine*—and superior for being a local product.

Stephens was certainly aware that she was the first female editor in Portland, which accounts, in part, for her discussion, in the first pages of *Portland Magazine*'s debut edition, of the woman's sphere. Stephens also states her belief that any accusations of presumptuousness leveled at her will not be because she is a woman, but because she is attempting a literary magazine in Portland, Maine. Here again she addresses the city's uncertain sense of itself and its relationship to the nation's other cultural centers. Portland has been "objected to as not being a literary city," Stephens explains in the inaugural edition's address to readers, then asks what other city of similar size has produced "so many great men, in theology, in law, fiction, and poetry?" To win the goodwill of her readers, Stephens highlights the achievements of Portland's great men, though even as she sings their praises she is, in a sense, positioning herself right alongside them. Well-read and -connected Portlanders felt their second-tier status as a city in relation to Boston; to have a woman like Stephens champion the city and its culture must have come as welcome validation. Stephens artfully and knowingly manipulates the allegiances of her readers to win them for herself, securing the success of *Portland Magazine* through a rhetoric of modesty, femininity, and local loyalties.

The rhetoric of femininity is often employed by Stephens through the paradigm of motherhood, and is one that would have strengthened her position as a moral authority. Stephens herself was not a mother at this time, though she would have two children in the early 1840s. Still, she comprehended the lofty role of mothers, and used the early nineteenth-century language of motherhood in her editorial addresses and notes, as well as in her fiction—several of her poems in *Portland Magazine* have titles such as "To My Mother" and "The Daughter." We have already seen how Stephens, in her opening address, associated women's writing with child-rearing, implying both provided a "foundation of character for the rising generation." In the February 2, 1835, edition of *Portland Magazine*, Stephens, admonishing a New Hampshire magazine to "appeal to the ladies," has this to say about motherhood:

> Women are beginning to feel their great importance in the world, and to act up to it. As a proof, compare the children of this to those of the last generation. Does not the contrast speak volumes in favor of the present mothers? Is not the high trust placed in their keeping by the Almighty, beginning to be

justly appreciated? Mothers now (or soon will) think of themselves as they should; as Jewellers, with whom that rich gem, the human soul is entrusted; not to remain in the natural mine of ignorance, but to be taken out, polished, and brightened, as an ornament for this world; while it is purified by them and prepared to return in its increased excellence to the great giver.

Stephens links the supreme importance of mothers, who cultivate their jewellike children, to their literary pursuits. In order to raise the best children possible, she argues, women must be educated and prepared for the role of motherhood. Her use of the rhetoric of exalted and respectable motherhood held obvious correlations for her role as editor/mother of *Portland Magazine*, as well, and shows that she knew how to speak to her audience. Stephens returns again and again to the theme of motherhood, in fiction and in editorials, using the archetype of mother-child relations to describe her literary work and to position herself as an advisor to her female readers. Her voice is so strong and holds such conviction that the fact that Stephens has little tangible authority to rest on (i.e., she is childless) hardly matters—she creates a literary persona of such unimpeachable strength that she becomes the ideal she projects.

Stephens further garnered respectability and cachet for herself and her magazine through her illustrious list of contributors. She solicited contributions from her general readership, but it was the select group of recognizable personalities whose works graced the pages of *Portland Magazine* who lent cultural power to the periodical. Lydia Sigourney, the "sweet singer of Hartford," contributed a poem called "The Muffled Knocker" to an early issue of *Portland Magazine*, while local luminaries writing for Stephens included John Neal and Henry Wadsworth Longfellow—gone from Portland but still claimed by the city—whose poem "The Indian Mother's Song" hints at the epic works he would complete in the future. The recognizable names in *Portland Magazine* certainly lent authority to the publication, but one should not conclude that Stephens sold magazines solely on the basis of her more notable contributors. Indeed, Stephens herself wrote many of the pieces in the first edition, and continued to supply a good deal of the stories and poems in later issues.

In a way, Stephens, through *Portland Magazine*, actually helped legitimate and constitute Portland's literary elite, reversing the process by which she and the magazine achieved legitimacy. By providing the city with its first forum devoted entirely to literature, Stephens, through her editorial control, was able to define the literary product of the city: what she chose to publish was what readers of *Portland Magazine* would consume; the names and works she allowed on her pages became Portland's literary culture. By the second issue of *Portland Magazine*, for instance, Stephens has already begun to define her own perception of cultural authority. She refers to her "brother editors" who have made "honorable mention" of her work, and thanks "some of our best writers" for contributing to the magazine. She also expresses her "warmest gratitude" to the ladies who have submitted pieces for consideration. That she makes special note of these women underscores her particular interest in women and literature; the comment also, of course, functions as yet another flattering remark aimed at her female audience. After these words of thanks, however, Stephens describes what it means to her to have such a notable panel of supporters: "The encouragement of men and women of known taste in the world of literature and fashion has a greater effect than the mere support of a literary work. They are its guardians, and give, by their approbation, a guarantee for the respectability and purity of its contents." At first, we might interpret Stephens's constant reference to her readers and patrons as insecurity and tentativeness about her own authority. She seems very much to want approval and is almost fawning in her praise for the genteel men and women who act as arbiters of taste in Portland and beyond. However, as we have seen in her opening address, Stephens is skilled at using the rhetoric of praise to her own ends. Because she is the agent of cultural authority here—that is, because she controls the cultural goods being produced—she is on a level with the "men and women of known taste" who read and judge her magazine. That these men and women are also, in some cases, the people who contribute the literary contents of Stephens's product further levels the contested terrain of cultural authority.

Stephens also marked the cultural landscape for her readers with extensive reviews of other periodicals and recent books in her editorial notes. In almost every issue of *Portland Magazine*, she expressed her opinions about other periodicals; generally her reviews were favorable, though a significant few were sharply critical. Stephens used these reviews not merely to advise her readers, but to demonstrate her familiarity with the periodical form. For instance, in the June 1, 1835, edition of *Portland Magazine*, she describes Boston's *Pearl* thusly:

> It gives us great pleasure to learn that this excellent work is properly appreciated. We never meet with its delicate pages on a centre-table but we think the better of the subscriber for the good taste thus displayed. The Pearl is a New England journal and a credit to New England, therefore our public should support it abundantly. . . . Indeed we do not know of a person better fitted for his responsible station, than Mr. Isaac C. Pray Jr. editor of the Boston Pearl.

In this review, Stephens manages not only to praise the magazine, but its subscribers and its editor as well. She offers a kind of moral and cultural advice here: the right sort of people subscribe to the *Pearl*, and so ought readers of *Portland Magazine* (not that the two are, by any means, mutually exclusive). By praising editor Isaac C. Pray, Jr., Stephens also manages to draw attention to the role of the editor in a successful publication, forcing recognition of her own importance to *Portland Magazine*. Stephens reviewed books as well, and even informed readers where to buy their copies. In the April 1, 1835, edition of the magazine, for instance, her brief, favorable review of *Recollections of a Housekeeper* by Mrs. Clarissa Packard ends with the advice, "it is to be found at Colman & Chisholm's." Not only did Stephens suggest reading materials to her audience, she directed them to the appropriate store where said materials might be purchased, mapping out a literary world for her readers and providing a compass for its navigation.

Stephens's reviews of books and other publications also helped to establish her as an authority in her field. Her constant references to countless periodicals, both literary and otherwise, mark her as a woman familiar with the work of her peers. The references inform readers that other important literary figures are reading Stephens's magazine; indeed, at times her editorial notes become a message board. In the March 1, 1836, edition of *Portland Magazine*, Stephens compliments the editors of *Godey's Lady's Book* and the *Passion Flower* and submits memos to each. "Mr. Godey is informed that his polite request shall be attended to," she writes, without revealing the nature of that request, "as soon as we can possibly command the time requisite for its accomplishment." To the editors of the *Passion Flower*, she sends a flirtatious, flattering request: "Will our lovely sister of the Passion Flower—for most lovely we take it for granted she is—forward to us numbers two and four, of her exquisite little periodical? They have never reached us, and our set will be incomplete without them." These communiqués with other editors depict Stephens as a member of a literary community, a participant in a far-reaching cultural exchange. The periodical was uniquely suited to this sort of professional and communal exchange, cultivating broad relationships between producer and consumer; editor, writer, and reader. Stephens used this web of relationships to create a sense of social and professional connectedness to her readers, and by so doing, drew those readers into the network of cultural production.

Indeed, readers of *Portland Magazine* often became contributors to the publication. Throughout the run of the magazine, stories and poems are described as written by "a lady of Bangor" or as otherwise submitted by local readers, and Stephens discusses her policy regarding unsolicited stories and poems on more than one occasion. While she invites readers to submit their work, however, Stephens cautions them not to expect publication and outlines her own high standards for the contents of *Portland Magazine*. In the second issue of the magazine, she explains that even "one bad sentence, without the liberty of alteration, will be sufficient reason for the rejection of the best written communication," but expresses the hope that "the rejection of one, two, or three articles, will not discourage the young writer." These are high standards, indeed, particularly as mandated by a woman whose own career had scarcely taken flight. Stephens is in an odd position here: In order for *Portland Magazine* to succeed, it must fill its pages—Stephens, must, therefore, encourage submissions. But to ensure the fine reputation of the magazine, Stephens must also cultivate an air of exclusivity. Once again we see Stephens asserting her own authority and carefully managing the participation of her readers (and contributors) in the literary world. This management was crucial, after all, to Stephens's own success in that arena.

Stephens was, in fact, an active participant in the literary arena beyond Portland. During her tenure with *Portland Magazine*, she published at least two stories in periodicals based outside the state. These stories, "The Dangerous Frolic" and "The Diamond Necklace," were each reprinted in *Portland Magazine* with prominent tag lines indicating where they had originally been published. By including works of her own that had been published in the same periodicals about which she frequently raved, Stephens enhanced her own cultural status and situated herself more centrally in the greater literary world.

Stephens was understandably very concerned at the outset with the reception of *Portland Magazine*, and she continued to address this concern throughout the life of the magazine. By the end of the publication's first year, her preoccupation with a positive reception is still evident, yet it remains coded in language that is undeniably pleased and confident. In the September 1, 1835, edition of *Portland Magazine*, Stephens thanks her patrons and contributors for helping to make the publication a success and expresses her hope that she will be able to "increase the literary excellence of the work, and . . . make it still more worthy of an extensive support." Of course, Stephens's success was, in purely economic terms, dependent on the continued patronage of her readers. She was a businesswoman, required to please and flatter her customers. Her self-effacing rhetoric is not unusual for her time; women writers, both in periodicals and in books, frequently began their works with an apology for their natural inferiority to those produced by men.

Ann Stephens was, then, a woman who shrewdly used the conventions of her time to establish herself as a cultural authority in Portland, Maine. Employing language and themes familiar to her audience, Stephens was able to create a virtually ideal image of mid-nineteenth-century womanhood. Even though she acted outside of the prescribed sphere of home and family and participated in the masculine domain of business and culture, Stephens found a way to articulate a role for herself in this domain that was neither intimidating nor suspect. By describing literature as a feminine province and linking it to women's domestic duties in the very first issue of *Portland Magazine*, Stephens seems to have successfully sidestepped potential criticism of her editorial role.

This apparently successful avoidance of controversy seems largely to have been due, as well, to Stephens's supremely confident tone and language. She understood herself to be suited to the roles of editor and cultural leader, and her language throughout *Portland Magazine* is nothing if not self-assured and self-satisfied. Stephens was always ready with an opinion on everything from the best drawing teacher in town ("those young ladies of our city who wish to perfect themselves [should] call at his rooms in Middle St.") to suggestions for improving a local debating society ("get higher desks, which will preclude the awkward necessity of stooping at each sentence to look at your notes"). She weighed in on national controversies and repeatedly championed the importance of literature to local and national culture. Ann Stephens found great success as a literary and cultural advisor largely because she believed in her power to act as such, and never gave her readers cause to doubt her.

Stephens's confident and businesslike tone also consistently betrays her concern with material matters alongside—and perhaps ahead of—moral matters. In one telling passage quoted above, Stephens refers to Boston as the nation's "literary emporium," a phrase that connotes the business, rather than the culture, of literature. Certainly Stephens was concerned with her own cultural status, and used *Portland Magazine* as a medium through which to espouse moral epigrams and advice, but art, to Stephens, was secondary to tangible advancement and success. She had a talent for literature, but she also had a superb talent for self-creation and self-promotion, a talent that would take her to the top of the American publishing industry.

At the end of the September 1, 1835, issue of *Portland Magazine*, Stephens writes emotionally about the first year of the publication:

> We could weep as we look back to the past year, that of incessant exertion and painful anxiety as it has been; yet we cannot but regret its departure.... Suffice it to say, that out of numerous notices forwarded to us from all parts of the country, two only have failed to speak of it in terms of praise, not faint, but warmly bearing every mark of sincerity.... With these advantages we confidently think we can furnish our subscribers a good second volume of

the Portland Magazine. At least our exertions shall not be spared in the promotion of its usefulness and interest.

Rallied by the success of the magazine's first volume, Stephens sounds enthusiastic about the dawn of the next. However, merely one month after Stephens reflected on *Portland Magazine*'s glorious first year, signs of decline began to seep into the publication. The October 1, 1835, edition has the anonymous "N" apologizing for any errors that may be found therein, explaining that "the Editor has been laboring all this month, under a severe indisposition, from which she is just now recovering." The next month finds Stephens back at the reins of the magazine, offering an apology to "our subscribers on the Penobscot" for the delayed delivery of October's issue. "Our publisher was absent, we were confined to our room, and by mistake the Magazines were placed on board a packet, instead of the steamboat which usually conveys them," she explains. After Stephens's absence, the polished, successful face of the magazine began to erode. Stephens's martyrlike dedication to the magazine, and "N"'s explanations that she was worn out by that very dedication, may well have functioned to gloss over the imminent deterioration of the magazine.

From late 1835 on, Stephens is constantly making excuses and apologies in her editorial notes. In January 1836 she seems to have suffered a bout of influenza from which she was unable to recover and because of which she had less strength and time to deal with *Portland Magazine*. Finally, in the June 1, 1836, issue, Ann Stephens announces the end of her reign as editor of the periodical:

> Late events have so combined, that a change in [the magazine] can now be effected with advantage to the work, and we hope with the entire approbation of our readers. . . . It has long been our desire to throw off the cares of the press, and to devote our attention exclusively to miscellaneous writing. This, together with a determination to travel during some portion of the ensuing season, has induced us to resign the supervision of the Magazine to another.[2]

Here Stephens ties together all the issues of her personal life that had made their way into the second volume of *Portland Magazine*. She had been ill, and needed time to recover. She wished to travel, and this desire, combined with her fatigue, superseded her interest in editing the magazine. The "late events" of illness, restlessness, and, perhaps, loneliness, had overcome Stephens and caused her to reevaluate her future.

Indeed, Stephens may have simply been ready for bigger and better things, for a new city in which to shine. Having gained confidence, experience, and exposure through her work on *Portland Magazine*, at age twenty-six, Stephens must certainly have seen a bright future for herself in the greater literary world. Her subsequent work on numerous magazines and on her novels reveals a more polished style, yet throughout her career Stephens's tone and agenda remain remarkably consistent with the work she did on *Portland Magazine*. Themes of femininity and motherhood still run through her essays and her fiction, and Stephens remains, throughout her career, eminently concerned with her own reputation and role among the literati, even as she gained an ever more prominent place for herself in that world. In her post–*Portland Magazine* work, Stephens continues to reveal herself as a savvy orchestrator of readers and of social expectations, a woman who fits easily in some ways and uncomfortably in others into the constructs of nineteenth-century womanhood.

By the end of the 1830s, Portland had lost its luster as a literary city; most of its writers had moved to Boston or New York and it became, as Lawrence Buell writes, "increasingly clear that Portland would be remembered in literary history as little more than a point of origin" (30). Stephens herself had her earliest success in Portland, but left when her ambitions grew too great. Not only is Stephens one of the many writers and poets who left Portland in the 1830s, but the ultimate failure of *Portland Magazine* epitomizes the waning literary success of the city. Stephens's attempt to establish and cultivate, in Portland, a literary publication—and, by extension, a literary culture—that replicated those found in Boston could not be maintained.

The *Portland Sketchbook*, an anthology of Portland writers edited by Stephens in 1836, just before she left the city, stands as a sort of valedictory not only to Stephens but to writers like John Neal, Nathaniel Parker Willis, and Henry Wadsworth Longfellow, who were by the late 1830s largely gone from Portland. Her preface to the anthology shows that her editorial control is more obvious and self-serving than it ever was in *Portland Magazine*. She writes at length about her attempts to be "fair" in the anthology, about how hard it was to cut pages from the stories of eminent writers, but how she did not discriminate in terms of *whose* pages she cut. However, only one author has more than one of his or her pieces collected in the anthology, and that is Stephens herself. She alludes unsatisfactorily to this inconsistency in the preface by writing that "though great exertions were made, the editor found much difficulty in collecting original materials" from authors, so that she was "obliged, however, unwillingly, to supply the deficiency" (*The Portland Sketchbook* v). Instead of cutting one of her own pieces, then, and leaving the stories she *was* able to procure from other writers as they were submitted, Stephens opted to edit the others and fill out the book with her own work. She ends her preface to the anthology with one of her signature addresses to readers, expressing her modest hopes for success and flattering local loyalties: "The Editor now submits her Portland Book to the public, with much solicitude that it may meet with approbation—feeling certain that indulgence would be extended to her, could it be known how much labor and difficulty have attended her slender exertions, in the literature of a city she has never ceased to love" (*The Portland Sketchbook* v).

Having completed the *Sketchbook* and handed over the reins to *Portland Magazine*, Ann and Edward set off on a recuperative trip to Ohio to visit the Winterbotham family, who had settled there in the early 1830s. By 1837, the Stephenses had returned east and settled in New York City, where Ann began work as an editor and contributor at the *Ladies' Companion*. Furnishing at least one story to nearly every edition of the magazine, Stephens was credited with increasing circulation from 3,000 to 17,000 during her tenure (Gemme 48). Two of the stories she wrote for the *Ladies' Companion*, "Malaeska," and "Mary Derwent," ultimately became popular novels.[3] Stephens left the *Ladies' Companion* in 1841 to work at *Graham's*, during which time she also wrote for many other periodicals, including *Frank Leslie's Ladies' Gazette of Fashion*, the *Ladies' Wreath*, and the *Columbian Lady's and Gentleman's Magazine*.

Despite what must have been intense demands on her time as she wrote for all of these publications, Stephens also, during the early 1840s, had two children and, in the 1850s, established another magazine of her own, *Mrs. Stephens' New Monthly*. This periodical ran from 1856 to 1858 and contained serialized stories by Stephens and others, poems, articles on travel and history, and extensive editorial commentary on everything from fashion to literature to politics. *Mrs. Stephens' New Monthly* enjoyed moderate popularity but was forced by its publisher's financial difficulties into an alliance with the greatly successful *Peterson's Magazine* of Philadelphia in 1858. *Peterson's*, modeled after *Godey's Lady's Book*, was that magazine's biggest competitor in the 1850s, and Stephens's attachment to the publication only increased its popularity (Bercovitch 79). Charles J. Peterson, founder of the magazine, became a key figure in Stephens's career. When she went to work for the magazine, Peterson secured exclusive rights to her stories and tied her to a contract in which she was not allowed to contribute to other publications. In return for this exclusive engagement, Peterson arranged for his brother's publishing company to reissue the stories Stephens wrote for *Peterson's* as clothbound novels (Stern 233).

In her stories and in her nonfiction contributions to her magazines, Stephens maintained an awareness of her position as a woman—and as a woman author—throughout her career. She continued to profess, as she had in her work for *Portland Magazine*, that the role of author was perfectly suited to the lifestyle of the (at least moderately) genteel wife and mother.

In an essay titled "Women of Genius" written for the *Ladies' Companion* in 1839, Stephens explained, "There are few American women . . . who, by a systematic arrangement of time, cannot command three or four hours out of each day" for writing, an "honorable" and "dignified" occupation (90). By asserting that any woman can, without disrupting her other duties, "command three or four hours out of each day" for writing, Stephens justifies her own career, making it sound as if the only time she herself claimed for writing was these three or four hours and that she spent the rest of her time raising her children and doing the other things her readers did. The sheer volume of writing she produced renders such a scenario impossible, of course. Yet just as she did in the earliest issues of *Portland Magazine*, Stephens feels the need to account for her work and to claim it as "honorable" and "dignified" and not at all inappropriate for a woman.

The New York portion of Stephens's life was marked by great success and popularity. She is said to have had the first salon in New York, where such personalities as Edgar Allan Poe and her old friend John Neal would congregate (Pearson 6). She wrote about cultural events for New York newspapers, and in 1859 responded, in a widely reprinted letter, to an editorial by Victor Hugo condemning the recent execution of John Brown (Stern 49).[4] In 1850, she set off for a trip around the world, during which she was fêted by royalty, both actual and literary. In his history of dime novels and novelists, Edmund Pearson writes that on this trip Stephens received "marked attentions from members of royal and noble families, as well as from Thackeray, Dickens, [Alexander von] Humboldt, and others eminent in literature and science" (6). Stephens also became a friend of various presidents of the United States. In the 1850s, she met and befriended James Buchanan, and carried on a long correspondence with him. After Edward Stephens died in 1862, Ann and her children began to spend winters at the National Hotel in Washington, D.C. During this time Ann became an acquaintance of President Abraham Lincoln, and even rushed to the White House late one night to report an assassination attempt she had heard was being planned. She was admitted to the president's chambers (though he had already retired and was not present), thanked, and dismissed by John Hay, the president's secretary. Hay later recounted the "yarn" to an amused Lincoln (Stern 42). This vignette, while demonstrating the full extent of Stephens's confidence in herself and in her authority, is also a bit sad. The story shows a woman who, despite her self-assurance (or, indeed, because of it), was not viewed by others as quite the authority she thought herself to be. She was laughed at behind her back in the White House. Whether she knew that she was the subject of amusement or not we do not know, but this story shows that Stephens was not always viewed by others as she viewed herself.

Despite the glamorous events and acquaintances of her later life, Stephens never forgot the early years in Portland and always remembered the city warmly. In 1886, the committee planning Portland's centennial festivities wrote to Stephens and other illustrious former Portlanders, inviting them to return for the celebration. Stephens, at the age of seventy-six, declined, but graciously thanked the committee for thinking of her. In her note of response, she describes Portland as "a place that has been warmly in my heart for half a century and will be so until that heart ceases its toil" (Hull 361). In typical Stephens fashion, this note expresses deep feeling and gratitude to her "fans" (in this case, the Portland anniversary committee) while actually focusing more on Stephens herself (the sentimentally regretful "until that heart ceases its toil" reminds the reader that she is aged and will, tragically, probably die before long).

The "toil" of Stephens's heart, her literary career, was indubitably nurtured in Portland; her vast oeuvre remained, over her fifty-year career, impressively consistent in tone and theme with her earliest work for *Portland Magazine*. Only three months after she wrote Portland's centennial celebration committee, Ann Sophia Winterbotham Stephens died at the Newport home of her longtime publisher, Charles J. Peterson. She was eulogized as "the first American woman novelist of note" and "a pioneer in the romance writing of the day," praise that she might have found just a bit stale and perfunctory (qtd. in Stern 53). In a way, however, these accolades are perfect, in that they both classify Stephens for what and who she truly was and yet fail to encapsulate her complex and utterly unique personality. These conflicts are the same as those Stephens experienced in her own life and dealt with in her writing, of course. For instance, Stephens might well have resented being characterized as a "woman novelist," as in the first line cited above. She believed in her own unqualified greatness, and might well have viewed this as somewhat of a snub. Of course, she also made a career out of being a "woman novelist," and would not have minded the approbation that she was the first notable American version of the same.

A woman who bared herself more through her fiction and other writings than in straight autobiography, Stephens left little of herself behind, other than her work, when she died. But Stephens's work was her voice, and her literary career was her life. The girl who had "made up her mind" to make books "long before she knew what authorship was" grew into a woman for whom the mythology of print held great allure, and for whom the idea, or *ideal*, of the literary life was the model to which she adhered throughout her career.

Notes

1. Gemme's article is the only major critical study of Ann Stephens and deals primarily with her later periodical work and her novels.

2. In 1836, Stephens handed *Portland Magazine* over to the publishers of Bangor's *Eastern Monthly* and left Portland. Without Stephens, the magazine, now called *Maine Monthly*, faltered and died after only a few months.

3. The house of Beadle premiered its dime novel series with Stephens's *Malaeska* on June 10, 1860, advertising it as "The Best Story of the Day" by the "Star of American Authors." An initial printing of 10,000 sold out immediately; by the end of the 1860s, nearly half a million copies had been sold. See Karen L. Rood, ed., *American Literary Almanac: From 1608 to the Present* (New York: Facts on File, 1988), 32.

4. Stephens called the execution an "inevitable necessity" in a country where "Liberty with us subjects herself to the laws she has inspired."

Works Cited

Bercovitch, Sacvan, ed. *The Cambridge History of American Literature*, Vol. 2, *1820–1865*. Cambridge: Cambridge University Press, 1995.

Buell, Lawrence. *New England Literary Culture: From Revolution through Renaissance*. Cambridge: Cambridge University Press, 1986.

Gemme, Paola. "Ann Sophia Winterbotham Stephens." *Legacy* 1 (Dec. 1995): 47–55.

Hull, John T., ed. *Centennial Celebration: An Account of the Municipal Celebration of the One Hundredth Anniversary of the Incorporation of the Town of Portland*. Portland, Maine: Owen, Strout & Co., 1886.

Neal, John. *Portland Illustrated*. Portland, Maine: W. S. Jones, 1874.

Okker, Patricia. *Our Sister Editors: Sarah J. Hale and the Tradition of Nineteenth-Century American Women Editors*. Athens: University of Georgia Press, 1995.

Pearson, Edmund. *Dime Novels*. Port Washington, N.Y.: Kennikat Press, 1929.

Stephens, Ann S., ed. *The Portland Sketchbook*. Portland, Maine: Colman & Chisholm, 1836.

Stern, Madeleine B. *Publishers for Mass Entertainment in Nineteenth-Century America*. Boston: G.K. Hall, 1980.

———. *We the Women: Career Firsts of Nineteenth-Century America*. New York: Schulte, 1963.

Thompson, Gwen. "Ann S. Stephens and The First *Portland Magazine*." *Portland* 6 (Sept. 1994): 9–15.

Tompkins, Jane. *Sensational Designs: The Cultural Work of American Fiction, 1790–1860*. New York: Oxford University Press, 1985.

"ADDRESS"[1]
Portland Magazine, 1 October 1834

Noah, when sending out the dove upon the waste of waters, could not have felt more anxiety for its safe return with the green leaf of promise in its bill, than is experienced for the success of the specimen number of the *Portland Magazine*, which we now offer to the Ladies of Maine. The editor is fully aware of all that can be said in opposition to the present undertaking. She knows that days and nights of application and anxiety will be but a small part of the task she has imposed upon herself. With no hopes of fame or personal distinction does she step into the field of literature. Well she knows that what could be attained through the medium of a magazine would be far outbalanced by the sacrifice of private ease and personal comfort, yet knowing this, she still undertakes the task, certain that her object is good, and feeling resolved to do her duty to her subscribers so far as her powers will admit.

The editor earnestly deprecates the unfair criticisms and ill will of sterner reapers in the literary field. Let them go on in the strength of great intellects, measuring pens in political strife. Their's it is to dig the bosom of the earth, to scour the mountains, to draw the lightning from the clouds, and pore with keen eye over the starry heavens, in their search for philosophical knowledge. Earth, ocean, air and sky, we willingly yield to them. The privilege of deep research is man's right; with it we have no wish to interfere. All we ask is permission to use the knowledge he has scattered over the enlightened world. But poetry, fiction, and the lighter branches of the sciences are woman's appropriate sphere, as much as the flower-garden, the drawing-room, and the nursery; and the use of these cannot be denied us with any show of reason, so long as woman is singled out by nature and custom to lay the foundation of character for the rising generation. Will man trust the budding intellect and unformed principles of his sons and daughters to the guidance and moulding of a woman's judgment, and still deny her the power of contributing to the amusement of his leisure hours? Not unless he considers the moral welfare of his child of less value than the hours he devotes to amusement.

In commencing this magazine we may be deemed presumptuous; and we may be so—but not because we are a woman. Women have done more than we are now attempting to accomplish, and done it nobly too. We mark out no new path; establish no precedent. Works of this description, conducted by women, are numerous in Europe, and not unknown here. The Ladies' Magazine, of Boston, has succeeded well in a city where it has been surrounded by competitors which the proud spirit of man might have yielded to; yet does the Magazine flourish there, in the centre of our literary emporium; and from the commencement until now, the American Ladies' Magazine has been edited by a woman.

In objection to the present undertaking, it has been said that Maine is not a fit field for a work such as the Portland Magazine is intended to be. Portland in particular has been objected to as not being a literary city. We are surprised that such an objection can be made; and answer, that no place in America of equal size, and containing the same number of inhabitants; can, without presumption, claim precedence of ours in point of literary merit. What city containing only sixteen thousand inhabitants has produced so many great men, in theology, in law, fiction and poetry? We answer, none. Of our landscape and portrait painters we may well be proud. Our schools are numerous and of a high order. All branches of commerce and industry are carried on vigorously by the enterprising merchants and mechanics of Maine. New towns are springing up rapidly around us, and the sound of manufacturing machinery is beginning to overpower the roar of our waterfalls. With all these advantages why should not our state be able to support a literary magazine? Its society is not deficient in intelligence or refinement; yet if we are not misinformed, Maine has no paper nor magazine devoted entirely to literature. It can, and we are encouraged to hope will, support one. Our specimen number is now submitted respectfully for examination.—
ANN S. STEPHENS

1. This selection is Ann Stephens's address to readers in the first issue of *Portland Magazine*. It appeared on the first two pages of the issue.

"Where Women May Speak for Themselves": Miriam Frank Leslie's "Ladies' Conversazione"

LINDA FROST

BY the time she died on September 18, 1914, Miriam Florence Follin Peacock Squier Leslie Wilde had taken on yet another name and identity, if not another husband. Renaming and refashioning herself as "the Baroness de Bazus," this once queen of Publishers' Row left almost two million dollars to "Mrs. Carrie Chapman Catt . . . to the furtherance of the cause of Woman's Suffrage"; word of the controversial legacy joined that of the war in Europe on the front pages of New York's newspapers (Stern, *Purple Passage* 182). Briefly a Southern belle and always a fashion aficionada, three-time divorceé and one-time widow of the powerful New York publisher Frank Leslie, successful writer, editor, and publisher in her own right, Miriam Leslie (the name by which she was perhaps best known) designed, launched, edited, and contributed to the 1865 story paper, *Frank Leslie's Chimney Corner*. Eventually attaining a circulation of 80,000, the *Chimney Corner* captured a yearly profit of over $72,000 for its publishers (Stern, *Purple Passage* 46). For the first five months of her editorship of the publication, Miriam Leslie arranged and composed a column that appeared on the eleventh page of the paper. Called "Ladies' Conversazione," it invited women readers to participate in a free exchange between the editor and themselves. It was to be, according to one columnist, a "place where women may speak for themselves" (3 June 1865, 11).

Although the cause to which Miriam Leslie would eventually will the bulk of her estate is never specifically mentioned in the column, "Ladies' Conversazione" nevertheless brings emotional attention to the issues the women's movement addressed more overtly and politically. The correspondents' letters that comprise these columns—letters selected and responded to by Miriam Leslie, if not actually composed by her as well—personalize the concerns dealt with by the promoters of women's rights and give them deeper resonance via the correspondents' often moving accounts of their own experiences.[1] Nevertheless, like its sister family papers, *Frank Leslie's Chimney Corner* devoted itself to the professedly impartial and apolitical instruction and amusement of "the young and old, in the family and by the fireside" (3 June 1865, 10). As a result, Miriam Leslie's "Ladies' Conversazione" columns provide us with a carefully contradictory dialogue concerning the situation of the archetypal white, middle-class American woman in the nineteenth century. At once supportive of a conventionally feminized domestic home and hearth, "that altar around which cluster our holiest and most cherished recollections," Miriam Leslie's editorial choices and contributions nevertheless call into question the concepts that make such a space possible (3 June 1865, 10). Readers send letters questioning the validity and possibility of happiness for women in marriage, letters that promote the personal value of public work for women, and letters that lament the tragedy of domestic violence. Through these texts, nineteenth-century readers could see for themselves the implications of an American class-gender system that ideologically, if not physically, relegated women to a claustrophobically private sphere.[2] While these letters exemplify the importance of public speech for women—in a space Miriam Leslie cleared for her readers as well as for herself—they also call into question the naturalness and validity of gendered behaviors and traits overall. "Ladies' Conversazione" is a fascinating example not only of nineteenth-century popular readership, but also of what could happen when an editor represented himself or herself as loosening the reins of his or her editorial practice and allowing his or her readers to speak for themselves.

Born in New Orleans in 1836, Miriam Florence Follin was schooled in Cincinnati and New York and published her first piece of journalistic prose in the *New York Herald* when she had barely turned fourteen.[3] Carefully grooming Miriam in matters of culture and intellect, her parents apparently never legalized their union—an issue that cropped up at inconvenient moments of Miriam's life. Not surprisingly then, perhaps, Miriam became someone who managed both to fly in the face of social convention and to maintain the superficial attributes her society deemed valuable and significant for women. In other words, she could divorce several husbands and *still* be the belle of Abraham Lincoln's first inaugural ball. Her first marriage was to a jeweler who lent her her first diamonds when she was seventeen; Miriam's mother forced the man, David Peacock, to marry Miriam, then swiftly had the marriage annulled. Miriam's next husband was Ephraim George Squier, an archeologist and later writer and editor for *Frank Leslie's Illustrated Newspaper* who lost his sanity along with his wife when they separated years later. Their divorce left Miriam free to marry the vivacious and successful Frank Leslie in 1874. By this time, she was editing three of the Leslie publications herself: *Frank Leslie's Lady's Magazine*, *Frank Leslie's Lady's Journal*, and *Frank Leslie's Chimney Corner*. Sometime after Leslie's death, Miriam was married for the last time, to Oscar Wilde's alcoholic brother, Willie, whom she divorced within two years.

Miriam was one of the most famous women in America by the end of the century. Not only had she defied the conventional constraints of nineteenth-century American marriage by using divorce to her own advantage, she was also one of the most successful publishers of her time. She went so far as to legally assume the name and identity of her third husband—Frank Leslie—when he pointedly left it to her in his will. (Leslie had died almost immediately following a court case in which his estranged son was barred from using the Leslie name in his own publishing ventures.) Along with his name, Miriam inherited Leslie's crippling debts, but by capitalizing on the event of President James Garfield's shooting, she was able to save *Frank Leslie's Illustrated Newspaper* and the rest of the Leslie establishment from bankruptcy.[4] Before Miriam saw the Leslie publishing house into the twentieth century, she rescued it from ruin one more time in 1898; her involvement with *Frank Leslie's Popular Monthly* was completely finished in 1905. She was a powerful figure in the world of nineteenth-century popular publishing but, as Patricia Okker puts it, despite the uniqueness of her particular editorial authority, Miriam Leslie, "like many other women editors, . . . claimed that authority to a great extent on the basis of her gender: as a fashionable woman, she was qualified to be a fashion editor; as a financially troubled widow, she turned to business to 'save' her husband's empire" (31).

In fact, there is even a bit of the feminine apologetic stance in Miriam's first "Ladies' Conversazione." According to "Mr. Editor," it is a letter from Maud Augusta that gives "him" the idea for the column overall. Maud writes:

> Mr. Editor— . . . I want you to devote a column in your journal to women in general—not to your remarks and views concerning them, be good enough to understand; you men have talked so much and so long, and never hit on the truth yet, that it is time you were silenced forever! What I want is a place where women may speak for themselves, in spite of all the slanders of you male creatures. It is seldom enough we get an opportunity. (3 June 1865, 11)

Mr. Editor encourages his readers to see this as an invitation to join the conversation, and to do so without fear of reprisal for a range of things:

§ Subject matter—"let it be distinctly understood that, in the way of subjects, our correspondents shall not meet with any sort of restriction—from grave to gay, from trifling to the most weighty affairs"

§ Disagreement with fellow correspondents—"there shall be space for the publication of letters, and an opportunity for replies given to any who dissent from opinions or views which anybody else may offer"

§ Potentially troublesome questions—"we promise to reply to questions as patiently as Job himself could have done"

§ Fear of exposure, despite the inherently public nature of the forum itself—"every woman knows the sanctity of an editor's drawer, so that she may write with the most perfect freedom." (3 June 1865, 11)

In fact, the only area the editor begs his/her readers to avoid is a very specific one:

> one thing we do hope, that nobody with a mathematical turn of mind will have the cruelty to ask any questions the answer to which would involve the slightest acquaintance of figures. Let us be frank and humble for once, and acknowledge that we have not the most distant idea in regard to the mysterious signs. (3 June 1865, 11)

Despite the fact that this particular editor is assumed to be male, here "he" invokes a curiously feminized fear of math by using what Okker calls the "sisterly editorial voice." According to Okker, this rhetorical stance demonstrates an equal valuing of the voices participating in the column, both editorial and correspondent, and, combined with the format of the column overall, it "broke down the barrier between editor and audience to create an actual dialogue" (31). As other scholars have noted, the letter itself was an emotionally charged textual vehicle in nineteenth-century America, a period of rapid demographic shift and greater social isolation. Ronald Zboray has explained the increase in circulation and importance of the letter in American culture as one result of the related increase in transience among Americans and immigrants in the early part of the nineteenth century: "As the whirlwind of economic development scattered these individuals all over America they struggled vainly to preserve these former affectional networks through correspondence" (31). In light of this, Miriam Leslie's column promised much more than simply advice; it offered an emotional oasis for the domestically isolated woman reader.

Weekly correspondence columns in story papers and miscellanies at this time largely functioned as a place where editors could publish their responses to writers' unsolicited submissions. When a weekly such as San Francisco's *Golden Era* or *The New York Mercury* did run a more substantive correspondence column, the editor seemed to favor a quality of unity in the voices included in it. Although "Mr. Mercury" of *The New York Mercury*'s "Ladies' Promenade" includes letters from all kinds of women living all over the country—even one from an avowed Cherokee writer—all seem to conform to an established aesthetic, one promoting a recognizable and consistent set of characteristics most often referred to as elements of sentimental discourse. The goal of writers like these seems to be inclusion in the pages of the paper itself, not a drive to challenge what's already been printed there. By enumerating all of the areas that might inhibit a potentially timid writer not accustomed to assuming the highly visible speaking position of a published correspondent, and by using the "sisterly editorial voice" to enhance the spirit of intimacy that will characterize "Ladies' Conversazione," "Mr. Editor" clears the way for women writers to take the stage, and to say whatever they want to once they get there. If the letters that were published in Leslie's column were not actually written by "real readers," they still accomplished something unique in the realm of mid-nineteenth-century popular periodicals. Whether written by correspondents or Miriam Leslie herself, the letters that comprise "Ladies' Conversazione" provide a textual shape for what "true" dialogue might look like, imaginatively forcing into being a gender-inflected conversation other periodicals of this time simply did not offer.

In fact, rather than promote the homogenizing force of sentimental discourse so obviously favored by other newspaper editors in similar columns, "Mr. Editor" actively promotes dialogue in the *Chimney Corner*, even going so far as to argue against assumptions of feminine homogeneity in the final segment of "Ladies' Conversazione":

> Who says "Every woman is alike?" Why, many benighted individuals affirm that such is the case. In how profound a darkness do they live and think, who believe that women are fashioned after one model more exclusively than are the other sex.
>
> Let him but occupy our own editorial chair, and spend an hour in perusing the various epistles which it is our good fortune to receive, and he will own himself mistaken *instanter*. (7 October 1865, 299)

While adamant that women do not fit one particular model, the *Chimney Corner*'s "Mr. Editor" still uses the device of the regular correspondent to highlight particular stereotypes of American women. "Schoolgirl" writes in several times to get answers for her lessons and in the process reveals the pains of schooling: "Couldn't you some time write an article about the way teachers behave, and I'd just leave it where [my governess] could find it. Maybe it would rouse her conscience, which is more than I can do, even if I cry till I am black in the face" (10 June 1865, 27). But again, in the spirit of dialogic exchange, "Ladies' Conversazione" later prints a letter from "Governess" herself: "The life of a teacher is hard enough at best—certainly it does not require to have its annoyances aggravated by ill-judged sympathy with rebellious young people, who are only too ready to consider anything in the shape of study and duty as synonymous with tyranny and ill usage" (8 July 1865, 91). Other types appear in this column—a pampered "Blanche" who misses out on a summer in Saratoga, a work-hungry "Edith" who longs for some productive duty, etc.—and each is met with another, equally questioning, conflicting voice. Almost all of the correspondents who contribute to Leslie's column wind up matched by such a voice, putting them all into "conversazione" and thereby allowing "Mr. Editor" to challenge the idea that any printed articulation of women's experience can be univocal and representative of all women.

Certainly the letters and dialogic exchanges printed in "Ladies' Conversazione" allow for the airing of some surprisingly charged issues; they appear even more so when we remember that they appeared in a venue supposedly designed to *preserve* rather than critique the middle-class family/fireside culture of nineteenth-century middlebrow America. The experiences, stories, and voices of these women offer themselves up on the page for their readers' sympathy. In addition, they raise the question of how satisfying expectations for women in America at this time really were. For instance, a June 24, 1865, letter from "Your blue friend, Edith" argues that women need some kind of productive work to do to keep them happy and whole:

> I sit in my cozy room, with its thousand pleasant surroundings, and a restlessness takes possession of me that I am ashamed of. Surely, there must be some work for me to do. I am not alone in this. I see all about me dyspeptic, sad-eyed, languid women—women never quite well, and unable to endure anything. They are *not* indolent; let them be thoroughly interested in any subject, and oftentimes their energy is wonderful to see; but they droop and fade.... [My] dear friends say to my growlings, "Why, you ought to be the happiest creature in the world, for you have nothing to do." I wish they could only know what hard work it is to do it. (59)

Edith here forcefully debunks the image of the mythologically delicate True Woman; it is clear to her that if women are sickly, it is a sickness born of boredom. When another correspondent, Monitor, writes in to chastise Edith for not undertaking the work right in front of her ("Couldn't . . . the fingers [be] employed in making something useful for those poor children, just round the corner . . . ?"), Edith responds to that as well, admonishing her for upholding yet another stereotype of the selfless work deemed most appropriate for women of this class (1 July 1865, 75):

> I don't much like what Monitor says. . . . She knows as well as I that we can't all be missionaries to the poor people round the corner, and that it don't take much serious thinking to get ready the slippers and paper for papa. (5 August 1865, 155)

A week after Edith's first call for worthwhile work, another correspondent reveals the kind of cruel discouragement women often received whenever they did try to do more of the type of work Edith craves. Viola Treadwell describes in painful detail her husband's contempt for her literary endeavors. She is writing something to send to the *Chimney Corner* when he

> banged on the door, as husbands always will, and asked me, with a look of ridicule, what I was doing.
> I answered, with some hesitation, "thinking." He repeated the words with a provoking sneer, and added—
> "Really, my dear, you had much better amuse yourself by getting the tangle out of Will's hair or mending the rents in Dick's pantaloons! Take my advice; try to be useful, and leave literature to heads that are better fitted for it."
> Of course I was very much disconcerted by this uncivil rebuke, but I kept as calm as possible, and told him I would not give up writing unless he absolutely forbade it. He burst into a loud laugh, desired me to recover my senses with all speed, and take care that the beef was not over-roasted. (1 July 1865, 75)

Another young newlywed writes in about the disappointment her marriage has been to her:

> ... baby is such a comforter. I sit at twilight with her in my lap, and tell her all my troubles, and she 'coo's' and 'sh's' in her soft little voice, and then I am happy. But when she is asleep it all comes back, and I wish I was lying in the graveyard opposite, with my baby in my arms. I believe, after all, that marriage is not best. I was happier before.—M.A.L. (2 September 1865, 219)

Rather than simply uphold the values of middle-class America and the ideological separation of the public and private spheres that papers like the *Chimney Corner* purportedly promoted, letters like these expose the dissatisfaction and even brutality such thinking could support. In Miriam Leslie's column, women conventionally separated from one another, locked into isolated, domestic spaces, both reach *and* speak out in the space "Mr. Editor" provides.

Other correspondents contest the image of women as the weak, fragile beings mythologized as the ideal woman of the time. "Wanderer" writes in with a question about the ease of women journeying in the Adirondacks and is reassured by the editor that "there is no serious obstacle to ladies undertaking the trip, provided they can make up their minds to leave crinolines and furbelows at home" (8 July 1865, 91). After complimenting the "dear sir" editor on "his" representation of men in his paper, correspondent "Susan Selina Snipes" points out the contradictions in women's representation and their actual movement in the public sphere:

> It is the universal custom to speak of women as a class of beings kept so completely under the shadow of the masculine wing as to be shielded entirely from the storms of life. We are spoken of as delicate creatures, unfit to battle with the stern realities of life; and did I live in the moon, and only *hear* of women, I should always think of them as tenderly cherished household pets, whose lives were one long summer day. I, however, am not a resident of the moon, and have no such poetical ideas with regard to the position of my sex. I do know, however, that the shadow of the wing masculine is, indeed, over us, and throws us so completely in the shade, that in the never-ceasing conflict for bread and butter, in which a great number of us are constantly engaged, we are treated as though we were possessed of a giant's strength, more patience than Job, and the simplicity of idiots.
>
> For example, we are expected to work in the mill, the shop, the household, the store or the school-room, as long and as well as men, but when pay-day comes we receive a mere trifle in comparison with them, and are railed at as silly, loud-voiced females, if we venture to ask for a more just award. (19 August 1865, 187)

While the topic of women's suffrage does not appear in the column *per se*, its implications are everywhere apparent in these letters' investigations of women's limitations and women's actual and potential capabilities. The correspondents who people this column bring individual force and emotion to the very issues that gave the women's movement of this time its lifeblood. The questions of women's work, women's position in the public sphere, women's satisfaction with traditional institutions such as marriage—all of these come under scrutiny via the stories of Edith, Viola Treadwell, M.A.L., and Susan Selina Snipes. The editor responds to Snipes simply by saying, "you are right and we are wrong. We acknowledge it, and hope fervently that the day will come when all this will be changed" (19 August 1865, 187).

* * *

> Dear ladies, as we shuffle over the white epistolary pile, a thousand pleasant fancies throng: Who wrote all these letters? How many of them were pretty; how many beautiful; how many noble and true? What portion of them should we admire if we beheld them? How many would regard approvingly our own *personnel?* Under what circumstances were they written? Some, we are sure, laughingly, gayly, by pretty fingers that *will* get ink-stained, and girlish brains, that come to a stand-still every half-dozen lines, demanding imperiously of their own wits, or a companion, "what *shall* I say next?"
>
> Some, we believe, are written in real perplexity—some in real distress—many in a state of dire indignation.
>
> But we are prosing, and shall have no space left for our letters. (30 September 1865, 283)

In as much as Miriam Leslie's column targets the problems of womanhood in the nineteenth century and the ideological constraints that compel these correspondents to call them into question, "Ladies' Conversazione" similarly enacts the constructedness of gendered roles and personal identity itself. As a literary text compiled and/or written by Leslie herself, "Ladies' Conversazione" makes clear the way in which language—and particularly the language of experiential, personal narrative—creates the self. The fact that "Mr. Editor" comments that the "prosing" he is doing will use up space intended for letters that are themselves constructions of different kinds of identity is wonderfully ironic, especially given the way in which Mr. Editor "himself" plays with his—or her—own identity in previous columns.[5]

In July, Mr. Editor experiences a confrontation of a more violent and potentially dangerous nature than any other printed thus far in the column. This particular episode emphasizes what will become a larger issue later on: the identity-constructing power of the written text itself. When Mr. Editor is confronted with the comments of an enraged and threatening "Injured Husband," he/she is ill-prepared for what waits inside this envelope:

> Tenderly we abstracted a dainty, well-filled envelope, from the white pyramid, and after gazing upon it a few moments, . . . we had decided that the writer must certainly possess blue eyes, auburn ringlets, . . . a complexion like—like—peaches and cream; judge, then, of our horror when the following met our eye . . . (15 July 1865, 107)

The following is a diatribe by "Injured Husband," who claims that he "caught" his wife

> writing a letter to you, beginning, "*Dear* Mr. Editor," and containing the most impertinent, the most false, the most abominable complaints and allegations against *me*, her husband. I snatched the pretty epistle from her, boxed her ears, and rushed frantically from the house. . . . And now, sir, what I have to say is simply this—that unless you stop writing such abominable trash to the women as you have so far, I shall take it upon myself to chastise you as you deserve. You ask them to write you an account of all their grievances. One wife was on the point of detailing what she imagined to be hers; her husband discovers her, and, in the rage of the moment, recalls her, through the medium of her ears, to a sense of duty. Let me tell you, sir, in that sensible country, England, a man is very properly and wisely allowed to use a stick, not thicker than his thumb, to recall his wife to reason, and I am told this is the reason why Englishwomen always prefer a man with small thumbs. (15 July 1865, 107)

The editor responds with dismay:

> Do you wonder now that we dread to answer those letters before us? Who knows what pistols and threats may rest in those silent quadrangles of paper?

If the box of Pandora had never been opened, man would have been spared infinite woe. (15 July 1865, 107)

What "Mr. Editor" reveals here is interesting; when readers join a writing community such as the one constructed in the paragraphs of "Ladies' Conversazione," there is simply no telling what they will bring to the table. Domestic violence here reaches far beyond the sacred confines of the home and into the very public world of the weekly newspaper. Despite the fact that "Mr. Editor" "begs" this man's wife to jump back in line and save herself a whipping, this editorial voice has already made clear the monstrosities that hover, hidden, in this most "sacred" private space—the home. Just as Mr. Editor is shocked and dismayed to see what might be—and in this case, is—revealed in the not so "silent quadrangles of paper" through which he rifles every week, so the readers too may be equally shocked to see what all goes on in their larger American community. As Mr. Editor says, "if the box of Pandora had never been opened, man would have been spared infinite woe" (15 July 1865, 107). Looking beneath these surfaces may upset everything we have come to believe about ourselves, and may further disturb the domestic foundations of the American family the *Chimney Corner* professed in its first issue to protect and promote.

It is perhaps no accident, then, that soon after this account, Mr. Editor reveals *her* true identity. Part of what the exchange with "Injured Husband" makes apparent is that writing allows the writer the possibility to represent him or herself in any number of ways; after all, his letter arrived "in a dainty . . . envelope" that suggested something other than an ear-boxing jealous husband. In a letter published on August 5, 1865, "Ethelinde" imagines Mr. Editor's countenance as "he" reads her letter detailing the fantasized moment when her words move "him" from disinterest to pleasure to publication. But while Ethelinde describes Mr. Editor's unequivocally "manly brow," in a different letter, "Laura" comments on her uncertainty regarding the editor's identity: "I hardly know whether I am writing to one of the *fair* or the *unfair* sex," she says, after complaining about her husband's unwillingness to take her out of town (155). Mr. Editor's response first equivocates regarding her/his gender, then "lets the cat out of the bag":

Will Laura excuse us if we own that, as one of the fair sex, we don't want a sister, and, as one of the sterner sex, we are equally unprepared to receive a wife and impromptu family. We are also reluctantly compelled to admit that . . . we cannot help thinking that her husband is right—seldom as we women—ah! we have let the cat out of the bag; but what's once said can't be recalled; and so let us say, in all womanly sincerity, . . . that if her husband does not wish to go out of town, she had much better to stay with him, and by her angelic behavior make him ashamed of himself. That is all an ill-used wife can do in the nineteenth century. (155)

Mr. Editor publishes a swift retraction of this statement in the next issue—"we took a savage pleasure in finding fault with everybody, and finished by giving the impression—need we say, a *wrong* one—that we had the honor of belonging to the 'fair sex'"—but the damage, so to speak, has really been done (12 August 1865, 171). Even as the editor refers to the powerlessness of the "ill-used wife" of the nineteenth century, "she" has clearly exempted herself from this definition by indicating the power she holds as Mr. Editor. Her subsequent retraction of this "coming out" merely reinforces the advice her own example offers: namely, women should—and can—use language to control their own self-fashioning.

Whatever else she may represent, Miriam Leslie's role as "Mr. Editor" undeniably demonstrates how writing afforded women an imaginative freedom perhaps nowhere else possible. Miriam herself would embody the process of linguistically reconfiguring one's identity by assuming the Frank Leslie name and persona—a name that was itself the result of the reinvention of a British engraver named Robert Carter.[6] The power of writing to recreate and rebirth the self is everywhere apparent in this narrative and it is probably the greatest legacy Miriam Frank Leslie could have possibly left her readers.

* * *

All the rest, residue and remainder of my estate, . . . I do give, devise and bequeath unto my friend MRS. CARRIE CHAPMAN CATT of the City of New York. It is my expectation and wish that she turn all of my said residuary estate into cash, and apply the whole thereof as she shall think most advisable to the furtherance of the cause of Women's Suffrage to which she has so worthily devoted so many years of her life. . . . (Article Twelve, The Will of Frank Leslie, 30 June 1881)

The letters and editorial commentary contained in the *Chimney Corner's* "Ladies' Conversazione" characterize the kind of complex cultural actor Miriam Frank Leslie was. Describing the impression left on her audiences during a lecture tour Miriam undertook in 1890 through the Midwest, biographer Madeleine Stern recounts these contradictions: "She had presented in person to the Middle West an extraordinary figure, part man, but all woman. . . . She was romance and opportunism rolled into one. She was brocade and diamond, artifice and subtlety, ingénue and sophisticate" (*Purple Passage* 152). Known to her death as both the most fashionable of belles and the most successful of businesswomen, Miriam Frank Leslie evinced in her life the same kind of questioning of gendered assumptions that she displayed in the voices of the letter writers contained in "Ladies' Conversazione." As she argued in a piece published in *The Ladies' Home Journal* in March of 1892, Miriam believed that while the innocence of girls and women should be maintained, it should always be informed: "I believe that many a woman of the world who has discreetly eaten of the fruit of the Tree of Knowledge of good and evil, is as pure, as innocent, and very far safer than the convent-bred girl who knows not tinsel from gold, nor apples of Sodom from wholesome fruit" (6).

It would be very tidy and even triumphant to end this essay with the simple but splendid proclamation with which I started: that upon her death, Miriam Leslie left just shy of two million dollars to further support the fight to win the vote for American women. While it would be fitting to end on that note, it would also be misleading. Through a range of complicated interpretations and rewrites of the language of Miriam Leslie's will (ones that include the attempt to "prove" that Miriam's relatives had no stake in her fortune because they had no "heritable blood" due to the "fact" that Miriam's mother had been a black slave when Miriam was born—a flashy bit of fiction that marks at least one place where race enters the Frank Leslie tale), various interested parties worked hard to write themselves into it, thereby shifting the suffragists' rewards into their own pockets. These attempts were only marginally thwarted by Miriam's own carefully worded clause prohibiting anyone who contested any part of the will from receiving any portion of the estate. But self-fashioning in language benefits parties other than those seeking political equality; enough was said and written in the end to whittle the final figure received by Catt to half of the original stated amount—$977,875.02. This could easily be another potential end to this story, a more justifiably enraged and politicized one that illustrates in specific figures the immense ideological and economic obstacles with which feminists (even after death) have had to contend. But the story need not be concluded here. In fact, despite successful contests of the will, almost a million dollars passed into the hands of one of feminism's most respected leaders at this time—Carrie Chapman Catt—and it is she who wrote the ending of Miriam Frank Leslie's story with which I want to close here.

With the money salvaged from Leslie's will, Catt formed the Leslie Woman Suffrage Commission, which established, among other things, the following:

The Leslie Bureau of Suffrage Education. This project's goal was "the education of the American public to the point of seeing woman suffrage as essential to democracy. . . . The task of the Bureau was the dissemination of suffrage material through every available avenue of publicity. It was to be news purveyor, publicity expert and propaganda carrier. The field of the Bureau was the American press in its most extended application," providing all forms of information regarding suffrage to the widest sweep of American dailies, weeklies, semi-weeklies, and monthlies humanly possible (Young 32). According to Rose Young, who compiled the Commission's final report in 1929, it was in part the attention paid to newspaper editors nationwide by the Bureau that shaped the kind of response they ultimately gave suffrage; "when at last suffrage was won for women, the number of outstanding papers that were editorially hostile was negligible" (35).

The *Woman Citizen*. The Leslie Commission consolidated three disparate suffrage-promoting newspapers into the weekly *Woman Citizen*. Its first issue, appearing on June 2, 1917, bore this inscription: "The *Woman Citizen* is published weekly by the Leslie Woman Suffrage Commission in the hope that it may prove a self-perpetuating memorial to Mrs. Frank Leslie's generosity toward the cause of woman suffrage and her faith in woman's progress" (Young 36).

It is difficult to imagine a more fitting continuation of the legacy—both financial *and* political—left by Miriam Leslie. What she had promoted in different ways all her life—the advancement of women, their successful movement in the public sphere, and greater awareness of the difficulties encountered by women attempting this movement—continued to be promoted even more overtly and more clearly with the help of her legacy. As Maud Audesly says in "Ladies' Conversazione," women needed a place to speak for themselves. Miriam Leslie certainly provided that place, both in her life and well beyond it.

Notes

1. "Ladies' Conversazione" ran from June 3 to October 7, 1865, when it was replaced by the promising, but ultimately less dialogic "A Gossip with Our Readers." Scholars such as Leslie's biographer Madeleine Stern have noted that it's more than likely that at least some of these letters were in fact written by Miriam Frank Leslie herself, which was not an uncommon practice at this moment in periodical publication (Stern, *Purple Passage*, 185). Regardless of the letters' authenticity, though, they still demonstrate a clear desire on Leslie's part to create a space where women could—and probably did—"converse" openly about issues of significance to them. Whether Leslie composed the letters herself or selected those to which she responded, the fact remains that she shaped and sanctioned this uniquely flavored public avenue for dialogue.

2. In her preface to "No More Separate Spheres!," a special issue of *American Literature* devoted to the reassessment of this historically problematic notion, Cathy N. Davidson claims that the essays in the volume work to break down "the binary of the 'separate spheres,' a retrospective construction that has had the effect of recreating a binaric gender division among contemporary critics that influences what books we write, read, teach, and cite in our own work" (443). Davidson goes on to explain that the idea of separate spheres

has not only spawned its own critical binary among scholars of nineteenth-century writing and culture, but was arguably never actually the historical condition scholars have hypothesized; she refers to the "metaphoric and explanatory nature" of the model to begin this dismantling of its hold on American literary studies (445). I certainly agree with Davidson and the essayists in this volume about the need to question the historical probability of the separate spheres model, but I would also argue that we can hardly ignore its existence in the realm of literary texts such as those that appeared in periodicals like *The Chimney Corner*. I see the notion of separate spheres as a metaphoric entity such as Davidson suggests and more potently, an ideological construction (in Althusser's terms, an ideological state apparatus or ISA) that certainly helped shape the conversations of the time regarding women's social movement and cultural positioning.

3. Along with her journalistic work, Miriam Leslie published several books, including an account of her and her penultimate husband's lavish trip west, *California: A Pleasure Trip from Gotham to the Golden Gate*. See Stern, *Purple Passage*, 185–188, for a complete bibliography of Miriam Leslie's publications.

4. As Donald Dale Jackson puts it, "issuing three editions of a pictorial in one week was unprecedented, and so were the rewards—an explosion in the paper's circulation from 30,000 to 200,000 and a chorus of praise for the enterprising editor" (160–161).

5. Susan K. Harris and Joyce W. Warren have similarly outlined the ways in which Fanny Fern (Sara Payson Willis) herself manipulated her own persona in her extremely popular and widely read periodical columns (particularly those for *The New York Ledger*) and her novel, *Ruth Hall*. For more on Fern's self-fashioning in her writing, see Harris, 111–127, and Warren, ix–xxxix.

6. Born Robert Carter, Leslie supervised the engraving department of the *London Illustrated News*, the model for most American illustrated newspapers, before coming to America. In the United States, Leslie worked for Frederick Gleason on one of the first illustrated weeklies in America, the Boston-based family miscellany *Gleason's Pictorial Drawing-Room Companion*. He also worked as an engraver for P. T. Barnum on the catalog for the American Museum, and during Barnum's brief foray into periodical publishing, on Barnum's *Illustrated News*. When Barnum sold the *Illustrated News* to Gleason after less than a year of publishing it under his own name, Leslie went on to make his own mark on the world of publishing with *Frank Leslie's Lady's Gazette Fashion*, the first of what would be some fifty Frank Leslie titles. For more on Leslie, see Stern, *Publishers for Mass Entertainment in Nineteenth-Century America*, 180–189, and Mott, 452–465.

Works Cited

Davidson, Cathy N. "Preface: No More Separate Spheres!" *American Literature* 70.3 (September 1998): 443–463.

Frank Leslie's Chimney Corner [New York], 1865.

Harris, Susan K. *Nineteenth-Century American Women's Novels: Interpretive Strategies*. Cambridge: Cambridge University Press, 1990.

Jackson, Donald Dale. "Miriam Leslie: Belle of the Boardroom." *Smithsonian* 28.8 (November 1997): 150–162.

Leslie, Mrs. Frank. "Are Our Girls Too Independent?" *The Ladies' Home Journal* 9.4 (March 1892): 6.

Mott, Frank Luther. *A History of American Magazines*. Vol. II, 1850–1865. Cambridge, Mass.: Harvard University Press, 1938.

Okker, Patricia. *Our Sister Editors: Sarah J. Hale and the Tradition of Nineteenth-Century American Women Editors*. Athens: University of Georgia Press, 1995.

Stern, Madeleine B. *Publishers for Mass Entertainment in Nineteenth-Century America*. Boston: G. K. Hall, 1980.

———. *Purple Passage: The Life of Mrs. Frank Leslie*. Norman, Okla.: University of Oklahoma Press, 1953.

Warren, Joyce W. "Introduction" in Fanny Fern, *Ruth Hall and Other Writings*. New Brunswick, N.J.: Rutgers University Press, 1986.

Young, Rose. "The record of the Leslie woman suffrage commission, inc., 1917–1929." Text available on the Library of Congress "American Memory" Web site: http:memory.loc.gov (Oct. 23, 2003).

Zboray, Ronald. "The Letter and the Fiction Reading Public in Antebellum America." *Journal of American Culture* 10.1 (1987): 27–34.

"Our prospectus"
Frank Leslie's Chimney Corner, 3 June 1865

WE present herewith, just as the aurora of peace irradiates the horizon, the first number of THE CHIMNEY CORNER. Its title was fixed four years ago, and was duly copyrighted at the time, and it would by this time have become an "institution" in the land had not the great Rebellion, now happily closing, intervened to put a stop to the enterprise. We now see our way clear to carry out a long-cherished design, that of establishing a weekly periodical, which shall be a welcome messenger of instruction and amusement to the young and old, in the family and by the fireside—that altar around which cluster our holiest and most cherished recollections.

THE CHIMNEY CORNER will always have a continued story of a superior and unexceptionable kind.

"CLEVELAND HALL," the opening chapters of which the present number contains, is a romance of great power, and cannot fail to enchain the attention of the reader.

Each number will also contain a variety of short stories from our best American writers, Sketches of Travel and Society, Anecdotes of Natural History, Biography, Poetry, Agricultural and Horticultural Directions, Family Medical Prescriptions, Notes and Queries, Parlor Pastimes, Comic Pictures, Portraits, and every other subject of Pictorial Art.

THE CHIMNEY CORNER starts with a select corps of upwards of two hundred contributors, and has a complete editorial staff of established ability and large experience. It starts assured of success, and of gathering together a circle of readers which will widen daily, and to which it will prove an instructor and an entertaining friend and guest.

In addition to these literary attractions THE CHIMNEY CORNER will be the most elaborately illustrated Family Paper ever published, the designs being made expressly for it by the most eminent artists.

New and attractive features will be from time to time introduced, so as to place THE CHIMNEY CORNER above all competition.

"Ladies' Conversazione"
Frank Leslie's Chimney Corner, 10 June 1865

We find that we were correct in the belief that giving up a column of the paper to the ladies, as we proposed in our first number, would meet with general approbation.

Already quite a summer shower of letters has poured upon us, several of which we intend to publish as a sort of dessert after the more serious portions of the journal, while a few others, which demand secresy, shall be treated with the confidence we promised in the beginning.

Among these letters there is one signed "Anita," the writer of which we intend giving no peace, since we have her address, until she permits us to give it a place among those "Hints to Conversations."

We confess, however, that we are a little puzzled in the start. We have been taken terribly in earnest. Our fair correspondents, permit themselves the widest latitude in their demands and queries, and we are afraid we shall be obliged to resort to looking wise as a Mussulman instead of replying very early in the day.

For instance, one lady wants to know if it is true that the Empress Eugenie has discarded crinoline. Now, the truth is, until the Atlantic cable is laid, and telegraphic communication with Europe established, it will be difficult to answer such important subjects in a satisfactory way. It is quite possible, however, that the fair Empress may favor us with a letter from her own royal hand before a great while. She does write for the papers, gossips say; and in that case, we have no doubt, from the charming frankness she displays on all occasions, that she will settle such weighty points clearly and decidedly.

Then, a boarding-school miss wants us to "be down" on Madame Chourtleur for giving the pupils rice pudding (we wish the little girl would remember the succulent preparation is spelled with two d's) five days out of a week.

Really, this is beyond us. We will appeal to Madame's feelings; we will remind her of the time when she was young herself and liked variety in the way of puddings (always with two d's, my dear), but beyond this we cannot venture. We are willing to compromise with Mademoiselle by sending her a box of caramels—you see, if we can't satisfy in one way we are ready to try another.

But of the letters before us which contain no bar against publication, it would be invidious to make a choice. We shut our eyes; we become as blind Fortune, or a Congressman to his constituents' interests, and draw one out of the pile at hazard:

"Dear Mr. Editor,—For a long time I have been wishing to express my feelings on a certain subject, and your kind offer gives me an opportunity which I seize at once. Do you know that there is a certain class of young men in New York who continue to make going in or out of church an exceedingly disagreeable affair? They collect about the doorways and on the steps, half of them furnished with eyeglasses, which they are obliged to look over the tops of in order to see at all; and there they stand, staring with faces that are divided between an expression of mental vacuity and intolerable impertinence.

"Don't you think that at least a respect for the place might check them somewhat? We are growing accustomed to the battery of glances we must run in theatres, cars or stages, but at least let them leave us one spot where their behavior will permit us to indulge in the belief that there is something approaching a soul under their preposterously long waistcoats and amazing neckties.

"Yours respectfully,

"May Fairthorn."

We have not a word to add. We leave the criminals to their consciences, if they are troubled with such things, and the stinging rebuke of a thorn that is certainly as sharp as fair . . .

"Ladies' Conversazione"
Frank Leslie's Chimney Corner, 17 June 1865

We have another letter from the lady whose epistle in our first number, it will be remembered, suggested the idea to us of allowing this speaking place to female human nature in general.

"Dear Mr. Editor,—I was decorously gratified—I don't think it would be dignified to acknowledge how pleased I was—to see that you accepted my suggestion in regard to the letters, with such promptitude and good nature.

"Really, if all you men would, on all occasions, pay the same attention to the hints and wishes of your guardian angels—meaning the particular women who are good natured enough to take an interest in you—I am sure you would be preserved from at least one half of the follies into which you fall now upon the slightest provocation.

"But it is the strangest thing—now, I don't say this in a fault-finding spirit, only from a sense of duty, to point out your short-comings—you never can, any of you, get anything exactly right. Even in the small matter of a name, either you or your proof-readers must needs make a mistake, and cause me to sign myself "Maud Augusta."

"Now do I write like a woman whose name is Augusta, and how could you twist Audesly into anything of the sort? It's all very well for Miss Juliet Capulet to ask, 'What's in a name?' From her haste to change hers, I should opine there was something in it she did not like! But I suppose I may have my opinion as well as Juliet, and I hope I have been better 'brought up' than to talk with a strange young man over a balcony at the hour she did, and I say distinctly, there is a great deal in a name.

"Why, an ugly name is like a pug nose—one of the most serious drawbacks in life; and if a man does conquer fate under the cloud of either dispensation, he certainly deserves an uncommon degree of credit.

"But what I wanted to say was, that I am so pleased you have given us this column, and I know ever so many young ladies who are going to write you letters. One of them is especially skilled in that line—dear me, didn't she write six different notes, each in a different hand, to a favorite actor, asking him to play a certain piece, and didn't he do it, thinking six separate young women had petitioned him out of the weakness of their hearts.

"The truth is, you men are so easily deceived, it is quite a shame to cheat you; but you'll never be better, that's one comfort, so we shall never be at a loss for amusement and occupation. With this satisfactory assurance I reiterate my pleasure and surprise at your being sensible enough to accept my suggestion, and take my leave, begging you to be at the trouble to print correctly the name of,

"Yours, truly,
"Maud Audesly."

We apologize most heartily to our correspondent for the mistake in regard to her cognomen; we can only console her as we often do our irascible friends of the quill, by saying that no one would ever have noticed the error if she had not herself pointed it out.

Frances Wright of the *Free Enquirer*: Woman Editor in a Man's World

CAROLYN KARCHER

FRANCES ("Fanny") Wright (1795–1852) defies all the paradigms literary historians have constructed to schematize women's entry into the professions of authorship, editorship, and journalism. When she shouldered the responsibility of coediting the *New-Harmony Gazette* with Robert Dale Owen in June 1828, Wright did not plant herself in the domestic sphere, unlike such predecessors as Lydia Maria Child and Sarah Josepha Hale, founding editors, respectively, of the *Juvenile Miscellany* (1826–1834) and the *Ladies Magazine* (1828–1836). Nor did Wright assume her editorship as a wife or daughter carrying on a family business—unlike most of the dozen-odd women who had published political newspapers before her. Nor did she hide for a strategic interval behind a male figurehead, as did Mary Ann Shadd Cary on launching the *Provincial Freeman* (1854–1860), a Black nationalist alternative to *Frederick Douglass's Paper*. Nor did Wright refrain from signing her editorials and articles, unlike Margaret Fuller, who used a star as her byline during her stint as the *New-York Tribune*'s literary editor (1844–1846). Nor, least of all, did Wright share the evangelical piety that inspired the *Advocate of Moral Reform*'s editors to challenge male authority in their crusade to save fallen women (1834–1850).[1]

Instead, Wright took over a controversial utopian colony's eight-page weekly newspaper, which she bought and reoriented toward a national audience. Addressing a predominantly male readership in an aggressively masculine voice, tackling such reputedly unfeminine subjects as economics, and flailing all the orthodoxies the American public held sacrosanct, she advocated sweeping reforms to transform the United States into the egalitarian republic it purported to be. Prior to her arrival on the scene, her "brother editor" Robert Dale Owen had been helping to run the *New-Harmony Gazette* as his father Robert Owen's mouthpiece—thereby ironically following the traditional female route into newspaper publishing that Wright herself avoided. In a reversal of roles, Wright dominated their collaborative enterprise and occupied the sites of maximum visibility on the masthead, the editorial pages, and the lecture circuit, which boosted subscriptions, while her male partner worked behind the scenes. Indeed, it was Fanny Wright's name, not Robert Dale Owen's, that gave the paper they retitled the *Free Enquirer* its notoriety. Wright and Owen chose this title to proclaim their commitment to rational investigation. In an era when whole regions were being "burned over" by revivals of religion as evangelical preachers threatened shrieking congregations with the fires of hell, Wright and Owen denounced the clergy as purveyors of "superstition" and urged readers to substitute reason for dogma.

Wright's striking deviations from what we have come to consider the norm for nineteenth-century women writers and editors have consigned her to the margins of literary history. Despite a series of biographies, culminating in Celia Morris Eckhardt's splendid *Fanny Wright: Rebel in America*, scholars have paid little attention to Wright's editorship of the *Free Enquirer* and still less to her trenchant journalism. Wright has survived in the pages of women's history texts primarily as a pioneering feminist theorist and lecturer—the first woman in the United States to assert from a public rostrum, in front of secular audiences comprising both sexes, that "until women assume the place in society which good sense and good feeling alike assign to them, human improvement must advance but feebly."[2] In emphasizing this aspect of Wright's career, twentieth-century scholars have taken their cue from Elizabeth Cady Stanton and her coauthors' *History of Woman Suffrage* (1881), which features a portrait of Wright as its fronticepiece and lists her second (after Mary Wollstonecraft) among the heroines whose "Earnest Lives and Fearless Words" instigated the campaign for women's "Political Rights."[3]

Yet the arguments in favor of sexual equality that Wright articulated in the speeches feminist historians have chosen to anthologize constitute only a subsidiary part of a much more ambitious agenda. That agenda, spelled out by the words "human improvement," in which Wright enveloped her call for raising women's status, emerges most clearly from the columns of her newspaper the *Free Enquirer*. Because Wright configured the paper to showcase her ideas, she expressed her views through multiple channels: her lectures and speeches, which she published in the *Free Enquirer*, alongside the commentaries they elicited in the press, and her responses to those commentaries; items written before and after her active tenure as editor—including poems, a play, a manifesto attacking the marriage institution and defending race-mixing, economic essays, and reportage on the European scene—all of which enhanced Wright's visibility even in her absence; a series of fables she composed especially for the *Free Enquirer*; and above all her editorials.

Thus, a study of the *Free Enquirer* reveals the full scope of Wright's political thought and program for social change, as well as the diversity of genres through which she promulgated her message. It also enables us to recover an alternative model of nineteenth-century women's authorship and editorship that broadens our understanding of the options available to those who sought to influence the public through the press. At the same time, the brevity of Wright's editorial career, the vicious baiting to which she was subjected, and the tragic vulnerability this powerful woman at last showed to the forces she had so boldly assailed help explain why hers remained a maverick voice among her "sister editors." Neither as editor of the *Free Enquirer* nor as lecturer did Wright betray the slightest sense of self-consciousness about usurping male prerogatives. Speaking as a disembodied citizen of the Enlightenment, she never acknowledged that her culture coded such citizenship as male. Yet her body would impose on her the same limitations other women of her era faced, regardless of how she wished to identify herself.

Wright brought to the *Free Enquirer* a sensibility molded by her birth in Dundee, Scotland, in 1795, which gave her a foreigner's perspective on the United States and an eighteenth-century faith in rationality; her upper-class status, which gave her economic security and psychological self-assurance; and the loss of her parents at age two, which taught her to "put her trust in ideas" rather than in "people who would die or betray," as Eckhardt puts it (12). In the third-person autobiographical sketch she published in 1844, Wright herself recognized "the heart solitude of orphanship" as a key factor in developing her intellectual independence by obliging her to spend her childhood among people with whose "views and characters" she felt no "sympathy."[4] While still in her teens, she rebelled against her class when she saw Scottish tenants being driven off land they had farmed for centuries, so that wealthy proprietors could raise sheep. Almost simultaneously, Wright recalled, she "awoke, as it were, to a new existence" when she learned about a "country consecrated to freedom" and equality—the newly independent United States. "To see that country was now, at the age of sixteen, her fixed but secret determination" (*Biography* 11). Before she embarked on her first trip to the United States in 1818, Wright also came under the influence of the utopian socialist Robert Owen, whose plans for eliminating the evils of capitalism by establishing model communities would shape her approach to social reform.[5] Wright was attracted not only to Owen's socialist philosophy, but to his belief in women's equality and to his religious freethinking. She would preach these values in her newspaper editorials and speeches.

Wright first gained a transnational audience by publishing an enthusiastic account of her travels, *Views of Society and Manners in America* (1821), which of course endeared her to Americans. Yet no matter how dazzled she was by the free institutions of the United States, Wright could not help noticing what she called "the anomaly presented . . . by the condition of the enslaved negro." As she later explained in a lecture published in the *Free Enquirer*, "I saw in the injury to the race of color the only stain upon the national honor; and sorrow for the injured fame of a republican country, mingled with my pity of the slave."[6]

Accordingly, Wright set out to investigate slavery on a second trip to the United States in 1824, this time accompanied part of the way by another eminent mentor, the Marquis de Lafayette, who was now making a triumphal tour of the nation he had helped liberate. During her travels through the South, Wright observed the workings of the slave system; interviewed such leading statesmen as Jefferson, Madison, Monroe, and Jackson; familiarized herself with the laws regulating slavery; and tried to ascertain how the evil might be phased out. By the end of her trip, she had decided to "devote [her] time and fortune" to a pilot project that would provide a model for gradual emancipation.

Wright's plan consisted in showing that slaves could be allowed to buy their freedom over a five-year period of apprenticeship to a remunerative trade, after which they could be transported to Haiti or elsewhere outside of the United States. The notion that white prejudice against race-mixing made it necessary to tie emancipation to expatriation was universal among whites during this period, as the many prominent politicians Wright consulted stressed. If prevailing opinion accounts for the approach to emancipation Wright chose in 1825, however, it surely does not account for the intrepidity that led her to act publicly against slavery at great personal and financial risk, nearly a decade before either the formation of a radical abolitionist movement, committed to "immediate emancipation" rather than colonization, or the rise of women antislavery writers and speakers.[7]

To test the feasibility of her scheme, Wright bought a plantation in Tennessee, which she called Nashoba, peopled it with approximately seventeen slaves (ten purchased and the others donated), and started trying to operate it on the principles of cooperative labor that Robert Owen was then implementing in his utopian community at New Harmony, Indiana. Over the next few years, Wright also tried to turn Nashoba into a laboratory for experimenting with other Owenite ideas, such as free love and schools segregating children from their parents, so that the new generation could be brought up uncontaminated by preutopian habits. Most daringly, she began arguing, contrary to her original premise and to everyone around her, that the ultimate solution to the problems of slavery and prejudice was for Blacks and whites to blend into one race. Her "Explanatory Notes, respecting the Nature and Objects of the Institution of Nashoba, and of the Principles upon which it is founded," state the case cogently:

> Idle indeed is the assertion that the mixture of the races is not in nature. If not in nature, it could not happen; and, being in nature, since it *does* happen, the only question is whether it shall take place in good taste and good feeling and be made at once the means of sealing the tranquillity, and perfecting the liberty of the country, and of peopling it with a race more suited to its southern climate than the pure European,—or whether it shall proceed, as it now does, viciously and degradingly, mingling hatred and fear with the ties of blood—denied indeed, but stamped by nature herself upon the skin.

Wright adds that she is laying special emphasis at Nashoba on the "education of the race of color" because it will hasten the "physical amalgamation of the two colors"—an outcome she considers "a good equally desirable for both" "when accompanied by a moral approximation."[8]

As if touting the benefits of transmuting the United States into a brown nation were not controversial enough, Wright's "Explanatory Notes" link her defense of racial "amalgamation" to a condemnation of "matrimonial law" as "tyranny." On the one hand, Wright points out, the institution of marriage and the definition of the marital bond as indissoluble force "unsuitable and unsuited parents" to stay together to the detriment of their offspring; on the other hand, the same code "stamps with infamy . . . the best-grounded and most generous attachments, which ever did honor to the human heart, simply because unlegalized by human ceremonies." Relationships outside of marriage, Wright implies, being "grounded" in love rather than coercion, actually deserve more "honor" than those sanctioned by law.[9]

Wright published the "Explanatory Notes" broadcasting her heterodox views as her first contribution to the *New-Harmony Gazette*, spread over three installments in January and February 1828. Though the editors of mainstream newspapers would cover Wright with infamy when her "Explanatory Notes" reached a larger audience, the *Gazette*'s Robert Dale Owen hailed her for her courage and wisdom. "Few would *dare* to express their opinions openly and fearlessly as she has done, when these opinions are completely at variance with many of the most deep-rooted prejudices which exist among us," he affirmed in an unsigned editorial note; "yet all who have examined the subject, with minds unwarped by prejudice, must confess the force and correctness of her arguments."[10] So began Wright's association with the *New-Harmony Gazette* and her collaboration with Robert Dale Owen.

Less than six months after the publication of her "Explanatory Notes," Wright left Nashoba for New Harmony and exchanged the running of an emancipationist colony for a new career as editor—a career that would be haunted and eventually destroyed by the ghost of her ill-fated antislavery venture. She would keep her promise of freeing her slaves and taking them to Haiti, but Nashoba had disastrously failed to demonstrate the viability of either ending slavery by Wright's method or farming a plantation on the cooperative system. A newspaper seemed to offer a more effective vehicle for reforming American society, and the *New-Harmony Gazette* was currently "the only one removed from party or sectarian influences"—at least so Wright characterized its utopian, anticlerical stance (*Biography* 34).

From the date of her editorial debut on 18 June 1828, Wright advertised her presence at the helm of the *New-Harmony Gazette*. Belying the modest statement that she had "undertaken the superintendence of the paper during a temporary absence of Robert Dale Owen," her name preceded his in the editorial box, an excerpt from her play *Altorf* filled the poetry column, and her articles—signed alternately with her initials or her full name (a policy to which she drew attention by announcing it)—dominated the editorial pages. Moreover, Wright indicated that she meant to occupy the superior position in her relationship with her "brother editor," and that she, not he, was best qualified to formulate the paper's ideology, as she underscored by chiding him for misusing the term "natural law" in one of his articles.[11]

Two weeks later, Wright was already extending her show of power and authority beyond the offices of the *New-Harmony Gazette*. When the editor of a rival newspaper, the *New York Correspondent*, flaunted a style she considered too belligerent, she lectured him:

> [Y]ou spend too much artillery against those whose foolishness is not worth the cost. . . . To correct errors, let us declare truths; to confound priests, let us enlighten the people; and to overthrow blind belief, let us lead men to think! . . . Let us then not spend our breath in scolding, nor our ink in disputing; and let us rather declare our own views than quarrel with other people's.[12]

Wright's call for a style of journalism that appealed to reason instead of passion and relied on "truth" instead of invective—though she did not necessarily live up to her professed ideals—points to one of her leading motives for wishing to edit a newspaper: to raise the level of the American press, which she found abysmally low. In words that typify her caustic editorial style and sound as timely today as in the 1820s, she complains: "[W]ere we to take the press for an organ of public sentiment, we might conceive that a mental palsy had fallen upon the nation, and that the whole people were engaged in quarrelling about trifles, libelling their public officers, insulting individuals, or sleeping away their intellects under the fumes of tobacco."[13] The American press is obsessed with "PERSONALITIES," she notes on another occasion, and "The motto of republics, '*Principles, not men,*' is but too universally violated and forgotten."[14]

Wright's ambition to create a model newspaper as an instrument for reforming the American press and its readers required a larger stage than a failing utopian colony in backwoods Indiana. It also required severing the *New-Harmony Gazette* from its parochial origins as the exponent of the elder Robert Owen's philosophy. Within six weeks of having stepped into the editorial chair, Wright proposed to buy, recast, and relocate the *Gazette*. The prospectus of the new paper appeared on 30 July. Designed "to aid in the diffusion of truth, in the spread of liberal principles, and in the dissipation of . . . prejudices," its editors pledged, the *Gazette*'s successor would be focused on education, as befitted a publication aimed at transforming readers' consciousness, but would encompass as well "[s]cience, agriculture, practical economy and general politics; sketches and anecdotes from real life; selected and original poetry; foreign and domestic news." The paper would also bear a new motto: "Just opinions are the result of just knowledge,—just practice of just opinions."[15]

It was Wright who chose New York City as the site from which to launch the *Free Enquirer* on 28 January 1829, because it seemed to offer such a central and vast "field" for her "exertions." As she explains in one of her inaugural editorials, "if free enquiry be impracticable in New York, it must be so every where, while, should it successfully elicit truth here, the same would spread far and wide."[16]

Wright's role in deciding on the paper's new home once again testifies to the unprecedented power and visibility she enjoyed, for she had observed New York's advantages in the course of a lecture tour—itself a milestone for women—that had taken her to most of the major cities in the United States; in the meantime, her coeditor had been running the *Gazette* from New Harmony, where he would remain until March 1829. During her months on the lecture circuit, the *Gazette* had maintained her visibility by reprinting extracts from her writings and by publishing her lectures in full, together with extensive reviews of them by other newspapers.

Editorializing and lecturing served Wright as complementary means of sowing the seeds of free inquiry in a nation subjected, she believed, to the thralldom of religious orthodoxy. Her combative editorial style provoked almost as much controversy as her lectures, which broke taboos against public speaking for women. The editorial that leads off the inaugural issue of the *Free Enquirer* minces no words articulating the paper's mission: to offer "antidotes" to the "nostrums" of the clergy Wright brands "spiritual quack[s]." These "quack[s]" have adapted their "priestly wares" to a variety of clienteles, Wright charges: they retail "solemn prayers, disputatious sermons, alarming denunciations, rhetorical discourses, pathetic appeals, hobgoblin stories, rhyming hymns, pealing organs, sonorous cursings, and sweet voices tuned to melody." She proceeds to damn Protestants along with Catholics and to affront her Protestant-born readers by pronouncing their religion the more repressive of the two.

> [Protestantism, too] could fine and imprison and starve and banish troublesome enquirers and stiff necked nonconformists; and even occasionally roast one at a slow fire, as Calvin did Servetus. And—alas for our ears! she has banished the swelling paeans and harmonious psalmistry of Romish music for the nasal twang of presbyterianism, and the groanings of entranced methodism. And—alas for our eyes! in lieu of glowing paintings and speaking sculpture and theatrical processions, we have large meeting houses, with blank whitewashed walls, and cold, stiff, starched faced preachers, preaching starvation and abnegation, and craving for Peter's pence all the same.

Revealingly, Wright personifies both religions as female—Protestantism as a "cunning dame," Catholicism as the whorish "lady of Babylon." By implication, she identifies the free inquiry she champions (and herself with it) as genderless, if not male.[17]

The "antidotes" to orthodoxy that Wright proposes to dispense in the *Free Enquirer* consist of precise counterparts to the poisons that pour from the orthodox press: "heterodox fables, . . . heterodox essays, heterodox histories and heterodox philosophy." The first of Wright's "heterodox fables," "The Owls," appears on page 2 of the same issue as her inaugural editorial, which may be said to intertwine essay, history, and philosophy. "The Owls" portrays the clergy as lazy, parasitical birds that sleep during the day but screech and hoot at night, terrorizing other birds into feeding them to propitiate the gods the owls claim to serve. Wright's fable thus anticipates and reinforces the anticlerical message of her editorial, which in turn recapitulates it.

The thematic coherence Wright creates in the paper's columns carries over into the editorials by Robert Dale Owen and Robert Jennings, who had briefly joined the staff of the *Free Enquirer*. Owen's, for example, explicate the title and motto of the paper (6–7), while Jennings's exults: "We again begin to breathe freely through our own columns, which is what we cannot do through any other paper in the city," rival editors having "very consistently . . . refused to publish any thing, be it ever so true, respecting Frances Wright, unless it be in raillery or abuse of her" (8). A further note by Jennings rounds out the issue—and again contributes to showcasing Wright—by announcing that she has "consented to redeliver her *Lectures on Knowl-*

edge at the request of a number of respectable citizens" (8). These lectures, of course, are duly reprinted in later issues, where they sometimes substitute for actual editorials by Wright.

Wright spells out her editorial strategy (and her control of the paper) in the next number. There she directs the attention of the "reflecting reader" first to a fable titled "The South Sea Islander in London," suggesting "that, in the social frame of civilized society, now so called, ALL IS NOT RIGHT," then to the article "Marriage" by her "brother editor, Robert Dale Owen, suggesting that MUCH IS WRONG." She urges readers to examine the "customs, laws, religion, and opinions" of their own society, and particularly its marriage institution, from the vantage point of the South Sea Islander. While elucidating the ideology embedded in her arrangement of the selections, Wright takes credit for her coeditor's critique of marriage. Its "substance," she coolly asserts, "was . . . first elicited by my own writings and conversation" and subsequently developed in the lecture she delivered some months ago "in the presence of at least one tenth of [the] whole population" of Cincinnati.[18]

Self-promotion, in fact, constituted a prominent element of Wright's editorial strategy, inextricable from her promotion of the newspaper that served as her organ. A communication signed "V." and a poem signed "Ada," both reprinted in the *Free Enquirer* of 19 November 1828, illustrate this puffery. V. describes how the office of the *Free Enquirer* was "literally beset with 'hungry expectants'" hours before its weekly edition was to come off the press. The "clamorous crowd," s/he reports, included "every class," from "the Saxony cloth of what is called '*good society*,' down to the independent homespun of economy and the threadbare of penury." All fortunate enough to secure copies of the paper, adds V., devoured it while walking, "as if fascinated by the charm of style, beauty of diction, and boldness of invective, which in so eminent a degree characterize" the *Free Enquirer*. Hoping that the crowd's response reflects the headway Wright's ideas are making, V. predicts that her "noble undertaking" will usher in the millennium, though she is now "at least a century before her time."[19]

Just as Wright's lectures complemented her editorials, so "Ada"'s jocular poem about the impact both media were having on Wright's audience complements "V."'s tribute to her newspaper. "What a panic has seized all the men!" exclaims "Ada," at the prospect "that we women should know/ Something more about handling a pen,/ Than our grandams, some ages ago!" The "fright" of men and the "fuss" of "bigots and priests," moreover, is well warranted, Ada affirms, "For the lectures of Miss Frances Wright/ Are received with unbounded applause" and are awakening women to their true powers: "She tells us, we women possess/ An intellect equal with them."[20]

Along with the paeans of her admirers, Wright reprinted the anathemas of her foes, apparently with almost equal relish. "*This female monster* blasphemes God and advocates licentiousness!" "She would repeal the marriage act." "A bold and eloquent woman lays siege to the very foundation of society—inflames and excites the public mind. . . . She avows that her object is a thorough and radical reform and change in every relation of life—even the dearest and most sacred. Father, mother, husband, wife, son, and daughter . . . are to be swept away equally with clergymen, churches, banks, parties and benevolent societies" by this "Red Harlot of Infidelity." Such attacks, Wright contends, merely reveal the weakness of her opponents: "Unable to confute the truths, which had been advanced, unable, also, to frighten from her post the reformer, who sought her weapons from the hand of reason alone, the only remaining resource was to frighten her hearers."[21]

As Wright's enemies recognize, the "radical reform" Wright preaches in the *Free Enquirer* indeed extends beyond the church and family to encompass the courts, the electoral system, and the economy. With reference to the courts, Wright editorializes against "judiciary executions" (capital punishment) as *"murders of the worst kind,"* because they amount to "shedding . . . human blood, with all the ceremony and deliberacy of law and religion." The purpose of law should be "the *prevention* and not the *punishment* of crime," she argues.[22] With reference to the electoral system, Wright advocates universal suffrage and contemptuously dismisses those who warn against it, like one of her chief antagonists, the editor of the *New-York Commercial Advertiser*. Such spokesmen of the mainstream press represent the "spirit of monied pretension" and understand neither "the country they inhabit" nor "the genius of its institutions or its people," Wright opines (apparently forgetting that she herself is a foreigner). They should study the Declaration of Independence and fulfill the proper role of an editor in a democratic nation: "To advise the people how *best to use* the power which is theirs, and *theirs alone.*"[23] Wright sought to act on this prescription when she entered the domain of the economy and intervened in the struggle for self-empowerment that the laboring classes were waging under the aegis of the Working Men's Party.

Of the causes Wright espoused as editor of the *Free Enquirer*, none better measures the extent—and the limits—of her radicalism. When the Working Men's Party formed in 1828, Wright's prolabor sympathies naturally drew her to it. Originating with skilled workers in Philadelphia, from which it spread to New York and other cities in the Northeast, the party served as a political vehicle through which the laboring classes could advance their own interests rather than remain hostage to the elites who controlled the Democrats and Whigs. The Working Men's Party fielded its own candidates in the November 1828 elections, polling as many as 6,090 out of 21,000 votes.[24] Its leaders attributed the "calamities of the poor" to the "unequal distribution" of wealth and demanded concrete measures "to equalize the possession of landed and of all other property." Wright, however, found herself unable to endorse what she saw as a program for "wresting violently the possessions of some to bestow them upon others, or to divide them among all." Through the *Free Enquirer* she and Robert Dale Owen attempted to steer the Working Men in a direction the two editors deemed more appropriate—one that unmistakably demarcated bourgeois reformers from workers.[25]

Editorializing from Auburn, New York, her latest stop on the lecture circuit, Wright admonishes the Working Men: "Reform ought never to travel faster than the public mind; whenever it does so it produces alarm and . . . confusion."[26] The proper place to begin, she insists, is not with economic redistribution but with education. In a subsequent editorial addressed "To the Intelligent among the Working Classes; and Generally, to All Honest Reformers," Wright urges them to unite behind a measure she considers far likelier to win the public's support: "NATIONAL, RATIONAL, REPUBLICAN EDUCATION; FREE FOR ALL, AT THE EXPENSE OF ALL." Elaborating on why her solution is preferable, she explains: "Until equality be planted in the mind, in the habits, in the manners, in the feelings, think not it can ever be in the condition. Equalize fortunes at this hour, and knavery in one year would have beggared honesty; improvidence would have dissipated its possessions."[27] In other words, without education the poor would soon waste or be cheated out of any property awarded them.

To inculcate egalitarian principles from early childhood, in isolation from the corrupting influences of students' social milieux, Wright recommends establishing a system of state-funded boarding schools where rich and poor, "*male and female*," can learn side by side "*without distinction of class*"—a utopian idea she derives from the elder Robert Owen. Such schools, she claims, would weld the American people into "but one class, and, as it were, but one family," in a single generation, thus achieving more effectively than any redistribution of property the "*equalization of our human condition.*"[28] Apparently it does not occur to Wright that American voters might resist surrendering their children even more than surrendering their property, or that they might fiercely oppose taxing themselves to pay for schools aimed at uprooting class distinctions and instilling values contrary to their own, or that teachers entirely free of the biases republican education was supposed to eliminate might be few and far between.

In her advice to the Working Men, Wright adopts the same authoritative tone as in her ripostes to clerical detractors, rival editors, and colleagues at the *Free Enquirer*, yet with different consequences. Now, instead of reversing the power relations of gender, she exploits the power relations of class. Wright and Owen's efforts to redirect the Working Men's Party touched off a schism that ultimately destroyed it.

Before witnessing this outcome, Wright herself succumbed to the restrictions on women's freedom that she had been defying in her career as editor and lecturer. She became pregnant on the trip to Haiti during which she made good her promise to her Nashoba slaves. Faced with the prospects of condemning her unborn child, as well as herself, to social ostracism and ignominy if she did not marry the father, a Frenchman named Phiquepal d'Arusmont, she left for France on 1 July 1830 and disappeared from circulation for many years.

Wright's editorship of the *Free Enquirer* did not officially end until 13 October 1832, however. As if acknowledging that the paper still depended on Wright's name for its reputation, Owen continued to list her before himself on the masthead as coeditor and proprietor, and he even consulted her in person before announcing her resignation.[29] Meanwhile, Wright continued to send articles to the *Free Enquirer*: a seven-part series on "Wealth and Money" and two dispatches on the French revolution of July 1830. Of these, "The People at War" represents Wright at her best. Foreshadowing Margaret Fuller's brilliant reportage on the Italian revolution of 1848, Wright displays a proto-Marxist insight into the conflict she describes as "openly and acknowledgedly, a *war of class*" in which the "ridden people of the earth . . . are struggling to throw from their backs the 'booted and spurred' riders whose legitimate title to starve as well as to work them to death will no longer pass current."[30]

Wright herself would never participate in the struggle she celebrated. "[P]ainful circumstance," she hinted in her October 1832 valedictory to readers, obliged her to relinquish the editorship of the *Free Enquirer*. Thereafter, embittered by an unwanted pregnancy, an unhappy marriage, and a life discordant with her youthful ideals, Wright turned increasingly conservative. Though she eventually came back to her adopted homeland without her estranged husband and daughter, settling in Cincinnati, she did not join any of the movements for social change that sprang up in the wake of her meteoric career as editor and lecturer. Yet the bold example Wright had set in her prime inspired countless other women, as the *History of Woman Suffrage*'s authors testified. Wright lived to see Sarah and Angelina Grimké,

Abby Kelley, and Lucy Stone mount the rostrum to call for abolishing slavery and emancipating women; Lydia Maria Child and Jane Swisshelm assume the editorship of antislavery newspapers that also championed the urban poor (in Child's case) and crusaded against capital punishment, as had the *Free Enquirer*; and Elizabeth Cady Stanton and Lucretia Mott organize the first women's rights convention at Seneca Falls, New York. A century and a half after Wright's death in 1852, as we confront the recrudescence of the religious and racial bigotry she indicted so scathingly, her legacy of free inquiry remains as vital as ever.

Notes

1. For paradigms of women's entry into authorship, see Douglas, *Feminization of American Culture*; Baym, *Woman's Fiction*; Kelley, *Private Woman, Public Stage*; and Fetterley, *Provisions*. For an excellent overview of nineteenth-century women editors, centered around Sarah Hale, see Okker, *Our Sister Editors*. For individual studies, see Karcher, *The First Woman in the Republic*; Rhodes, *Mary Ann Shadd Cary*; and Mitchell, *Margaret Fuller's New York Journalism*. On the *Advocate of Moral Reform* see Smith-Rosenberg, "Beauty, the Beast, and the Militant Woman" in *Disorderly Conduct*; and Ritter, "Insurrection Behind the Veil," Chap. 2.

2. Wright, "Lecture II. Of Free Enquiry Considered as a Mean[s] for Obtaining Just Knowledge," *Free Enquirer*, 25 Mar. 1829, 169; reprinted in her *Course of Popular Lectures* (1829: 41–62) and in the compilation *Life, Letters and Lectures, 1834/1844* (21–37) and excerpted in Rossi, *Feminist Papers* (108–17), and Lerner, *Female Experience* (224–29).

3. See especially Spender, *Women of Ideas*, which reproduces the frontispiece and title page of the *History of Woman Suffrage* on its cover.

4. *Biography, Notes, and Political Letters of Frances Wright D'Arusmont* 9, included in *Life, Letters and Lectures*.

5. For an excellent study of Owen's ideas and their influence on Wright and other women, see Taylor, *Eve and the New Jerusalem*.

6. "Address Delivered at the New York Hall of Science on Sunday the 18th of October 1829, by Frances Wright," *Free Enquirer*, 31 Oct. 1829, 1. The quotation in the next paragraph is also from this address.

7. William Lloyd Garrison first issued the call for "immediate emancipation" on American soil in his newspaper the *Liberator* in 1831. Lydia Maria Child's *An Appeal in Favor of That Class of Americans Called Africans* (1833) provided a full-length argument for incorporating African Americans as equal citizens, and the American Anti-Slavery Society was founded later the same year. Angelina and Sarah Grimké began giving public lectures against slavery to mixed audiences of men and women in 1837.

8. "Nashoba," *New-Harmony Gazette*, 6 Feb. 1828, 133. For historical accounts of Nashoba, see Eckhardt, Chaps. 5–6; and Woloch, *Women and the American Experience*, Chap. 7.

9. "Nashoba," *New-Harmony Gazette*, 6 Feb. 1828, 132.

10. Owen, untitled editorial, *New-Harmony Gazette*, 30 Jan. 1828, 126.

11. *New-Harmony Gazette*, 18 June 1828, 270–71, 272. See especially "To R. D. Owen: suggested by the perusal of his article in the 129th number of the Gazette . . ." (270–71).

12. "To the Editor of the *Correspondent*," *New-Harmony Gazette*, 2 July 1828, 284.

13. Untitled editorial, *Free Enquirer* 29 Jan. 1829: 8. Wright's editorials are dated 28 January 1829, while the early sections of this number are dated 29 October 1828. According to Eckhardt (190–91), this confusing discrepancy, which lasts for several months, arises

because Wright reprints editorials from the New Harmony edition of the *Free Enquirer* while she is editing the paper from New York.

14. "Anonymous Writing," *Free Enquirer*, 15 Feb. 1829, 48. Again, the editorial appears in a number dated 3 Dec. 1828.

15. "Prospectus of the *New-Harmony and Nashoba Gazette*, in Continuation of the *New-Harmony Gazette*," 30 July 1828, 318–19. The Prospectus continues to appear in subsequent issues of the *New-Harmony Gazette*, as well as in the opening issues of the *Free Enquirer*, the title on which Wright and Owen eventually settled. The old motto of the *Gazette* was "If we cannot reconcile all opinions, let us endeavor to unite all hearts."

16. Eckhardt asserts that Wright "had announced her decision to stay in New York" and to base the newspaper there "without consulting Robert Dale" (190). The quotation is from Wright's second untitled editorial of 28 Jan. 1829 (29 Oct. 1828), 7.

17. Untitled editorial, *Free Enquirer*, 29 Oct. 1828, 5–6. For a fine analysis of the ambivalent attitudes toward women that characterized freethinkers and made theirs a predominantly male movement, see Ginzberg, "'The Hearts of Your Readers Will Shudder.'"

18. Untitled editorial, *Free Enquirer*, 1 Feb. 1829 (5 Nov. 1828), 15–16. The fable is on the first two pages (9–10). The articles "Romantic Devotion of a Wife" and "Domestic Life in Persia" (11–12), reprinted from other sources, extend the focus on marriage.

19. V., "Communicated," *Free Enquirer*, 8 Feb. 1829 (19 Nov. 1828), 32.

20. Ada, "The Panic," *Free Enquirer*, 8 Feb. 1829 (19 Nov. 1828), 32.

21. Wright quotes and replies to her enemies at length in her editorials "Answer to Vindicia, Being Applicable to the Times, and Prefatory to a Series of Essays on the Causes of Existing Evils" and "A Caricature," *Free Enquirer*, 4 March 1829, 150–51 and 19 June 1830, 267–68.

22. "Richard Johnson," *Free Enquirer*, 20 May 1829, 236. Johnson had just been executed in Philadelphia while Wright was lecturing in the city.

23. "American Politicians Versus The American People. Or Aristocracy Vs. Democracy," *Free Enquirer*, 29 July 1829, 318–19.

24. On Wright and Owen's involvement in the politics of the Working Men's Party, see Eckhardt 215–20; also Streitmatter, "Origins of the American Labor Press," *Journalism History* 25 (Autumn 1999): 99–106.

25. Quotations are from Eckhardt 216 and Owen's "Mechanics' Meeting," 31 Oct. 1829, 7–8, which summarize the Working Men's demands; and from Wright's "Parting Address," *Free Enquirer*, 21 and 28 Aug. 1830, 338, 345, which critiques them.

26. "From Auburn," 21 Nov. 1829, 31–32.

27. "To the Intelligent among the Working Classes," *Free Enquirer*, 5 Dec. 1829, 46.

28. "The New York Daily Sentinel" and "Parting Address," *Free Enquirer*, 22 May and 21 and 28 Aug. 1830, 239–40, 338, 345–46.

29. See his editorial "Proposed Change," *Free Enquirer*, 13 Oct. 1832, 407, where he says he "abstained" from announcing the transfer of editorial responsibilities earlier because "I did not consider myself at liberty to decide any thing on the subject, except in conjunction with my sister editor."

30. "The People at War," *Free Enquirer*, 27 Nov. 1830, 38. See also "Wealth and Money," 25 Sept. and 2, 9, 16, and 23 Oct. 1830, 382–83, 390–91, 397–98, 402–407, and 410–12; and "A Few Words on Passing Events in Europe," 16 Oct. 1830, 407–408.

Works Cited

Ada. "The Panic." *Free Enquirer*, 8 Feb. 1829 (19 Nov. 1828): 32.

Baym, Nina. *Woman's Fiction: A Guide to Novels by and about Women in America, 1820–1870.* Ithaca, N.Y.: Cornell University Press, 1978.

Douglas, Ann. *The Feminization of American Culture.* New York: Knopf, 1977.

Eckhardt, Celia Morris. *Fanny Wright: Rebel in America*. Cambridge, Mass.: Harvard University Press, 1984.
Fetterley, Judith. *Provisions: A Reader from 19th-Century American Women*. Bloomington: Indiana University Press, 1985.
Ginzberg, Lori D. "'The Hearts of Your Readers Will Shudder': Fanny Wright, Infidelity, and American Freethought." *American Quarterly* 46 (June 1994): 195–226.
Jennings, Robert L. Untitled editorial notes. *Free Enquirer*, 28 Jan. 1829 (29 Oct. 1828): 8.
Karcher, Carolyn L. *The First Woman in the Republic: A Cultural Biography of Lydia Maria Child*. Durham, N.C.: Duke University Press, 1994.
Kelley, Mary. *Private Woman, Public Stage: Literary Domesticity in Nineteenth-Century America*. New York: Oxford University Press, 1984.
Lerner, Gerda. *The Female Experience: An American Documentary*. Indianapolis: Bobbs-Merrill, 1977.
Mitchell, Catherine C. *Margaret Fuller's New York Journalism: A Biographical Essay and Key Writings*. Knoxville: University of Tennessee Press, 1995.
Okker, Patricia. *Our Sister Editors: Sarah J. Hale and the Tradition of Nineteenth-Century American Women Editors*. Athens: University of Georgia Press, 1995.
Owen, Robert Dale. "Mechanics' Meeting." *Free Enquirer*, 31 Oct. 1829: 7–8.
———. "Our Title." *Free Enquirer*, 29 Oct. 1828, 6.
———. "Our Motto." *Free Enquirer*, 29 Oct. 1828, 6–7.
———. "Proposed Change." *Free Enquirer*, 13 Oct. 1832, 406–407.
———. Untitled editorial. *New-Harmony Gazette*, 30 Jan. 1828, 126.
Rhodes, Jane. *Mary Ann Shadd Cary: The Black Press and Protest in the Nineteenth Century*. Bloomington: Indiana University Press, 1998.
Ritter, Carla Rineer. "Insurrection Behind the Veil: Religious Heterodoxy in Sedgwick, Child, and Stowe." Ph.D. diss., Temple University, 2000.
Rossi, Alice S., ed. *The Feminist Papers: From Adams to de Beauvoir*. Rev. ed. Boston: Northeastern University Press, 1988.
Smith-Rosenberg, Carroll. *Disorderly Conduct: Visions of Gender in Victorian America*. New York: Knopf, 1985.
Spender, Dale. *Women of Ideas (and What Men Have Done to Them): From Aphra Behn to Adrienne Rich*. London: Routledge, 1982.
Streitmatter, Rodger. "Origins of the American Labor Press." *Journalism History* 25 (Autumn 1999): 99–106.
Taylor, Barbara. *Eve and the New Jerusalem: Socialism and Feminism in the Nineteenth Century*. New York: Pantheon, 1983.
V. "Communicated." *Free Enquirer*, 8 Feb. 1829 (19 Nov. 1828), 32.
Woloch, Nancy. *Women and the American Experience*. New York: Knopf, 1984.
Wright [D'Arusmont], Frances. "A Caricature." *Free Enquirer*, 19 June 1830, 267.
———. "Address Delivered at the New York Hall of Science on Sunday the 18th October 1829, by Frances Wright." *Free Enquirer*, 31 Oct. 1829, 1–5.
———. "American Politicians Versus the American People. Or Aristocracy Vs. Democracy." *Free Enquirer*, 29 July 1829, 318–19.
———. "Anonymous Writing." *Free Enquirer*, 15 Feb. 1829 (3 Dec. 1828), 48.
———. "Answer to Vindicia, Being Applicable to the Times, and Prefatory to a Series of Essays on the Causes of Existing Evils." *Free Enquirer*, 4 Mar. 1829, 150–51.
———. "From Auburn." *Free Enquirer*, 21 Nov. 1829, 31–32.
———. "Lectures on Knowledge. By Frances Wright. As Delivered in the Park Theatre, City of New York. Lecture II. Of Free Enquiry Considered as a Mean[s] for Obtaining Just Knowledge." *Free Enquirer*, 25 Mar. 1829, 169–71.
———. *Life, Letters and Lectures, 1834/1844*. New York: Arno Press, 1972.
———. "Nashoba. Explanatory Notes, respecting the Nature and Objects of the Institution

of Nashoba, and of the Principles upon which it is founded . . ." *New-Harmony Gazette,* 30 Jan., 6 Feb., and 13 Feb. 1828, 124–25, 132–33, 140–41.

———. "The New York Daily Sentinel." *Free Enquirer,* 22 May 1830, 239–40.

———. "The Owls." *Free Enquirer,* 29 Oct. 1828, 2.

———. "Parting Address As delivered in the Bowery Theatre, to the People of New York, in June, 1830. By Frances Wright." *Free Enquirer,* 21 and 28 Aug. 1830, 337–39, 345–47.

———. "The People at War." *Free Enquirer,* 27 Nov. 1830, 38.

———. "Richard Johnson." *Free Enquirer,* 20 May 1829, 236.

———. "The South Sea Islander in London." *Free Enquirer,* 29 Oct. 1828, 9–10.

———. "To R. D. Owen: suggested by the perusal of his article in the 129th number of the Gazette . . ." *New-Harmony Gazette,* 18 June 1828, 270–71.

———. "To the Editor of the Correspondent." *New-Harmony Gazette,* 2 July 1828, 284.

———. "To the Intelligent among the Working Classes; and Generally, to All Honest Reformers." *Free Enquirer,* 5 Dec. 1829, 46–47.

———. Untitled editorial note. *New-Harmony Gazette,* 18 June 1828, 270.

———. Untitled editorial. *Free Enquirer,* 29 Oct. 1828, 5–6.

———. Untitled editorial. *Free Enquirer,* 28 Jan. 1829 (29 Oct. 1828), 7–8.

———. Untitled editorial. *Free Enquirer,* 1 Feb. 1829 (5 Nov. 1828), 15–16.

———. Untitled valedictory. *Free Enquirer,* 13 Oct. 1832, 407.

[Wright, Frances and Robert Dale Owen]. "Prospectus of *The New-Harmony and Nashoba Gazette,* in Continuation of *The New-Harmony Gazette.*" *New-Harmony Gazette,* 30 July 1828, 318–19.

Untitled Editorial
Free Enquirer, 29 October 1828

—"Have at ye, then!
A needle or nine pounder—choose, my lieges!"
OLD PLAY.

The advocates of error have at least the merit of well earning their pay. It matters not to enquire if this be with the hope of increasing their percentage of profits. Let the motive sleep: the fact is all with which we have to do; and the fact speaks loudly for their activity, ingenuity, and perseverance.

To their activity all the earth bears testimony. Scarcely an acre of its remotest regions but is harassed by their footsteps; and scarcely a human ear, savage or civilized, but is stunned by the Babel of their doctrines, anathemas, and disputes. Their ingenuity has forced all the arts useful or useless, to the furtherance of their craft, and the increase of their gains. According to the taste of the age or the people, we find the servants of religion casting their idols in the moulds of attractive grace, terrific power, or incongruous absurdity. All the passions of men are worked on by turns. The superstitions of ignorance, the credulity of folly, the imaginations of youth, the weakness of age, the idleness of dissipation, the tremulousness of disease—all are addressed in appropriate style and befitting language. Without adverting to the religions of antiquity, or to those of remote regions, we find full exemplification of the worldly wisdom of heavenly traders within the precincts of modern times and modern superstitions. Our priestly wares are of all kinds, for all tastes and conditions. We have solemn prayers, disputatious sermons, alarming denunciations, rhetorical discourses, pathetic appeals, hobgoblin stories, rhyming hymns, pealing organs, sonorous cursings, and sweet voices tuned to melody.

The spiritual quack has nostrums of every species and quality, according to country, clime, and government. Under the bright sun and brighter fancy of Italy, Christianity decked her sombre features with the pleasing knaveries of the graceful mythology she supplanted. And the Romish clergy, the most learned and talented of which the modern superstition can boast, has ever fitted its pomps and its pageantries, its humor and its coat, the tune of its songs and the temper of its tyranny, to the character of the people with whom it had to deal. In Italy, as we have observed, the sons of the temple spake to the imagination in the light notes of pleasure. Popes, cardinals, monks and friars were all fine gentlemen or pleasant fellows; just looking serious at high mass, issuing bulls and excommunications against those who alarmed or attracted their ambition; and sprinkling their discourse with no more fire and brimstone than was absolutely necessary to ensure the payment of Peter's pence, and the undisturbed tenure of thrones, churches, palaces, and fat lands. In Spain, the tribe of Levi were all grave Spaniards, haughty and taciturn as the princes and people they had to govern. Here the jesuits took their rise, and the inquistion reigned in all its grim silence and mysterious terror. In France the clergy were courtly and noisy, agreeable, vain, ambitious, and presuming. In Germany they grew with the nation mystical and disputatious, and so turned reformers. Then up rose Protestantism with all her varying sects and never ending dogmas.

This cunning dame, having ostensibly made war against the pomps and vanities of the lady of Babylon, had of necessity to shorten her own robe and show less finery. But men soon learnt, that if she had dropt some pleasant fooleries, she had adopted many dull ones, and that if the times forbade her to kindle as many *auto-da-fes* and dig as many dungeons as her ancient rival, she could fine and imprison and starve and banish troublesome enquirers and stiff necked nonconformists; and even occasionally roast one at a slow fire, as Calvin did Servetus. And—alas for our ears! she has banished the swelling paeans and harmonious psalmistry of Romish music for the nasal twang of presbyterianism, and the groanings of entranced methodism. And—alas for our eyes! in lieu of glowing paintings and speaking sculpture and theatrical processions, we have large meeting houses, with blank whitewashed walls, and cold, stiff, starched faced preachers, preaching starvation and abnegation, and craving for Peter's pence all the same. And—alas for our nostrils! instead of graceful clouds of odor breathing incense, we have the hot breaths of crowded, sighing devotees; and the steam of brimstone, fresh extracted by priestly alchemy from the infernal cauldron.

But in varying some tricks and ringing the changes on some tunes, the *reformed* tribe of Levi have husbanded all the spirit of the trade and secret of the craft. If they have bad music, they forbid the making of better; if they have no Carnival, they enact a law against all dancing and masking and merriment; and make one long Lent of the year round. If men and women fall asleep under their sermons, they forbid to better orators the use of the rostrum. If they write heavy folios, too dull to be read, they debar sprightlier authors from the use of the press. Bibles and psalm books and pious tracts cover the high ways as pebbles, and the fields as daisies; and they who will not read them or buy them are sent to the devil. Awkward manufacturers though they be, they hold the monopoly of all trade and custom. They work all the presses, make all the books, rhyme all the songs, tune all the fiddles, and make all the world move to their dull time.

But we may begin to change the tense of the verb. They *have done* all this; but, by the hope and the strength and the improving sense of the age, they are about to share the market with more able, and I trust, more honest artisans. And, alas for them! when once well shared, it is well lost. And yet, could they but see it, they might be gainers by their own bankruptcy. They will have nothing to do but to write sense instead of nonsense, preach wisdom instead of folly, and sing good songs instead of bad psalms. So doing, if they have not more followers, they will have more listeners; and should they even get less pay, they will get more praise.

With a view of hastening this change in public affairs, I have determined to subscribe my quota of exertions in every style possible to my invention. And, seeing that the servants of the old temple have been accustomed to deal in all wares, giving us orthodox creeds, orthodox histories, orthodox philosophy, and even orthodox novels and nursery tales, I have thought it advisable to prepare antidotes to the same; and, with this view, have prepared a series of heterodox fables, the first of which, under the title of *The Owls*, appears in our present number. Should any of our readers of the old school object to laughing, I or my co-editors will be happy to meet their taste under the graver form of heterodox essays, heterodox histories and heterodox philosophy, F. W.

Lucy Stone and *The Woman's Journal*

KATHARINE RODIER

BETTER known as a political force through her oratory skill than as a literary figure, reformer Lucy Stone nonetheless featured prominently in the world of nineteenth-century American letters in a number of ways: as a self-publisher who circulated print versions of her speeches on abolition and woman's rights; as the subject of others' editorials, tributes, and lampoons; and perhaps most significantly as the cofounder, publisher, and coeditor of *The Woman's Journal*, a weekly newspaper dedicated to women's issues that drew subscribers from all states and thirty-nine countries by 1875. Although she became noted first for her speeches against slavery, Stone also stood with Susan B. Anthony and Elizabeth Cady Stanton as one of the century's most influential crusaders for women's equality. Stone's biographers document how disagreements among the three led Stanton and her staff in their monumental *History of Woman Suffrage* to downplay Stone's contributions to their cause, leading in turn to her virtual erasure from the public record that celebrated the others' achievements. Only recently have scholars begun to reappraise Stone's larger importance both as an activist and as a considerable presence in the history of women's publishing. Her political and commercial investment in *The Woman's Journal* arose not only from her liberal convictions and a shrewd appreciation of how she might circulate them in print, but from a growing personal focus on marital fidelity and family cohesion, loyalties that in the late 1860s and early 1870s she had seen jeopardized in her own marriage to Henry Brown Blackwell. Stone's inception of *The Woman's Journal* suggests one instance where the nominally separate spheres of nineteenth-century gender ideology in the United States could manage to fuse: on the one hand it reinscribed the conservative "family values" that voices into the twenty-first century have continued to tout, but on the other it reasserted a woman's right—if not her duty—to articulate and to change the persistent inequities that she apprehended in her world.

In 1843, Stone carried her liberal convictions to Oberlin Collegiate Institute in Ohio, the first four-year college in the United States to admit women. Despite Oberlin's professions to support the emancipation of women and of blacks, Stone's fervent advocacy of social reform for these groups set her apart from much of her community, as had been the case earlier in her education in Massachusetts at Mount Holyoke Female Seminary under Mary Lyons. Nonetheless, during this time, she intensified her efforts as a human rights activist, seeking various venues including debate for her public expression. After abolitionists Stephen and Abby Kelley Foster visited the college in 1846, Stone first became involved with the print media: serving as an agent for the *Anti-Slavery Bugle* of Salem, Ohio, she contributed an article opposing the proslavery stance of the local church. Upon her graduation in August 1847, she was invited to write a commencement essay for her class, but as only males in her program were allowed to publicly read their statements, she declined the ostensible honor. Certainly, while Stone had begun to value the persuasive immediacy of public appearance, she did not at this time fashion herself as a journalist, or even as a writer. Yet she could appreciate—and might hope to exploit, albeit in this instance through omission—the potential power of the written word to extend the audience for any spoken statement that she might make.

By 1848, Lucy Stone had started a bold career lecturing on issues that concerned her, her primary occupation for the next decade, despite vehement and recurring opposition. In June of that year, she joined Foster as an agent for the Massachusetts Anti-Slavery Society (MASS). Inclined to infuse her passion for women's rights into her abolitionist lectures, Stone met resistance from MASS officials who urged a more singular focus on their stated cause. Initially, she replied, "I was a woman before I was an abolitionist. I must speak for the women" (qtd. in Blackwell, *Pioneer*). Not wishing to lose this compelling lecturer, the society worked out a compromise: Stone would speak for their agenda on weekends, but could devote her own time during the week to lecturing on other concerns. With a consistent urgency, Stone would then amplify her public statements by introducing a print component. After her appearances, versions of her lectures circulated as printed tracts, which she herself would distribute, or in newspaper reprints, even though she made her speeches largely without written scripts. In this manner, as a pamphleteer but also as a subject who inspired publicity, Stone used the power of print to help create a public record of her remarks, earning further recognition, if not notoriety, for the causes that thereby became affiliated with her name. Touring several states to speak, she met crowds as likely to call her a "raving she hyena" and to burn pepper in her face, spit or throw hymnbooks at her, or douse her through an open church window, as to embrace her eloquent but plainspoken message of equality (qtd. in Taylor A1). Despite such physical threats, her will to give voice to her convictions, sometimes through multiple or complementary media, remained unyielding.

After her wedding in 1855 to Henry Brown Blackwell, the couple joined efforts to advance Stone's preferred causes. To an extent, Stone would curtail her public activism as lecturer at her husband's behest when in 1857 she gave birth to the couple's only child, Alice Stone Blackwell. But she did not immediately turn to print expression as a possibly less physically demanding alternative to public speaking. By the late 1860s, the cataclysm of the Civil War and the ensuing upheavals of Reconstruction had splintered countless antebellum political affiliations, especially in the controversy over whether the long-vexed "woman question" demanded priority over suffrage for freedmen. These frictions helped spark Stone's disaffection from former woman's rights allies, a volatile dynamic that, when she resumed public activism, would impel her to seek her own means and venues beyond the lecture hall to publicize her opinions. Unwilling to subordinate their woman's cause to any other, Anthony and Stanton called for educated suffrage, which would grant most white women the vote ahead of unschooled ex-slaves. In the midst of this conflict, Stone traveled to Kansas in 1867 to fight for a dual referendum, which would strike both "white" and "male" restrictions from that state's voting standards. By 1869, at the American Equal Rights Association Convention in New York (AERA), Stone remarked that the problems of discrimination based on race and on gender were parallel:

> Woman has an ocean of wrongs too deep for any plummet, and the negro, too, has an ocean of wrongs that can not be fathomed. There are two great oceans. . . . But I thank God for that Fifteenth Amendment, and hope that it will be adopted in every state. I will be thankful in my soul if *anybody* can get out of the terrible pit. (qtd. in Goldsmith 182)

Notably, at this time Stone lamented to Anthony her disappointment in the tepid East Coast news coverage of the struggle by Horace Greeley's *New York Tribune* and Theodore Tilton's *Independent*, whose efforts she saw as ineffectual: "What a power to hold, and not use!" (qtd. in Kerr 125). Clearly, Stone had recognized both the potential and the potential shortcomings of the print media as a source of publicity, but also as an influence on readers: a remotely controlled force more far-reaching than even the most charismatic human voice.

After both Kansas referenda failed, Stone determined that Anthony and Stanton's absolutism may have damaged their own vehement campaign, further fraying any alliance among the three of them and compelling Stone to redefine the purposes of her activism and her preferred modes of conveying her convictions. The growing tensions between Stone and her colleagues Anthony and Stanton had not stopped the others from affirming Stone's insight into the power of the press, as they had already founded their own suffrage newspaper, *The Revolution*, in New York in 1868. Significantly, Stone also thought that the support and funding of Anthony and Stanton's New York-based operations by the ostentatiously racist Democrat George F. Train betrayed both moral principles and Republican loyalty (Lasser and Merrill 165). Moreover, Train—who opposed black voting rights, and whom Stone had labeled "a charlatan" and "a lunatic, wild and ranting" (qtd. in Goldsmith 137; Kerr 129)—also financed the appearance of *The Revolution*, which advocated, "Men, their rights and nothing more; women, their rights, and nothing less" (qtd. in Kerr 129). As Andrea Kerr and Barbara Goldsmith point out, *The Revolution* also promoted topics such as educated suffrage, labor and wage equity, an eight-hour workday, paper currency, "The Abolition of Standing Armies and Party Despotism," and a tax on foreign goods, while it exposed the "misconduct" of Wall Street entrepreneurs, the clergy, politicians, and the well-to-do (Kerr 131; Goldsmith 177). In Stanton's not-uncertain words, *The Revolution*'s pages proclaimed, "Society as organized today is one grand rape of womanhood under the man power" (qtd. in Goldsmith 177). Before the 1869 AERA convention in New York, Stone and Mary Livermore—herself a journalist by this time, having helped establish *The Agitator* in Chicago in 1868— would work to convince Anthony to disengage Train from *The Revolution*. Interestingly, this action occurred after Anthony had taunted Stone on a personal level, "I know what is the matter with you. It is envy, and spleen, and hate, because I have a paper and you have not" (qtd. in Kerr 130). Not only did these developing factions each see the utility of a newspaper to their cause, *The Revolution* had itself become a point of sneering contention, at least from Anthony's corner. Thereafter, Stone resolved to dissociate her office from Anthony's paper. As late as 1871, however, Anthony feared that Stone might acquire the publication, "the results of all my hardest 20 years" (qtd. in Goldsmith 261), giving further evidence of the personal and ethical stake that each woman had claimed in much more than a public relations struggle.

If these tensions between AERA's New York and New England factions had seemed to diminish at any point, they reescalated at the 1869 New York convention, when Livermore read a counterresolution against what she designated as the "Free Love" platform that, in truth, the New York group only ambiguously affirmed. Characteristically, Stone had intended not to address the free love issue—which Livermore had deemed "horrible and mischievous to society" (qtd. in Goldsmith 183)—and sought to redirect the AERA's attention back to focus on suffrage and legal equity for men and women:

> I am unwilling that it should be suggested that this great, sacred cause of ours means anything but what we have said it does. If anyone says to me,

"Oh, I know what you mean, you mean Free Love by this agitation," let the lie stick in his throat. You may talk about Free Love, if you please, but we are to have the right to vote. Today we are fined, imprisoned, and hanged without a jury trial by our peers. You shall not cheat us by getting us off to talk about something else. (qtd. in Goldsmith 184)

Nonetheless, after Livermore, Stone, and Blackwell left the convention, Anthony and Stanton began in reaction to plan and recruit members for a separate organization, the National Woman Suffrage Association (NWSA). As they envisaged it, NWSA would oppose the by-then nearly ratified Fifteenth Amendment because it excluded women, demand that a Sixteenth Amendment enfranchise women, battle for woman suffrage and equal labor conditions, and encourage equal rights between spouses in marriage as well as more liberal divorce laws (Goldsmith 186). Later, Stone would label as "underhanded" her colleagues' founding of the NWSA. Subsequently, she countered them by helping to organize and direct an alternative group, the American Woman Suffrage Association (AWSA), rooted in her support by the regionally based New England Woman Suffrage Association (NEWSA). Although Stone claimed that despite its different orientations, AWSA would not constitute "an enemy or antagonist . . . in any way" to NWSA, few seemed inclined to accept without question her rationalization that the work of each office would complement that of the other (qtd. in Goldsmith 201). In the meantime, spurred by these differences, and perhaps inspired by Livermore, Stone stepped up fundraising efforts toward starting a suffrage paper of her own (Kerr 142).

Writing to Antoinette Brown Blackwell, her friend and sister-in-law, in October of that year, Stone foreshadowed the more definitive split between woman's rights proponents that would occur in November after the NEWSA rally in Cleveland. Remarkably, her letter also documents a concurrent schism in her family situation:

> Col. Higginson, either influenced by Theodore Tilton, or from a feeling of (what shall I say,) mistaken magnanimity, perhaps, told Mrs. Stanton, and Susan, that he expected to see them at Cleveland.
> They neither of them intended to go—I do not know that they will—But it will be so dreadful an incubus, to take them up again! tho' perhaps there will be no help for it if they go. But I do very much wish you could plan to be there, so that we may counsel.
> You know Alice goes to Newburyport this week. I think it is the best thing for her, but I feel crushed and torn and homeless—But I shall make myself very busy. (Lasser and Merrill 175)

This was not the only instance in which Stone would use the sexually charged, predatory image of "an incubus" to denigrate her opponents, regardless of their gender. And characteristically, Stone here imagines that industry, personal and professional, can compensate for the absence of her child—a recurring reality in this family at this time, despite the anxiety it caused Stone—and the planned relocation of her own home. Such conflicts between personal and public commitments would persist for Stone over the remainder of her nonetheless determined life.

In the same letter, Stone also outlined her plans for a publication, especially significant because she conceived of it as a shared effort with her husband, then involved with another woman, Abby Hutchinson Patton. Patton presented yet another face of the nineteenth-century public woman who allied her talents with reform: as the "rose-bud of a sister" in the singing Hutchinson family, Abby Hutchinson had appeared across the United States at many a rally where Lucy Stone would lecture (Hutchinson 1, 82). More recently, Patton and her husband, a successful businessman and sometime associate of Blackwell's, had resided near Stone's family in Roseville, New Jersey. By the occasion of Stone's letter, Blackwell and Stone had sometimes lived and worked apart, affected by what Patton referred to as Blackwell's "grand and secret love" for her (qtd. in Goldsmith 184). Barbara Goldsmith reports that Blackwell's sisters, physicians Elizabeth and Emily Blackwell, believed that Stone's public activism had caused her to ignore her husband, and also that Stone proposed the joint publishing effort to him as part of an "ultimatum"—a word that Stone's biographer Andrea Kerr also uses—to ensure his reinvestment in their marriage (184–185).

In such a context, as Stone's own language in the letter suggests, a word like "reinvestment" would bear multiple meanings—financial, as well as marital or emotional:

> Harry will join me at Newburyport, and we shall set to, to raise $10,000 to start a paper. I suppose you know the N. E. Woman Suffrage Association propose to take the "Agitator"—call it the "Woman's Journal," with Mrs. [Mary] Livermore, Mrs. [Julia Ward] Howe, T. W. Higginson & Mr. [William Lloyd] Garrison as Editors—*If we can raise the money*. If we do I shall try and work through the paper, for the future, and quit this lecturing field nearly altogether.
>
> It is not consistent with any home life, or any proper care of my family. I feel it more and more, and shall certainly not continue this mode of work—tho' it is my natural way.
>
> But I long for a snug home, by myself, from which I can send out, what I think, in some shape not so effective for me perhaps, but on the whole better, under the circumstances—If I were only a ready writer, I should be so glad!— (Lasser and Merrill 175)

Tellingly, Stone conjoins a *mea culpa* attitude with a pragmatic program, determining for him what her *husband* will do. But tensions in her language further betray her internal conflict. Can a person indeed "quit" an endeavor *"nearly* altogether" (italics mine)? Can a "home life"—the "proper care of my family" in a "snug home"—necessarily enable her work *"by myself* ?" Such a collective goal would seem in most cases to negate claims to autonomy. Moreover, recognizing that founding a newspaper might be "not so effective" a means of expression for Stone "but on the whole better, under the circumstances" than her "natural way" admits the personal compromise involved in this particular quest for a projected greater good.

Envisioned as a substitute for her brilliant but exhausting career as an orator—an increasingly demanding undertaking as Stone grew older, and one seen by at least some observers, including her husband and in-laws, as threatening to her family—*The Woman's Journal* came to function essentially as a "diary of [her] public life" (Hays 221), although she never fully gave up the lectern. To found and to maintain the *Journal* required a huge monetary investment, which was underwritten by a joint-stock company whose members, mostly Stone's colleagues and supporters, initially purchased two hundred shares in the venture at fifty dollars each. While Blackwell owned the greatest number of shares in the *Journal* and would work there in various capacities from business manager to associate editor, his commitment to the enterprise fluctuated, especially in its earliest days, when he continued to travel frequently between Boston and New York and elsewhere. Blackwell's sister Emily describes his own struggle over working on Stone's publication: "He VOWS he won't go into the paper but will come back to Roseville and go into business but in the next breath he discusses the possibility of his taking up the paper, and I rather incline to think he will be drawn into it" (qtd. in Kerr 145). In spring 1870, Blackwell cast his involvement with the *Journal* with irritation, in a far from altruistic light: "I am sure I don't know why *I* am working hard here without even a salary and for no earthly reason but to try to make Lucy happy" (qtd. in Kerr 150). By early 1872, when Antoinette Brown Blackwell asked who indeed functioned as the *Journal's* editor, Stone responded assertively, yet once again not without qualification, "Harry! But he means to go to Santo Domingo next month, and then I shall edit it" (qtd. in Kerr 169–70). Understandably, the boundaries of a highly politicized collective effort, grounded in private and unresolved interpersonal issues, proved difficult even for the absolute Stone to draw.

Designating the *Journal's* editorial board required of Lucy Stone emotional and professional trust: wryly, she would come to refer to the publication as "a big baby which never grew up, and always had to be fed" (qtd. in Kerr 167), a familial if monstrously domesticated and insatiable construct. Men and women collaborated in the *Journal's* production. Its staff eventually grew to include not only Stone's husband and her former abolitionist allies (themselves no strangers to publishing)—such as Thomas Wentworth Higginson and William Lloyd Garrison—but also, her own daughter, Alice. By the fourth issue, Mary Livermore, whose Chicago suffrage journal was absorbed by the *Woman's Journal*, was listed on the masthead as the publication's editor, above associate editors Stone, Higginson, Garrison, and the renowned writer, Julia Ward Howe. Livermore would hold that title until December 1871, when, reversing Stone's own career direction, she returned full-time to a lecturing career, continuing with the *Journal* as a corresponding editor. Among the other important figures who contributed to Stone's *Journal*, only Higginson, who became the weekly newspaper's lead writer, was offered a regular salary for his columns, an even more striking distinction after the Panic of 1873 and the ensuing five-year depression shook the country's financial foundation and the *Journal's* economic future. When Garrison resigned in the first year, Henry Blackwell's name joined those on the list of editors. By the mid 1870s, Howe, Stone, and Blackwell were listed as editors, with Higginson and Livermore designated as editorial contributors. By 1881, Stone, Blackwell, and Higginson were supplying the bulk of the *Journal's* editorials.

Obtaining reliable financial backing remained a concern for the enterprise. An 1870 letter signed by the *Journal's* staff suggests the personal and professional strategies that Stone coordinated to help build support for this publishing venture:

> Dear Friend:
> We send you specimen copies of the "WOMAN'S JOURNAL" by mail.
> Will you oblige us by calling upon your friends and neighbors as soon as convenient, and making us up a large list of subscribers?
> The price of the paper is $3.00 a year, payable invariably in advance. We allow fifty cents cash commission upon each new subscriber obtained; or we will send seven copies for the price of six.
> For the sake of the cause of Woman's Equality, we hope that you will be able to engage in this important work at once.
> If not, please try to find someone who will do so.
> Hoping for an early reply.
>   We remain,
>   Yours very truly,
>   Mary A. Livermore
>   Julia Ward Howe
>   Lucy Stone
>   Wm. Lloyd Garrison
>   T. W. Higginson
>   Henry B. Blackwell

Approaching the addressee cordially, as "Dear Friend," the signers enclosed a sample product, aiming to increase future sales through informal social networking: "calling upon your friends and neighbors." They initially cast their pitch as a request, in accommodating language, asking rather than urging, "Will you oblige us . . . as soon as convenient." Yet the staff states a desired outcome directly: they profess to seek "a large list of subscribers" rather than a lending library of casual if like-minded readers. As the letter progresses, it discloses its financial purposes, designating costs and payment structure before it reverts to a loftier appeal to subscribers based on *ethos*, "[f]or the sake of the cause." Pragmatically, but again politely, the writers close by anticipating a reader's possible refusal, yet they do not absolve the recipient of responsibility for conveying the request to others, now "at once," rather than "as convenient." Engineering "New Woman" results by reiterating some "True Woman" appeals, this letter documents as well a promotional strategy that would come to define the ideological composition of the *Journal* itself.

Stone's own involvement with the *Journal* was equally complex. Besides writing her own columns for the paper, she oversaw the *Journal*'s finances, administering accounts and salaries; recruited editors and writers; identified newsworthy issues, ranging from Rosa Bonheur's paintings to the 1871 Chicago fire, but also from protests over detrimental working conditions and low wages to legislative records of state and local prosuffrage votes; oversaw the paper's layout, its delivery to its female printers, and its mailing; staged bazaars and sales to raise crucial income and garner publicity; and managed subscribers. Stone would also handle manuscripts and correspondence, enlarge the scope of the paper through an international as well as national news outreach, and publish relevant patent information (Kerr 167, 194). By pursuing a vocation in print she may have removed herself from the likelihood of physical assault, which she had faced as a speaker before the Civil War, but her work remained physically demanding. As late as 1877, she recounted "pounding the pavement" herself to collect advertisements: "I walked miles to picture stores, crockery stores, grocery stores, book stores, to 'special sales' going up flight after flight of stairs, only to find the men out, or not ready to advertise, and for all my day's toil, I did not get a cent" (qtd. in Kerr 194). The first issue appeared on January 8, 1870, which was, significantly, the second anniversary of its main competitor, *The Revolution*.

As a forum for the AWSA, which welcomed men into its ranks (the NWSA initially resisted admitting men), *The Woman's Journal* purported to "champion the passage of the Fifteenth Amendment, to defend the family, and to preserve the institution of marriage" (Tuttleton 41). Focusing on local and state suffrage campaigns rather than on the federal battle, the *Journal* would promote expanded roles for women within fundamentally conventional settings and muted discussion of current controversies over divorce, adultery, infanticide, and free love, which raged in NWSA circles. It proclaimed itself "Devoted to the interests of woman, to her educational, industrial, legal and political equality, and especially to her right of suffrage," but whereas it monitored working conditions for women, it reflected little sustained commitment to larger social issues, such as labor struggles or the burgeoning unemployment in the 1870s (qtd. in Lasser and Merrill 167). When Elizabeth Cady Stanton, taking her cue from Stone's earlier rhetorical direction, charged that *The Woman's Journal* only examined suffrage, Stone detailed her publication's more comprehensive coverage: "every question, fact, and interest that concerns woman. Education, work, clothing, food, health, training of children, marriage" (qtd. in Kerr 156). Regularly, the *Journal* printed the AWSA constitution and the names of its officers, many of which appeared also on the newspaper's masthead.

Publishing literary reviews, social tidbits, poetry, fiction, and ads for sarsaparilla and the "Emancipation Waist"—a "strictly hygienic dress reform garment," along with its editorials and suffrage news, *The Woman's Journal* did not sell itself as a radical publication (XV. 32, 3). In 1876, Stone summarized its perspective by paraphrasing Higginson: "we dont (sic) think women are better than men, or that their suffrage will bring the millennium" (qtd. in Wheeler 256). As *The Woman's Journal* founder, Stone relied on the versatility of her staff, and appreciated their dedication to the ideals that they shared. Published every Saturday in Boston and Chicago, and later in St. Louis, the *Journal* featured columns such as "What Women Are Doing," which might include items about the former Queen of Spain's "autobiography in the shape of a novel" (I. 3, 19); Maria Mitchell's lectures on astronomy, expatriate American women sculptors in Rome, and "Mrs. Stonewall Jackson's sister" and her work as an architect designing a "hexagonal apartment" (I. 4, 27); or George Sand's action for defamation against an adultery charge (I. 8, 59), but also "Harriet Miner, colored, widow of Wm. Purvis, a wealthy South Carolina planter, died in Philadelphia, Friday, aged eighty-five, and worth $200,000. When a slave, she discovered a plot to murder her master, and disclosed it to him, and he, in gratitude, married her, leaving all his property to her at his death" (I. 2, 11), and "Miss Lucy Bliss has taught school eight years at Stockbridge, without the loss of single day. As she lives two miles from the school-house, she must have walked more than 13,000 miles in that time." (I. 4, 27)

In addition, the *Journal* included dispatches from state and local sources under "Suffrage Items"; foreign correspondence and international perspectives on women's issues; and "Just For Fun." The latter ran jokes, such as "A sick young lady in Worcester, Mass., has been attended by thirteen physicians, and still lives"; "A young lady in Cavendish recently killed a skunk with a butcher knife. She says the battle is not always to the strong"; and "Josh Billings says that the mosquito was born of poor, but honest, parents who had in their veins some of the best blood in the country" (I. 8, 59). In the same early issue (26 February 1870), publishers Lee & Shepard advertised "Mrs. Stowe's New Book—*Lady Byron Vindicated*"; *The Nursery—A Monthly Magazine for Youngest Children*; and *Tracts for the People* by educators, clergymen, and the author of *Farm Talk*. Similarly, NEWSA advertised *Woman's Suffrage Tracts* by Henry Ward Beecher, John Stuart Mill, and others, published by Charles K. Whipple. Despite Stone's will to eschew feminized clichés—"no fashion plates, no household hints, no recipes" (Kerr 199)—homey hints surfaced in its pages, especially before 1871: "A little beef's gall will not only set, but heighten, yellow and purple tints, and has a good effect upon green" (qtd. in Hays 218).

Besides featuring articles by the well-known literati on its editorial staff, *The Woman's Journal* featured original works and reprints from some of the era's most notable and in some cases most popular writers. The *Journal*'s poetic selections often played to the romantic or inspirational, and included poems such as Elizabeth Barrett Browning's "My Heart and I" (I. 32, 249), Lucy Larcom's "Better" (I. 2, 14), John Greenleaf Whittier's "In School Days" and Alice Cary's "A Passing Wish" (I. 4, 27), Celia Thaxter's "Regret" (II. 15, 118) and "Her Eyes" (I. 9, 70), and poems by "H. H.," who eventually published as Helen Hunt Jackson. Prose selections included Bret Harte's comic adventure "Miggles: Episode on a California Stage Ride" (I. 1, 6–7) in the inaugural issue, Louise Chandler Moulton's "Story of an Old Young Man" (I. 3, 22), and Rebecca Harding Davis's "A November Afternoon" (I. 4, 30). According to Madeleine B. Stern, between November 14, 1874, and 1887 Louisa May Alcott would contribute eighteen letters, articles, stories, and poems, including nine feminist tracts, which Stern reprints in *Louisa May Alcott: From Blood and Thunder to Hearth and Home* (1998). The importance of Alcott's work for the *Journal* led to her listing on its masthead as one of its "occasional correspondents" (Stern 147). In the *Journal* pages, Alcott commented with typical irony on persistent gender inequities in her native Concord in particular, which she called "a town which ought to lead as if it really possesses all the intelligence claimed for it" (11 October 1879, qtd. in Stern 161). On February 26, 1887, shortly before Alcott's death in 1888, the *Journal* began to offer copies of Alcott's *Jo's Boys* as an incentive for new subscribers (XVIII. 8, 20), printing a recurring endorsement from the popular author drawn from her May 12, 1885, letter to Stone's publication: "It is the only paper I take, and I find it invaluable to me."

Some years before, on January 23, 1875, Alcott had provided a tribute to *The Woman's Journal*—then housed at Number Three, Tremont Place, in Boston—as one of its front page poems (VI. 4, 23):

> AN ADVERTISEMENT
> by Louise (sic) M. Alcott
>
> Ho! All you nervous women folk
> Who sigh that you were born;
> Come, try a sovereign remedy
> For half the ills you mourn.
> I, lately, have discovered it,
> And proved its potency,
> By tasting at the fountain-head—
> Tremont Place, Number Three.
>
> Here, at this moral restaurant,
> Our sex may always find,
> When weary of domestic stews,
> Nice lunches for the mind.
> Essays are served at certain hours,
> Gossip, of course, is free;
> Discussion always is on tap,
> And once a month, Club Tea.
>
> I know whereof I speak, my friends,
> For at the Woman's Club
> I found a pleasant mingling
> Of heaven and the Hub.
> No wine, cigars or gambling,
> But wisdom, wit, and fun,
> The matrons knit their husband's (sic) hose,
> And quoted Emerson.
>
> Wise virgins had their lamps well trimmed
> And lighted up the rooms
> With luster of brave words and deeds,—
> Worthy the noblest grooms;
> Yet strong enough to stand alone,
> (In hygienic boots),
> And bear life's burdens, for they wore
> The famous "freedom suits."
>
> "Home" was the dish we feasted on,
> The evening I was there;

Garnished with eloquence, and served
On finest *Cheney* ware,
Porter was sipped to soothe the brains
Beneath each lofty bonnet;
No pewter pot the liquor held,
But it had a good "head" on it.

Flowers were there, and one I saw
That bore an honored name;
In Boston it has flourished long,
And with the Pilgrims came.
The plant a worthy scion was,
Stately and strong and gay;
'Twill make the modest posy blush
To add, it blooms in *May*.

Among the hills the farmers think
The Peabody bird sings ever,
"Sow your wheat! sow your wheat!" as if
To rouse all to endeavor.
Two Peabody birds this Club possessed,
One did cheerily sing
"We've gained our seats at last!" and one
"Let Kindergarten spring!"

I looked about me for the queen
Who ruled this busy hive,
Where work and play, reform and fun,
Together seemed to thrive.
I said, "I wish their magic spell
These blithe souls would avow."
A dozen voices answered me—
"Look round and you'll see *Howe*."

I said, "Can strangers enter here,
Led by some friendly *Star*?"
They answered, "If their *Ames* be good,
We care not who they are;
The young, the old, the rich, the poor,
And if a noble male
We *Ferrette* out, we welcome him,
With "Worthy brother, *Hale!*"

Then hasten, all ye women folk:
Tuck up your skirts and walk.
Here's food for hungry hearts and souls,
Here mind with mind may talk.
Here spirits of the best are found,

> Here flows the true Club Tea,
> And the cream of human kindness,
> At Tremont Place, Number Three.
> January, 1875.

Characteristically infusing this fifth-anniversary piece for the *Journal* with wit, warmth, and cheer, Alcott delineates the paper's office as an idealized, domesticated scene, humming with Emerson-espousing, knitting matrons, and marriageable but nonetheless independent "wise virgins," garbed sturdily in "hygienic boots" (l. 30) and "freedom suits" (l. 32). Here intellect proves not only nourishing, but delectable; not only restorative, but liberating. At the same time, the all-star enterprise is collegial, even familial. Presumably, Alcott's elusive "queen" (l. 49) might represent Stone herself. Punning references in italics more clearly identify others on hand as Stone's coeditor Howe, as well as Ednah Dow Cheney, Bronson Alcott's protégée and his daughter's own 1889 biographer. Another figure in the poem may represent Maria S. Porter, poet and local school committee member, to whom Alcott had written in 1874,

> Let us hear no more of "woman's sphere" either from our wise (?) legislators beneath the State House dome, or from our clergymen in their pulpits. I am tired, year after year, of hearing such twaddle about sturdy oaks and clinging vines and man's chivalric protection of woman. Let woman find out her own limitations, and if, as is so confidently asserted, nature has defined her sphere, she will be guided accordingly; but in heaven's name give her a chance! (190)

Alcott also features in this setting her mother's family, the Mays, with Alcott's late uncle, the abolitionist and Unitarian minister Samuel Joseph May, known in particular for his liberal leanings. Other noteworthy members of the coterie may be identified as educators Elizabeth Palmer Peabody and Mary Peabody Mann; C. H. Ames, mentioned in Alcott's correspondence as having educated two sisters (209); and Edward Everett Hale, Unitarian pastor, reformer, and author of *The Man Without A Country*. As "An Advertisement," Alcott's rollicking but homespun meeting of the minds would serve to promote Stone's publication as certifiably wholesome, energized, and inviting, a corollary of sorts to Alcott's own wildly popular young people's fiction.

Beginning with the *Journal*'s first issues, Stone herself supplied a sampling of such "food for hungry hearts and souls." Her earliest writings indicate the range of the commentary over her twenty-year commitment to the paper, running from the sober "Laws in Relation to the Property Rights of Married Women in Massachusetts" (I. 1, 8) to a profile of "Our Office" on January 15, 1870. Prefiguring in ways Alcott's congenial depiction in

"An Advertisement," Stone begins with a charming description of the workspace and its furnishings. But Stone's piece concludes with no uncertain bid for active support, advancing the dually personal and pragmatic direction of her staff's 1870 letter to potential subscribers:

> To this office the friends of the cause are always welcome. Through it we hope not only to make acquaintances all over the country, who have common interest with us in our work, but who will cooperate actively with us in extending the circulation of our journal, who will take responsibility in carrying tracts and petitions to every house in the neighborhood, who will open the way for lectures, and by every just means induce all the friends of the cause to unite in the long, strong pull, which is necessary to take woman above the political level she now shares with idiots, lunatics, paupers, felons, and unpardoned rebels, and to put her on the same plane with other decent taxpaying citizens. (I. 2, 13)

Stone's call for unity and recognition in "Our Office" resounds further through a biographical footnote: at the time of this printing, until their move in December 1870 to their large Dorchester home, Pope's Hill, her family resided literally in the same Boston building, in quarters above the *Journal*'s here so lovingly rendered, apparently welcoming office. Alice Stone Blackwell described the Tremont Place accommodations as "one room and a cupboard": these were not expansive conditions for a family under duress (qtd. in Hays 215). But for a woman determined to fulfill her commitments to her family and to her work, such a location might seem not only convenient, but an auspicious place to base her dual mission.

Aptly, Stone took responsibility for inaugurating her daughter's contributions to the *Journal* in 1872 (III. 10, 73). As Alice recalled:

> In the afternoon Mama brought home my surprise. It actually *is* that Toby thing, altered and put on the first page of the *Journal*, with A. S. B. at the bottom ["Pussy Cat" 2/22/1872}. I was prepared for it, yet sat down and shrieked, after my usual style. Mama seems rather disgusted that I am not pleased, and showed signs of turning blue; so I decided to be pleased, and abated my wrath. (*Growing* 43)

Already a shareholder in the *Journal*, the young Alice Blackwell would come more willingly to contribute to her mother's publication in other ways, including by making deliveries and taking the paper to the printer when the family moved across town. Extending the *Journal*'s literal "family" further, Alice's cousin Emma Lawrence helped out in the office, "clipping slips" and eventually writing reviews of books and plays (*Growing* 49). A candid as well as loyal recorder of family events during the initial publication of the *Journal*, Alice began her extant Boston diaries on her parents' anniversary in 1872, after a fire had damaged Pope's Hill and sent the

Stone-Blackwells to a small house on the same premises during rebuilding. During this period, she proudly defended her mother to people who "rile me so" about her politics (*Growing* 57). But Alice also notes frequently the comings and goings during these days by both her parents, for Stone ultimately did not cease lecturing for her causes after starting the *Journal*, and Blackwell pursued various business ventures in the wake of his liaison with Patton. Moreover, Alice mentions often her mother's headaches and "blues" despite her engagement with her work (68), and registers a telling picture of domestic unhappiness even after Stone's *Journal* had gained full operation: "Mama is getting to be just like Aunt Sarah, snarling all the time. I could stand it well enough . . . but that Papa looks so tired and worn that I think I should cry if I didn't feel so much like swearing" (31). Even so, following Stone's best intentions, the *Journal* enterprise survived persistent family frictions as well as financial growing pains.

Not surprisingly, considering the luminaries on the *Journal* staff and their ongoing concerns and aspirations, their own public conflicts would form part of its material, much as they constituted targets for others' assaults. In the January 22, 1870, issue, concerning Harriet Beecher Stowe's *Lady Byron Vindicated*, which the *Journal* also steadily advertised, Mary Livermore countered Julia Ward Howe's defense of "the woman who loved Byron." Posting Livermore's more conservative judgment on the front page, the *Journal* might appear to advocate her impressions. At the same time, however, the paper's layout not only preserved the controversy, it indirectly shifted the reader's attention to Howe's opinion "in another column" by Livermore's imprecise cross-reference. In fact, Howe's essay appeared in the same issue a few pages later (I. 2, 20):

> But will we say for her, "Is she not a woman and a sister?" Must her memory endure the burning hell of flame rather than that Lady Byron's Arctic should be considered a little under temperature for a luxuriant and tropical imagination? We shall emphatically answer, NO. If the opposition between Byron and his wife can be accounted for on any ground less monstrous, the common plea of uncongeniality must stand, and this dark spectre must be dismissed, to rank with other phantoms which sore distress will conjure in an overwrought brain.

Livermore's piece had urged those who would take sides on the matter to read Stowe's book, itself less than impartial, rather than its critiques, before affiliating themselves with either faction. But all the *Journal*'s treatments of popular controversy were not always contrived to encourage its reader to weigh perspectives.

Stone's moral positions would soon withstand their own public assault in print from the sensational *Woodhull & Claflin's Weekly*. Having begun her own liberal newspaper on May 14, 1871, Victoria Woodhull later that year in its pages would take to task what she deemed the prudish, hypocritical "Boston" contingent, as represented by AWSA and in particular by Stone's *Journal*:

> For our part we should be very glad to have the movement for suffrage receive the support of all persons who are honest advocates of it; but we maintain now, as Mrs. Livermore did in 1869, that whoever (sic) rejects aid, let it come from whatever source it may, is not for suffrage but against it; and Mrs. Livermore and the rest of the clique know it is so. And when they say that the 150,000 readers of a paper which advocates suffrage earnestly and persistently, are not representatives of the movement, and, in fact do not belong to it at all, simply because they advocate a paper which advocates Lucy Stone's former marriage theory in preference to the *Journal*, they know they speak a lie of which they are liable to convict themselves, whenever the spirit of truth predominates over their assumed policy of falsehood. ("Boston")

Stone and Henry Blackwell had expressed that "former marriage theory" in a six-point protest that as newlyweds in 1855, they had lodged against contemporary marriage laws, printed then in *The Worcester Spy* and in *The Liberator*. Their legalistic argument—against marriage construed as "custody," "control," and "sole ownership" by the husband—advocated a woman's right to "the product of her industry," and sought to extinguish the precedent that "the legal existence of the wife is suspended during marriage." They had asserted:

> We believe that personal independence and equal human rights can never be forfeited, except for crime; that marriage should be an equal and permanent partnership, and so recognized by law; that until it is so recognized, married partners should provide against the radical injustice of present laws, by every means in their power. (qtd. in Hays 128–129)

While the substance of the protest itself then provoked controversy, perhaps its most remarked outcome was that Lucy Stone did not change her last name to her husband's, a detail that even Susan B. Anthony had found difficult to apprehend.

To ground her objections, Woodhull had fixed on what she read as Stone's advocacy of "marriage for life" (qtd. in Kerr 156), which seemed to Woodhull more a harsh sentence than an ideal. In her wrath at "Boston" and in the face of her own wavering support by once-captivated supporters like Anthony, Woodhull would expose the adulterous Tilton-Beecher scandal, implicating not only AWSA's president—and brother of the noted *Journal* contributor, Stowe, herself a vindicator of the wronged Lady Byron—but irreparably undermining the public's reception of woman suffrage for decades. The *Journal* took up the Beecher-Tilton matter with a strong denial. Julia Ward Howe would attack Henry Ward Beecher's accuser, Theodore Tilton, while Stone would write in sympathy with Tilton's wife, Beecher's lover—although Stone would not identify her as such: "Elizabeth Tilton said what her tormentors required her to say, against herself, against her pastor, to her apparent certain ruin, to escape the torturing flames, leap from the top to certain death" (qtd. in Hays 235). Assertive on the issue yet oblique in addressing the scandal's details, the *Journal* here managed to perpetuate its moral purpose largely by eschewing Woodhull's tactics of exposure.

Other personally based conflicts would also embroil the *Journal*'s staff, sometimes matching them against one another in equally righteous stances. In 1883, Thomas Wentworth Higginson, a seemingly doubtless ally of Stone, would himself confront an antagonistic aspect of his colleague when he opposed her support of Democrat Benjamin Butler in a Massachusetts governor's race. Stone and Blackwell appreciated Butler's support of woman suffrage, but Higginson distrusted the candidate's uncertain business record, unclear party loyalties, and opposition to temperance (Lasser and Merrill 230). Higginson supported Butler's opponent Robert Bishop partly out of Republican loyalty, but more for his advocacy of civil service reforms. Looking ahead to a votership overwhelmingly—and vulnerably—expanded by women's suffrage, Higginson thought policies should first be mandated to preclude electoral corruption. Despite its ostensible political neutrality, *The Woman's Journal* published the ongoing disagreement between Stone and Higginson, prefiguring their far more serious quarrel during the next presidential election. As Butler took office, Stone and Blackwell printed in the *Journal* a "biting reply" to Higginson's attacks, followed by the lead writer's brief vacation from its pages (Hays 277).

In the 1884 presidential election, it was Higginson who joined independent Republicans, or Mugwumps, to side against mainstream Republican James G. Blaine. Higginson's cousin, Democrat Grover Cleveland, had an impressive service record as mayor of Buffalo, New York, and appealed to Higginson's sense of civic reform. Stone objected to Cleveland on moral grounds: as one letter in *The Woman's Journal* alleged, he had been accused of forming "an irregular connection" (XV. 44). Reportedly the father of an illegitimate son, Cleveland represented a threat to the family for Stone, whose own sometimes difficult marriage had survived her husband's attraction to Patton, as well as the aftershocks of the Tilton-Beecher affair. Publicly, Stone rallied support in the *Journal*, writing in one pronouncement, "Women must be opposed at all cost, to that which is the destruction of the home. They know with an unerring instinct that the purity and safety of the home means purity and safety to the State and Nation" (qtd. in Wheeler 286). As the election drew closer, Higginson and Stone faced off once more in *Journal* columns, each claiming superior moral ground for his or her candidate, and by implication, for his or her ethical views. According to Hays, Higginson intimated that both men and women might be equal partners in any sexual question, whereas Stone asserted woman's purity as an absolute unless violated by man's lechery (Hays 288).

Their exchange of October 9, 1884, suggests the crux of their opposition. In his weekly commentary, Higginson argued in Cleveland's case for the authority of public opinion. "L. S." coolly countered:

> If, by testimony of credible witnesses, it is clear that he is a man of dissolute life, as is affirmed, then he should be dropped at once. If such testimony is not found, there will be no need of apology or excuse for Grover Cleveland. But there should be no doubt in the case. (*Journal* XV. 32, 1)

Despite such open doubts, Cleveland won the election, an outcome Stone blamed on "the need of a moral force in politics that can come only when women have their equal political rights" (*Journal* XV. 45, 2). As Stone urged women even more strongly to seek the ballot, implying it was their moral imperative, Higginson withdrew his contributions as the *Journal*'s regular head writer.

On 18 December 1884, Stone wrote to Higginson a civil farewell:

> As the time draws near when we shall not see every week the well-known initials, I trust we shall all remember on how many of our respective articles we have all agreed, and on how few we have differed in this long pull for an unpopular reform, and "something must be pardoned in the spirit of liberty."
>
> No difference that has occurred makes the least difference in my feeling toward you. No one will give you more cordial good wishes than I shall always, nor more sincerely wish success to you and to all yours, as I do now. (Wheeler 288–289)

A more personal, more candid letter written to her friend Cornelia Hussey three weeks earlier suggests the true extent of Stone's perturbation with Higginson, down to her resentment over his salary, and her protection of his vanity against unfavorable subscriber reactions:

> Mr. Higginson has sent us a short note saying that he should resign his connection with the Woman's Journal at the close of this year. He gave no reason, and his note was very brief. This was followed very soon by another, asking not to re elect him a vice president of the American suffrage ass. & he gave no reason. I am told that he is to write for Harper's Bazaar hereafter. He has always been paid $600 a year—$50 each month. This he has never failed to get when the Journal was so poor that H.B.B. and I gave all our time for nine years without a cent of compensation. We shall save the $600, but

we shall miss his good articles, (and the bad ones too), and some subscribers who say they only took the Journal for his articles. But the cause grows and flourishes, and it will continue to do so no matter who falls out.... I want to thank you for your offer to make good the six subscribers who stopped their Journal on account of the ground we took about Cleveland. Some have stopped for the side *we* took and some for the side T. W. H. took, but not many of either. We had ever so many letters and articles on sides, bitter, and personal. We quietly put them in the waste basket. T. W. H. will never know the service we rendered him in that way. So many were *mad* with him. Rev. Mr. Gilbert at Chicago told us that Judge Thacher had a friend whose own niece was seduced and ruined by Cleveland. Mr. Ball says he is a gross sensualist "preying wherever he can find prey." Think of it, a male prostitute in the White House, & no woman a voter! (Wheeler 288)

In Stone's proprietary construction, "T. W. H." appears remote, protected, and unaware of her efforts on his behalf, the antithesis of the eager younger man who had revered the actions of the colleague he called a "dear little stainless saint." At the same time, she assumes the earlier supervisory role that he had once played for her, rendering her "service" on his now-vulnerable behalf.

Apparently, though, Higginson had not irrevocably offended the moral but business-minded Stone, as his work soon reappeared in the *Journal*, excerpted from *Harper's*, although not as reliably as before the Grover Cleveland contretemps. A March 15, 1887, letter from Stone to her husband indicates her continued exasperation by Higginson's vanity, in this case over his request for an elaborate layout for an article. As an enduring composite of its staff's commercial, political, social, aesthetic, and philanthropic perspectives, the *Journal* undoubtedly signified a different personal territory for each contributing editor. If Stone thought of the weekly as a substitute for her lecture career—and as something she could seek to control even when alienated from members of her own family—any such tension within her self-constructed *Journal* "family" must have touched her individually as well as professionally, as her miffed private remarks attest. But as a woman powerful enough to control her own weekly publication, not to mention as a long-time Higginson colleague, Stone stood in a rare position to criticize a writer and personality whom many other women, from Emily Dickinson to Helen Hunt Jackson, had looked to as a possible mentor or patron. Through her influence, her attainment would outlive her. After her death in 1893, under Alice Stone Blackwell's direction, the *Journal* would publish until 1917, when it merged with two other papers. In 1920, the United States ratified the Nineteenth Amendment, guaranteeing women the right to vote.

Despite Stone's political and social achievements, including these decades with *The Woman's Journal*, her own characteristic diffidence, combined with her moral rectitude, undoubtedly contributed to her partial exclusion from the historical limelight. In 1876, when Stanton, Anthony, and Matilda Joslyn Gage asked Stone for information to include in their *History of Woman Suffrage*, she admitted,

> I have never kept a diary or any record of my work, and so am unable to furnish you the required dates . . . I commenced my regular public work for anti slavery and woman's rights in 1848. I have continued it to the best of my ability ever since, except when the care of my child, and the war prevented. . . . I cannot furnish a biographical sketch, and trust you will not try to make one. (qtd. in Hays 289)

To others, she confided that she felt "more than content to be left entirely out of any history that those ladies may publish of the suffrage work," and elaborated, "It is a shame to publish such a one sided history—But the good work exists all the same and will just as truly have done its part in the great movement." The "good work" of reconstructing Stone's contributions to women's history in the United States is owed primarily to her letters, to the memoirs and written accounts by contemporaries and fellow reformers who included her daughter, and especially to the print legacy of Stone's nearly twenty-three years with *The Woman's Journal*, from 1870 to the end of her life. On many levels, then, Lucy Stone's work as editor of *The Woman's Journal* documents one woman's will to put into action, even against personal bonds and tensions, an individual vision of a larger public good. She had charged as much in 1854, anticipating by twenty years Louisa May Alcott's more detailed directive on the subject to Maria S. Porter: "Too much has already been said and written about women's sphere. Leave women, then, to find their sphere" ("Disappointed" 67).

Works Cited

Alcott, Louisa May. *The Selected Letters of Louisa May Alcott*, ed. Joel Myerson and Daniel Shealy. Boston: Little, Brown, and Co., 1987.

Blackwell, Alice Stone. *Growing Up in Boston's Gilded Age: The Journal of Alice Stone Blackwell, 1872–1874*, ed. Marlene Diehl Merrill. New Haven: Yale University Press, 1990.

———. *Lucy Stone*. Boston: The Woman's Journal, 1893.

———. *Lucy Stone: Pioneer of Woman's Rights*. Boston: Little, Brown, 1930.

"The Boston Exclusives Again." *Woodhull & Claflin's Weekly*. 28 October 1871. Archived at Victoria Woodhull & Company; Jackson, Mich.: http://victoriawoodhull.com/wc archive.htm (July 27, 2001).

Goldsmith, Barbara. *Other Powers: The Age of Suffrage, Spiritualism, and the Scandalous Victoria Woodhull*. New York: Knopf, 1998.

Hays, Elinor Rice. *Morning Star: A Biography of Lucy Stone 1818–1893*. New York: Harcourt, Brace & World, Inc.

Hutchinson, John W. *Story of the Hutchinsons (Tribe of Jesse)*. New York: Da Capo Press, 1977.
Kerr, Andrea. *Lucy Stone: Speaking Out for Equality*. New Brunswick, N.J.: Rutgers University Press, 1992.
Lasser, Carol, and Marlene Diehl Merrill, eds. *Friends and Sisters: Letters between Lucy Stone and Antoinette Brown Blackwell*. Urbana: University of Illinois Press, 1987.
Livermore, Mary A., et al. Letter. Jan. 1870. American Antiquarian Society.
Stern, Madeleine B. *Louisa May Alcott: From Blood and Thunder to Hearth and Home*. Boston: Northeastern University Press, 1998.
Stone, Lucy. "A Disappointed Woman." *Great American Speeches*, ed. Gregory R. Soriano. New York: Gramercy Books, 1993. 66–68.
Taylor, Robert. "The Fight for Woman's Vote Spearheaded by Rabid Radicals." *Boston Sunday Globe*. 15 December 1968, A-25.
Tuttleton, James W. *Thomas Wentworth Higginson*. Boston: Twayne, 1978.
Wheeler, Leslie, ed. *Loving Warriors: Selected Letters of Lucy Stone and Henry B. Blackwell, 1853 to 1893*. New York: Dial Press, 1981.
The Woman's Journal (Boston and Chicago), 1870–1893.

"Our Office"
The Woman's Journal, 15 January 1870

Would the readers of the WOMAN'S JOURNAL like a peep into our office?

It occupies the entire first floor, at No. 3 Tremont place. The rear room is used for folding, directing and mailing the paper. The front room is the especial *sanctum* of the Editors. Its carpet has a small, neat pattern, of quiet colors. It is the only article we have had to purchase. The substantial and comely black-walnut chairs were the gift of a pleasant young furniture merchant, who will be sure to supply his customers precisely as he agrees. The sofa, upholstered in green rep, the center-table, the card-table, the desk, with pigeon-holes and drawers, the *étagère* and the clock are all furnished by one of the earliest friends of the cause, and who will stand by it to the last. That the room may be pleasant, as well as comfortable, she has covered the walls with pictures. Forest scenes, glowing with autumn colors, are on one end of the room, and "Coming Home" on the other. Landseer's companion pieces, "The Challenge" and "The Sanctuary," hang one each side of a fine portrait of Mr. Garrison. The shelves of the *étagère* are supplied with tracts of all the kinds published by the New England Woman Suffrage Association; with petitions for a sixteenth amendment to the United States Constitution, and also the Legislature of the State. A large grate, with an open fire, gives a look of cosy home-likeness to "our office."

So much for what is in the room. Now, for what is done there. The first of the two days we occupied it, came early in the morning a young woman doctor, to subscribe for the WOMAN'S JOURNAL. She was soon followed by an active young man, who would like to canvass for advertising and who, before the day was over, had brought a good paying list, with promise of more the next day. Men and women long familiar with our cause came in to exchange greetings, to congratulate us, and to subscribe for the WOMAN'S JOURNAL. Pleasant faces of men and women whom we did not know, but who knew us, looked in, with manifest cordial good-will and sympathy. There were pleasant chats about the old times—the hard times—when even our best friends warned us that we were sadly mistaken. There were pleasanter chats about the more cheerful and hopeful prospect now. All day long, there was coming and going of earnest men and women interested in our cause: and when, just at night, a lady called and subscribed for the JOURNAL, as many others had done, and left us, in addition, $50 as a donation, it seemed a fitting close of the first week of the new year, during which so many things had occurred which we shall always hold in grateful remembrance.

To this office the friends of the cause are always welcome. Through it we hope not only to make acquaintances all over the country, who have common interest with us in our work, but who will coöperate with us actively in extending the circulation of our journal, who will take responsibility in carrying tracts and petitions to every house in their neighborhood, who will open the way for lectures, and by every just means induce all the friends of the cause to unite in the long, strong pull, which is necessary to take woman above the political level she now occupies, with idiots, lunatics, paupers, felons, and unpardoned rebels, and to put her on the same plane with other decent tax-paying citizens. —L.S.

Eyes in the Text: Marianna Burgess and *The Indian Helper*

JACQUELINE FEAR-SEGAL

Introduction

IN 1879, Captain Richard Henry Pratt was indefinitely relieved of active duty in the United States Army to organize a living experiment. In the lush valley of the Susquehanna River in central Pennsylvania, Pratt founded the Carlisle Indian Industrial School. He hoped to demonstrate that Native American children from all tribes could successfully be stripped of their traditional cultures and transformed into material fit for American citizenship. After five years of academic and practical training in a boarding school far from home, Pratt postulated that Indian children would dress, talk, behave and think like white Americans. But, just three years after the Battle of the Little Bighorn, few in the United States were ready to concede that Indians either could or should be made citizens. Carlisle needed to publicize its mission and from the outset the Print Shop was given a key role.

Less than three months after the school opened, its first publication was cranked off a small press set up in a converted stable. Readers of *Eadle Keahtah Toh* [*The Morning Star* in Lakota], a four-page, two-column paper, were informed, "we are enabled to give information of this work to many friends," thanks to the gift of the press and the fortuitous blessing that "one of the lady teachers is a practical printer."[1] The "lady teacher" was Marianna Burgess, who would become a shadowy but increasingly powerful presence in the stream of publications that emanated from the Carlisle presses.

To begin with, Pratt invited a military colleague, Lieutenant Leroy Brown, to edit the first two issues of *Eadle Keahtah Toh*. When Brown returned to active service, Marianna Burgess stepped in and published the next two issues, and then Pratt appointed his son, Mason, as editor.[2] Over the years, Burgess's name was given for all business correspondence, and she was sometimes featured as a joint editor. But Burgess never acted as sole publisher of Carlisle's main paper.[3] This monthly periodical (which changed its name several times over the years) was published almost continuously during the life of the school (1879–1918).[4] It was the public voice of Carlisle. Examining and elucidating the finer points of Indian policy, it trumpeted and displayed Carlisle's successes to a skeptical white public, whose support was vital to the school's survival.

Then, when the Carlisle Indian School was five years old, a second publication suddenly appeared. One among many of the new periodicals in what has been described as "a mania of magazine starting," *The Indian Helper* would be more successful than countless similar endeavors. Against the trend of the time, instead of soliciting advertisements, it enlisted the support of over ten thousand subscribers, who sustained the magazine for over fifteen years (Mott 5). Running parallel with Carlisle's main paper, *The Indian Helper* came out weekly. Both its title and subtitle, "FOR OUR INDIAN BOYS AND GIRLS," made clear its targeted readership was not the general public, but Indian children. Pupils at Carlisle, children who had gone to work for families in the Pennsylvania area in what Pratt called the "outing system," and a growing body of Carlisle-educated Indians who had returned to their reservation homes, made up the bulk of readers. But white supporters of the Carlisle Indian School, including many children, were also eagerly courted and added to the list.

For all its readers, one of the most distinctive and baffling aspects of *The Indian Helper* was its editor. Each week a notice on the second page announced:

> The INDIAN HELPER is PRINTED by Indian boys, but
> EDITED by The-Man-on-the-band-stand, who is NOT an Indian.[5]

For fifteen years no one, besides this unexplained white male persona, claimed editorship of the paper. *The Indian Helper* presented itself in the guise of a school magazine and featured stories and articles about schoolwork, events, and day-to-day activities. But reverberating through its pages was the voice of the mysterious Man-on-the-band-stand. Sometimes he would analyze or criticize an issue, but he did not restrict himself to a traditional editorial column. His preferred style was to interject his comments and opinions all through the paper, briefly but unexpectedly, in little homilies and asides. His attention focused on the children. Few things about their dress, deportment, manners, physical appearance, or behavior escaped his comment. From his "home" on the bandstand, which stood in the middle of the school grounds, this "man" watched them. He eavesdropped on their conversations and then reported and spoke out in pages of *The Indian Helper*. Interspersed amongst commonplace school news, the minutiae of the children's lives were described and placed on public display. They were his subjects, observed and reported on, as well as exhibits to demonstrate the success of the educational experiment.

The Man-on-the-band-stand and Marianna Burgess

Who was the-Man-on-the-band-stand? Why was he invisible, ubiquitous, unnamed, and so secretive? What was his function in a school ostensibly committed to teaching Indian children how to find a place in American society? For readers living far from Carlisle or with few links to the school, the identity of the Man-on-the-band-stand remained a perpetual puzzle, and their letters, printed in *The Indian Helper*, were used to further this sense of mystery. Anyone who lived and worked at the school, or spoke to the Indian boys who worked at the Print Shop, was well aware that supervision of all school publications lay in the hands of Miss Marianna Burgess. So was Marianna Burgess the Man-on-the-band-stand? The question was posed directly one week and then answered negatively in a section of *The Indian Helper* called "Question Box":

> Q. Who is the Man-on-the-band-stand? Is it Miss Burgess? L.D.
>
> Ans. The Man-on-the-band-stand is the editor of the INDIAN HELPER, who sees *everything*, but does not print all he sees. The Man-on-the-band-stand is not Miss Burgess.[6]

This answer was confusing, but it contained a truth. Marianna Burgess almost certainly wrote the Man-on-the-band-stand. She might share his initials, and she played on this in the paper, constantly energizing the mystery surrounding his identity, but she and he were not one and the same person. The Man-on-the-band-stand was a constructed persona, far more ubiquitous and powerful than Marianna Burgess could ever hope to be. All-seeing, all-hearing, but selectively revealing in the columns of *The Indian Helper*, this imaginary persona strutted across the pages that allowed for his construction: a commanding, authoritative, omnipotent, but illusory presence. Full appreciation of how he claimed and wielded his power requires knowledge of the school's layout and we will return to consider this later. Nothing about the Man-on-the-band-stand was straightforward or stable. Just as the answer given to the question above was direct yet evasive, so too was the discourse of the Man-on-the-band-stand and much of the paper over which he presided. Every week in *The Indian Helper* there was a "Puzzle Corner," with conundrums, enigma, and riddles for readers to solve. Often this was placed at the end of the paper, almost as if it were the Man-on-the-band-stand's signature, because of course the biggest ongoing mystery was the question of his identity.

In this essay I will confront the Man-on-the-band-stand, explore how and why he was constructed, and unpack the role he played in the campaign to "civilize" Indian children. To do this we will also need to scrutinize closely the role Marianna Burgess played in this enterprise. No record survives to tell us whose idea it was to invent an unseen resident for the bandstand and sustain his invisible existence for over fifteen years, but all available information points unequivocally to Marianna Burgess. One week, when she was away from the school, she openly revealed to readers of *The Indian Helper* the part she regularly played in the production of the paper, as well as her intimate association with the Man-on-the-band-stand:

> The Indian printer boys received many deserved compliments on last week's HELPER, which they issued in the absence of the Man-on-the-band-stand's chief clerk. The old man *thought* they would do well if they tried.[7]

Marianna Burgess's relationship to the M.O.T.B.S. (as he was often called in *The Indian Helper*) was intense, complicated, and shifting. In *The Morning Star/Red Man* she was always listed as manager or superintendent of printing. In *The Indian Helper* she generally described herself as the Man-on-the-band-stand's chief clerk. On occasions, however, a Mrs. M.O.T.B.S. was mentioned, with the suggestive implication that this was Burgess. It was certainly she who constructed his multiple personalities and developed his voice. He was her creature. In the pages of *The Indian Helper*, where she created, paraded, operated, played, and flirted with him, we find her delighting in his power, ambiguity, and numerous roles. Through him she attempted to control, intimidate, and manipulate the children. From behind the safety of his undetectable facade, she claimed the freedom to report, uncensored, her own version of all that went on in the school. He allowed her to live a vicarious life. The imaginary persona she had invented had voice, power, and prominence at Carlisle, and Carlisle was Burgess's world. She had arrived at the school when just twenty-six. When she was thirty-one, the Man-on-the-band-stand took up residence on his bandstand, only fifteen yards from Burgess's room in the teachers' quarters. The two of them did not "part company" for nearly twenty years. I will later consider the demise of the Man-on-the-band-stand, but notwithstanding his equivocations and ambiguity, through *The Indian Helper* we gain more insights into his "life" than we are ever granted from the effaced details of Burgess's biography. So although, in essence, this is a study of an extraordinary woman editor of the nineteenth century, I will concentrate more on her editorial doppelganger than on Marianna Burgess herself.

Some fragments of Burgess's biography can be pieced together. Although the picture is very incomplete, the Carlisle Indian School supplied the frame of her life. Here she lived and worked for nearly twenty-five years, organizing and running the Print Shop. Burgess was a hands-on printer. At Carlisle she ran a succession of ever-more-complicated presses and trained dozens of Indian boys in the print trade. The Print Shop at the Indian School might, at first glance, have appeared amateurish. Opening in a converted stable with a donated press, it remained dependent on antiquated equipment and inadequate charitable donations of second-hand print face. Yet it operated under the authority of Captain Pratt, who would often position himself on the bandstand, seen and seeing. Although Pratt was not the Man-on-the-band-stand, his imposing six-foot-high figure, silhouetted on the bandstand, gave a shadowy reality to this imaginary figure. Pratt's presence at Carlisle was essential to the Man-on-the-band-stand's existence; behind Pratt, who had been seconded from the U.S. Army and War Department, stood the full apparatus of the American state.

Carlisle was spawned by the expansionist territorial ambitions of the United States. As the United States commandeered and engulfed Indian lands, Indian nations were concentrated on reservations and their children packed off to white-run schools. The first pupils at Carlisle came to the school after spending three years as prisoners in Fort Marion, Florida, where Pratt had been their jailer. Most of those who followed were not strictly prisoners, but they were hostages for their parents' good behavior out West. Even students who attended willingly were participating in an educational experiment approved, bolstered, and largely financed by the federal government. It is within this power structure that the Print Shop, *The Indian Helper*, and the persona of the Man-on-the-band-stand have to be configured. This constellation of power transformed what might have been only an imaginary, laughable, chameleon-like character into a sinister and threatening force.

The Man-on-the-band-stand's traffic in enigmas, evasions, secrecy, and mystery was merely the cloak for a monstrous power game. He was, as he frequently reminded his readers, unknowable (like God) and chided them for believing otherwise. Reveling in his own mystery, he gave away tantalizing hints and tips about his identity, teasing and tormenting his readers. Perhaps the most bizarre was a small diagrammatic drawing of a face, published under the heading:

> THE MAN-ON-THE-BAND-STAND
> WOULD LIKE TO KNOW
>
> Who took this picture of him?[8]
>
> . .
>
> |
> —

The picture was meaningless, an apparently harmless enigmatic joke. But within the context of the Carlisle Indian School it carried a hidden, ominous message about power and visibility. This supposed "photograph" of the Man-on-the-band-stand divulged nothing about its alleged subject. The mocking request "The Man-on-the-band-stand would like to know who took this picture of him?" suggested indignation that someone might have caught a glimpse of him and even had the audacity to take a photograph. The sketched lines of this diagrammatic cipher, however, teasingly confirmed his identity as both unknowable and invisible. By contrast, every feature of the children and their new American identities were regularly exhibited in the many photographs taken by local photographer J. R. Choat.

Photographs were one of the main weapons in the armory of the Indian School. They were used to illustrate the transformation from "savage" to "civilized" the school boasted it could accomplish.[9] A series of "before" and "after" photographs, of individuals and groups, was published to exhibit the supposed transformation wrought by a Carlisle education. *The Indian Helper* was one of the vehicles by which they reached the outside world. Repeatedly offered for sale or handed out to readers in exchange for securing subscriptions to the paper, these photographs of the children presented them scrubbed, dressed, arranged, and displayed for the public eye. While close-up photographic images of the Indian children were paraded for everyone to look at, an enigmatic drawing was all that was seen of the Man-on-the-band-stand, a mask for his shifting and multiple personalities.

The Bandstand

The layout of the school buildings provides an important key to understanding his influence. When a subscriber allegedly asked, "Will you please explain why you are called the 'Man-on-the-band-stand'?" The answer came:

> If the questioner were at Carlisle, he would know why.
> The Band-stand commands the whole situation. From it he can see all the quarters, the printing office, the chapel, the grounds, everything and everybody, all the girls and the boys on the walks, at the windows, everywhere. Nothing escapes the Man-on-the-band-stand. Already he sees into the homes of the boys and girls who go out upon the farms.[10]

Situated at the symbolic as well as architectural hub of Carlisle, the bandstand commanded panoramic views of the whole school, but its full potential for voyeurism was realized only when it was made the permanent "home" of an invisible, vigilant observer.[11] When not stationed at his post, the Man-on-the-band-stand led them to believe he moved unseen amongst the children, observing their activities and eavesdropping on their conversations. He could drop in, undetected, on any event, innocent or otherwise. In fact the more innocent his visitations, the more ominous they feel:

> The Man-on-the-band-stand pricked up his ears when he heard strains of music on Friday evening. Then looking toward the sewing room, and seeing a bright light shining through the window, he stepped over to see what might be going on. He stole in so quietly that no-one saw or heard him.[12]

From his sheltered vantagepoint, the Man-on-the-band-stand observed and discussed the lives of Indian children in the pages of *The Indian Helper*. When they left Carlisle, with the help of the U.S. Postal Service, he followed them back to their reservation homes. His location at the center of the school transformed an innocent bandstand into an inspection tower. Had he been a silent observer, his presence might have been disturbing but without threat. His ability to publish details of his sightings made the Man-on-the-band-stand menacing.

Today it is impossible to imagine the Man-on-the-band-stand stationed at his post without being reminded of both the design and purpose of Jeremy Bentham's panopticon.[13] A radical new method for simultaneously punishing and reforming prisoners, the architecture of the panopticon allowed surveillance and recorded evidence to substitute for force. Fundamental to its design was the inspection tower, constructed at the center. From here the subduing gaze of authority would look out, seeing without being seen and thus affording an asymmetry of knowledge and power.[14] Although Bentham's twenty-year campaign for the construction of his Panopticon Penitentiary failed in England, he had publicized a concept and provided architects with a circular design laid out to promote discipline through surveillance. On the outskirts of Philadelphia, in 1821, Bentham's concept and design was to merge with Quaker ideas about institutional reform and criminal behavior and become enshrined in the rows of cells that radiated out from the central tower at the new Eastern State Penitentiary.[15] By this time the panopticon had become a commonly known and understood mechanism.[16]

Two hundred miles from Philadelphia's pioneering prison, the Indian School in Carlisle represented a much later and more circumscribed reform drive than the one that built the penitentiary. Yet the task of "civilizing" Indian children, as projected by reformers, shared something in common with earlier schemes to reform prisoners. Both relied for success on the subject imbibing a new morality. To experience the demanded inner transformation, he had to participate in the process of his own correction. At Carlisle, no carefully crafted inspection tower looked out over the pupils until the bandstand was commandeered to perform this function.

In the days when the Carlisle Barracks was home to the U.S. Cavalry School, where young cavalry recruits were trained to fight Indian tribes out West,[17] its commonplace bandstand had seemed an innocuous structure and a very far cry from the inspection tower we have been discussing. But by a series of ingenious strategies, this inoffensive gazebo was converted into an inspection tower with greater potency than Bentham ever dreamed and powers more diverse than those exercised at Eastern State Penitentiary.

The invention of an invisible man who made the bandstand his home and watched the children continuously from its raised platform, turned this roofed structure into a quasi-inspection tower. (I will return later to the significance of the occupant of the bandstand being male and not female.) Unlike Bentham's panopticon, the bandstand's architecture did not declare its purpose; to the uninformed eye, it still looked like a pretty, pagoda-shaped bandstand. But to anyone made aware of its unseen resident, its open-sided, octagonal shape, and elevated platform could never look the same again. It is important to remember that in his first version of the panopticon, Bentham planned to supplement visual surveillance with a parallel system of acoustic surveillance, made possible by a system of pipes leading from the prisoners' cells to the central tower. The difficulties of ensuring that sound only traveled in one direction and therefore of preventing the prisoners from listening to the inspectors, led Bentham to abandon this part of his scheme.[18] Bentham, when designing his panopticon, was bound by the constraints of real life. For the Man-on-the-band-stand, who resided in a world of fantasy and make-believe, issues of feasibility imposed no such limits. Capable of single-handedly maintaining his constant vigil from the center of the school, he had the power both to see and listen to the children. Equally important was his ability to step down from his bandstand. This meant his surveillance was not confined to a single, central viewing point. He could mingle unseen amongst the children on the grounds, prowl through the classrooms and dormitories, or gate-crash a school picnic undetected. In him the voyeuristic powers of the panopticon reached new phantasmagoric heights, which he flagged and indulged in the column entitled, "What I See and Hear" in *The Indian Helper*. To understand how the Man-on-the-bandstand acquired and used his special powers, we need to turn our attention to the particular historical and social circumstances that allowed for his creation and ongoing life at Carlisle, and here it is the differences between Bentham's prisoners and Carlisle's Indian children that are instructive.

While neither Bentham nor the Philadelphia Quakers ever doubted that the gaze of authority possessed the power to induce guilt and contrition, this was a supposition rooted in a Christian notion of conscience and the individual soul. Indian children did not share in this Christian cosmology. Despite the differences in their separate tribal cultures, they had all grown up in societies where community lay at the core of all definitions of good and evil. To them the concept of individual salvation or damnation was completely alien, as their fate was inseparable from that of family and kin. The gaze of authority, as envisaged by Bentham, might be able to intimidate, but it would fail to trigger the personal remorse and guilt essential for inner transformation. At the Carlisle Indian School, therefore, inspection would have little effect, unless it was accompanied by an interpretive voice that was able to furnish this inner narrative for Indian children. The motto at Carlisle was "God helps those who help themselves." In the pages of *The Indian Helper*, the Man-on-the-band-stand outlined and detailed this creed in its daily detail. His voice was as vital as his gaze.

The Voice of the Man-on-the-band-stand

Voice, of course, was the Man-on-the-band-stand's only tangible feature. Or to be more accurate, voices, because his shifting personality was echoed in the numerous different voices he used to address the children. He could abandon his posture of authority, step from his bandstand and assume a variety of different identities as he moved among them, matching these identities with the range of styles and voices which simultaneously created them. But where a subject stands, what identity it there assumes, and by what values it is marked makes a political difference, and for this reason the Man-on-the-band-stand always made clear that at the drop of a hat he could climb back into his stand and reclaim the voice of authority.[19] In the pages of *The Indian Helper* he claimed a dizzying array of personalities and voices. Sometimes he gave counsel, like a wise uncle, pointing out the children's frailties as Indians and suggesting the best way for them to live their lives. Often he lectured them from his podium about the proper conduct and manners necessary for achieving success in America, or assumed the role of school monitor and, in slightly threatening tones, reiterated the school rules."[20] Giving praise and approval to re-enforce the lessons of civilization taught at Carlisle, he could sound like a patronizing auntie:

> The girls are buying rugs for their rooms when they have a little spare cash and the Man-on-the-band-stand is pleased to see the bright, cheery and home like effect it has upon their rooms.[21]

But just as easily, in the semblance of a disappointed parent, he could single out individual students for humiliation or embarrassment.[22] Using wheedling and insinuating tones, he would invite returnees to inform on their compatriots when they left Carlisle and went back to their reservation homes: "Let the boys and girls who go home, write to the Man-on-the-band-stand something about what our other pupils are doing who returned before."[23]

In a breathtaking change of role, the Man-on-the-band-stand could become sulky, petulant, and sorry for himself over small, banal incidents and sound like a spoiled child excluded from the party or a demanding geriatric denied his whim.[24] When speaking in this voice, instead of reproaching the children he would attempt to solicit their sympathy. Indulging in an exploitative reversal of the power-balance, he demanded that they nurture and care for him, bring him presents and acknowledge his stoicism in staying on his bandstand in all kinds of weather.[25] An equally dramatic change of style took place when the Man-on-the-band-stand moved openly into fantasy. Always located in a realm of semi-make-believe, when he became privy to the thoughts of Father Christmas or struck up conversations with fairies, the world of whimsy he inhabited progressed one stage further in its mix of the weird and infantile:

> The Man-on-the-band-stand stood for a few moments with closed eyes, one warm day this week, and as he was thus apparently in deep thought, a little fairy came along and called out to him, "Grandpa, what are you thinking about?"[26]

Having heard a story, which gave evidence of how the Man-on-the-band-stand could watch a group of boys rowing on a river, far away in Ohio, "the little fairy ran away to tell her playmates what she had seen and heard." This soft, intimate tone of storytelling was poles apart from his booming voice of authority. His varying discourses simultaneously reflected and created his multiple and fluid personality. He could veer from congratulatory to instructional, from teasing to critical, from friendly to sinister, from open to secretive, and from practical to fantastic. Speaking with the concern and familiarity of a friend at one moment, he could switch into the stern tone of a strict parent, then swing into the teasing manner of a companion. He could indulge in fantasy and make-believe and just as quickly shift into a voice of authority to remind readers of his powers to see, hear, and report everything that happened at Carlisle.

One function of these multiple discourses was intimately linked to Carlisle's mission to substitute U.S. goals and values for the ones Indian children had grown up with. In the minutiae of his remarks, the Man-on-the-band-stand informed the children about behavior that would make them acceptable in U.S. society. At a more personal level, he provided stories and anecdotes to tell them who they were and how they should behave. In the aching silence experienced by every far-from-home child, where the voice of grandfathers and elders would have spoken, the Man-on-the-band-stand sought to make his own voice resound. He sought to change loyalties as well as values. Myriad references to the school, to staff, to individual children, to the activities of Carlisle alumni, as well as the ever-growing list of *Helper* subscribers, contributed to the interest and appeal of *The Indian Helper* but also worked to create a new "imagined community," to use Benedict Anderson's term, of educated Indians, with Carlisle at its center. In substituting his written narrative for their oral stories, he drew them into a world no longer shared by elders and relations. Reading *The Indian Helper*, whether at school, on an outing, or back home on the reservation, provided a link between every subscriber, the Man-on-the-band-stand, Carlisle, and a broad-based Indian world very different from the one embraced by tribal affiliation. At this level, the Man-on-the-band-stand functioned ingeniously and consistently to further the goals of the Carlisle Indian School and the federal campaign to assimilate Native American children. But it is clear that some of his more baffling antics were driven by quite different motivations. To understand these motives, we need to look more closely at the Man-on-the-band-stand's creator, Marianna Burgess, and the ways she used her invention to gratify the demands of her own personal agenda.

Marianna Burgess at Carlisle

The Dakota writer Zitkala-Ŝa (Gertrude Simmons) spent two years (1898–1900) teaching at Carlisle, and her reflections on the personal lives of the staff there help us see Marianna Burgess from a different perspective. "I slowly comprehended," Zitkala-Ŝa writes, "that the large army of white teachers in Indian schools had a larger missionary creed than I had suspected. It was one which included self-preservation quite as much as Indian education." As a single working woman who shared her life with a female companion, Burgess lived outside the traditional domestic structures enjoyed by the majority of women in the United States at this time, over 90 percent of whom were married. Many in comparable situations gravitated to the new women's colleges and built their lives in the security of these communities. At age nineteen, however, Burgess journeyed not to college, but to the Pawnee Manual Labor School in Nebraska, where for four years she taught Indian children. Under Grant's Peace Policy, her Quaker father had been appointed Pawnee agent. So in 1873, after fourteen years as head of Millville School, Pennsylvania, William Burgess moved his whole family out West. This experience would stand Marianna in good stead as training.

The Burgess family returned to Pennsylvania just four years later, and when the Carlisle Indian School opened, Marianna and her companion,

Miss Annie Ely, applied to be teachers. The two women's rare experience of teaching Indian children convinced Pratt to accept them (Milner 51–60).[27] For the next twenty-five years, the life of Burgess became inseparable from the Carlisle Indian School, which she made her home. Here, with Annie Ely and a team of mostly Quaker women, she forged a new kind of family. As a working woman, separation from the conventional women's roles of child care, cooking, and entertaining placed her outside traditional structures and social arrangements, while affording her new freedoms and power (Smith-Rosenberg 245–68). Her lifestyle violated late Victorian norms, challenging accepted gender relations and distributions of power. Her espousal of the cause of Indian education muted this challenge because the lessons and examples she held up to Indian children so perfectly mirrored social convention. Marginalized by her marital status as much as her sexuality, in her work with Indian children at Carlisle she found a way not to challenge the dominant discourse. A socially liminal figure, she aligned herself with the powers of authority and establishment by teaching those more deviant than herself.

Marianna Burgess's relationship with Annie Ely was never a secret. They arrived together and lived in the teachers' quarters during all their years at Carlisle. In *The Indian Helper* their liaison was openly talked about and on one occasion the school band is mentioned serenading the two of them.[28] The Carlisle Indian School, a social experiment that challenged received wisdom about the racial inferiority of Indians, provided a safe haven for these two women, who were challenging the received wisdom about the natural place of women in society. Close, loving relationships between women were accepted as perfectly normal for most of the nineteenth century, even if by 1900, as Carroll Smith-Rosenberg has shown us, the perceived "innocence" of this type of friendship was coming under scrutiny.

For most of her time at Carlisle, Marianna Burgess's association with Annie Ely, a woman twenty years her senior, would have been judged as eccentric but not aberrant. At a time when "devotion to and love of other women [was] a plausible and socially acceptable form of human interaction," it did not openly upset accepted notions of binarity or put into question the categories of "female" and "male" (Smith-Rosenberg 60). Yet in *The Indian Helper*, Burgess's decision to create an invisible, male persona—to cross-dress, unseen and unknown in print—suggests a desire to blur and deconstruct the boundaries of both her gender and her identity. On a photographic postcard published at the Indian School in 1909, five years after Burgess left Carlisle, a group of girls are pictured playing croquet beside the bandstand. The lettering on the front reads, "Indian girls and summerhouse." Seeing the bandstand rendered so feminized and benign, after its years of male occupation, prompts me to ask, what might the voice of the woman-on-the-bandstand have sounded like, or even the-woman-in-the-summer-house? Whether she presented as witch, statue/decoration, or whore, her identity would have been severely socially constricted. It is hard to imagine her with more than one-dimensional power or voice, and she certainly could not have commanded the authority or versatility of the Man-on-the-band-stand. By ascribing male attributes to her editorial doppelganger, Burgess was able to claim the power and control identified with masculinity as well as the multiple voices and personalities it incorporated. In the context of a school that insisted that Indian children adopt a single, clearly discernable, "white" identity, she created an invisible male alter ego with shifting and multiple identities. She displaced the axis of gender onto the axis of race, prescribing a fixed borderline for Indian children while claiming a permeable borderline for herself.

This dynamic is well illustrated in Burgess's insistence that Indians stick to one name. On arrival at Carlisle, Indian children were invariably given American names, or their own names were translated into English. This single act had multiple impacts: it severed their connection to their personal and communal pasts, allowed them to be addressed in English without problem, incorporated them into a patriarchal system of ownership and heredity, and attached to them fixed and stable designation and identity. Within many native cultures it was common for an individual to be known by a series of different names during his/her lifetime, reflecting stages of life or deeds accomplished. At Carlisle this practice was condemned, and in the pages of *The Indian Helper* the Man-on-the-band-stand constantly stressed the need for Indians to adhere to one name. In an article entitled "Who is Mr. Robe?" Burgess used the excuse of a letter from a Mr. Robe, published in the Fort Lewis *Outlook*, to allow the Man-on-the-band-stand to pontificate on the question:

> Naturally we wonder if this is our Mr. Yellowrobe, class '95, who went sometime since to Ft. Lewis. There are various Robes among the Indians, such as Bearrobe, Buffalorobe, etc., and it seems important to the Man-on-the-bandstand for a man to retain his family or surname if he does not wish to lose his identity and lineal descent. If Mr. Wheelock should begin to sign his name Mr. D.W. Lock, he would soon lose his identity. If the Mr. Robe is our Mr. Yellowrobe we congratulate him and hope that he will hereafter allow no question about his name, but write the surname in full.[29]

Coming from a "man" who allowed himself the freedom and luxury of no name, just a list of alternating nicknames and abbreviation—M.O.T.B.S., Mr. See, Mr. See-All, Watch Dog—to accompany a range of assorted identities, this seems audacious. When we remember that Burgess also claimed the same right to anonymity, accompanied by ambiguous and shifting identities, it shows her double standards. In the pages of *The Indian Helper*, Burgess ducked and dived behind the posturing security of her shadowy alter ego. In 1891, when she published a fictional didactic text, once again she veiled her real identity.

Stiya: *The Pocket Bandstand*

Stiya: A Carlisle Indian Girl at Home (1891) announced on its title page that the book was written "by Embe." This, of course, was a species of acronym for Burgess's initials, M.B., and she was playfully laying claim to a long established tradition of women writers assuming pseudonyms to veil their true identity. But the line beneath the title: "FOUNDED ON THE AUTHOR'S ACTUAL OBSERVATIONS," signaled that she was also endeavoring to confer authenticity on what lay inside. Written in the first person, *Stiya* is ostensibly the true story of a Pueblo girl's return to her family and her courageous efforts, against all odds, to live the lessons learned at Carlisle. It is presented as a composite but nevertheless genuine biography. Yet even before we look at the book's content, we discover that Burgess is once again not only playing fast and loose with her own name, but also with the face, name, and identity of Stiya. "We have a little Stiya with us at present and use her name because it strikes our fancy," she reported in *The Indian Helper*.[30] The photographic studio portrait on the frontispiece of *Stiya* shows a young Indian woman wearing a long-sleeved, waisted, buttoned-to-the-neck dress, leaning on the back of an ornate Victorian chair. The caption reads, "STIYA, CARLISLE INDIAN GIRL." This picture, however, is not of Stiya Kowacura, the Pueblo girl whose name Burgess had fancied and taken. It is a photograph of Lucy Tsinah, an Apache.[31] In the first two pages of her book, Burgess had already collapsed the identities of two individual women from two very different tribes. She sent "little Stiya" out into the world with a fabricated biography, a multiple identity, and her family name (which Burgess herself had linked to identity) obliterated.

In *Stiya*, Burgess once again wrote in an assumed voice. Critics of the educational experiment spearheaded by Carlisle constantly reported that when students went home to the reservation, they reverted to traditional ways and "went back to the blanket." To reach these returned students and in an effort to shape the behavior of Indian girls far from Carlisle, Burgess anticipated the situations they would encounter on their return and then wrote the script for how they should respond. Stiya is portrayed as disgusted by the meanness of her home and the filth and superstition that surround it. Instead of joy, her homecoming is accompanied by revulsion:

"*My* father? *My* mother?" cried I desperately within. "No, never!" I thought, and I actually turned my back upon them. I had forgotten that home Indians had such grimy faces. I had forgotten that my mother's hair always looked as though it had never seen a comb. . . . I rushed frantically into the arms of my *school*-mother, who had taken me home. (2–3)

In the voice of Stiya, female, intimate, guileless, and fresh, Burgess sought to bring the Carlisle message closer to home. In *The Indian Helper*, the voice of the Man-on-the-band-stand might be able to command and even commiserate, but his was the male voice of white authority, emanating always from his bandstand and located at Carlisle. Using a very different messenger and purportedly identifying and empathizing with a Pueblo girl, Burgess created for herself an opportunity to speak as an Indian from inside Pueblo society. Sold for fifty cents through the pages of *The Indian Helper* and carried home by many returning students, *Stiya* was the closest Burgess could come to crafting a pocket bandstand.

This book, Laguna Pueblo author Leslie Marmon Silko tells us, "was the cause of the only big quarrel my great grandmother ever had with her daughter-in-law, Aunt Susie." Both women were horrified by Burgess's "libelous portrayal of Pueblo life and people." Aunt Susie wanted the defamatory text preserved, as "important evidence of the lies and the racism and bad faith of the U.S. Government with the Pueblo people." Grandma A'mooh wanted the book's lies burned, "just as witchcraft paraphernalia is destroyed." Silko estimates that their dispute took place around 1900, and the story was then passed orally down the generations, until Silko made it public in 1994. Its emergence affords us rare insight into how two Indian women responded to Burgess when she assumed the voice of a Pueblo girl (Silko n.p.).*

The Children and the Man-on-the-band-stand

Regrettably, no comparable record was left by the children at Carlisle telling us how they reacted to Burgess when she spoke to them through the Man-on-the-band-stand. Did they find him creepy? Were they confused by his various guises? Was he an intimidating presence haunting the campus? Or did they dismiss him as the silly pastime of a batty white woman and laugh when their own antics were publicized in the pages of *The Indian Helper*? If we comb through the pages of the paper, we can find fragmentary hints of how some of the students responded. Inevitably, when much of *The*

---

*Leslie Marmon Silko, "Introduction," in *Native American Literature: Catalog I*, Lopez Books, 1994, http://www/lopezbooks.com/articles/silko.html (11 November 2003).

Indian Helper's readership was in the process of acquitting both literacy and English, the Man-on-the-band-stand's activities often generated bewilderment. Yet, if we read between the carefully regulated lines, we can also find evidence of secret acts of insubordination and protest, of the kind E. P. Thompson has termed "acts of darkness."³² Much of this resistance is disguised, muted, or veiled for safety's sake, and its perpetrator is untraceable. Ink scribbles in a Bible, stolen food, broken windows, and paint deliberately chipped off the bandstand provide confirmation of many small, anonymous acts of resistance. But sometimes the battlelines are openly drawn between the children and the Man-on-the-band-stand. The children refuse to keep time with the piano as they march out of chapel; a small, apparently insignificant infraction, but the Man-on-the-band-stand recognizes it as a deliberate flouting of the rules and returns to it again and again.³³ A similar wrangle erupts over their persistent refusal to keep to the pathways and stay off the grass. The Man-on-the-band-stand tries to put the frighteners on them, warning how wet feet can lead to pneumonia and death, but by wearing tracks on the parade ground, the children were, quite literally, stamping their collective defiance onto the face of the campus.³⁴ Descriptions of these ongoing struggles drew attention to what James C. Scott has helped us to interpret as "hidden transcripts" of rebellion. Unwittingly, *The Indian Helper* became a vehicle for publicizing these recurring acts of insubordination, while simultaneously exposing the Man-on-the-band-stand's, and Carlisle's, powerlessness to stop them.

Few issues of *The Indian Helper* failed to include details of such "crimes." Some were recurrent, like the habitual Saturday ritual of naming and shaming those who had lapsed into speaking "Indian." Others were individual transgressions, as when seven boys were caught stealing apples from the tree behind the teachers' quarters.³⁵ The plethora of petty offenses reported included a mixed bag of disobedience, high spirits, and pranks. Yet persistent focus on these minor infractions served as a smoke screen for a range of far more serious offences: drunkenness, arson, and escape. These the Man-on-the-band-stand rarely mentioned, reflecting the propagandistic purpose of the paper, but also signalling awareness of the real risks associated with publicizing defiance. Yet, when news of Indian misdeeds was already in the public domain, it might gain a mention in *The Indian Helper*. Readers were told, for example, that "Disciplinarian Thompson spent Tuesday in Harrisburg attending Federal court in the settling of liquor cases," and also learned about the many fires that broke out at the school. From recent scholarship we know that some of these were likely to be the result of students torching the buildings.³⁶ But except when cases went to court, the Man-on-the-band-stand never gives us a whiff of arson, preferring to concentrate on the speed and efficiency of the school's firefighting force in dealing with the problem. One of the most serious offenses a Carlisle student could commit was to run away. This was a crime outside the scope of the federal courts and invariably punished by a spell in the school guardhouse. It was a serious and persistent problem at Carlisle, and yet the Man-on-the-band-stand only mentions runaways tangentially. "A True Story of Three Indian Lads Who Tried Running Away from School" is about children who supposedly attended a western school in a previous decade. The story serves a moral rather than informative purpose because the boys end up with frostbite.[37] This is the closest the Man-on-the-band-stand dares approach the issue of runaways. Despite his bluster and posturing, his evasive denial of all serious problems at the school reflects the fragility of his power.

For the Man-on-the-band-stand to command genuine authority, it was not only necessary that he speak from a position of power, but also that the Indian children concede him that power when they responded to his voice in the pages of *The Indian Helper*. Although he worked to furnish the children with an inner voice of conscience, it was never certain that this voice would not be drowned out by older, deeper Indian voices. One of the fundamental tasks of the Man-on-the-band-stand was to instill in each and every Carlisle pupil that inner voice of Christian conscience. In its absence, he was a mere man-of-straw and the experiment in Indian education at Carlisle destined to fail.

The End of the Man-on-the-band-stand

When Pratt founded the Carlisle Indian Industrial School, he claimed his reform program would accomplish its task in a single generation. Twenty years later, after thousands of Indian children had been corralled in boarding schools, the "Indian Problem" still persisted. Both the public and government started to lose confidence in the school's capacity to transform Indians. They subjected Carlisle and its expensive program to close scrutiny. To address this issue directly in July 1900 Pratt merged Carlisle's two publications, *The Red Man* and *The Indian Helper*, into a larger, single weekly. The Man-on-the-band-stand did not immediately disappear, but he was restricted to a single column, "The Man-on-the-band-stand's Domain." Denied the freedom to strut and roam all over the paper, he became less expansive, speaking in short paragraphs and terse one-liners.[38]

New attitudes toward Indian education, combined with Pratt's cavalier behavior toward the Bureau of Indian Affairs, provoked a crisis at Carlisle. On June 30, 1904, after less than three weeks' notice, the War Department relieved Pratt of his duties as superintend of the Carlisle Indian School. For Burgess and the Man-on-the-band-stand, this was a catastrophe. She had never before allowed any technical hitch to interrupt publication, but she signaled the extent of the disaster in the diminished size and thickness of the June 17 *Red Man and Helper*; it measured less than half its normal dimensions and featured Pratt's letter of dismissal on the front page. Beside the letter, Burgess wrote a paragraph entitled "WHY WE HAVE A SMALL PAPER THIS WEEK." At this stressful time, she took refuge in the technology and language of print and used a complicated description of the printing press to stand as a metaphor for the state of affairs:

> The standard on the feed side of the Babcock press in which are the studs and rollers that operate the grippers, broke on account of a screw working loose. The pieces had to be sent to the manufacturers in New London, Connecticut, for recasting and have not returned. If the grippers can not operate, there is no way to pull the paper from the type after the impression is made. We do not wish to disappoint our readers altogether; so print a paper this week which can be run on our half-medium platen press.[39]

That week, on page three of the shrunken paper, the Man-on-the-band-stand filled a column with banal news. It was his final appearance. Without farewells, he unceremoniously vanished.

The following two editions of *The Red Man and Helper* were merged in a bumper paper, giving a full account of Pratt's defense of his position. The next week, the paper announced the arrival of Captain William A. Mercer, and a section entitled "Miscellaneous" took the place of "The Man-on-the-band-stand's Domain." The Carlisle Indian School was obviously under new management, and Burgess was not herself. She had to ask "the Carlisle Sentinel publishing house [to come] to our rescue and run off this week's issue." This was to be the last *Red Man and Helper*. In it, a notice informed readers the paper would resume publication as *The Arrow*, after taking "a vacation for a brief period."[40]

Marianna Burgess stayed on at Carlisle for a few months and even supervised production of the first dozen issues of *The Arrow*. But this paper was a far cry from the old *Indian Helper*. Its huge pages were peppered throughout with local advertisements, and readers were encouraged to patronize the advertisers and recognize that "reciprocity is the order of the day."[41] The intimacy of *The Indian Helper* and Burgess's "imagined community" of Carlisle-educated Indians had entirely disappeared. In its place stood a paper that had unashamedly joined the twentieth-century world of commerce. Without Pratt and her Man-on-the-band-stand, there was no longer a place for Burgess at the Carlisle Indian School. At Thanksgiving, when time came for her annual holiday, Burgess went to visit her brothers in Chicago and she never returned.⁴² By the time she died, aged seventy-eight, both *The Arrow* and the Carlisle Indian School had long since gone. No obituary was published for Marianna Burgess. Instead, her memorial is carried in the surviving copies of over seven hundred issues of *The Indian Helper* and, obliquely, as she would have enjoyed, in the reconstructed bandstand, built in 1980, now standing on the exact site of the Man-on-the-band-stand's original home.⁴³

Notes

1. *Eadle Keahtah Toh*, January 1880, Vol. I, No.1.
2. *Eadle Keahtah Toh*, May 1880, Vol. I, No. 3; *Eadle Keahtah Toh*, Vol. I, No. 4 (July 1880). She listed herself as "M. Burgess, Publisher"
3. From August 1880 to June 1881 *Eadle Keahtah Toh* is "edited by the Indian Training School and Published by Mason D. Pratt." After that date, no publisher is consistently named and its production often appears to have been a team venture, for example, R. H. Pratt, A. J. Standing, and M. Burgess are listed as joint editors of Vol. VIII, No. 5 (March 1888).
4. After 1882, *Eadle Keahtah Toh* appeared under its translated name, *The Morning Star*, and in 1888 was renamed *The Red Man*. In 1904 it became *The Arrow* and then reverted back to being called *The Red Man*.
5. This as nearly as possible reproduces the style of the text as it appeared in *The Indian Helper*.
6. *The Indian Helper*, Vol. II, No. 38 (29 April 1887).
7. *The Indian Helper*, Vol. II, No. 41 (20 May 1887).
8. *The Indian Helper*, Vol. I, No. 27 (12 February 1886). This picture is half an inch high.
9. For an analysis of these photographs, see Malmsheimer, "'Imitation White Man.'"
10. *The Indian Helper*, Vol. III, No. 30 (9 March 1888).
11. For maps showing the layout of the Carlisle Indian School, see http://www.uea.ac.uk/eas/People/fear-segal/carlisleindiansch.htm (July 1, 2001).
12. *The Indian Helper*, Vol. III, No. 22 (13 January 1888).
13. For Michel Foucault's reflections on panopticism see, *Discipline and Punishment*, 195–228.
14. For Foucault it is this asymmetry that is the very essence of power, because ultimately the power to dominate rests on the differential possession of knowledge. Cf Foucault, "The Subject and Power," the afterword in *Michel Foucault: Beyond Structuralism and Hermeneutics*, 208–26.
15. Norman Johnston, *Eastern State Penitentiary: Crucible of Good Intentions*, Phila.: Philadelphia Museum of Art, 1994; Negley Teeters, *The Prison at Philadelphia: Cherry Hill, a History of Eastern State Penitentiary* (New York: Temple University Publications and Columbia University Press), 1957.
16. David Rothman's *The Discovery of the Asylum* is the seminal book that analyzes the development and spread of this idea.
17. An unsettling historical symmetry was set up when the children of many of the Indian warriors were sent to Carlisle.
18. Foucault points this out in a footnote, op. cit., 317.
19. See Kaja Silverman, *Male subjectivity at the margins*, 1–8, for an interesting psychological analysis of the relationship between voyeurism and power.
20. *The Indian Helper*, Vol. III, No. 9 (7 October 1887).
21. *The Indian Helper*, Vol. XIII, No. 1 (15 October 1897).
22. *The Indian Helper*, Vol. II, No. 1 (13 August 1886).

23. *The Indian Helper*, Vol. I, No. 45 (18 June 1886).
24. *The Indian Helper*, Vol III, No. 34 (6 April 1888).
25. For a lucid psychoanalytical discussion of how a parent can subvert the parental role and demand that the child take care of the parent see, Alice Miller, *The Drama of the Gifted Child*.
26. *The Indian Helper*, Vol. IV, No. 40 (24 May 1889).
27. Milner mistakenly refers to Millersville, Pa., as Millville: Richard Henry Pratt, *Battlefield and Classroom*, 232.
28. *The Indian Helper*, Vol. III, No. 30 (9 March 1888).
29. *The Indian Helper*, Vol. XIV, No. 14 (27 January 1899).
30. *The Indian Helper*, Vol. VI, No. 17 (26 December 1890).
31. Lucy Tsinah was married to Burdette Tsinah, and both were students at Carlisle. Thank you to Barbara Landis for this biographical information.
32. *The Indian Helper*, Vol. III, No. 25 (3 February 1888).
33. *The Indian Helper*, Vol. XIV, No. 16 (10 February 1899).
34. *The Indian Helper*, Vol. XIV, No. 39 (21 July 1899); *The Red Man and Helper*, Vol. XIX, No. 24 (15 January 1904).
35. *The Indian Helper*, Vol. XIV, No. 25 (30 June 1899).
36. For details of arson attacks, see David Wallace Adams, *Education for Extinction* and Genevieve Bell, *Telling Tales out of School*.
37. *The Indian Helper*, Vol. VIII, No. 25 (10 March 1893).
38. *The Red Man and Helper*, Vol. XVI, No. 4 and Vol. XV, No. 37 (13 July 1900; the paper retained the two separate volume numbers).
39. *The Red Man and Helper*, Vol. XIX, No. 40 and Vol. V, No. 42 (17 June 1904).
40. *The Red Man and Helper*, Vol. XIX, No. 52 and Vol. V, No. 48 (29 July 1904).
41. *The Arrow*, No. 12 (10 November 1904).
42. *The Arrow*, No. 13 (17 November 1904).
43. In 1980, a replica of the original bandstand was built in the middle of the parade ground and surviving buildings of the Carlisle Indian School. The teachers' building, where Burgess lived, is still standing.

Works Cited

Adams, David Wallace. *Education for Extinction: American Indians and the Boarding-school Experience, 1875–1928*. Lawrence: University Press of Kansas, 1995.
Bell, Genevieve. "Telling Tales out of School: Remembering the Carlisle Indian Industrial School, 1879–1918." Ph.D. Dissertation, Stanford University, (1998).
Embe. *Stiya: A Carlisle Indian Girl at Home*. Cambridge: Riverside Press, 1891.
Foucault, Michel. *Discipline and Punishment*, New York: Vintage, 1975.
———. *Michel Foucault: Beyond Structuralism and Hermeneutics*, 2d ed., ed. Hubert Dreyfus and Paul Rainbow. Chicago: University of Chicago Press, 1983.
Johnston, Norman. *Eastern State Penitentiary: Crucible of Good Intentions*. Philadelphia: Philadelphia Museum of Art, 1994.
Malmsheimer, Lonna. "'Imitation White Man': Images of Transformation at the Carlisle Indian School," *Studies in Visual Communication* 2.4 (Fall 1985): 54–74.
Miller, Alice. *The Drama of the Gifted Child*, New York: Basic Books, 1981, 1990.
Milner, Clyde A. *With Good Intentions: Quaker Work Among the Pawnees, Otos and Omahas in the 1870s*. Lincoln: University of Nebraska Press, 1982.
Mott, Frank Luther. *A History of American Magazines, Vol. III*. Cambridge, Mass.: Harvard University Press, 1938–68.
Pratt, Richard Henry. *Battlefield and Classroom: Four Decades with the American Indian 1867–1904*. New Haven, Conn.: Yale University Press, 1964.

Rothman, David. *The Discovery of the Asylum: Social Order and Disorder in the New Republic.* Boston: Little Brown, 1971.
Scott, James C. *Domination and the Arts of Resistance: Hidden Transcript.* New Haven, Conn.: Yale University Press, 1990.
Silverman, Kaja. *Male subjectivity at the margins.* New York: Routledge, 1992.
Smith-Rosenberg, Carroll. *Disorderly Conduct: Visions of Gender in Victorian America.* New York: Alfred Knopf, 1985.
Teeters, Negley. *The Prison at Philadelphia: Cherry Hill, a History of Eastern State Penitentiary.* New York: Temple University Publications and Columbia University Press, 1957.

"The Story of a Peach Tree"
The Indian Helper, 12 August 1887

In front of the north end of the dining-room there is a little peach tree growing among Miss Noble's flowers.... This tree came from a peach seed, which chanced to be dropped into the hard ground, among stones back of the dining-room. When found a year ago last spring, it was a puny, yellow-leafed, little tree, with many shoots going off in all directions and many would have supposed it would never amount to anything.

It was taken up and planted in the flower bed, for the purpose of showing what a difference the changed conditions would make in it. The change has been brought about in a little more than a year, by good care and proper attention to the natural wants of a fruit tree. If it had been left in the hard ground among the stones, it might have lived and have had peaches on it, after a while, but no-one will pretend to say that it would have made as strong and thrifty a tree as it is now or would have had as good peaches as it will have.

When found, it was hidden away among the weeds, in an out of the way place and stood many chances of being trampled down. There is not much danger of that where it is now, for besides the good care it gets, there are posts and a chain around the plot of grass where the flower bed is. When it was transplanted, there was a stake put in beside it and the tree tied to it, that it might be held up until it would be strong enough to stand alone. Now the stake is taken away; it would be a hindrance if kept any longer. When the wind blows it makes the roots of the tree strike down deeper and makes it all the stronger. The next time you pass the dining room take a good look at it and imagine it saying:

"Don't I look much better than if I was away back among the stones and weeds where Dr. Given found me? See how I hold up my head and see what nice neighbours I have all around here. I look at these pretty flowers, this green grass and trees and think, well, this is a good place to be, I am glad I was taken up and brought here. It was pretty hard at first. Why, the Doctor even took his knife and cut off some of my branches. But I see now that he knew better than I did. It makes a better looking tree of me. I don't think I want to be taken back. I don't know of any trees behind the dining-room that look as thrifty as I do. One tree back there died this summer. It stood among the stones and had no chance to grow. Some little ones were cut down by the boys when they were cutting weeds. Some others are struggling and trying to grow, but I don't think they will ever amount to much."

The readers of the *Helper* will think this is a long story about a little tree. So it is. But the writer has given it because he thinks it very like the history of many of the boys and girls in this Indian School. When found in their reservation homes by Capt. Pratt and others who have gone for them, they are poorly fed, living in dirt, with long hair and blankets, surrounded by ignorance and evils of all kinds,—weeds, WEEDS, **WEEDS**—stones, STONES, **STONES!** everywhere. Hard to grow to be good men and women in such places.

Here in the east, the conditions are all favorable. Good schools and family homes, kind teachers and friends. Supports are kept about you for a time, but soon you must begin to do for yourselves. Must not lean too long on the props. Some of your branches (long hair and blankets) have been trimmed off. At first you thought it was hard, but now I think you like it. You look better and *are* better, I don't believe you want to go back very badly. If you do, you won't see any boys and girls that look as well as you do. You won't see any who have as good chances to make good men and women as you have. There are hundreds of Indian boys and girls who ought to be brought out from among the weeds and put into the flower beds.

Dear boys and girls, stay among the FLOWERS.

Pauline E. Hopkins as Editor and Journalist: An African American Story of Success and Failure

HANNA WALLINGER

"I WAS engaged as literary editor because I was well-known as a race writer, had gained the confidence of my people, and also because there seemed to be at that time, no one else as well qualified to fill the position, for as yet the editing of a high-class magazine was puzzling work even to our best scholars." This is how Pauline E. Hopkins interpreted her position as editor and contributor to the *Colored American Magazine* in a letter to William Monroe Trotter, racial activist and owner-editor of Boston's *Guardian*, in 1905. R. S. Elliott, a white man in charge of the technical management of the magazine in its early years, includes, probably upon her request, this information:

> Pauline Hopkins has struggled to the position which she now holds in the same fashion that ALL Northern colored women have to struggle—through hardships, disappointments, and with very little encouragement. What she has accomplished has been done by a grim determination to "stick at it," even though failure might await her at the end. (47)

Elliott then adds the laudatory sentence: "Let us have a few more Pauline Hopkins to help forward the brighter and better day for the race" (47).

Her previous reputation as a performer and writer, a certain financial stability, and "grim determination," as Elliott chose to call it, allowed Pauline Hopkins to grasp one of the few opportunities available to her when the *Colored American Magazine* was founded in Boston in 1900. This position put Hopkins at the center of crucial debates about the cultural politics of magazine editing, the cultural politics of radical activism, and the early feminist movement. She was on the scene when race consciousness was being redefined. She was one of the few early African American women editors, journalists, and writers who prepared the path for future generations. An analysis of her negotiations with the "famous men" of her race, in particular with Booker T. Washington, entails a description of the sale of the magazine and its removal to New York. Details of this development are now made available by a set of letters recently discovered at Fisk University.

Her achievements at the *Colored American Magazine* and her eventual failure there invite a discussion of the cultural politics of magazine editing and the role of African American women involved in it.

The *Colored American Magazine* was founded by a group of Virginians who had migrated to Boston: Walter W. Wallace, Jesse W. Watkins, Harper S. Fortune, and Walter Alexander Johnson. The magazine was published by the Colored Co-operative Publishing Company, which also published four books, among them Hopkins's first novel, *Contending Forces*. The magazine was issued in May 1900 and announced itself to be "devoted to the higher culture of Religion, Literature, Science, Music and Art of the Negro, universally" ("Announcement"). The first editorial and publishers' announcement called for contributions from everyone interested in the race, "A vast and almost unexplored treasury of biography, history, adventure, tradition, folk lore poetry and song, the accumulations of centuries of such experiences as have never befallen any other people lies open to us and to you" (Editorial, May 1900, 60). The political purpose of the magazine was defined plainly: "What we desire, what we require, what we demand to aid in the onward march of progress and advancement is justice; merely this and nothing more" (ibid. 61).[1]

The *Colored American Magazine* contained elements of the mass magazine, such as articles that reflect evangelical piety (for example a long series of biblical stories), or address childrearing and health issues (for example, an article about the importance of healthy teeth). At the same time, it catered to the interests of a kind of social elite with articles about particular social classes (e.g. about "Boston's Smart Set" in January 1901), with occasional fashion notes, and even occasional pieces about vacation traveling.[2] One of its main concerns was education and related information about schools, educators, and famous graduates, an emphasis that increased after the magazine came under the control of Booker T. Washington. But it is mainly its inclusion of numerous poems, short stories, and serial novels that turned it into a quality journal. It offered literary access to writers such as Pauline Hopkins, who seized the opportunity and gained some degree of public prominence. When writing is, as Richard Brodhead sees it, an "acculturated activity,"[3] the many extraliterary factors that make the production and marketing of literature possible have to be taken into account in order to explain the rise to prominence of a certain writer or a group of writers at certain times.

Pauline Hopkins seized the possibility that the *Colored American Magazine* offered. Her interest in various forms of literature was clearly established before the year 1900, and her literary tastes and her wide knowledge were certainly acquired in the formative years when she toured the country and wrote various versions of the play she performed. She also wrote the first chapter of *Hagar's Daughter* and all of *Contending Forces* before she began at the *Colored American Magazine*. But without a channel for her literary activities, she would have been denied even the short-lived public prominence that she gained through the publication of her work in the magazine. Her genius would have been lost to the annals of history.

Hopkins contributed numerous editorials and biographical articles, one chapter of her already published first novel *Contending Forces*, and a total of seven stories and three serial novels to the magazine. The serial novels were *Hagar's Daughter: A Story of Southern Caste Prejudice* (1901–02), *Winona: A Tale of Negro Life in the South and Southwest* (1902), and *Of One Blood. Or, The Hidden Self* (1902–03). Her four novels and her short stories demonstrate the main concerns of Hopkins around the turn of the century: the amalgamation of the races, ancient history, the women's movement, the legacy of slavery, and the potential for heroism of African Americans.

The years 1900 to 1904 were her most prolific. Her novel *Contending Forces* was frequently praised in announcements and offered at a special rate to new subscribers. Some of her writings were published under the pseudonym Sarah Allen, her mother's maiden name. Another pseudonym she used was J. Shirley Shadrach.[4] In all this, she and the entire staff of the journal strove to turn the *Colored American Magazine* into a "quality national journal" (Johnson and Johnson, *Propaganda* 4). Hopkins had considerable influence, as Abby Arthur Johnson and Ronald Maberry Johnson note: "More and better fiction and poetry was published by the *Colored American Magazine* during the years Pauline Hopkins was editor than at any other time in its history" (*Propaganda* 6). Claudia Tate calls her a "leading proponent of activist black journalism during the post-Reconstruction period" (366), and William Braithwaite, a Boston poet and journalist, remembers that Hopkins introduced the practice of paying for contributions in order to attract more and better fiction and poetry (24f.). Hazel Carby concludes from the available evidence that Hopkins "had the power to influence the magazine's editorial politics" and called her position an "enviable place in the world of African American journalism" (4). Carby names as Hopkins's goals "the creation of an African American art and literature that would demonstrate the talents and skills of the group and prove to the rest of the world that black people, only recently released from slavery, were already as culturally advanced as other groups" (5).

A discussion of Hopkins's role and position at the *Colored American Magazine* is incomplete without a detailed analysis of her journalism, especially as it sheds light on aspects of her biography. Her "Famous Men of the Negro Race" series is the best starting point for a discussion of her negotiations with one of the most influential race leaders of her time, Booker T. Washington, and of her position as a radical African American in the Boston of her time. Similar to most women who aspired to obtain positions of prominence, Hopkins faced a power structure working against her.

In November 1900, Hopkins started her series on "Famous Men of the Negro Race" with a statement of purpose: "Races should be judged by the great men they produce, and by the average value of the masses" ("Toussaint" 11). Hopkins's view of the famous men of her race was shaped by her era's concepts of perfect manhood and her own beliefs in a common descent and a common purpose, which she once called "the quest for the Holy Grail" ("Robert Morris" 337). Like many of her contemporaries, Hopkins felt the need to move away from the definition of races as inferior or superior, civilized or uncivilized, of races as determined only by skin color, shape of the head, texture of the hair, or shape of the nose.⁵ Famous men and women, according to her and most other African American intellectuals of her time, possessed reliable and verifiable records of achievements that could be documented. In writing these sketches, Hopkins drew upon her profound knowledge of the political and social climate of her immediate surroundings, Boston, and of African American history in general.

Hopkins's biographical essays may be read as comments on the contemporary situation of African Americans. The many references to Booker T. Washington reflect her and the journal's dependence on his support and goodwill. Since Booker T. Washington was a very controversial figure, provoking wholehearted approval or bitter disapproval, she could not avoid taking sides. It will be observed that she often did so indirectly and tried to prevent an open conflict, but she lost her position as editor despite her caution.

The first editorial of the *Colored American Magazine* advocates the "bonds of that racial brotherhood, which alone can enable a people, to assert their racial rights as men, and demand their privileges as citizens" (Editorial, May 1900, 60). While calling for progress, activism, and justice, it also carefully praises the aims and personality of Booker T. Washington. The editorial ends, for example, with the following comparison of Washington and Christ: "Surely whatever else he deserves, he does not deserve censure, criticism and calumny. Sad would it be, indeed, if it were said of him as it was said of another of earth's greatest benefactors 'He came unto his own and his own received him not'" (ibid. 62; see also Schneider, *Boston* 64).

Booker T. Washington was the "wizard" of Tuskegee, the founder of the Tuskegee Institute in Alabama—an institution dedicated mostly to industrial education—and its principal from 1881 until his death in 1915. Controversial as a race leader, he warned African Americans against political agitation and promoted industrial education and agricultural expertise, which would guarantee them a secure position in society. From his humble southern origin, he achieved a place of prominence in part through clever maneuvers, which were not always publicly known, that won him the support of Tuskegee and gave him considerable political influence.[6] Washington published his autobiography *Up from Slavery* in 1901; it included a lengthy description of his "Atlanta Exposition Address," given only six years earlier. In this speech Washington called upon African Americans to work for their salvation through industrial progress and, to repeat his well-worn metaphor, to cast down their buckets where they were, in the American South. Agriculture, mechanics, commerce, domestic service, and the professions were the fields in which they should work. The southern white people were asked to help this "most patient, faithful, law-abiding, and unresentful people" (*Up from Slavery* 148). In an attempt to assure the support of his white audience, he spoke against civil equality: "In all things that are purely social we can be as separate as the fingers, yet one as the hand in all things essential to mutual progress" (148). His politics of racial accommodation through segregation alienated many contemporary African Americans who thought that voting rights, higher education, and equal opportunities were essential to the progress of the race. His disdain of political activism and his conciliatory attitude about voting rights guaranteed him, however, the prominent position and political influence that helped him maintain the Tuskegee Institute and pursue a number of other political aims. The fact that he had many followers is also reflected in the political climate that preceded the passing of *Plessy v. Ferguson* in 1896, the Supreme Court decision that legalized segregation on a large scale.

There are numerous examples of African Americans involved in education, politics, and journalism whose careers depended on the approval or disapproval of what is now called the "Tuskegee Machine." In his substantial study of Booker T. Washington's life, Louis R. Harlan claims that Washington "actually entered patronage politics with gusto and with a remarkable talent for its trivial details" (*Wizard* 6). Harlan quotes examples of Washington's influence on President Roosevelt and his power to further or squash the career of an African American politician or intellectual. He lists names of famous African American men and women who were directly or indirectly on the payroll of the "Tuskegee Machine."[7]

Although W. E. B. Du Bois was the most prominent opponent of Booker T. Washington on the question of industrial training versus the classical curriculum, the ramifications of this controversy can be detected in many other places and careers. The high-profile careers of Anna Julia Cooper, writer and educator in Washington, D.C.; Ida B. Wells-Barnett, radical antilynching crusader, civil rights activist, and suffragist based in Chicago; Fanny J. Coppin, educator and school principal in Philadelphia; and Mary Church Terrell, famous club woman and wife of Judge Robert Terrell, a loyal follower of Booker T. Washington, were dependent upon the goodwill of Washington.[8] In these cases, an ideological difference was infused with gender problematics. Pauline Hopkins is a good example of the merging of race, class, gender, and ideological questions. She was one of the few prominent women to oppose Booker T. Washington. Although she had to choose oblique criticism rather than open confrontation, she risked her career because of her political views.

When we read her biographical sketches with an eye upon Booker T. Washington, the choices she made about whom to include in her series and the order of appearance are significant. To begin with Toussaint L'Ouverture was certainly an excellent choice because he was recognized by most of her contemporaries as an exemplary man. She continued the series with a loving and reverent portrait of Frederick Douglass, and she placed this portrait in the December issue of 1900, at the beginning of the new century. Hopkins portrays him as a national heroic figure and as her personal hero. There is no doubt that he influenced her decisively. In the introduction to a pamphlet that he and Ida B. Wells-Barnett wrote for the 1893 World's Columbian Exposition in Chicago, Douglass states: "We are men and our aim is perfect manhood, to be men among men. Our situation demands faith in ourselves, faith in the power of truth, faith in work and faith in the influence of manly character" (qtd. in Bederman 39). Hopkins pays her respect to the man whom she admired and whose activist political ideals she tried to emulate. She certainly had him in mind when she put down her views on "perfected manhood."

In the next issue, January 1901, she discusses William Wells Brown (1814–1884), who had influenced her early writing so much. Typical of the organizing principles in her biographical sketches, she narrates his life partly by giving facts and partly by telling anecdotes that point out the subject's brave soul or his wit or humor.[9] Her conclusion about Brown is that such self-made men of the race are still needed today: "How many of us today can occupy and fill their vacant places? Not alone *occupy*, but *fill* them. Alas! how few, when we consider our advantages. If much is given, much is required. An ignorant man will trust to luck for success; an educated man will *make* success. God helps those who help themselves" (236).

Given Hopkins's divided attitude toward Booker T. Washington, it comes as no surprise that she did not immediately name him as one of those who could "fill" the place of William Wells Brown. Yet considering that in 1901 readers might have expected Booker T. Washington to be at least fourth in this series, it is remarkable that months would pass till she would write about Washington in this series about famous men of the race. Instead, she continued with a discussion of Robert Browne Elliott, a politician and race leader whose life gave her the opportunity to analyze more recent history and criticize racism and intolerance.

In the biographical sketch about Washington that finally appears in October 1901, Hopkins writes that no one will question "that Dr. Washington and Tuskegee are one" (436). Now this is no surprising statement, but what follows takes it literally: "Tuskegee is the soul of the man outlined in wood, in brick and stone, pulsating with the life of the human hive within on whom he has stamped his individuality" (436). The guiding images here, that of the soul as brick and stone and that of the beehive, indicate the hardness of the man's soul and the busyness of the bee that works hard. While the image remains within the realm of convention, it takes on extra meaning when we know that Washington's enterprising activities and influence, his individuality, which leaves its mark on many who depend on him, would eventually be directed against the journalist and oust her from her position as editor. It is also interesting to note that Hopkins gives two long quotations from an 1895 speech by Washington on "Industrial Education" that emphasize the achievements of black people in America, but that she does not quote from his more famous "Atlanta Exposition Address." She only refers to it as "his great speech" and says that it "received many flattering encomiums from leading men all over the country" (439). She comes back to this point when she says that Washington is "without a peer" in "attracting the attention of the monied element" (439).

Hopkins emphasizes his wealth once more when she calls him one of the most remarkable men of this age and mentions "his humble birth and rise to eminence and wealth" (441). The whole essay is permeated by references to money and wealth, mainly payments he received for Tuskegee, for his lectures, or the amount of money invested in such and such a part of Tuskegee. In her essay about John Mercer Langston, by contrast, there is whole-hearted praise of his achievements, but no reference to financial matters. In comparison to her unambiguous and genuine praise of Langston, her praise of Washington sounds flat and forced, at least to readers who read between the lines. Unlike the earlier essays, there are no references to "perfected manhood," common descent ("of one blood"), or the quest for the Holy Grail. Towards the end of this five-page sketch of Washington she says: "View his career in whatever light we may, be we for or against his theories, his personality is striking, his life uncommon, and the magnetic influence which radiates from him in all directions, bending and swaying great minds and pointing the ultimate conclusion of colossal schemes as the wind the leaves of the trees, is stupendous" (441). Syntactically, her praise of his striking personality and uncommon life is all but subsumed by the second part of the sentence, where his magnetic influence is compared to the force of a storm. Hopkins leaves it to the reader to conclude whom the great minds were that Washington bent and swayed. The "colossal" influence of the man would not only strip the trees of leaves but force many of his contemporaries to succumb to his views.

The essay highlights Hopkins's dilemma of criticizing a man who she felt was taking African Americans in a wrong direction, while in general praising him as a race leader who had achieved a position of wealth and prominence. While she repeatedly argued that the identity and power of the race depended on its manly men and worthy women, she could not fully condemn one of its most prominent contemporary leaders. At the same time she could not wholeheartedly endorse his program and, as early as 1901, must have felt her own position at risk because of this.

Hopkins's "Famous Men" series concluded in November 1901, but her dealings with Washington did not. Her career continued to be shaped by dealings with men who rarely showed an appreciation of her efforts and achievements. The question of Hopkins's attitude towards Booker T. Washington is not whether she was right or wrong from a historical standpoint in her assessment of his role and influence. Even if Booker T. Washington was perhaps less of an accommodationist than is usually acknowledged, since he organized legal battles against segregation and disfranchisement behind the scenes,[10] Hopkins could not have known about it at the time. To her, it appeared that Washington was the driving force behind people who sought to antagonize her.

In 1903 growing financial problems forced Walter Wallace to sell the magazine. It was bought by William Dupree, a Civil War hero and leader in civic organizations, who was assisted by William O. West and Jesse W. Watkins. Hopkins was officially listed as literary editor in the May/June issue of 1903. The magazine functioned as the journal of the Colored American League, founded the same year in order to raise more money. However, the financial situation of the *Colored American Magazine* was not stabilized permanently and, therefore, Dupree's ownership turned out to be only a transitional solution that did not guarantee its continued existence.

In the May/June issue of 1903, the three owners and editors are profiled in an article, "Biographies of the Officers of the New Management of Our Magazine," which is written in Hopkins's style, although it is not signed with her name. This article emphasizes the need to "renew the battle for equal and exact justice for all races and all men" and to present exemplary lives (such as that of William Dupree) which may serve to prove the "integrity, industry and character" of the race ("Biographies" 443). The "Editorial and Publishers' Announcements" in this same issue detail the possible hardships and months of doubt and uncertainty that preceded the reorganization and show the dedication of the managers to the publication:

> At the cost of many anxious moments and sleepless nights, when not a star of hope was visible on the horizon, God has permitted us to save this enterprise to our race. Envy and covetousness have sat with us in council, but even as did the Christian martyrs of old forgive their tormentors the tortures inflicted upon them, so do we forgive our enemies. At some future day we hope to be able to tell our true story to our readers, who will then give us the full sympathy of their warm hearts. (446)

In November 1903, Dupree suggested to Hopkins that he could solicit the white New York publisher and music critic John C. Freund for a series of articles on Jamaica. In the earlier months of his involvement with the magazine, Freund won Hopkins's confidence because she saw his engagement as "a case of pure philanthropy, one of those rare cases which are sometimes found among wealthy, generous and eccentric white men" (Hopkins-Trotter letter 2). She soon learned that he was instrumental in maligning and discrediting her as editor. Within months it became clear to her that Freund was backed by Booker T. Washington and was striving to transfer the magazine to New York.

This evaluation is based upon the April 16, 1905, letter from Hopkins to Trotter that Ann Allen Shockley had located at Fisk and included in the Hopkins papers (referred to as Hopkins-Trotter letter). In the ten pages of this letter, Hopkins clarifies the background information about the sale of the magazine from the original owners to William Dupree in the spring of 1903, the constant financial and organizational problems this change entailed, and then moves on to discuss the involvement of John C. Freund, the foundation of the Colored American League, and the eventual transfer of the magazine to New York under the editorship of Fred R. Moore. The general tone of this long letter is one of despair and bitter disappointment about the treatment she received from the white patron and her African American colleagues.

Within the letter there are references such as "See accompanying letter marked '1'" (see 2). These accompanying letters, twenty in number, are now available for study.[11] All of them are from John C. Freund, five of them are addressed to William Dupree, the rest to Hopkins herself. Although their numbering does not always correspond to that mentioned in the Hopkins-Trotter letter, it is necessary to list them according to writer and addressee and dates so that they can be identified more easily. Three letters are written by John C. Freund to Mr. William L Dupree, Superintendent, Station A, Post Office, Boston, Mass, dated November 19, 1903; January 27, 1904; and January 28, 1904. Letters marked 4 to 15 are from Freund directed to Miss Pauline E. Hopkins, Editor, "The Colored American Magazine," 82 West Concord St., Boston, Mass., with the following dates: February 11, 1904; February 18, 1904; March 5, 1904; March 12, 1904; March 14, 1904; March 16, 1904; March 17, 1904; March 18, 1904; March 24, 1904; March 25, 1904; March 28, 1904. Letters 16 and 17 are from Freund to Dupree, dated March 31, 1904, and April 6, 1904. Three more letters are addressed to Hopkins on April 7, April 11, and April 16, 1904. The last two are directed to her home at 53 Clifton St., North Cambridge, Mass. In the Hopkins-Trotter letter there are additional references to the March 1904 issue of the *Colored American Magazine*, especially Hopkins's article about the foundation of the Colored American League, "How a New York Newspaper Man Entertained a Number of Colored Ladies and Gentlemen at Dinner in the Revere House, Boston, and How the Colored American League Was Started."

Hopkins's motivation for documenting her experiences at the *Colored American Magazine* and for sending the accompanying letters to Trotter a year after all this had happened is stated in her opening paragraph:

> Herewith I send you a detailed account of my experiences with the Colored American Magazine as its editor and, incidentally, with Mr. Booker T. Washington in the taking over of the magazine to New York by his agents. It is necessarily long and perhaps tedious at the outset, but I trust that you will peruse it to the end. I have held these facts for a year, but as my rights are ignored in my own property, and I am persistently hedged about by the revengeful tactics of Mr. Washington's men, I feel that I must ask the advice of some one who will give me a respectful hearing, and judgment as to the best way to deal with this complicated case. (1)

This opening passage shows Hopkins's bitterness and her understanding of the role Booker T. Washington played in this transaction.

The letter does not give information about how she got hold of the letters to Dupree, but it can be assumed that Dupree had given her a copy of them because he wanted her to understand the role Freund had played from the outset. She names him and Jesse Watkins and William West as potential witnesses, who would substantiate the truth of her testimony if Trotter asked them. She adds about the position of Dupree: "Mr. Dupree, of course, knows more of the facts than I do, and I have no doubt would be willing to tell all that he knows if he were guaranteed protection from the malice of Mr. Washington's friends" (Hopkins-Trotter letter 10). This latter assessment shows that she felt Dupree to be sympathetic towards her position and that she trusted him.

When John C. Freund first joined the *Colored American Magazine* with a series of articles on Jamaica, he seemed to be genuinely interested in the publication. In his second letter to Dupree (Jan. 27, 1903), he uses the collective first person plural ("to get us clear by the First of March") to show his identification with the editors. He suggests the formation of a league to raise money and support the magazine's goals. Yet there is already a hint of his attempt not only to finance the magazine but also to exercise control over its content. He informs Dupree: "I have also written to Miss Hopkins urging her to do her utmost to keep out of the magazine anything that might be construed into antagonism to the whites. We must take high ground in order to disarm opposition and bring out the good will of the white people who are not only with you now, but have always been with you only you have not known it." In addition to constantly urging Dupree and later Hopkins to be more astute about business matters, the third letter to Dupree reveals his belief that the magazine should contain news, essays about famous men and women, organizations, and universities, rather than literature and critical articles. He assumed the role of spokesman for all the editors: "What we want to do is to get to work and show what the colored people are doing for themselves; how they are raising themselves up, and to do this, not by means of glittering generalities, but by making up individual cases" (Freund-Dupree, Jan. 28, 1904). He presses his argument again in his February 18, 1904, letter to Hopkins: "The magazine should therefore, in my judgment, contain some fiction, some interesting articles which will appeal to the general mass of the colored people, but particularly, it should treat of the work being done by the Negro people." All of this entails a curtailing of the editors' rights to "argue and fight prejudice on general lines or with glittering generalities" (same letter). Hopkins recognized Booker T. Washington's rhetoric in this letter, although it obviously took her some time to find out Freund's motives and his connections. Freund continued to compliment her on her ability and competence, but she could not but doubt his intentions after the receipt of these letters.

At about the same time, in January 1904, Freund invited Hopkins, Mr. and Mrs. Dupree, and some other people engaged in the *Colored American Magazine* to a dinner at the Revere House, Boston. This event is described by Hopkins in "How a New York Newspaper Man Entertained a Number of Colored Ladies and Gentlemen at Dinner in the Revere House, Boston, and How the Colored American League Was Started," a most interesting article publicizing her views and the role of John C. Freund to the *Colored*

American Magazine readership. The article contains Freund's speech at the dinner, which not only illustrates his motivations but also the often difficult relationships between white patrons and African American entrepreneurs and artists.

Freund justifies his participation in this enterprise: "I took an ever increasing interest in what is called the colored race problem, not because, let me be frank, I have any particular interest in the colored people as such, but because of the principles which had appealed to me, and because I believed that a man should be what he makes himself, whether his face be white or black, his hair straight or kinky, his eyes blue or brown, whether his nose curves one way or the other" (153). Despite the lack of personal interest Freund, in openly paternalistic rhetoric, proceeds to give good advice to the colored race in general and points out the important educational function of the magazine: "What you have to do is to put up such a proposition to the heart, the conscience, the chivalry, not only of the South, but of the people of the whole United States, that justice must—and will be done you" (154).

Thus far Freund does not differ from any other liberal white who thinks that the problem can be solved with good will and a determined effort on both sides. Then he criticizes the editor, Hopkins:

> I notice, in one of the articles written by your worthy, most talented and self-sacrificing editress, Miss Hopkins, a tendency to refer to her people as a 'proscribed race.'
>
> You must cease to speak of yourselves as a proscribed people. You must cease to dwell upon your wrongs in the past, however bitter, however cruel.
>
> How shall the barriers that hold you in be broken down, if you insist upon living behind them? Your duty is to forget the past, at least, to put it behind you and to advance bravely, with your faces to the dawn and the light. (155)

Freund here attacks not only Hopkins herself, but a whole generation of writers who insist on dealing with past cruelty to explain the present situation and who think that "to advance bravely" involves the backward glance as well. This is a generation of writers refusing to forgive the nation's wrongs by politely talking about future possibilities instead of demanding a collective responsibility. His praise of Hopkins as a talented and self-sacrificing editor sounds more than perfunctory when he then attacks her fiction. The term "proscribed race" features prominently in her novel *Contending Forces*, which begins with this dedication: "To the Friends of Humanity Everywhere I offer this humble tribute written by one of a proscribed race." Hopkins correctly understood Freund's intention: "'Proscribed race,' was a hit at my book 'Contending Forces' and my serial story

'Hagar's Daughter' both of which had aroused the ire of the white South, male and female, against me many of whom had paid me their compliments in newspapers squibs and insulting personal letters sent to the old management of the magazine" (Hopkins-Trotter letter 6).

Freund then urges the colored people not to consider their position as unique in the world and not to think that all they need to do is to make it known to the white people how far they have advanced in the arts, sciences, and education. He points out that the race problem gets adequate coverage in some of the leading white journals. He speaks about the brave and noble President Theodore Roosevelt and the people's great interest in and aid to Tuskegee. His solution to the problem is self-help. Safe and sound in his white skin, Freund closes by talking about the fact that every race has had to struggle, but that it can win and overcome adversity when it applies itself diligently enough.

It is difficult to imagine the reaction of the audience to this speech. Hopkins only notes that it was "cordially received" (158). The other speeches are not reprinted in full. She only mentions the speech of Mr. Butler R. Wilson, a lawyer, "who said that it gave him great pleasure to be present, and while he would not agree with all that had been said, he readily admitted that there was much food for thought" (158f.). Behind the scenes, Hopkins writes to Trotter, there was strict opposition to Freund's plan to transfer the magazine to New York (see Hopkins-Trotter letter 2f.) Given Hopkins's writings, it is safe to assume that she was offended by the paternalistic tone of Freund's address and especially did not like its blunt praise of Booker T. Washington. The friction between Freund and Hopkins may be seen as well in her letter to Trotter, where she laments that he "held with each one of us the patriarchal relation of ancient days" (Hopkins-Trotter letter 3).

The problems of financing and running the *Colored American Magazine* were acute most of the time. At the same foundational meeting of the Colored American League, where Freund hinted at the new editorial policies, Hopkins addressed the audience, and her report is summarized in the following way:

> Miss Pauline E. Hopkins, the editress of the Magazine, gave a most eloquent and touching account of the struggles of the magazine, with which she has been connected almost from its inception. She said that there were times when there was not a dollar in the treasury, and when the darkness of despair settled upon the little band of men and women who had devoted themselves to the cause, but even in the worst days, when everything seemed to have gone against them, they never despaired. ("How a New York Newspaper Man" 159)

In February 1904 Hopkins received a bouquet of violets, a book, and a twenty-five-dollar check from Freund. She was greatly puzzled by this preferential treatment because it made her position in the office uncomfortable. In her account of this she offers us a rare glimpse of her personal situation at this time. She refers to her bedridden mother as one of her "burdens at home" (Hopkins-Trotter letter 3) and says of herself: "As I am not a woman who attracts the attention of the opposite sex in any way, Mr. Freund's philanthropy with regard to myself puzzled me" (Hopkins-Trotter letter 3). In time Hopkins realized that the gifts must have been meant as a bribe just as she would later be offered a raise in salary to cover up Washington's role in the purchase of the magazine and its relocation to New York.

In order to solicit contributions and advance sales, the *Colored American Magazine* started a series at the beginning of 1904, "Industrial Education; Will It Solve the Negro Problem? Answered Each Month by the Greatest Thinkers of the Black Race" (Jan. 1904). Basically this series is a discussion of Washington's policies, and if a contributor did not want to avoid the issue, as John Edward Bruce did by concentrating instead on the problem of what the Negro question really was, he or she had to take sides. According to Hopkins, these articles "created consternation in the ranks of the Southern supporters because they were written by writers of so high a standing in the literary world as to prove that the policy of industrial education solely for the Negro was not popular, and was doomed to failure in the end" (Hopkins-Trotter letter 9).

From the beginning Booker T. Washington seemed to be behind the attempt to destroy the *Colored American Magazine* and transfer it from the supportive environment of Boston to New York, although it could not have been obvious to all that he was involved. In March 1904, Freund asked Hopkins to write a letter to introduce Freund to Washington, and Hopkins reluctantly does so: "Mr. Dupree and the staff requested me to comply strictly with Mr. Freund's request, so, although I had NO PERSONAL ACQUAINTANCE WITH MR. WASHINGTON, I wrote a letter to him detailing our situation, recounting Mr. Freund's kind acts and craving Mr. Washington's good offices as a race man in our favor" (Hopkins-Trotter letter 5). On March 25 and March 28, Freund informed Hopkins that he had met Mr. Washington and, in a letter referred to but not included in the available material, he told her that Washington had called upon him. In her own résumé of this part of her acquaintance with Freund, Hopkins doubted the fact that Freund and Washington had not met before: "The great question is,—Did Mr. Freund intend to help the enterprise when he took it up at the beginning and was he turned from his purpose by the influence of Mr. Washington's expressed views and desires, or was it a mutual understanding between these gentlemen from the beginning?" (Hopkins-Trotter letter 9).

The letter dated March 31, 1904, was dubbed by Hopkins "The Washington Letter," and was written by Freund to Dupree. In this letter Freund frankly admits his aversion to literary work and what he calls "political arguments." The magazine's aim should be: "first—to record the work the colored people are doing; second—to make the whites acquainted with it." In the final paragraph Freund writes, "With any literary magazine, let me tell you frankly, Booker Washington has absolutely no sympathy. Neither he nor I have the least hope for its future, but for a magazine which will do as I say, there is every hope and certain help." The following letter, April 6, 1904, again addressed to Dupree sets down the law:

> Either Miss Hopkins will follow our suggestion ... and put live matter into the magazine, eliminating anything, which may create offense, stop talking about wrongs and a proscribed race, or you must count me out absolutely from this day forth. I will neither personally endorse nor help a business proposition, which my common sense tells me is foredoomed to failure. Every person that I have spoken to on the subject is with me. IT IS MR. BOOKER WASHINGTON'S IDEA. (also quoted in the Hopkins-Trotter letter 5)

Hopkins notes that this letter "threw a firebrand into the office and made [her] position unbearable" (Hopkins-Trotter letter 5). The letter confirmed to her what she had suspected, namely that Freund "was curtailing my work from the broad field of international union and uplift for the Blacks in all quarters of the globe, to the narrow confines of the question as affecting solely the Afro-American" (Hopkins-Trotter letter 4). She suspects that Freund and Washington were offended by a number of solicited articles on President Roosevelt's Philippine policy and William Lloyd Garrison's criticism of industrial education in the April issue of 1904. She notes that she had committed herself to these articles previously and did not want to alienate and offend these renowned contributors to the *Colored American Magazine*.

The relationship between Hopkins and Freund turned from one of benevolence on Freund's side and tolerance and gratitude on Hopkins's side to one of mutual reproach and distrust. On March 24, 1904, Freund writes to her: "I note your amiable disposition to crown me, if not here then hereafter. You are like all your people; your hearts' blood isn't good enough for anybody who gives you a kind word or does you a friendly act." In later letters he questions her competence as editor and criticizes her for her lack of business sense and her obstinacy.

Hopkins's assessment of the fate of the magazine unequivocally places the blame at Washington's door. Her final words in the ten-page letter condemn his role and character:

> With the knowledge which we possess, can we be expected to worship Mr. Washington as a pure and noble soul?
>
> Can we be expected to join in paeans of praise to his spotless character and high principles?
>
> One cannot help a feeling of honest indignation and contempt for a man who would be a party to defraud a helpless race of an organ of free speech, a band of men of their legal property and a woman of her means of earning a living. (Hopkins-Trotter letter 10)

In late April/early May of 1904 the magazine was sold again, and Fred R. Moore, the national organizer and recording secretary of the National Negro Business League, which was financed and backed by Booker T. Washington, assumed the position of owner and editor. Although Washington's exact involvement in the purchase and restructuring of the *Colored American Magazine* was kept a secret, rumors of his having invested a large amount of money in a number of African American magazines had been spread in 1903 and denied by him fervently.[12]

Hopkins decided to move to New York, accept a salary of twelve dollars a week, and "succumb to the powers that were, and do all [she] could to keep the magazine alive unless they asked [her] to publicly renounce the rights of [her] people" (Hopkins-Trotter letter 7). The new owner of the magazine also held the rights to her novel *Contending Forces,* and she was not willing to forsake the money still promised to her. In New York she learned the system of manipulations behind the scenes of magazine publishing. She recapitulates the activities of Washington's active agents and trusted allies: "Plans are laid for 'downing' opposing Negroes, wires are pulled for paying political jobs, and 'ward-heeling' schemes are constantly resorted to" (Hopkins-Trotter letter 8).

The May 1904 issue is the first in which we find no article attributed to Pauline Hopkins or any of her pseudonyms. In the next issue, Fred R. Moore appears solo on the masthead above his "Publisher's Announcements." The address given is now Pearl Street in New York, the general manager is Moore. The struggle for leadership had obviously been decided. Simultaneous with a new layout of the title page, Hopkins's name disappeared from the magazine until November 1904, when Moore reported that she was in "ill health" ("Publishers' Announcements," Nov. 1904, 700). The same announcement names as associate editor Roscoe Conkling Simmons, who was Mrs. Margaret Murray Washington's nephew and a zealous supporter of his "Uncle Booker."[13] In a later retrospective detailing the development of the magazine under his editorship, Moore mentions that Miss Hopkins and Jesse W. Watkins "rendered good service until September 1904" (Editorial, June 1905, 342), when Hopkins left because of ill health and Watkins was dismissed for undisclosed reasons. Hopkins most probably stayed in New York for another few months to prepare the essay about the city's subway system, which she published in *The Voice of the Negro* in December 1904.

The change in editorial policy is apparent in the column "In the Editor's Sanctum" of May 1904: "What the nation desires to know about the Southern Negro is not how many votes he casts so much as whether he is bringing himself into such a position that he can discharge his social and personal duties as an American citizen" (382). Civil rights here are discarded for material wealth because it is more important to become a "peasant proprietor of the soil" than to vote (382). The white man is asked to become a brotherly and protective friend of the black man:

> We implore the white men of the North and the white men of the South to deal with the Negro question soberly, tenderly, discerningly; and throw their strong arms about the Negro, and protect and counsel him, and be his elder brother, and help him get education, and pour soothing oil into his wounds, and work hand in hand with him, and employ him, and put him on his feet, and teach him that he is a man. (383)

This paternalistic rhetoric must have alienated many readers who were used to race pride in the magazine. Moore's editorial in the June issue of 1905, one year after the magazine relocated to New York, is explicit about the new editorial politics:

> We shall support the policies of Dr. Booker T. Washington, irrespective of harping critics, because we believe in them, and we shall endeavor to make friends for the race wherever possible. We shall continue to publish the doings of the race in business and what is being done along educational lines; and at all times we shall reserve the right to criticise, in a dignified way, those policies that do not seem to be for our best interest. (June 1905, 342)

While the emphasis of the magazine shifted from literature to current affairs, news of fraternal orders, education, and business affairs, it lost a great part of its readership (see Bullock 113–15). Its circulation dropped considerably. While sales used to average from 800 to 1,500 copies in New York, it dropped to 200 a month (see Hopkins-Trotter letter 8). The new motto was now: "Prejudice will be erased through education, character and money" ("Publishers' Announcements," March 1905, 164). Hopkins's political positions and commitment to African American literature clearly conflicted with the magazine's new editorial policies.

Pauline Hopkins as Editor and Journalist

What the controversy among Hopkins, Moore, and Washington shows more clearly than anything else is that despite her competence and popularity, Hopkins lacked the financial backing and political influence that would have ensured a longer career. As a woman undertaking the nearly unprecedented career of editor, she was further at a disadvantage. The *Colored American Magazine* gave her access to the public, advertised her writings, and published her fiction and nonfiction, but it also effectively ended her career when she was ousted from it.

Hopkins tried to stay with the *Colored American Magazine* for a short time after its transfer to New York, but returned to Boston after a few months. For a short period of time she wrote for the *Voice of the Negro*, the first African American journal published in the South, in Atlanta. Its editorial policies under J. Max Barber were much more radical, closer to the position of W. E. B. Du Bois and thus more in accordance with her own preferences. In late 1904 and early 1905, Hopkins published a six-month sociocultural survey, "The Dark Races of the Twentieth Century," and an essay "The New York Subway." The editor announced her association with the journal in the November issue of 1904 by saying: "Miss Pauline E. Hopkins is a well-known literary star among the Boston magazine writers. By any amount of coaxing and begging and paying we have been able to secure her services as one of our regular contributors." He adds, "Miss Hopkins was by far the best staff writer on The Colored American Magazine when it was published in Boston. She has made her mark and is entitled to be considered as one of the best young writers in the race. Be sure to see her first article. Miss Hopkins is no longer connected with The Colored American Magazine" ("Our Christmas Number," Nov. 1904, 467). Hopkins ceased to publish with the *Voice of the Negro* after the July 1905 issue, but there is no explanation for this in the magazine itself.

The *Voice of the Negro* repeated some of the successful editorial policies of the *Colored American Magazine*. It included, for example, a large number of articles by famous African American women. The July 1904 number even announced an entire issue devoted mainly to the voices of African American women, in which they could answer "Mrs. Felton, Thomas Nelson Page, William Hannibal Thomas," and others about their unfair accusation of a lack of morality among colored women. There was also a large number of portraits of notable men and women, some fashion and society notes, and a serial novel by Gardner Goldsby called "The Welding of the Link" (July 1905 to July 1906). The *Voice of the Negro* had to move from Atlanta to Chicago after the Atlanta Riot in 1906 and the accusations that the editors of the magazine were treating this riot unfairly. The October 1906 issue asks on its opening page "Shall the Press Be Free?" and states:

"In certain parts of this country Truth is literally gagged and bound and lies dumb and helpless in the dust while the lie is haughty and mighty and wields the sceptre in all the regions round about" (Barber 391). J. Max Barber defends himself: "The Voice of the Negro has told the truth, the plain unvarnished truth for nearly three years in the city of Atlanta and the heart of the South. The time came when that section could no longer endure sound doctrine" (391).

At the same time that she wrote for the *Voice of the Negro*, Hopkins self-published her historical treatise, *A Primer of Facts Pertaining to the Early Greatness of the African Race and the Possibility of Restoration by Its Descendants—with Epilogue*. This treatise is Hopkins's call for black nationalism and establishes her place firmly in a line of writers who became famous for their Ethiopianism, a movement that tried to vindicate the early greatness of the African peoples and explain their achievements in the diaspora. In her "Dark Races" series and *A Primer of Facts*, Hopkins combines the gender problematic with the race question and tries to negotiate her way within a central paradox of her time: the denial of race difference coupled with an emphasis on the special role of the African American.

Hopkins made a brief comeback as editor of the Boston-based *New Era Magazine* in 1916, together with Walter Wallace, her former colleague from the *Colored American Magazine*. The magazine attempted to recreate and revitalize the goals of the former publication, with a series on "Men of Vision" and the fragment of a novel, "Topsy Templeton." Hopkins also planned a column, entitled "Helps for Young Artists," which showed her continuing concern for their advancement. Meta Warrick-Fuller, the magazine's art editor, called for some kind of new writers' union when she "urged black artists to form groups in order to experiment with suggestions advanced in the column" (Johnson and Johnson, *Propaganda*, 67). *New Era Magazine* ceased publication after two issues and received hardly any comment, not even by Du Bois, who had commented on the changes and passing of the *Colored American Magazine* earlier. Johnson and Johnson speculate that he might have seen the *New Era Magazine* as a potential rival to his own *Crisis* (68).

The *New Era Magazine* is subtitled "An Illustrated Monthly Devoted to the World-Wide Interests of the Colored Race." Its flyleaf announces that it is

> devoted exclusively to the best interests of the colored race, not alone in this country, but throughout the world. The rapid progress made by the race in this country during the past twenty to twenty-five years, as well as present-day progress will be fully and accurately shown. The magazine will deal fully and frankly with all questions affecting the real progress of the race, and will

do its utmost to assist in developing the literature, science, music, art, religion, facts, fiction and tradition of the race throughout the world. (April 1916)

Articles that were being prepared included essays about Africa, Puerto Rico, Haiti, color prejudice, mechanic arts, colored masonry, women of color and the suffrage movement, Negro artists in Europe, reforms in Liberia, education, music, practical help for young men in business, hints to young artists, reminiscences of early days, and business. The international and national concerns clearly distinguish it from the *Colored American Magazine* under Fred R. Moore. The overall design of the magazine also documents Hopkins's continuing concern with matters of race, politics, and literature well beyond her more famous years at the *Colored American Magazine*.

Hopkins can be credited with two articles about "Men of Vision," which continue the earlier "Famous Men of the Negro Race" series. The articles treat Mark René Demortie and Reverend Leonard Andrew Grimes, while an article planned for the Easter number was to be about Henry Highland Garnet. Hopkins wrote a serial novel, "Topsy Templeton," of which two installments still exist. One short story, "Converting Fanny," is signed Sarah A. Allen and shows a considerable development in subject matter and writing style. It is likely that she wrote the sketch about Crispus Attucks that opened the second number of the magazine. The prospectus also mentions a series called "Facts Pertaining to the Early Greatness of the African Race," planned for future issues. The title and contents were directly taken from Hopkins's *Primer of Facts*. It is not clear why the magazine failed after only two issues, especially since the third number was well planned and organized.

Passionately committed as she was to racial uplift, black history, and the concerns of colored women, her life seemed to lose its momentum after the failure of the *New Era Magazine*. The years of relative silence about her between 1905 and 1916, and the years of absolute silence about her from 1916 to 1930 cannot be reconstructed. The silence enveloping Hopkins in her later years is a frustrating one. Her early career as a singer, playwright, and performer and her later career as a writer and journalist were dependent upon the presence of an audience. To be forced to give up all this must have demanded a high price on her part. I see the fifty-seven-year-old Hopkins frantically trying to get the money to start another magazine. Much thinking and time went into the organization of a group of supporters and contributors. The fact that she managed to put out at least two issues speaks of her passionate commitment. The quality of the journal speaks of her highly developed intellect and the restlessness that made it all possible. Her failure, however, if we can see it as such at all, speaks of the relentless world of business, where success is measured in financial, not in ideological, figures. If we say that Hopkins failed in putting out more issues of the magazine or more of her own writing, we can reverse this line of thinking and argue that she succeeded against great odds in doing what she did: editing two journals and publishing four novels, several short stories, one play, and numerous articles.

Notes

1. For general information about the *Colored American Magazine*, see Johnson and Johnson, *Propaganda* 1–16; Johnson and Johnson, "Away from Accommodation"; Bullock 106–118; Charles S. Johnson; Braithwaite; Meier; Du Bois; Schneider 57–81.

2. For a discussion of the so-called "quality journals"—the *Atlantic Monthly*, *The Century Magazine*, and *Harper's Monthly Magazine*—see Brodhead, *Cultures*, esp. 107–141.

3. Brodhead argues: "Writing always takes place within some completely concrete cultural situation, a situation that surrounds it with some particular landscape of institutional structures, affiliates it with some particular group from among the array of contemporary groupings, and installs it in some group-based world of understandings, practices, and values. But this setting provides writing with more than backdrop. A work of writing comes to its particular form of existence in interaction with the network of relations that surround it: in any actual instance, writing orients itself in or against some understanding of what writing is, does, and is good for that is culturally composed and derived" (*Cultures* 8).

4. This article is part of a book-length project on the life and literature of Pauline E. Hopkins. Her use of Shirley S. Shadrach as another pen name can be proven beyond doubt.

5. The development of scientific racism in the nineteenth century and its various movements and uses have been explored in numerous studies, among which I consider those by Gossett, Fredrickson, and Stanton especially helpful.

6. Much of my information about Washington is taken from Louis R. Harlan's two-volume biography.

7. For detailed information, see Harlan, *Wizard* 32–62, esp. 44–48; and Lewis, esp. 299–304. See also Scheiner, esp. 172, for Booker T. Washington's influence on Theodore Roosevelt.

8. For information on Cooper, see Gabel and Hutchinson. Details about the works of Coppin, Wells-Barnett, and Terrell can be obtained from their autobiographies: *Reminiscences of School Life, and Hints on Teaching* (Coppin), *Crusade for Justice* (Wells-Barnett's autobiography, edited by her daughter Alfreda M. Duster), and *A Colored Woman in a White World* (Terrell).

9. See Doreski; and Lois Brown, 169–206, for a discussion of these essays. Brown's dissertation (1993) contains valuable and reliable information about Hopkins and a very good evaluation of her career.

10. See Schneider 58; Harlan, *Booker T. Washington: The Making of a Leader* 291; Meier, esp. 77–79.

11. My great thanks go to Jessica Metzler from Florida State University for calling my attention to the discovery of these letters at Fisk and to Ms. Beth Howse from Special Collections at Fisk University for sending them to me.

12. For the influence of Booker T. Washington on African American magazines, see Johnson and Johnson, *Propaganda and Aesthetics* and "Away from Accomodation"; Meier; Thornbrough.

13. See Roscoe Conkling Simmons's letter to Booker T. Washington of December 13,

1904 (Harlan and Smock, ed., *Booker T. Washington Papers*, v. 8, 154–56), in which he writes, for example: "The world has long ago placed the laurel wreath of leadership, not only of a race, but of a thought, on your brow, and as long as I can see to write, none, shall disturb it" (155). This fulsome praise was caused by some unfavorable remarks about Washington in the *Voice of the Negro*. See also Braithwaite 26; Meier 70.

Works Cited

"Announcement." *Colored American Magazine* 1.1 (May 1900): n.p.
"Biographies of the Officers of the New Management of Our Magazine." *Colored American Magazine* 6.6 (May/June 1903): 443–49.
Barber, J. Max. "Shall the Press Be Free?" *Voice of the Negro* 3.10 (Oct. 1906): 391.
Bederman, Gail. *Manliness and Civilization: A Cultural History of Gender and Race in the United States, 1880–1917*. Chicago: University of Chicago Press, 1995.
Braithwaite, William Stanley. "Negro America's First Magazine." *Negro Digest* (Dec. 1947): 21–26.
Brodhead, Richard. *Cultures of Letters: Scenes of Reading and Writing in Nineteenth-Century America*. Chicago: University of Chicago Press, 1993.
Brown, Lois A. "Essential Histories / Determined Identities: Images of Race and Origin in the Works of Pauline Hopkins." Ph.D. dissertation, Boston College, 1993.
Bullock, Penelope. *The Afro-American Press, 1938–1909*. Baton Rouge: Louisiana University Press, 1981.
Carby, Hazel. *Reconstructing Womanhood: The Emergence of the Afro-American Woman Novelist*. New York: Oxford University Press, 1987.
———. *Contending Forces: A Romance Illustrative of Negro Life North and South*. Boston: Colored Co-operative Publishing Company, 1900. Rpt. Miami: Mnemosyne, 1969. Rpt. with afterword by Gwendolyn Brooks, Carbondale: Southern Illinois University Press, 1978. Rpt., ed. Richard Yarborough, Schomburg Library of Nineteenth-Century Black Women Writers, New York: Oxford University Press, 1988.
Coppin, Fanny Jackson. *Reminiscences of School Life, and Hints on Teaching*. Vol. 13, *Women in American Protestant Religion 1800–1930*. New York: Garland, 1987.
Doreski, C. K. *Writing America Black: Race Rhetoric in the Public Sphere*. Cambridge: Cambridge University Press, 1998.
Du Bois, W. E. B. "The Colored Magazine in America." *Crisis* 5–6 (Nov. 1912): 33–35.
Duster, Alfreda M., ed. *Crusade for Justice: The Autobiography of Ida B. Wells*. Negro American Biographies and Autobiographies. Chicago: University of Chicago Press, 1970.
"Editorial and Publishers' Announcements." *Colored American Magazine* 1.1 (May 1900): 60–64.
"Editorial and Publishers' Announcements." *Colored American Magazine* 6.6 (May/June 1903): 466–67.
Editorial. *Colored American Magazine* 8.6 (June 1905): 342–43.
Elliott, R. S. "The Story of Our Magazine." *Colored American Magazine* 3.1 (May 1901): 43–77.
Fredrickson, George M. *The Black Image in the White Mind: The Debate on Afro-American Character and Destiny, 1817–1914*. New York: Harper, 1971.
Gabel, Leona C. *From Slavery to the Sorbonne and Beyond: The Life and Writings of Anna J. Cooper*. Northampton, Mass.: Smith College, 1982.
Gossett, Thomas F. *Race: The History of an Idea in America*. Dallas: Southern Methodist University Press, 1963.
Harlan, Louis R. "Booker T. Washington and *The Voice of the Negro*, 1904–1907." *Journal of Southern History* 45 (Feb. 1979): 45–62.
———. *Booker T. Washington: The Making of a Leader. 1856–1901*. New York: Oxford University Press, 1972.

———. *Booker T. Washington: The Wizard of Tuskegee. 1901–1915.* New York: Oxford University Press, 1983.
Harlan, Louis R., and Raymond W. Smock, eds. *The Booker T. Washington Papers*, 13 vols. Urbana: University of Illinois Press, 1977.
Hopkins, Pauline E. "Converting Fanny." *New Era Magazine* (Feb. 1916): 33–34. Published under the name Sarah A. Allen.
———. "The Dark Races of the Twentieth Century," a series published in *Voice of the Negro*: I. Oceania: The Dark-Hued Inhabitants of New Guinea, the Bismarck Archipelago, New Hebrides, Solomon Islands, Fiji Islands, Polynesia, Samoa and Hawaii," 2.2 (Feb. 1905): 108–15; II. "The Malay Peninsula, Borneo, Java, Sumatra and the Philippines," 2.3 (March 05): 187–91; III. "The Yellow Race: Siam, China, Japan, Korea, Thibet," 2.5 (May 05): 330–35; IV. "Africa: Abysinians, Egyptians, Nilotic Class, Berbers, Kaffirs, Hottentots, Africans of Northern Tropics (including Negroes of Central, Eastern and Western Africa), Negroes of the United States," 2.6 (June 05): 415–18; VI. "The North American Indian," Conclusion, 2.7 (July 05): 459–63.
———. "Famous Men of the Negro Race," a series published in the *Colored American Magazine*: "Toussaint L'Overture," 2.1 (Nov. 1900): 9–24; "Hon. Frederick Douglass," 2.2 (Dec. 1900): 121–32; "William Wells Brown," 2.3 (Jan. 1901): 232–36; "Robert Browne Elliott," 2.4 (Feb. 1901): 294–301; "Edwin Garrison Walker," 2.5 (Mar. 1901): 358–66; "Lewis Hayden," 2.6 (Apr. 1901): 473–77; "Charles Lenox Remond," 3.1 (May 1901): 34–39; "Sargeant Wm. H. Carney," 3.2 (June 1901): 84–89; "Hon. John Mercer Langston," 3.3 (July 1901): 177–84; "Senator Blanche K. Bruce," 3.4 (Aug. 1901): 257–61; "Robert Morris," 3.5 (Sept. 1901): 337–42; "Booker T. Washington," 3.6 (Oct. 1901): 436–41.
———. "How a New York Newspaper Man Entertained a Number of Colored Ladies and Gentlemen at Dinner in the Revere House, Boston, and How the Colored American League Was Started." *Colored American Magazine* 7.1 (Jan. 1904): 151–60.
———. *The Magazine Novels of Pauline Hopkins*, ed. Hazel Carby. Schomburg Library of Nineteenth-Century Black Women Writers. New York: Oxford University Press, 1988.
———. "Men of Vision: I. Mark Rene Demortie." *New Era Magazine* 1.1 (Feb. 1916): 35–39.
———. "Men of Vision: II. Leonard A. Grimes." *New Era Magazine* 1.2 (Mar. 1916): 99–105.
———. "The New York Subway." *Voice of the Negro* (Dec. 1904): 605, 608–12.
———. *A Primer of Facts Pertaining to the Early Greatness of the African Race and the Possibility of Restoration by Its Descendants—with Epilogue.* Cambridge, Mass.: P. E. Hopkins, 1905.
———. "Topsy Templeton." *New Era Magazine* (Feb. 1916): 11–20, 48; Mar. 1916, 75–84.
Hutchinson, Louise Daniel. *Anna Julia Cooper: A Voice from the South.* Washington, D.C.: Smithsonian, 1981.
"In the Editor's Sanctum." *Colored American Magazine* 7.5 (May 1904): 382–83.
Johnson, Abby Arthur, and Ronald M. Johnson. "Away from Accommodation: Radical Editors and Protest Journalism, 1900–1910." *Journal of Negro History* 62 (1977): 325–38.
Johnson, Abby Arthur and Ronald Maberry Johnson. *Propaganda and Aesthetics: The Literary Politics of Afro-American Magazines in the Twentieth Century.* Amherst: University of Massachusetts Press, 1979.
Johnson, Charles S. "The Rise of the Negro Magazine." *Journal of Negro History* 13 (1928): 7–21.
Lewis, David Levering, ed. *W. E. B. Du Bois: A Reader.* New York: Henry Holt, 1995.
Meier, August. "Booker T. Washington and the Negro Press." *Journal of Negro History* 13 (Jan. 1953): 67–90.
"Our Christmas Number." *Voice of the Negro* 1.11 (Nov. 1904): 467.
"Publishers' Announcements." *Colored American Magazine* 7.11 (Nov. 1904): 700.
"Publishers' Announcements." *Colored American Magazine* 8.3 (March 1905): 164.
Scheiner, Seth M. "President Theodore Roosevelt and the Negro, 1901–1908." *Journal of Negro History* 47 (1962): 169–82.

Schneider, Mark R. *Boston Confronts Jim Crow, 1890–1920.* Boston: Northeastern University Press, 1997.

Shockley, Ann Allen. *Afro-American Women Writers 1746–1933: An Anthology and Critical Guide.* Boston: G. K. Hall, 1988.

Stanton, William. *The Leopard's Spots: Scientific Attitudes Toward Race in America 1815–59.* Chicago: University of Chicago Press, 1960.

Tate, Claudia. "Hopkins, Pauline E." In *The Oxford Companion to African American Literature*, ed. Andrews et al., 366–67.

Terrell, Mary Church. *A Colored Woman in a White World.* 1940. Rpt., ed. Nellie McKay, African-American Women Writers, 1910–1940. New York: Hall, 1996.

Thornbrough, Emma L. "More Light on Booker T. Washington and the New York *Age*." *Journal of Negro History* 43 (1958): 34–49.

Washington, Booker T. *Up from Slavery. Three Negro Classics.* New York: Avon, 1965. 203–205.

Letters (Fisk University Library, Special Collection):
John C. Freund to William L. Dupree, 19 November 1903
John C. Freund to William L. Dupree, 27 January 1904
John C. Freund to William L. Dupree, 28 January 1904
John C. Freund to Pauline E. Hopkins, 11 February 1904
John C. Freund to Pauline E. Hopkins, 18 February 1904
John C. Freund to Pauline E. Hopkins, 5 March 1904
John C. Freund to Pauline E. Hopkins, 12 March 1904
John C. Freund to Pauline E. Hopkins, 14 March 1904
John C. Freund to Pauline E. Hopkins, 16 March 1904
John C. Freund to Pauline E. Hopkins, 17 March 1904
John C. Freund to Pauline E. Hopkins, 18 March 1904
John C. Freund to Pauline E. Hopkins, 24 March 1904
John C. Freund to Pauline E. Hopkins, 25 March 1904
John C. Freund to Pauline E. Hopkins, 28 March 1904
John C. Freund to William L. Dupree, 31 March 1904
John C. Freund to William L. Dupree, 6 April 1904
John C. Freund to Pauline E. Hopkins, 7 April 1904
John C. Freund to Pauline E. Hopkins, 11 April 1904
John C. Freund to Pauline E. Hopkins, 16 April 1904
Pauline E. Hopkins to William Monroe Trotter, 16 April 1905

"Editorial and Publishers' Announcements"
Colored American Magazine, May/June 1903

It is with great pleasure and satisfaction that Messrs. William H. Dupree, William O. West and Jesse W. Watkins, the new management of the Colored Co-operative Publishing Company, are enabled to announce the fact that on May 15, 1903, they purchased the copyright, title, and all bookrights, records, plates, cuts and other property of the Colored Co-operative Publishing Company, and will continue issuing the magazine under its old name, THE COLORED AMERICAN MAGAZINE.

Owing to legal complications arising in settling the affairs of the old board of directors, the April number did not appear, and we find it advisable to issue the May and June numbers as a double number.

At the cost of many anxious moments and sleepless nights, when not a star of hope was visible in the horizon, God has permitted us to save this enterprise to our race. Envy and covetousness have sat with us in council, but even as did the Christian martyrs of old forgive their tormentors the tortures inflicted upon them, so do we forgive our enemies. At some future day we hope to be able to tell our true story to our readers, who will then give us the full sympathy of their warm hearts. We know that this is their due because of the patience they have always exhibited when we have asked their kind indulgence for apparent negligence on our part. But, at present, we can only ask that our friends will trust us, feeling that the new management will do its best to restore public confidence in this enterprise and satisfy the demands of all those who have honored us with their patronage. When adversity presses on every side we realize that "a friend in need is a friend indeed."

For three years this enterprise has been an inspiring example of race progress; the new management hope to make it a greater inspiration to the race than it has been in the past. Its future success and length of life depend much on the energy, capability and honesty of its new management, but more largely upon the earnest, sincere and generous interest of its friends and the public. We shall continue the publication of the magazine under the direction of some of those who gave the best of their time and talents to promote its former growth.

Recognizing the immediate need of a race journal of high standard, we appeal to the generous public to aid us in our endeavor to uphold the banner of race progress. We recognize, also, that public confidence has been strained, but not by those who now seek to establish the magazine on a basis of honesty and integrity toward all.

We shall endeavor, after the first issue, to have the magazine ready for delivery, promptly two or three days before the first of every month, thereby insuring all patrons their copies absolutely ON TIME.

Only partly satisfied with the success of the magazine in the past, we shall endeavor to excel all former efforts.

We shall print only that literature which is helpful, practical and beneficial to good home influences by the best known colored authors. Our stories will be clean and healthy. Our articles will have in them the sparkle and freshness of originality. Expense will be secondary to the wishes of our readers. Religion, science, music and art will, in every respect, represent what is best in a permanent literary success. Miss Hopkins' serial, "Of One Blood," will be continued in the double number for May and June, and readers will be able to take up the thread of the story from where it was broken when the April issue was suspended.

The entire management and office force will consist of colored Americans of high standing in the community.

Correspondents are requested to write concerning manuscripts, already forwarded or prospective, photographs and all other matter of interest to themselves and the management. The removal from Park Square to W. Concord Street has, of course, caused some confusion in office routine, but we hope to be in good business trim in a few weeks. Manuscript should be written on one side only. Enclose postage when wishing its return. If in sympathy with us, write us a letter of approval. Address all communications to

THE COLORED AMERICAN MAGAZINE is not only National but International in character. Our correspondents include patrons in China, Hawaii, Manila, West Indies and Africa. We consider it our highest privilege to do whatever we have the power to do to advance the best interests of the race everywhere. All that God wishes us to do is what we can. This we do gladly. Some time ago we received the following letter from Mr. A. Kirkland Soga, editor of "Izwi Labanut" (The Voice of the People), a weekly native organ published in England at East London, South Africa, and the sole medium of native opinion in the colony.

After receiving this letter we perfected arrangements with Mr. Soga for a series of articles on "The Ethiopian of the Twentieth Century," fully illustrated by special photographs. The series begins with this number.

Dear Miss Hopkins:—

Our attention has been drawn to your work in the COLORED AMERICAN MAGAZINE by Mr. Harry Dean, a young American travelling in this country, who gives us a very flattering account of your work on behalf of the colored race. We have therefore considered the question of enlisting your sympathies and your pen through the columns of the magazine, on behalf of your black and colored brethren in South Africa. We are sending you a bundle of our paper 'Izwi Labantu,' from which you will see that the conditions in this country are similar to those existing in the reconstruction days in Southern America, with the difference that, at present, there are only two papers representing the native press in South Africa, viz., our own, which is not yet in a position to combat successfully the phalanx of opposition of the anti-native press in South Africa, and the 'South African Spectator,' which is run in a small way by Mr. F. L. S. Pereguino at No. 10 Hanover Street, Cape Town. You will see therefore, that the natives of this country are poorly represented. After reading the papers which will give you an insight into the main questions of education, franchise, religion and tenure conditions, etc., we would be glad if you would communicate with us on any topic on which you require enlightenment. You might apply to His Majesty's Stationery Department, London, for the Blue Books of the Cape, Natal and Rhodesia, which are usually compiled as favorably to the Government side as possible. But there is, of course, the other side which I intend, if possible, to present to the American and British public in the form of a book which I would like to complete early next year. Meantime we wish that the attention of the reading public of America should be directed to South Africa, and that we should co-operate by extending hands across the sea.

A. KIRKLAND SOGA.

"Yours for the Indian Cause": Gertrude Bonnin's Activist Editing at *The American Indian Magazine*, 1915–1919

JAMES H. COX

GERTRUDE Simmons Bonnin's current literary reputation rests on her work in the years 1900 to 1902, when Bonnin, in her midtwenties and under the self-given Lakota name Zitkala-Ša (Red Bird), published articles in *Harper's Magazine*, *Atlantic Monthly*, and *Everybody's Magazine*, and a collection of *ohunkakan* entitled *Old Indian Legends* (1901).[1] The articles were collected and published as *American Indian Stories* (1921). Literary scholars have assessed Bonnin's work by focusing their attention on this three-year period of literary production that precedes her conversion to Catholicism, her role as an activist and public intellectual in the pro-assimilation Society of American Indians (S.A.I.), and her campaign with General Richard Henry Pratt, the founder of Carlisle Industrial Training School, against the Native religious practices that involved peyote. The "old legends" and "stories" tell only a small part of Bonnin's history. From 1915 to 1919, Bonnin was also a contributing editor and, for four issues, the editor general of the S.A.I.'s magazine. A consideration of her service as an editor provides the opportunity to review her work as a writer of fiction and autobiographical essays from a broader political and intellectual context. The expanded focus on her entire career as author and activist illustrates that her relationship to both Native and non-Native cultural and intellectual traditions was a constant negotiation characterized by many shifts between acceptance of, resistance to, and compromise with those traditions. In many camps and, simultaneously, in a camp all her own, Bonnin moved between coalitions and alliances, between the West and the East, and between tribe and pan-Indian community, in a career as activist and writer that continued until her death. Any attempt by scholars to construct Bonnin as consistently defying or accommodating a single ideology will not succeed in revealing the complexities of her search for a viable future for American Indians in the United States.

Several issues of concern to many contemporary Native intellectuals must be addressed before proceeding with a discussion of Bonnin. Much recent scholarly work in Native studies addresses a consistent shortcoming in many articles and books published on Native Americans and Native American literature: the scholar's lack of familiarity with tribal and Native intellectual contexts. The most serious scholarly transgression involves writing about Native Americans and Native American literature without privileging, or even acknowledging, the work of Native scholars and other Native creative writers.[2] Native literary studies is an area in which a lack of wide reading in the field is still forgiven by conference organizers, editors at scholarly journals, and university presses. Robert Allen Warrior (Osage), in *Tribal Secrets: Recovering American Indian Intellectual Traditions* (1995), proposes that in any study of work by Native authors, the "critical interpretation of those writings can proceed primarily from Indian sources" (xvi). He is interested in "the ways American Indian intellectuals write about and speak to each other about the role of intellectual work in the social, political, economic, cultural, and spiritual struggle for an American Indian future" (xvi). In contrast to much academic discourse that either forecloses on an American Indian future or writes toward the perceived "end" (removal, Wounded Knee) of a particular kind of Indian existence, Warrior orients his work toward the future, even though his work is historical.

Relevant to this study of Bonnin is the first of four major periods, identified by Warrior, for public Native intellectuals in the twentieth century. During this period, which for the purposes of Warrior's study runs from 1890 to 1916, prominent Native intellectuals such as Carlos Montezuma (Apache) and Charles Alexander Eastman (Mdewakanton Dakota) helped form the S.A.I. The members of the S.A.I., Warrior explains, were part of a generation "[f]aced with the prospect of total dispossession if Natives continued to resist the U.S. government" (7), and their efforts to organize represented "the first coming together of Native intellectuals in a specific political project" (10). This project was integrationist and assimilationist, though the history of the S.A.I.'s magazine, first called *The Quarterly Journal of the Society of American Indians* and then *The American Indian Magazine*, reveals a lively public discussion between Indians about what integration and assimilation meant. In particular, the accommodationist tone of the early issues shifts substantially when, in 1918, the year Carlisle closes as an Indian boarding school and the Native American Church is incorporated in Oklahoma, Gertrude Bonnin becomes the editor for four of the final five issues. A principal critical premise of this article is that we can understand Bonnin's work as an editor most clearly by focusing on her role within the context of continuing and emerging Native intellectual traditions in the era in which assimilation was federal policy. The discussion will benefit most clearly from the work of Native scholars and creative writers who addressed or are addressing the same issues as Bonnin: education, religious worship, literary self-representation, political self-determination, treaty rights, sovereignty, the legal status of Indians, the social and cultural status of Native women, and the social and cultural disruption of Native lives that Bonnin understood to be caused by the Indian boarding school system, the government ward status of most Indians, the dictatorship of a corrupt Bureau of Indian Affairs (B.I.A.), the reservation system, and peyote use.

Bonnin's life spanned a series of often abrupt changes in Indian Country that helped define the historical context in which she addressed these issues. She was born in 1876, the year that Lakota and Cheyenne warriors under the command of the Hunkpapa Lakota leader Sitting Bull defeated General George Armstrong Custer at the Battle of the Greasy Grass.[3] The military victory over invading U.S. troops was not prophetic of future successes for the Plains Indians and the many bands of the Sioux, including Bonnin's own people on the Yankton Reservation.[4] The assassination the following summer of the Oglala Lakota leader Crazy Horse, and, in 1890, the assassination of Sitting Bull and the massacre of Big Foot's band of Minneconjou Lakotas at Wounded Knee, helped to make continued military resistance on the Plains difficult. In terms of education, Bonnin experienced first hand the federal government's assimilation policy as a student at boarding schools and as a teacher at Carlisle. In the area of religion, she saw the height of Sioux participation in the Ghost Dance, the suppression of traditional Native religious practices, such as the Sun Dance on the Uintah-Ouray Ute Reservation, where she spent fourteen years, and the creation of the Native American Church. She also defended in print her "pagan" beliefs, then converted to Catholicism and, possibly, was a practicing Mormon at some time during her life.[5] In the political arena, Congress passed both the Manypenny Agreement, which claimed the Black Hills for the United States and reinforced Sioux dependence on the federal government, and the General Allotment Act, which instituted a policy that continued until 1934 of alloting tribal lands to families and individuals. In 1924, Congress granted citizenship to all Native Americans. Self-representation and other identity issues were also at stake during this period. The Wild West shows, in which Sitting Bull participated, gained international popularity, while non-Native scholars and "friends of the Indian" reform organizations dominated by non-Natives continued to have a vast influence on the ways in which the general public viewed Indians. The reform organizations also had influence on federal policy. Bonnin saw the publication in 1928 of the Meriam Report, which contributed substantially to a reform of Indian policy that became the Indian New Deal. Before Bonnin died in 1938, the Collier administration at the B.I.A. began, and in 1934, Congress passed the Wheeler-Howard/Indian Reorganization Act, which ended allotment and sanctioned the reconstitution of tribal governments.[6] This brief history should suggest neither unremitting disaster nor that Bonnin's life ended at a point of clear reversal of the U.S. government's policies of assimilation, treaty abrogation, land seizure, and cultural warfare. But as a Native intellectual and community activist throughout much of her life, Bonnin was often actively engaged in these events, and her writings were always embedded in this history.

Negotiating with the Civilizing Machine, 1900 to 1915

Two critical readings of Zitkala-Ša's work during the three years she published in mainstream magazines tend to dominate recent scholarship. There is interest in her subversion of sentimental literary modes and in the ways in which *American Indian Stories* is overtly defiant of the federal government's assimilation program in the Indian boarding schools. These articles assess Zitkala-Ša in relation to Anglo women authors, with the exception of P. Jane Hafen's (Taos Pueblo) "Zitkala Ša: Sentimentality and Sovereignty," in which Hafen situates Zitkala-Ša's work within the context of her commitment to tribal sovereignty, and an article by Dorothea Susag that traces the influence of Zitkala-Ša's Native language and culture in the autobiographical essays.[7] The orientation of the articles is toward finding Zitkala-Ša's place in the canon, rather than her place in Indian Country, which Craig Womack (Oklahoma Creek-Cherokee) insists is a more important project for our understanding of Native writers.[8] Generally, scholars view *Old Indian Legends* as an affirmation of Sioux culture and a subversive critique of colonialism. Jeanne Smith reads *Old Indian Legends* from a more specifically Native critical position by explaining the ways in which "Zitkala-Ša explores both the enabling and the destructive potential of the trickster for the future of her culture" (47). These articles contribute to our understanding of Zitkala-Ša during the years when her writing is more interesting in a contemporary critical context, in which finding subversion in the work of marginalized authors is a common project. Zitkala-Ša's rejection of assimilation, of the violence of the "civilizing machine," help to establish her critical reputation as an anti-assimilationist (*American Indian Stories* 66). In the final line of her series of three essays about her experience as a student and teacher, she writes, "few there are who have paused to question whether real life or long-lasting death lies beneath this semblance of civilization" (99). Following her two years as a teacher at Carlisle, Bonnin intended to collect stories at Yankton in an effort of cultural affirmation that directly challenges her boarding school experience.

Bonnin's literary career does not end with the publication of the legends and stories, her marriage at Yankton in 1902 to Captain Raymond T. Bonnin (Yankton Dakota), and her subsequent move to Utah. In addition to the poems she published in the S.A.I.'s periodical, Bonnin collaborated in 1913 with William F. Hanson, a music professor at Brigham Young University, on *The Sun Dance Opera*. The opera is another attempt to negotiate different cultural traditions, to alter both traditions in order to validate Native lives and beliefs within the context of a medium of creative expression privileged by the majority culture. Hafen writes, "*The Sun Dance Opera* reveals the sometimes turbulent cultural waters that Bonnin navigated in her life. Often she seemed caught between validating her indigenous beliefs and seeking public approval" (xx). The performance of a sacred ritual in a Western medium and for a mostly non-Native audience would have made the *Opera* controversial even in the second decade of the twentieth century, and this kind of exploitation is frequently under scrutiny in contemporary Native intellectual contexts. In *Manifest Manners* (1994), Gerald Vizenor (Anishinabe) critiques what he calls "the consumer sun dances" that for some members of the American Indian Movement became a performance of resistance rather than a spiritual ceremony (154). The consumer sun dances are also popular with "wannabes," non-Native cultural tourists who make playing Indian a weekend hobby.[9] Vizenor's point is that a religious ceremony in a nonreligious context—on a theatre stage, in front of television cameras, or for the benefit of tourists—is no longer a religious ceremony. Though Bonnin and Hanson reserved places in the opera for the performance of traditional Native songs and dances, the possibility of the exploitation of Native peoples and cultures might have troubled her future colleagues in the S.A.I., particularly another Sioux, Chauncey Yellow Robe, who contributed a critique of Wild West shows to the magazine.[10] The *Opera* relies on a sentimental plot with a male villain, Sweet Singer, and two women under duress, the abandoned Shoshone Maid and Winona, who loves Ohiya but has Sweet Singer's unwanted courtship with which to contend. Contemporary Native scholars such as Womack and Elizabeth Cook-Lynn (Crow Creek Dakota) suggest that aesthetic success or failure might be less important than the fact that Bonnin fashions a response to colonial incursions into Indian Country, in this case the suppression of the Sun Dance in Utah. The opera includes cultural traditions that have been substantially compromised, but there is an insistence, however muted, that the Sun Dance has meaning. This affirmation of meaning is both a refusal to capitulate to the majority culture's aesthetic expectations and a refusal to surrender a tribal worldview.[11]

Vizenor's discussion of Luther Standing Bear (Oglala Lakota), the author, actor, teacher, and activist whose shifting critiques and accommodations of the majority culture are similar to Bonnin's, suggests a way to read Bonnin's pre-S.A.I. work through the lens of a Native intellectual. Vizenor writes: "The postindian warriors encounter their enemies with the same courage in literature as their ancestors once evinced on horses, and they create their stories with a new sense of survivance. The warriors bear the simulations of their time and counter the manifest manners of domination" (3–4). Zitkala-Ša performs similar acts of courage, as she works in her early stories toward survival and resistance (survivance). Though Zitkala-Ša makes different literary decisions than Ella Deloria, another author from Yankton, she counters domination of her culture and people by making strategic forays into the enemy's territory: sentimental literature and opera.[12] Survivance, to use Vizenor's term, *is* the negotiation, not a permanent solution or "terminal creed," but a process that requires constant vigilance and frequent adjustments of strategy. The opera is the only creative work Bonnin made public during her fourteen years in Utah, where her work in the community of Uintah-Ouray eventually leads her to membership in the S.A.I. and a national presence in American Indian politics.

Liberating the "Little Peoples," 1915–1919

The official beginning of the S.A.I. was a meeting organized by Fayette A. McKenzie, a professor of economics and sociology, in April 1911 at Ohio State University.[13] The group McKenzie invited to campus was comprised of "progressives," those American Indians who desired a reform organization run by Indians and who, Hazel Hertzberg explains, "believed in education, hard work, and in adapting their attitudes, values, and habits of life to those of the larger American society" (31).[14] They were proassimilation and prointegration, often to the point of being overtly antitribal, and when they began publishing their magazine in 1913, the editorials maintained a focus on this central ideological message.

Bonnin became an editor during the tenure of Arthur C. Parker (Seneca), and we can most clearly understand her editorial work in contrast to his vision for the magazine and his ideas about the future of American Indians.[15] Parker edited the magazine during its first five and one-half years of publication. He insisted that the responsibility for solving the "Indian problem" rested with Indians, who needed to "awaken" and "improve" themselves. "Awaken" and "improve" were key terms in the era's reform discourse and code words for assimilation. Parker's other interests included the need for Indians to have equal access to all levels of education and to be granted status as U.S. citizens. He also advocated for the creation of a court of claims specifically for Indians, a codification of the laws and policies that applied to Indians, and the gradual termination of the B.I.A. Most urgently, he believed in the value of the organization as a pan-Indian community, as a group of American Indians determining their own future, and he protected the S.A.I. by muting criticism of non-Natives, demanding loyalty to the organization, and struggling vigorously to obviate any factionalism.

When Bonnin became editor, she was less willing than Parker to forgive any kind of attack on Native Americans, more strident in her condemnation of injustice and corruption, and more willing to pursue the resolution of local, tribal grievances rather than reiterate the organization's national platform. The magazine's content, whether or not authored by Bonnin, became less conciliatory, but more romanticized. As editor, Bonnin also foregrounded her interests in literature and community activism, and in terms of policy, she used her position as editor to publicize her antipeyote stance. Finally, in the issues she edited, Bonnin gave a more prominent position to the Native and non-Native women who played a role in local, national, and global affairs. An overall assessment of her editorial work suggests she understood editing as a continuation of her role as an activist invested in the future of Native communities. However, like her literary production, her editorial work was neither consistently resistant to nor accommodating of non-Native attempts to compromise, assault, or annihilate those same Native communities.

Parker's voice dominates the magazine, beginning with the first issue in January–April 1913. Though the initial all-male editorial board included influential thinkers and writers such as Montezuma and John M. Oskison (Cherokee), who published three novels in the 1920s, Parker appears to have been the sole author of the frequently long editorials (twenty or more pages) that begin each issue. He established the ideological position of the magazine by focusing his editorials on the "uplift" of the race and its necessary assimilation into the society and culture of the United States. He writes in the "Editorial Comment" in the first issue that the aim of the all-Indian organization is "to place the race in the position of a constructing, producing factor in civilization" (7). Along with many of the writers published in the magazine, Parker believed that education was the key to uplifting the race. By education, he did not mean the limited curriculum at Indian boarding schools, but the formalized Western education to which Anglos had greater access. The vocational education of the Indian boarding schools was inadequate, in the S.A.I.'s opinion, to prepare Indians to compete in a world largely controlled by non-Natives. Parker actually wanted access to more, not less, Western education.

Parker's carefully constructed argument for assimilation was defensive, apologetic, and paternalistic. In the April–June 1913 issue, he writes, "The fundamental principle of Americanism since its earliest beginning has been to produce a uniform civilization. The base of that civilization, better termed *ethnic* culture, was and is English" (104). He continues by discussing a hypothetical immigrant from Finland: "Later, as he became acculturated, he might return to a consideration of the ways of his fathers and seek to commemorate them, but purely as a matter of racial pride or patriotic interest, and not as something to be revived and made again an active culture to be lived and followed" (104). Parker's nonthreatening posture assures his Native and Anglo audience that Indians have little interest in remaining Indians. Following complete assimilation, Parker suggests, any identification of a person of Native heritage as Indian will be intellectual, not actively cultural. In addition, his editorial inquiry into the future of American Indians is as paternalistic as the voices of the non-Native reform organizations. In his second editorial, in a section subtitled "The Social Tyranny of Tribal Life," Parker even distances himself rhetorically from "the Indian people":

> It is not difficult to see why the student carefully educated, trained and taught in all the ways of civilized life does not prosper as he should normally in normal communities when he returns to the reservation. He alone can not always compel all the rest of the community to see that he is right and that they are wrong. This brings [sic] to the proposition, then, that to bring about the civilization we desire to the Indian people, where they are, we must make the social life of the reservation the same as that found in communities we are pleased to call civilized. (108)

For Parker, Anglo culture is normative, and he was antitribal in that he saw no future in the social segregation of the reservation system. Though the S.A.I. advocated for the settlement of land claims, their concern was that the Department of the Interior allow "competent" Indians to control individual allotments.[16]

Throughout his tenure as editor, Parker qualifies his theories of assimilation and race relations by making contrasts between American Indians, African Americans, and recent groups of immigrants, for example, but he steadfastly maintains his focus on the issues important to him and the S.A.I. More direct critiques of Anglo settlers, Indian agents, and other government officials increase with each issue, both in his own editorials and in the magazine. Parker's most earnest critiques of European culture occur when he is discussing World War I. In the January–March 1917 editorial, he wonders if "the civilization of which the European has boasted is after all a defective thing" (8). But in the Spring 1918 issue, he returns to commenting upon the ignorance and superstition of "savage tribes" and insisting that complete loyalty to the United States is the only hope for Indians (7). Fearful of creating factions within and political difficulties outside the organization, Parker attempted to avoid controversy by maintaining a clear alliance with the organization's platform of assimilation and integration.

As soon as she became a contributing editor in the October–December 1915 issue, the last under the title *The Quarterly Journal of the Society of American Indians*, Bonnin makes her first appearance in its pages as a community organizer and activist. Her presence as a contributing editor does not change the magazine's format and content except in terms of the promotion of her community center project and the publication of her poems. In the first mention of Bonnin, Parker uses her as an example of those Indians who have benefited from education in non-Indian schools. The next two references to her reveal her interest in publicizing the community work she was doing at Uintay-Ouray. In a section devoted to the S.A.I.'s fifth annual conference, held that year in Lawrence, Kansas, the editors note that the community center is an example of what Indians can do to help themselves. Regardless of Bonnin's own ideas about the role of the center, the editors interpret her work according to the S.A.I.'s platform of Indian self-help.

Bonnin describes the community center from her own perspective in the same issue in "A Christmas Letter From Zit-kal-a-sa: Describes Her Community Improvement Work Among the Utes." Her primary concern is the welfare of the community's women elders, for whom the community center sewing class made some garments, though Bonnin also requested that the women pay for the materials. The sewing class also began serving lunch to those Indians who came to the agency for the Monday disbursal of government checks. Prior to the intervention of the sewing class, the underpaid Native government employees at the agency were overburdened by requests for hospitality. The remainder of the letter articulates her opposition to peyote. In this section of the letter, Bonnin most closely approximates Parker's condescension toward Indians on reservations: she writes that the Utes are "easy victims because of their ignorance, superstitions and degradation" (324). She has, she notes, asked a state senator, a Mr. Colton, to join the S.A.I. as an associate member and to help with legislation to prohibit the importing of peyote into Utah.[17]

Bonnin's antipeyote position was intimately connected to her community center efforts. Her article "Chipeta, Widow of Chief Ouray, With a Word About a Deal in Blankets" appears in the July–September 1917 issue, following Ouray's obituary. The inclusion of the obituary establishes the context for the antipeyote statement. First, Bonnin assures her readers that both Ouray and Chipeta were friends and even defenders of white settlers. Then she describes her visit to Chipeta to warn her of the destructive effects of peyote. Bonnin's concern is that neither Chipeta nor her brother, McCook, will stop using peyote because the government has not told them that, like liquor, peyote is bad. After she critiques the government's attempt to honor Ouray's widow with a gift of two trading-store shawls that they make the Ute tribe and, therefore, Chipeta, purchase, Bonnin constructs Chipeta as an infantile and abused loyalist to the government and an uninformed abuser of peyote. As in her previous statements against peyote use, Bonnin uses the conventional social reform discourses of Indian inferiority and helplessness. Her use of this discourse advances her political interest in prohibiting the use of peyote, but undermines other attempts to illustrate the strength of Native women. She concludes her article by explaining that water rights, title to Ute land, or a letter from the government against peyote use would have been better gifts than two shawls. To an early twenty-first century reader, the list is an interesting mix of demands for sovereignty (water rights, land claims) and a request for colonial imposition (the prohibition of Native religious practices). Bonnin saw no contradiction in these requests. The American Indian future she envisioned included self-determination in terms of ownership and control of the land, but no peyote use, which she believed militated against the ability to own and control the land "wisely."

Bonnin's literary contributions to the magazine when she is on the editorial board promote the S.A.I.'s stated goals but occasionally challenge Parker's more conciliatory position. "The Red Man's America" offers revised lyrics to "My Country 'Tis of Thee" that change the song into a request for citizenship and voting rights and a demand for passage of bills that would abolish a corrupt B.I.A. and criminalize peyote use. "A Sioux Woman's Love for Her Grandmother" appears in what came to be known as the "Sioux Number" in October–December 1917. In the poem, set just prior to the Battle of the Greasy Grass, Bonnin focuses on the relationships between women as constitutive of Native communities: a grandmother, defying Custer's troops, remains behind as her community retreats to wait for her lost granddaughter. "The Indian's Awakening" is Bonnin's most ideologically complex literary contribution. "Awakening" was a familiar word in the discourse of racial progress, and Parker uses the word in his editorials, for example, to indicate his belief in the superiority of Western culture. If there has been an awakening in the poem, however, the poetic persona has emerged from sleep into a nightmare. The opening lines recall her first days at boarding school, when school employees cut her long hair into an Anglo style and took her traditional clothing. But those who attempted this external imposition of Anglo cultural signifiers "Left heart all unchanged; / the work incomplete" (line 3). These lines indicate that assimilation is far more complicated than succeeding as a student in Anglo terms.

The following lines offer a greater challenge to Parker's editorials and other articles in the magazine, such as the award-winning essays written by boarding school students about the value of their educations. The second and third stanzas repudiate Bonnin's boarding school experience and the title of the poem:

> My light has grown dim, and black the abyss
> That yawns at my feet. No bordering shore;
> No bottom e'er found by hopes sunk before.
> Despair I of good from deeds gone amiss.
> My people, may God have pity on you!
> The learning I hoped in you to imbue
> Turns bitterly vain to meet both our needs.
> No Sun for the flowers, vain planting seeds.
>
> I've lost my long hair; my eagle plumes too.
> From you my own people, I've gone astray.
> A wanderer now, with no where to stay.
> The Will-o-the-wisp learning, it brought me rue.
> It brings no admittance. Where I have knocked
> Some evil imps, hearts, have bolted and locked.
> Alone with the night and fearful Abyss
> I stand isolated, life gone amiss. (lines 9–24)

There has not been an enlightenment or awakening; her learning helps neither herself nor her people. If they read it carefully, the poem must have made Parker, Eastman, Montezuma, Pratt, and the other regular contributors wonder about Bonnin's ideological affiliations. However, Bonnin also uses a note of excessively articulated anguish at cultural loss that is prevalent in non-Native literary endeavors about Indians. This conventional tone might have made the poem more acceptable.

The rest of the poem refigures the meaning of a racial "awakening" as used by Parker and many of the other contributors to the magazine. In the poem, the persona's awakening is spiritual and requires a journey to visit her ancestors. Bonnin converses with a divine voice that, first, assures her there is meaning in life and, then, refreshes her before she climbs on a saddled horse and rides through the cosmos, the realm of what she calls the Great Spirit. In this cosmos, there is "A village of Indians, / camped as of old. / Earth-legends by their fires, some did review, / While flowers and trees more radiant grew" (lines 66–68). At this camp, an elder tells her that the people she sees are now souls, distant from their life on earth in traditional Dakota lands, but still connected to the living by memory. The persona's return to earth is joyous. The poem is a figurative "going back to the blanket," the expression used by the boarding school system and its adherents to describe a student who has returned to the reservation and rejected Western education. There is a suggestion, too, of the promise of the Ghost Dance in the persona's discovery of a spirit world in which her ancestors live in the old ways without Europeans.

Bonnin's writings on her community work and the poems illustrate two of the many ways that she engages the social and cultural issues that influence her life and the life of Indian communities. The letter is part of Bonnin's increasing attempt to use the organization and the magazine to make direct interventions in the daily lives of American Indians, a strategy that differs from Parker's priority of cultivating the organization. The Christmas letter shows Bonnin as a social activist who organizes B.I.A. employees, missionaries, and Utes in order to alleviate a strain on the community's resources. However, Bonnin's antipeyote position contrasts with the image of a village of elders living an idealistic existence in the poem. The poem does not suggest that traditional Native belief systems are superstitions or that Indians unfamiliar with Western educational expectations are ignorant or degraded. The positions appear to be inconsistent, but we must read her paternalistic comments within the context of her strident antipeyote stance. She employs the assimilationist rhetoric in order to convince the state senator, and any other member of her audience, that the Utes are helpless, in spite of the fact that in the first part of her letter, she illustrates a vibrant community willing to address concerns created by an intrusive government bureaucracy.

Bonnin's role as contributing editor and eventual election as the S.A.I.'s secretary and treasurer provides her with the opportunity to interject herself more forcefully into debates within the S.A.I. In July–September 1916, the editors publish a transcription of a debate, which occurred at the S.A.I.'s sixth annual conference in Cedar Rapids, on the loyalty of the Indian employees of the B.I.A. to "the race." Against the attacks of those who want to abolish the B.I.A. immediately, Bonnin defends those who work for the government so they can stay on the reservation. Her contribution to the debate, embedded in the context of her own sometime employment by the government and her work at Uintah-Ouray, is a critique of those who have not remained "in the wilderness" in order to help their people with daily needs. She says, "In justice to those Indians who wish to be citizens of our beloved America, to be true to the Government of America, to be civilized men and women, to be loyal to their own who are not so far along as they are, these Indian employees are glad to work under the Indian Bureau" (255). This statement provides an important clue to Bonnin's view of Indian affairs. She approves of working inside communities, which is why she might have shifted focus from her literary efforts. Bonnin's positions herself as a "communitist" in the sense Jace Weaver (Cherokee) uses the term in reference to literature. Weaver writes: "I would contend that the single thing that most defines Indian literatures relates to this sense of community and commitment to it. It is what I term communitism.... It is formed from a combination of the words 'community' and 'activism' or 'activist.' Literature is communitist to the extent that it has a proactive commitment to [the] Native community, including the wider community" (43). Contemporary readers are left, however, without a clear conception of what Bonnin envisioned for this and other Native communities. The S.A.I., for example, had members who often argued for the dismantling of all reservations, and if Bonnin agreed with this position, her activism was preparing Uintah-Ouray for this eventuality. On the other hand, Bonnin had great respect for her elders, including Chipeta, and, literarily, articulated a desire to revisit their world, idealized as it often is in her writings. Even the words "not so far along," which imply an acceptance of assimilationist doctrine and Western cultural superiority, do not clarify the issue, for the tone of her contribution to the debate indicates we could read her comments as facetious.

The context in which Bonnin becomes editor illustrates her willingness to risk aggravating factions in order to address specifically tribal rather than more generally pan-Indian concerns. Hertzberg explains that Parker's frustration with factionalism led him to consider taking the magazine from the S.A.I. and having it published by a different group or making the S.A.I. subsidiary to the magazine. As political disagreements and personal animosity exacerbated the conflicts over the abolition of the B.I.A. and peyote use at the Cedar Rapids conference, Parker grew increasingly anxious about the organization. With Parker engrossed in the factionalism, Bonnin began to assert her position on the editorial board in late 1917 with the publication of the "Sioux Number." Hertzberg writes that this issue was

> [i]n all likelihood ... evidence of Gertrude Bonnin's Sioux patriotism. For as Parker took less interest and devoted less time to the affairs of the Society, Mrs. Bonnin gave more.... She was by no means willing to sit by and watch the Society expire or allow it to become merely an adjunct of the *American Indian Magazine*. While she agreed with Parker on many issues, being especially vehement against peyote, she was increasingly inclined to take a stronger line against the Indian Bureau than he did. (173)

Following the publication of the "Sioux Number," Bonnin aligned with Eastman to organize a conference in 1918 in Pierre, South Dakota, in the middle of Sioux country. Parker did not attend the conference, where he was ousted as president. The ensuing issues of the magazine include an unprecedented emphasis on a single American Indian group, the Sioux: Bonnin includes pictures of Dr. Eastman and Captain Bonnin; adds Margaret Frazier (Sioux), Ben Brave (Lower Brule Sioux), and Elaine Goodale Eastman, an author and Charles Eastman's Anglo wife, to the editorial staff; and foregrounds past (Sitting Bull's assassination) and present (the Black Hills land claim, the death of the Eastman's daughter) events in the Sioux region. This shift in focus shows strong tribal ties for these members of the S.A.I., even if returning to their communities permanently was not a choice either Bonnin or Eastman made.

The voice of the magazine, if not necessarily its ideology, changed abruptly when Bonnin claimed the editorship of the Autumn Number in 1918, following the Pierre conference. Hertzberg explains that in Pierre, "Parker was asked to remain as editor of the *Magazine* should he desire to do so; otherwise, Mrs. Bonnin was to become editor, as she informed him shortly after the conference. . . . While he hesitated, Mrs. Bonnin acted, notifying him that since she had received no reply from him, she was assuming the editorship herself" (176). Bonnin offers a different narrative in her first editorial, which begins by explaining that Parker did not attend the conference because he was on military duty. Her description of the conference also puts a benign public facade on the factionalism that led to Parker's ousting. Bonnin writes, "The spirit of a great united American brotherhood fighting in a common cause,—the defense of world democracy, pervaded the whole affair" (113). Like Parker, Bonnin read the war in Europe as directly relevant to the status of American Indians, but her articulation of this position was more strident rhetorically:

> Surely, the flaming shafts of light typifying political and legal equality and justice,—
> government by the people, now penetrating the dark cloud of Europe are a continuous revelation. The light grows more effulgent, emanating as it does from the greatest of democracies,—America. The sunburst of democratic ideals cannot bring new hope and courage to the small peoples of the earth without reaching the remotest corners within America's own bounds. (114)

This insistent demand for liberation, which Bonnin offers in the characteristic paternalism of reform discourse, illustrates the most clear difference between Parker's and Bonnin's editorial approaches to addressing issues pertinent to Indian Country.

Bonnin situates her interest in tribal activism in a global context. In her second editorial, she reiterates her position on the recently ended war in Europe. The exultant tone is far removed from Parker's long pieces on the need to embrace the organization's "ideals." Bonnin writes, "Under the sun a new epoch is being staged! Little peoples are to be granted the right of self-determination! Small nations and remnants of nations are to sit beside their great allies at the Peace Table; and their just claims are to be duly incorporated in the terms of a righteous peace" (161). Bonnin's optimism about the Peace conference implies an equal hope that American Indians will have their "just claims" addressed in the United States. She continues, "The universal cry for freedom from injustice is the voice of a multitude united by afflictions. To appease this human cry the application of democratic principles must be flexible enough to be universal. Belgium is leading a historic procession of little peoples seeking freedom!" (161–62). The subtext, as articulated for years by the S.A.I., in the editorial by Bonnin, and by Eastman in an article that followed, is that the B.I.A. produces afflictions by defying the democratic principles to which Bonnin refers. She ends her editorial with a request for citizenship for American Indians and a query as to who will represent her people in Paris. With a more tribally oriented editorial board providing a message in a broader global context, Bonnin locates herself in a political and intellectual place that contrasts with Parker's tighter focus on pan-Indian efforts to legislate American Indians into the mainstream.

Bonnin is also more unapologetically interested in the "old ways" than Parker, who rarely mentions older generations in an effort to keep his intellectual focus on the future "awakening" of his race.[18] She follows her first editorial with an article entitled "Indian Gifts to Civilized Man," which had been published in the July *Indian Sentinel*. The article foregrounds American Indian beliefs: the powerful Navajo deity Changing Woman, Bonnin explains, is the source of both corn and potatoes, which help to alleviate the hunger around the world that is one consequence of the war. After Bonnin reads global events through the lens of Navajo oral traditions, she defends Indians as patriotic and loyal, even if they are not citizens, and offers gratitude that the Indian soldiers were not segregated. She believes "a close companionship promises mutual benefits," as Indians, in her estimation, have an inherited sense of direction that makes them good guides (116). Bonnin suggests the possibility of a mutual and equal, perhaps idealized, cultural exchange within the context of a prointegration position that refuses to privilege non-Native worldviews and is, therefore, not necessarily antitribal. In apparent contradiction, however, she publishes in the same issue a letter she wrote to the third assistant secretary of war requesting that he not close Carlisle as an Indian boarding school. The letter reflects

Bonnin's shift in alliances to her former nemesis, Pratt, who was also staunchly antipeyote. Any pleasure a traditionalist or an assimilationist would have while reading Bonnin's contributions to the magazine would eventually be muted.

Bonnin's greater willingness to honor American Indian beliefs complements her construction of herself as a well-read, politically and intellectually engaged American Indian woman involved in world events. In the second issue she edits, she includes "America, Home of the Red Man," a personal narrative about her trip to the Pierre conference, which she originally wrote for *The Home Mission Monthly*. In the narrative, a "paleface" traveler accosts Bonnin in order to ask about a service pin she is wearing. Bonnin explains that the pin belongs to her husband, "a member of the great Sioux Nation, who is a volunteer in Uncle Sam's Army" (165). The man replies, "Oh! Yes! You are an Indian! Well, I knew when I first saw you that you must be a foreigner" (165). Rather than responding to the man, Bonnin has a vision of thousands of Indian soldiers in France. She watches the soldiers and thinks, "The Red Man of America loves democracy and hates mutilated treaties" (165). The vision continues with the image of an Ute grandmother donating five hundred dollars to the Red Cross, an Indian soldier who refuses to quit after he receives multiple wounds, and "little French orphans, babes with soft buckskin moccasins on their tiny feet. Moccasins that Indian women of America had made for them, with so much loving sympathy for an anguished humanity" (166). After she places orphaned but recently liberated French children in Native American shoes, the culmination of the vision calls for American Indians to be emancipated from the B.I.A. and the paternalism of the U. S. government. Bonnin then interrogates the traveler about what he has read recently, but, obviously intimidated, he withdraws, and she suggests that the world will pass by the traveler and leave him behind. The white man, like so many literary Indians before him, fades off the page in the face of the politically and intellectually astute Indian woman.

With the male traveler retreating under the scrutiny of a strong Indian woman's interrogation, Bonnin captures the image of another editorial goal: providing a greater presence for a favored constituency, Native and non-Native women. Bonnin alters the content of the magazine by the cumulative influence of her editorial decisions regarding women: she includes pictures of and eulogies to Angel DeCora Dietz (Winnebago), the artist who illustrated *Old Indian Legends*; newspaper clippings on women's temperance and suffrage movements; and excerpts from a speech in which she insists that more women, the teachers of Native children, should be involved in the S.A.I. She also uses the term "sisters" to describe her companions in reform. In her third contribution to the Winter Number of 1919, "The Coronation of Chief Powhatan Retold," Bonnin privileges the role of women in global affairs and shows the subversive rhetorical moves she used so frequently in the autobiographical essays and *ohunkakan*. The topic is a European visit by the President and Mrs. Wilson. Bonnin explains that the First Lady, Edith Bolling Galt Wilson, is a direct descendant of Pocahontas, and, therefore, that the hosting of the Wilsons by the royal families of Europe is a reenactment of the reception given to Pocahontas and John Rolfe three centuries before.[19] Bonnin, however, is less interested in international diplomacy than in reiterating her message in the previous editorial. She places the Wilson's visit in historical context: "Springing from the tribal democracies of the new world, Pocahontas was the first emissary of democratic ideas to cast-ridden Europe. She must have suffered untold anguish when King James was offended with her sweetheart husband, Rolfe, for his presumption in marrying the daughter of a king—a crowned head too!" (179). In this historically subversive narrative, Bonnin suggests that Europeans destroyed democracy in the Americas, just as they have done in Europe during World War I. European claims about bringing civilization to the Americas, Bonnin implies, is an historical inaccuracy. Rather, a Native woman, Pocahontas, brought civilization to Europe, and Mrs. Wilson, her descendant and the wife of the man trying to establish the League of Nations, occupies the same role contemporarily. The second part of the article establishes the same point: Powhatan, a "liberty loving soul," was not impressed by the crown and royal costume sent by King James I through John Smith (180). Bonnin says the English "resorted to trickery" to get Powhatan to accept the gifts and dress as a European monarch (180). In Bonnin's narrative, liberty resides in the "primeval forest," not the European metropolis, and to coerce Powhatan to mimic the metropolis in the forest is an act of aggression that, for Bonnin, signals the beginning of the European attempt to remake the Americas in its image. Pocahontas and Mrs. Wilson, with help from their male relatives, offer the greatest resistance to European barbarism. The Pocahontas article explores all the issues of interest to Bonnin and the S.A.I., from education to treaty rights to citizenship. The citizenship issue, for example, when read through the lens of this article, becomes a request for *re*-entrance into a democratic world destroyed by Europeans.

Bonnin's final contribution to the Winter 1919 issue, "Letter to the Chiefs and Headmen of the Tribes," illustrates the risk of identifying her either as the proponent of a more traditional or more assimilationist ideology. The title of the letter has an asterisk that alerts readers to a message from Bonnin at the bottom of the page: "Dear Reader into whose hands this letter has fallen, will you do a kind act by reading and explaining it to an Indian who cannot read or speak English?" (196). The message solicits sympathy for the "poor Indians" of conventional reform discourse, the same stereotype that Parker mocked by referring to his representative Indian by the first name "Lo," as in "Lo, the Poor Indian." Bonnin, then, connects the issue of language use to land. Learning English, she implies, will help Indians to retain ownership of their land "for the future children of our race" (197). She contextualizes her argument with a description of a memory of "the open Indian country in which I played as a child," and then signs the letter "Yours for the Indian Cause" (197). In contemporary intellectual contexts, Bonnin's defense of Indian land would take high precedence, while her insistence on speaking English would militate against efforts at recuperating to maintain Native languages. However, foremost in Bonnin's mind is that she is working for a specifically Indian cause in order to ensure a specifically Indian future. In the Summer 1919, issue, Bonnin publishes part of an address to the Minneapolis conference in October of the same year. The future she envisions includes children who will "be proud of their Indian blood" (154). This conception of an American Indian future is not intellectual, like Parker's, but biological and, by implication, cultural. Indians will become responsible Americans, Bonnin writes in language similar to Parker's, but they will do so as Indians, not imitation Anglos.

Bonnin's final issue as editor includes an increased emphasis on spirituality, though she still addresses many of the topics that held her interest in the previous issues: her tribe, the loyalty of Indian soldiers, the benefits of integration, and blatant racial discrimination, in this case against Eastman, who was prevented from entering the Menominee Reservation during a speaking tour on Indian citizenship. In "An Indian Praying on the Hilltop," Bonnin thanks the Great Spirit for providing her with individual consciousness and protecting her. The next two paragraphs state that this same power awakens her, friendless and impoverished, from nightmares in a dangerous land. The context is so general, however, that a reader could interpret this dangerous land as an America invaded by colonial European powers, as the factionalized S.A.I., or as reservations, which Bonnin saw as unpleasant living environments. The prayer ends with Bonnin rejoicing: "I see the dawn of justice to the Indian, even upon earth: and now, Great Spirit, my heart is full of joy!" (92). The optimism following a statement of potential despair is familiar in Bonnin's work in the magazine, but she leaves many questions unanswered. Readers might take the prayer as a statement in support of traditional American Indian spiritual practices, though only the reference to a Great Spirit instead of God keeps the prayer from being more readily identifiable as Christian, or she might be performing "the humble Indian" for her acquaintances in Christian reform organizations. Whether Bonnin intended the "Prayer" to be read as autobiographical or fictional is not even clear. The ambiguity of the message, however, is an appropriate representation of her complex intellectual and ideological understanding of American Indian life in the early twentieth century.

The report on the S.A.I. conference at the end of the issue includes an address by Bonnin in which God, rather than the Great Spirit, plays a significant role within the context of Bonnin's belated insistence that the organization, which she says has doubled in membership in the last year, remains united. In apparent contradiction to her optimism about the organization, the conference was the culmination of her career in it. In the elections for president, Thomas Sloan, a well-known peyotist, defeated Eastman and Captain Bonnin by a vote of 25 to 8 to 5. The following transcription of events shows Bonnin declining her nomination by Sloan to remain as secretary and treasurer. Her protest of ill health also serves as her resignation as editor of the magazine. Bonnin says:

> I feel that I must at this time make a public statement about my own health which, under ordinary circumstances, I would not mention. I have been glad to serve in some capacity these past four years and I think you all know it but I have continued the work against my physician's instructions. I have been very ill and he says that if I expect to recover or keep well I must rest. I shall not be able to serve you in any way I fear. I am honored to have my name mentioned again but my name will have to be withdrawn because of my health. (180)

Following her statement, Captain Bonnin declines a nomination, too, and Eastman and Montezuma both decline, "absolutely," to be editors of the magazine (181). The hasty withdrawal of this group, led by Bonnin, appears to be a result of Sloan's election as president. As quickly as Bonnin claimed the editorship from Parker, she lost it and her power within the organization to Sloan.

Sloan's differences with the outgoing officers and editors manifests itself in a vastly revised ideological orientation for the magazine. In the next issue, non-Native writers predominate. Parker's and Bonnin's efforts to cultivate Native voices makes an abrupt retreat as authors such as Mary Roberts Rinehart, a European American initiated into the Blackfeet tribe and given the name "Pitamakan," or Running Eagle; Walter Hough, the curator of ethnology at the United States National Museum; Clark Wissler, a faculty member at the University of Indiana; and Lew Sarett, a "noted author of Indian verse," reproduce conventional vanishing-race discourse and exoticized Indians. Sloan even included advertisements at the end, such as the one for Stetson. The large format, commercial issue dominated by non-Native writers was the last of *The American Indian Magazine*.

Lobbying and Organizing for the Indian Cause, 1920–1938

Though her involvement with the S.A.I. ended, Bonnin's career helping what she called, patronizingly, the "little peoples," continued. In 1921 and 1922, she lobbied for Indian causes, often under the auspices of the General Federation of Women's Clubs (G.F.W.C.), which added a national committee on Indian welfare. As William Willard (Oklahoma Cherokee) explains in his discussion of Bonnin's political activism, the chair of the G.F.W.C.'s Indian welfare committee hired John Collier, the future commissioner of the B.I.A., to research the social conditions of American Indians. While Collier was in New Mexico fighting the Bursum Bill, which was intended to dispossess Pueblos of their land, Bonnin was in Oklahoma investigating scandals that resulted following the discovery of oil on Indian land, which led to the publication by the Indian Rights Association of "Oklahoma's Poor Rich Indians" (1924), coauthored by Bonnin. Willard's research shows that Bonnin's political activity increased dramatically following her exit from the S.A.I. Willard explains that Bonnin used her connections with Republicans, including wealthy philanthropists such as the DuPonts and Rockefellers, in the "efforts of the Yankton Sioux tribal government to secure claims reparations from the federal government for land lost and infringed upon in Minnesota, Iowa, and South Dakota" (12). With her husband, she campaigned in the West for Congressional candidates, and in 1928, their efforts led to the addition of a plank in the Republican platform that included "(1) a presidentially appointed commission to investigate and report to Congress on the administration of Indian affairs: (2) guarantees of treaty and property rights to the Indians of the United States. Any law or administrative practice which was prejudicial to these rights should be repealed" (Willard 12). She eventually served in Collier's American Indian Defense Association, and then formed, in 1926, the National Council of American Indians, her own organization with individual reservation chapters. Hafen writes that the Bonnins "argued that of the various Pan-Indian groups only the NCAI could claim Indians as executive officers" (*Dreams* xxi). In 1932 Bonnin gave testimony before the Senate Indian Committee on the topic of the abuse by reservation superintendents of the power they had to lease Indian land to non-Indians. In the same year, she supported Roosevelt, who chose Collier as his B.I.A. Commissioner. Collier's administration involved the attempt to address many of the grievances that the leaders of the S.A.I. expended so much effort publicizing more than a decade earlier.

Bonnin's activist editing, inextricably connected to the literary efforts that preceded and the lobbying efforts that followed, regained her a national readership and earned her access to a new constituency, which she continued serving after she left the S.A.I. As activist and editor, Bonnin viewed her work as occurring within the context of a struggle for liberation, and her devotion was to the alleviation of immediate suffering without reference to a particular ideology. Her role as editor most clearly illustrates Bonnin's tendency to defy the work of late-twentieth century scholars seeking to align her with various groups of Native writers and intellectuals. Bonnin fulfills the demands of some of the more "traditional" *and* "progressive" of twenty-first-century Native intellectuals, all of whom are addressing issues similar to Bonnin's. Her editorial conflicts with Parker replicate themselves in contemporary debates at conferences and in the pages of scholarly journals devoted to Native literature and culture. Rarely focusing on a single ideological position for an extended period, often contradicting and qualifying what appear initially as clear statements against assimilation or against Native religious practices, as a Native intellectual Bonnin deploys many strategies in her negotiation of the colonial context that shaped and still informs the relationship between Native Americans and the federal government. Whether she abandoned some of these strategies as only temporarily or marginally successful is less important than that she was always ready to act for the survival of Native communities.

Notes

1. Agnes M. Picotte (Lakota) describes *ohunkakan* as "tales regarded as having some fictional elements" in the foreword to *Old Indian Legends* (xi). Dexter Fisher, in the foreword to *American Indian Stories*, cites a letter Bonnin wrote to Carlos Montezuma in which she explains the name change as the result of a family quarrel about Bonnin's departure from the community to receive an education at a boarding school.

2. Until very recently, scholarly work on Native Americans without any reference to Native critics was the norm. The transgression is much more difficult to understand now that the work of Native critics is readily available. Examples of scholars who generally ignore the work of Native intellectuals and contemporary creative writers include Cheryl Walker, in *Indian Nation: Native American Literature and Nineteenth-Century Nationalisms* (1997), and Joshua David Bellin, in *The Demon of the Continent: Indians and the Shaping of American Literature* (2000). Even a work with a title such as Arnold Krupat's *Red Matters: Native American Studies* (2002) privileges to a large extent non-Native scholars and critics. Warrior cites Greg Sarris (Coast Miwok/Pomo) for the same transgression in *Keeping Slug Woman Alive: A Holistic Approach to American Indian Texts* (1993), which, as Warrior notes, "all but eschews references to critical writings by American Indians" (xix). One consequence of the lack of interest in Native scholarship by non–Native studies scholars is the repetition of Native scholarship by higher-profile non-Native authors who work in more privileged aca-

demic environments and have access to more powerful publishers. Reading Native creative writers is of equal importance, as their work often includes the critique of colonialism and other forms of oppression that occupy the attention of many late-twentieth- and early-twenty-first-century critics.

3. Identifying members of what is commonly called the Sioux Nation involves making distinctions according to council division and band. For example, Sitting Bull was from the Hunkpapa band of the western Lakotas, also called the Tetons. I will identify people from the Sioux Nation as specifically as possible, and will use "Sioux" only when I have been unable to find other information.

4. In identifying Bonnin's affiliations, I will follow the guidance of P. Jane Hafen (Taos Pueblo). Hafen explains that Beatrice Medicine (Lakota) and Vine Deloria, Jr., (Standing Rock Dakota) classify the Yanktons as Dakotas. However, Bonnin probably spoke the Nakota dialect, while her pen name is Lakota. When she wrote in a Native language, she used Dakota. As Nakota is most frequently a linguistic classification, Hafen uses the term *Yankton* (*Dreams* xiv).

5. Bonnin had a Mormon burial in Arlington, Virginia. Hafen also cites from the manuscripts of Bonnin's collaborator on *The Sun Dance Opera*, William Hanson, who writes that Bonnin was a "faithful Mormon" ("Zitkala Ŝa" 41).

6. Standing Rock Dakota author Vine Deloria, Jr., writes that the Wheeler-Howard Act "gave the reservations their first taste of self-government in nearly half a century" (*Custer* 55). Deloria discusses the Meriam Report and Wheeler-Howard in detail in Chapter 9 of *Behind the Trail of Broken Treaties: An Indian Declaration of Independence* (1974). He generally applauds the results of the I.R.A. and Collier's efforts as commissioner of the B.I.A. Historian James J. Rawls explains that while 181 tribes ratified the I.R.A., another 78 rejected it. Many Native Americans viewed the I.R.A. as an attempt to impose on the tribes a non-Native system of government.

7. For discussions of Zitkala-Ŝa's use of sentimental literary modes, see the articles by Susan Bernardin and Laura Wexler. Bernardin views much of Zitkala-Ŝa's writing as using the language of domesticity to challenge "sentimental ideology's foundational role in compulsory Indian education as well as its related participation in national efforts to 'Americanize' the Indian" (213). Wexler positions her argument in reference to the debate between Jane Tompkins and Ann Douglas on the literary value of domestic fiction, but refocuses on "the expansive, imperial project of sentimentalism," and how this project fails Zitkala-Ŝa (15). Ruth Spack, in an article she frames critically by the work of Kenneth Lincoln, Renato Rosaldo, and Eric Cheyfitz, sees Zitkala-Ŝa's writing as subverting the boarding school education she received by using English to reconstruct Native women in positive ways. In her discussion of what work by Zitkala-Ŝa has been included in the canon, Patricia Okker considers Zitkala-Ŝa's writing career in terms of European American literary modes, or movements, such as realism, naturalism, and modernism.

8. Womack writes that the argument of *Red on Red: Native American Literary Separatism* (1999) is "that Native literatures deserve to be judged by their own criteria, in their own terms, not merely in agreement with, or reaction against, European literature and theory. The Native Americanist does not bury her head in the sand and pretend that European history and thought do not affect Native literature, nor does she ignore the fact that Native literature has quite distinctive features of its own that call for new forms of analyses" (242–43).

9. Rayna Green writes that "the living performance of 'playing Indian' by non-Indian peoples depends upon the physical and psychological removal, even the death, of real Indians" (31). Philip Deloria's *Playing Indian* (1998) is a history of non-Natives playing Indian, from the Boston Tea Party to the New Age movement.

10. Yellow Robe's article appears in the January–March 1914 issue. Yellow Robe asks, "What benefit has the Indian derived from these Wild West Shows? None, but what are degrading, demoralizing and degenerating, and all their influences fall far short of accomp-

lishing the ideals of citizenship and civilized state of affairs which we most need to know" (39).

11. Womack writes that in the discussion of Native literatures, "autonomy, self-determination, and sovereignty serve as useful literary concepts" (11). Cook-Lynn criticizes contemporary Native authors who do not foreground in their work a defense of tribal nationhood and sovereignty.

12. Ella Deloria wrote an ethnographic novel, *Waterlily* (1988), and in *Dakota Texts* (1932), she translated stories from the same oral traditions as those in *Old Indian Legends*. A discussion of Zitkala-Ša's work alongside that of Luther Standing Bear, Charles Alexander Eastman, and Ella Deloria, for example, in addition to Native women authors such as E. Pauline Johnson (Mohawk), Alice Callahan (Muscogee), and Mourning Dove (Okanogan), would provide a greater understanding of Indian literary and intellectual traditions. In its entirety and in terms of content, though not literary mode, *Waterlily* reads much like the chapters "The Legends," "The Beadwork," and "The Coffee-Making" in *American Indian Stories*.

13. Hertzberg explains that Charles A. Eastman and his brother, the Reverend John Eastman, along with the Revered Sherman Coolidge (Arapaho), considered founding an organization of American Indians at the beginning of the century. Simultaneously, in a letter dated 1 June 1901, Bonnin appears to be continuing a discussion with Montezuma about a similar organization. P. Jane Hafen made Bonnin's letters to Montezuma, which she transcribed, available to me.

14. Non-Natives with an interest in participating were nonvoting members called "associates."

15. Parker was a great nephew of Colonel Ely S. Parker, the author of the surrender ending the Civil War and the first American Indian to serve as commissioner of the B.I.A.

16. Deloria, Jr., explains the connection between the Department of the Interior's use of certificates of competency and the loss of Native land in *Behind the Trail of Broken Treaties* (189–90).

17. Bonnin revises the Christmas letter in the next issue, though she adds a section in which she locates her work in the context of "the uplift of the race" (309–10). The tone of this revised report suggest her efforts are motivated by Christian duty, yet also emphasizes that at this point, Bonnin prefers direct community activism to literary interventions or, later, to activism on a national scale.

18. Parker published a history of the Seneca and a collection of Seneca stories during the 1920s. His career, literarily, is the reverse of Bonnin's.

19. Edith Wilson, as Bonnin notes, claimed to be an ancestor of Pocahontas. Many of the oldest European Virginian families made the same claim, perhaps to suggest that they were biological rather than colonial inheritors of the region.

Works Cited

Bernardin, Susan. "The Lessons of a Sentimental Education: Zitkala-Ša's Autobiographical Narratives." *Western American Literature* 32 (1997): 212–38.

Bonnin, Gertrude. "America, Home of the Red Man." *The American Indian Magazine* (Winter 1919): 165–67.

———. "Chipeta, Widow of Chief Ouray, With a Word About a Deal in Blankets." *The American Indian Magazine* (July–Sept. 1917): 168–70.

———. "A Christmas Letter From Zit-kal-a-sa: Describes Her Community Improvement Work Among the Utes." *The Quarterly Journal of the Society of American Indians* (Oct.–Dec. 1915): 322–25.

———. "The Coronation of Chief Powhatan Retold." *The American Indian Magazine* (Winter 1919): 179–80.

———. "The Indian's Awakening." *The Quarterly Journal of the Society of American Indians* (Jan.–Mar. 1916): 57–59.

———. "Indian Gifts to Civilized Man." *The American Indian Magazine* (July–Sept. 1918): 115–16.

———. "An Indian Praying on the Hilltop." *The American Indian Magazine* (Summer 1919): 92.

———. "Letter to the Chiefs and Headmen of the Tribes." *The American Indian Magazine* (Winter 1919): 196–97.

———. "The Red Man's America." *The American Indian Magazine* (Jan.–Mar. 1917): 64.

———. "A Sioux Woman's Love for Her Grandmother." *The American Indian Magazine* (Oct.–Dec. 1917): 230–31.

Cook-Lynn, Elizabeth. "American Indian Intellectualism and the New Indian Story." In *Natives and Academics: Researching and Writing About Native Americans*, ed. Devon A. Mihesuah. Lincoln: University of Nebraska Press, 1998.

Deloria, Ella. *Waterlily*. Lincoln: University of Nebraska Press, 1988.

Deloria, Philip J. *Playing Indian*. New Haven, Conn.: Yale University Press, 1998.

Deloria, Vine, Jr. *Behind the Trail of Broken Treaties: An Indian Declaration of Independence*. Austin: University of Texas Press, 1974.

———. *Custer Died for Your Sins*. 1970. Reprint, Norman: Oklahoma University Press, 1988.

Green, Rayna. "The Tribe Called Wannabee: Playing Indian in America and Europe." *Folkore* 99 (1988): 30–55.

Hafen, P. Jane. *Dreams and Thunder: Stories, Poems, and the Sun Dance Opera*. Lincoln: University of Nebraska Press, 2001.

———. "Zitkala-Ŝa: Sentimentality and Sovereignty." *Wicazo Sa Review* 12 (1997): 31–42.

Hertzberg, Hazel W. *The Search for an American Indian Identity: Modern Pan-Indian Movements*. Syracuse, N.Y.: Syracuse University Press, 1971.

Okker, Patricia. "Native American Literatures and the Canon: The Case of Zitkala-Ŝa." In *American Realism and the Canon*, ed. Tom Quirk and Gary Scharnhorst. Newark: Delaware University Press, 1994. 87–101.

Parker, Arthur C. "Editorial Comment." *The American Indian Magazine* (Jan.–Apr. 1913): 1–12.

———. "The Editor's Viewpoint." *The American Indian Magazine* (Apr.–June 1913): 103–16.

———. "Editorial Comment." *The American Indian Magazine* (Jan.–Mar. 1917): 5–11.

———. "Editorials." *The American Indian Magazine* (Spring 1918): 5–12.

Rawls, James J. *Chief Red Fox is Dead: A History of Native Americans Since 1945*. Fort Worth: Harcourt, 1996.

Spack, Ruth. "Re-visioning Women: Zitkala-Ŝa's Revolutionary *American Indian Stories*." *Legacy* 14 (1997): 25–42.

Smith, Jeanne. "'A Second Tongue': The Trickster's Voice in the Works of Zitkala-Ŝa." In *Tricksterism in Turn-of-the-Century American Literature: A Multicultural Perspective*, ed. Elizabeth Ammons and Annette White-Parks. Hanover, N.H.: University Press of New England, 1994.

Susag, Dorothea M. "Zitkala-Sa (Gertrude Simmons Bonnin): A Power(full) Literary Voice." *Studies in American Indian Literatures* (Fall 1993): 3–24.

Vizenor, Gerald. *Manifest Manners: Postindian Warriors of Survivance*. Hanover, N.H.: University Press of New England, 1994.

Warrior, Robert Allen. *Tribal Secrets: Recovering American Indian Intellectual Traditions*. Minneapolis: University of Minnesota Press, 1995.

Weaver, Jace. *That the People Might Live: Native American Literatures and Native American Community*. New York: Oxford University Press, 1997.

Wexler, Laura. "Tender Violence: Literary Eavesdropping, Domestic Fiction, and Educational Reform." In *The Culture of Sentiment: Race, Gender, and Sentimentality in Nineteenth-Century America*, ed. Shirley Samuels. New York: Oxford, 1992.

Willard, William. "Zitkala-Ša: A Woman Who Would Be Heard!" *Wicazo Sa* 1 (1985): 11–16.
Womack, Craig S. *Red on Red: Native American Literary Separatism*. Minneapolis: University of Minnesota Press, 1999.
Yellow Robe, Chauncey. "The Indian and the Wild West Show." *The Quarterly Journal of the Society of American Indians* (Jan.–Mar. 1913): 39–40.
Zitkala-Ša. *American Indian Stories*. 1921. Reprint, with a foreword by Dexter Fisher, Lincoln: University of Nebraska Press, 1985.
———. *Old Indian Legends*. 1901. Reprint, with a foreword by Agnes M. Picotte, Lincoln: University of Nebraska Press, 1985.

"Editorial Comment, by Gertrude Bonnin, Acting Editor"
The American Indian Magazine, July–September 1918

The Pierre, (S.D.) Conference is an accomplished fact. In these trying war times it was a privileged sacrifice to journey there.

Three of the S.A.I. officers absent are in military service. Arthur C. Parker, President, is on military duty "Somewhere in America"; John M. Oskison, First Vice-President, is serving "Somewhere in France"; Margaret Frazier, Vice-President on Membership, is a trained nurse in the Red Cross work at Camp Bowie, Texas.

The Honorary President, Rev. Sherman Coolidge, presided over the meetings.

The delegation of members though numerically small, was strikingly representative. There were gathered together in behalf of Indian welfare work—Arapahoe, Apache, Oklahoman, Ojibway, Ute, Pottowatomie, Sioux from different tribes and others.

It was gratifying and significant that in the face of the Conference dates having been designated for country fairs on all Indian reservations under Indian Bureau management, a successful conference was possible. Faithful Associate members cross the continent to attend the American Indian Conference. Many new members were added to the rolls during the meeting.

The hospitality of the citizens of Pierre will ever be cherished in memory.

The spirit of a great united American brotherhood fighting in a common cause—the defense of world democracy, pervaded the whole affair. American Indians are watching democracy, baptized in fire and blood overseas. They are watching the christening with mingled feelings of deepest concern,—the thing lies so close to their hearts it is difficult to give it expression. Indian soldiers lie dead on European battlefields, having intermingled their blood with that of every other race in the supreme sacrifice for an ideal.

Surely, the flaming shafts of light typifying political and legal equality and justice,—government by the people, now penetrating the dark cloud of Europe are a continuous revelation. The light grows more effulgent, emanating as it does from the greatest of democracies,—America. The sunburst of democratic ideals cannot bring new hope and courage to the small peoples of the earth without reaching the remotest corners within America's own bounds.

Frank discussions are apt to call forth suppressed emotions of the American Indian but need not thereby create ruffled feelings. The Society of American Indians is compelled by the stress of the times to consider and discuss higher education for the Red Man and the rights of small peoples at its Annual Conference.

It is needful to thrash out the truth about Indian matters. Truth and justice are inseparable component parts of American ideals. As America has declared democracy abroad, so must we consistently practise it at home.

The American government is one where the voice of the people is heard. It is therefore not a radical step nor a presumption for the native Red Man today to raise his voice about the welfare of his race. The Red Man has been mute too long. He must speak for himself as others cannot, nor should he be afraid to speak the truth and to insist upon a hearing for the utterance of truth can harm no one but must bless all mankind.

The future success of the Indian as a full-fledged American citizen depends largely upon what he does for himself today. If he is good enough to fight for American ideals he is good enough for American citizenship now.

Our Conference was honored by the presence of an Indian Bureau official, Mrs. Wilma R. Rhodes, Field Supervisor. This representative of our government repeatedly took the floor of the Conference to differ from the expressed opinions of the Indian members. These debates were marked with intense feeling. The difference seemed to be the natural result of a different viewpoint and interest.

The Indian Bureau system was naturally defended by its representative. The members of the Conference expressed a decided preference for Public Schools and American institutions. The Bureau representative advocated the alleged sweet oil of Government Schools under the Bureau System, while the Conference members protested against what they believed to be the fat fly of paternalism in this particular brand of ointment.

The Society of American Indians appreciates every true friend but were the organization to begin naming them it would be an undertaking. The great object and purpose of the Conference is to study the interest of the race as a whole and to devise means and methods for its practical advancement and the attainment of its rightful position among the peoples of the world.

"The Coronation of Chief Powhatan Retold"
The American Indian Magazine, Winter 1919

Mrs. Woodrow Wilson, wife of the President of the United States, is a lineal descendant of Pocahontas. Wide acclaim has been given Mrs. Wilson in Europe where, preliminary to the world's Peace Conference, both she and her distinguished husband have been enthusiastically welcomed and sumptuously banqueted by the royal families.

It is a remarkable coincidence that three centuries ago, Pocahontas was also received in Court by the King and Queen of England. It is recorded in history "that the most flattering marks of attention" were paid to the daughter of Chief Powhatan. Springing from the tribal democracies of the new world, Pocahontas was the first emissary of democratic ideas to cast-ridden Europe. She must have suffered untold anguish when King James was offended with her sweetheart husband, Rolfe, for his presumption in marrying the daughter of a king—a crowned head too!

Through weary miles of tangled forests of the eastern coast, Captain John Smith with four escorts carried word to Powhatan that new presents for him had arrived from England; and that Captain Newport sent him an invitation to come to Jamestown to receive them.

The stately Indian chief, having just returned from a journey, was very likely reclining upon "his bed of mats, his pillow of dressed skin lying beside him with its brilliant embroidery of shells and beads," dressed in a handsome fur robe, "as large as an Irish mantel." It was the fall of 1608: and the air was damp and cool. With grave dignity he replied to the messengers—"If your king has sent me presents, I also am a king and this is my land. Here I will stay eight days to receive them." As for the cunning proposal that he join the settlers in a common campaign against another tribe of Indians, he said "I can avenge my own injuries." Proud and sagacious was Powhatan, even Captain John Smith had to admit.

When Jamestown learned that Chief Powhatan would be at home to receive the King's gifts, Captain Newport with fifty men immediately set out to the chief's dwelling. Among the many gifts presented at that memorable time, was a royal crown sent by King James I of England. It was a disappointment to Captain Newport that this unusual present brought to the Indian Chief no glad thrills at all. But the faithful subjects of England knew that the old chief was exceedingly whimsical. They thought so because he was more interested in trifling trinkets and bright colored beads which appealed more to the artistic eye of the aborigine. He was grossly ignorant of the world's rank and power associated with particular pieces of the white man's articles of dress and decoration. One time, the chief admired a string of blue beads so much that he bought them from Captain Smith, paying three hundred bushels of corn, every kernel of which was worth more than gold to the hungry colonists.

It was not surprising then that the scarlet robe and royal crown did not happen to please his unspoiled taste. Perhaps brooding over the encroachments of the pale-faces upon his territory might have caused him to question the real significance of these King's garments and crown. To the liberty loving soul of Powhatan, this royal camouflage was no comparison to the gorgeous array of Autumn in that primeval forest where he roamed at will.

However, by dint of persuasion, the coronation day was chosen. When the time came for the performance of the solemn ceremony, the courage of Powhatan failed. Such a parley as was held under those ancient trees can scarcely be imagined. The Indian Chief was incorrigible. It were really laughable, did it not in later years prove to be so tragic. After hours of reassurance that the king's garments would not injure him, he reluctantly permitted himself to be dragged into them. The greatest difficulty was encountered when Powhatan stubbornly refused to kneel to receive the crown, as he was requested.

The patience of his visitors was exhausted. Still they who would move heaven and earth to execute their king's command must find a way to move this American aborigine. They resorted to trickery. "One leaned hard upon his shoulder to make him stoop a little and three stood ready to fix the royal gewgaw on his head." At the signal of the pistol shot, a volley of musketry was fired as a salute.

With a muttered growl of surprise, the warrior chieftain tore himself loose from their hands. His eagle eye flashed the wireless "Are you come to trifle with me and to kill?"

Again Powhatan, now a crowned head, was reassured that all was well. Upon recovering his composure, it is told that he generously gave his old shoes and mantle to Captain Newport for his courtesy.

PART III
CAREER EDITORS

Antebellum Lady Editors and the Language of Authority

STEVEN FINK

IN Fanny Fern's 1855 novel *Ruth Hall*, the title character finds herself compelled by circumstances to transgress the boundaries of her woman's sphere and visit a story paper's editorial office: she hopes to sell one of her articles in order to feed her fatherless children (thereby returning to and fulfilling the duties of her domestic, feminine role, and so justifying the temporary transgression of her sphere). When she inquires of a printer's boy whom she encounters on the stairway, "Is this 'The Daily Type' office?" the "little ruffian" replies, "All you have to do is ask, mem. You've got a tongue in your head, haven't ye? women folks generally has."

Any deference Ruth, or the reader, might have expected from the boy, based on age, class, or gender, is nullified by the fact that Ruth has transgressed her proper sphere. The boy is not simply uncouth; he is asserting his rightful authority over her *in this place*, since, even as a menial and a child, he belongs here and she does not. Moreover, while the boy's rude reply centers upon the stereotype of female loquacity, the effect of the encounter is to demonstrate that Fanny does not know what language to use in this male milieu, and so she remains tongue-tied. When her timid knock at the office door goes unheeded, she steels herself and, penetrating the "whir of machinery, and a bad odor of damp paper and cigar smoke," she walks in, where "she found herself in the midst of a group of smokers, who, in slippered feet, and with heels higher than their heads, were whiffing and laughing, amid the pauses of conversation, most uproariously. Ruth's face crimsoned as heels and cigars remained, in *status quo*, and her glance was met by a rude stare" (120).[1] Like the boy, the men in the office feel no obligation to defer to her gentility or her femininity. When Ruth bravely but ineffectively proceeds to ask if they might be interested in any of her contributions, she is even more rudely dismissed.

As represented here, the editor's office is a men's den of the crudest sort, and no *lady* belongs there. Ruth Hall's creator, Fanny Fern, was, of course, only one of many antebellum women writers to actually cross that threshold, and with considerable success. We have a rich body of more or less recent criticism describing the negotiation of separate spheres by literary women—particularly those whom Mary Kelley describes in her book

Private Women, Public Stage as "literary domestics." In actuality, as Susan Coultrap-McQuin has argued, "the literary marketplace was not particularly alienating to women," and that rather than the crude den of male exclusivity encountered by Ruth Hall, the editorial offices of antebelllum America were dominated instead by the figure of the "Gentleman publisher," who took a paternal interest in guiding the careers of women writers (x, 33–35). This, in fact, is a fair description of Fanny Fern's character, Mr. John Walters, who recruits Ruth to his *Household Messenger* and guides Ruth's subsequent professional career.

But in either case, whether civilly or uncivilly, the line between men's and women's spheres was preserved—at least in appearance. As Ann Douglas describes women writers of the period, "they were professionals masquerading as amateurs. They evaded or at least mitigated just those restrictions imposed by pastoral and domestic duties which they celebrated in print; in disseminating praises of the private virtues, they gained access to the public realm" (85).² The masquerade was not just on the part of the woman writer, of course—the "gentleman publisher" (and the male writer in general, in the role of "gentleman amateur") participated in a kind of masquerade by which his overt (and often exaggerated) gentility cloaked his underlying commercial and professional interests. Clearly, *class* was an important component in the elaborate construction of both the literary lady *and* the literary gentleman.

Nevertheless, the literary *marketplace*—that is, the *business* of literary production—was at least within the province of men's sphere, so when male editors and publishers needed to *talk* about the bottom line, they could do it. Business, professionalism, and money were, on the other hand, precisely not part of the literary lady's vocabulary. As Mary Kelley points out, Catharine Maria Sedgwick's brother negotiated on her behalf with publishers and editors; Mary Virginia Terhune and Susan Warner were represented by their fathers (12–18). Women might write, and even have considerable commercial success; and they might also exert a great deal of public influence; but the masquerade of separate spheres required that *business* be left out of their public conversation. Early in her career, even the notable feminist Margaret Fuller could write to Elizabeth Peabody in 1839, seeking a periodical outlet for her writing, "The Democratic Review is not what I want, yet I might like to put something there occasionally, and should like to be asked. As to what my answer would be I would only ask of you, . . . Are they good pay (for I have heard the contrary)—? Will they pay me *unasked*? Or torture all my lady like feelings as almost all other persons with whom I have been concerned—" (2:91–92). While Fuller could be perfectly frank about her monetary concerns in her private correspondence with another (progressive) woman writer, she shrank at the prospect of having to acknowledge them openly. While Fuller understood the nature of the public role she was expected to play, there was nevertheless nothing cynical about this masquerade, for she had genuinely internalized the values which made discussions about money an offense to her "lady like feelings." As Sarah J. Hale remarked in the *Ladies' Magazine* in 1830, "Our men are sufficiently money-making. Let us keep our women and children from the contagion as long as possible."[3]

Yet women *writers* became women *editors* surprisingly early in the nineteenth century, even as this complicated their relation to the world of commerce and to the ideology of separate spheres. At first, and not surprisingly, they were editors of juvenile magazines, such as the *Juvenile Miscellany*, which Lydia Maria Child established and edited from 1826 to 1833; or the *Rose-Bud*, established and edited by Caroline Howard Gilman beginning in 1832; or they were editors of ladies' periodicals, such as *The Ladies' Magazine*, which Sarah Hale edited from 1828 to 1836, before becoming editor of *Godey's Lady's Book*. But it was not long before women editors expanded into family and general-audience popular magazines, such as the *Portland Magazine*, established and edited by Ann Stephens from 1834 to 1836; or the *Union Magazine*, edited by Caroline Kirkland from 1847 to 1849. Caroline Gilman, too, had expanded her *Rose-Bud* into a family magazine, the *Southern Rose*, in 1835. Moreover, Lydia Child became the editor of the *National Anti-Slavery Standard* from 1841 to 1843, and Margaret Fuller became editor of the transcendentalist journal *The Dial* in 1840—only a year after writing the letter quoted earlier about the vulnerability of her "lady like feelings." Yet the emergence of these women editors did not significantly alter the fact that editing itself remained a profession identified with the male world. As Susan Coultrap-McQuin has argued, "Sarah Josepha Hale, Caroline Gilman, Ann Stephens, Amelia Bloomer, and others certainly made their mark as editors and publishers, but there were too few women involved in the trade for anyone to think the ideal of the Gentleman Publisher was inappropriate for the industry as a whole" (33–34).

My overarching question in this essay, then, is what happens when the editor's chair itself is occupied by a woman—and a *lady*—rather than by either a contemptuous cigar-smoker *or* by a solicitous, paternalistic literary gentleman? How did they manage to fulfill the more public and overtly professional role of editor (as opposed to the masquerade of amateur affected by the literary domestics)? Did their gender limit or reconfigure their editorial authority? How did they represent themselves and their role as editors? And, in particular, what language did they find that enabled them to conduct business without violating the tacit restrictions on their identities as "ladies"? When Sarah Hale advises, "Let us keep our women and children from the [money-making] contagion," her "us" is ironically ambiguous. Is she speaking here as a woman to and among women readers (as distinct from "our men," from whom she distances herself)? Or is she using the (implicitly male-inflected) editorial "we," speaking as an editor among editors, who as cultural guardians adopt an essentially paternalistic attitude toward "our women"? If the ambiguity obscures the fact that Hale herself was writing as the professional editor of the *Ladies' Magazine*, this only underscores the fact that women—and especially women editors—needed to be extremely discreet, if not duplicitous, about the very business in which they were engaged.

Periodical editors in fact needed to deal with business and financial matters on several fronts: with the owners/publishers of the magazine, who both financed and oversaw its physical production (if the editors were not themselves the owners); with contributors, who produced the literary matter and at least hoped for monetary remuneration; and with readers, as subscribers to and purchasers of the magazines. In what follows, I consider what seem to me revealing examples of women periodical editors engaged in the *business* of periodical publication on each of these fronts.

Nominally, at least, the editor exerted primary authority over the contents of the magazine—she articulated its scope and mission, she solicited contributions, she exercised critical judgment in evaluating the appropriateness and the quality of submissions, and she often determined what, if any, extraliterary material should be included. But in fact, the publisher, who financed the periodical and who hired the editor, could exercise considerable control over the contents, and the publisher's bottom line was, invariably, sales. This was, of course, the case for both men and women editors, but in the case of women editors, the relationship between publisher and editor took some unique twists. One of the more interesting and ironic examples is the case of the controversial inclusion of colored fashion plates in several of the ladies' magazines. Sarah Hale undertook the editorship of the new *Ladies' Magazine* with strong convictions about the proper education and cultivation of American women, and she was an outspoken opponent of magazines' pandering to fashion. For the first two years of the *Ladies' Magazine*'s existence, therefore (while it was published by Putnam and Hunt of Boston), Hale refused to include fashion plates, even though they were beginning to appear in competing magazines at just this time.[4] By 1830, however, competition from other women's periodicals had intensified (chief among these was Louis A. Godey's *The Lady's Book*, which, from its very first number in July 1830, built its reputation largely on its colored fashion engravings). From November 1830 through 1833, therefore,

Hale reluctantly capitulated to market demands and pressure from her publisher: she now included fashion plates as a feature of her magazine, though she manipulated their role by adding editorial comments suggesting that these plates illustrated the antirepublican and corrupting influence of foreign fashions.[5] At the end of 1833, the *Ladies' Magazine* was taken over by a new owner, James B. Dow, and Hale herself became a part owner of her magazine (Entrikin 51, 53). Thus, Hale's antifashion principles again prevailed, and no more fashion plates appeared in her magazine until 1837, when Louis Godey bought her magazine, folded it into his own, and hired her as his new editor. With Godey as her publisher, Hale now had no choice but to accede to his demands that the magazine feature colored fashion plates.[6]

We find an even clearer example of a publisher's pressuring an editor to play to the market in the relation between Caroline Kirkland, as editor of the *Union Magazine*, and its publisher, Israel Post. In soliciting a contribution for the inaugural issue from her friend William Cullen Bryant, Kirkland confidently assured him that she had "sole editorial charge" of the literary matter, and hinted, moreover, that she should like to distinguish the *Union* from the popular magazines on which it was modeled, "to modify it a little in conformity with my own notions of what should be."[7] To another friend and potential contributor she declared, "I long to make [it] spirited and original and *insinuative* of much good."[8] Yet after only a month, she would write to Evert Duyckinck, "Are you disgusted with me because I have not been able to make the Magazine more purely Literary— There are many reasons for this—one of the principal of which is that I feel in honor bound to make the thing in some degree what the people expected it to be when they engaged me—but I shall elevate it as fast as I can with their concurrence."[9] But Israel Post was seeking the most popular, not the most elevated matter; and soon Kirkland was referring to him as "that old troglodyte,"[10] whom she dreaded to encounter in the office. After Post sold the magazine, and Kirkland was no long an editor, she expressed her frustration in an essay on "Reading for Amusement":

> It is not only, as is sometimes said, the fashion-plates that give a frivolous and vulgar aspect to certain handsome monthlies. It is the prevailing, almost exclusive use of amusing matter, with hardly a grain of ballast in the shape of actual information. It is in vain to say the style and matter of these things must be adapted to the taste of the readers.... [T]he duty of those who write for the public, is to aim at raising the standard of taste and improving the judgment of those who read; and publishers who disregard this will be repaid in the end by neglect. The declining state of most of our monthlies is to be traced to the forgetfulness of this necessity; and our experience and observation both lead us to feel sure that not to editors or writers is this owing so

much as to proprietors of the magazine, who, holding the purse-strings, short-sightedly refuse to pay for any but 'amusing' articles, and look upon what is technically termed 'heavy matter' as unsaleable.[11]

In the cases of both Hale and Kirkland, it is, ironically, *male* publishers who compel these women editors to emphasize fashion plates and love stories; but the point is that such pressure is driven not by a commitment to an ideology of separate spheres but, as Kirkland pointed out, by the bottom line of what is saleable.

Another marketable feature of the magazines, however, was the publication of works by "name" authors, which to a certain extent, at least, countered the leveling impulse from publishers. So even as Israel Post resisted Kirkland's literary ambitions, he also relentlessly urged her to exploit her literary connections to obtain contributions from prestigious writers. In this case, the interests of publisher and editor were more likely to coincide, but again, it was marketability, not literary quality, that mattered. In this context, we find women editors, off the public record, speaking and writing quite frankly about money and the commodification of literary matter. That is, one linguistic manifestation of the split identity of the "lady editor" was to use the language of commerce to conduct the magazine's business behind the scenes, and to use the quite different language of conventional, genteel femininity for public consumption in the pages of the magazine itself. Thus, when Kirkland writes to Bryant for a contribution to the first number of the *Union Magazine*, she explains quite frankly what is at stake: "Now as my own compensation in this matter is to be mainly dependent on the success of the attempt—(a circumstance which I would not like to have mentioned—) I hope you will not refuse a contribution to our first number, likely to be of important service to me—."[12] Kirkland genuinely wished to publish "spirited and original" literature of high quality—that is what her "own notions" of the magazine called for, and the impediments created by obtuse publishers rankled her for years. But in this letter to Bryant, she casts her appeal in terms of a personal favor, necessitated by the contingent nature of her own salary, the fact that the publisher holds the purse-strings, and the market value of Bryant's name (rather than the literary value of his work). Writing to Bryant again, several months later, she made the matter even more explicit:

> My publisher is so truly orthodox that he declares we must be saved by a *name*—and that if I should fill the pages of the magazine with the best literary matter that ever illuminated type it would be of no use (pecuniarily) if written by Tom, Dick & Harry—Now under these circumstances can not you come to the rescue in the shape of *one single page* of prose? On any conceivable

subject.... Whatever you choose to ask will be gladly paid for an article of any—no matter what—length."¹³

Kirkland was less expansive, but equally frank, in her request for a contribution from Bayard Taylor (with whom she was also personally acquainted): "It is quite an object with us to obtain known and popular *names* for our Jan. No—the *quality* of this article is secondary—(This is for your private ear as a mem. From the publisher—)."¹⁴ Again it is the publisher who speaks for the bottom line, but of particular interest is Kirkland's self-conscious, parenthetical comments, in which she distinguishes between the discourse of business transactions and the discourse of public self-representation. Kirkland did not lift the veil this way with writers whom she did not know personally. To Longfellow, for example, she simply wrote, with noticeably greater formality than to Bryant or Taylor, "Mrs. Kirkland's compliments to Mr. Longfellow—ventures to ask of him a contribution to the Union Magazine to which she is anxious to give a high character by the aid of the best writers." She was frank enough to add, however, that "The pay of the Union is the same as that of other Magazines—that is to say whatever eminent writers choose to ask."¹⁵

But Kirkland was not always so comfortable dealing with the money end of her job. In a letter to a friend, she described "three ladies who call here occasionally hoping to get something put into the Magazine." All three are well-bred and educated women who bear unmistakable marks of hard times or abuse, and Kirkland concedes, "One of the most unpleasant parts of my new employment is the necessity of dealing with such people in a mere business way, as I am obliged to do. The sight of their hope and fears requires strong nerves, or a very long purse."¹⁶

It is particularly in instances like this that the *role* of lady and the *job* of editing a periodical are revealed to be not entirely compatible. The ideology of separate spheres was promoted precisely so that women could exercise their moral, nurturing, compassionate impulses; they were to be protected by the boundaries that defined the private and domestic—as in a kind of moral incubator—from the threat of contamination or corruption by the harsh, rational materialism of the public sphere of business and politics. In her role as editor, however, Kirkland recognized that it was precisely her nurturing and compassionate impulses that she needed to suppress in the face of the "hope and fears" of these women. A "long purse" might have enabled her to keep the lines blurred between philanthropy and business, and so between the roles of lady and editor; but because the publisher, not the editor, held the purse strings, Kirkland recognized the "necessity of dealing with such people in a mere business way." The issue being forced,

Kirkland implicitly acknowledged that she was an editor, a businessperson, who adopted or maintained the role of *lady* only so long as it was feasible or desirable, and not a lady—i.e., a representative of "woman's sphere" and its attendant values—who chose to act in the role of editor.

In saying that Kirkland was "not a lady," I emphatically do not mean to cast aspersions on her character—though that is indeed how women's forays into the public sphere were treated by the most conservative adherents of the ideology of separate spheres. I mean only to underscore the fact that the concept of "lady" was itself a construct of the ideology of separate spheres and so became an increasingly precarious role to sustain the farther women ventured into the public sphere. That the ideology of separate spheres was flawed and actually pernicious is evident by the very condition of Kirkland's three would-be contributors—their status as "ladies" not only failed to protect them from abuse and destitution,[17] but in fact made them more vulnerable, and left them ill-equipped when they—like Ruth Hall—were compelled to compromise themselves and approach an editor in the hopes of selling their literary wares. They may have thought that a lady editor would be more sympathetic than a man, and Kirkland was indeed deeply pained by their plight, but the laws of the marketplace prevailed.

Perhaps the most striking and overt example of Kirkland's awareness of her bifurcated discourse appears in a letter she wrote to Bayard Taylor, who had stepped in as acting editor of the *Union Magazine* in the spring of 1848, while Kirkland embarked on a European tour. In a hurried note to Taylor written just before leaving New York, Kirkland addresses some last-minute editorial business: "I have written all I could—if I can I will yet finish a scrap of Editorial for the *June* head—If I don't accomplish it, will you write something as foolish and feminine as you can—that it may pass for mine."[18] Kirkland apparently understood that it ought to be no more difficult for Taylor to assume the masquerade of lady editor than it was for her to do so.

Kirkland also seems to have understood that the role of "lady editor" was a *marketable* image for those magazines that targeted female readers and consumers. The illusion of disinterested gentility, which was affected to some degree by almost all literary workers, both male and female, editors and writers, was that much easier to project for women, whose "proper" sphere reinforced such expectations. Israel Post had most likely been inclined to offer Kirkland the editorship of his magazine because she was a woman, as well as because she was a popular and well-connected writer. Certainly Louis Godey knew the value of acquiring Sarah Hale as editor of his magazine, and William Snowdon, publisher and editor of a *Godey's* competitor, *The Ladies' Companion* (1834–1844), enlisted frequent contributors Ann Stephens, Frances Osgood, Lydia Sigourney, and Emma Embury onto his editorial board at various times. Sigourney and Embury "saw their names printed on the title page of each volume; no other editors received such notice.... Poe reported that Snowdon pays his editresses $2 per week each for their names solely" (Weathersby 197). To underscore the obvious irony, it was the very masquerade of feminine gentility, which eschewed the taint of business, that constituted these women's literary capital and made them a marketable commodity on the covers of these magazines.

There was generally little reason, of course, for editors to publicly address money matters with contributors in the pages of their magazines. Gentility dictated discretion, and business negotiations were conducted chiefly through private correspondence. But occasionally editors found it expedient to state general commercial policies in print, and even lady editors were sometimes driven to transgress the strict bounds of propriety, or drop the masquerade of nonprofessionalism momentarily, as when Sarah Hale felt compelled to explain in the pages of *Godey's* the underlying market forces of authorship and publication: "We want it distinctly understood that, unless by previous understanding to that effect, no articles published in this magazine will be paid for. Young writers and those who have not acquired a literary reputation must remember that the mere insertion of their articles . . . is quite a compensation in itself."[19] And in cases such as Caroline Gilman's *Rose-Bud*, where the editor was also the publisher (that is, she hired a printer herself, and was not the paid employee of an owner-publisher who underwrote the venture), printed replies to potential contributors could reveal just how closely the editor kept her eye on the account books: Acknowledging in an editorial notice the receipt of a contribution, Gilman adds, "While we thank our Correspondent and beg his continued interest in the Rose Bud, we would request him to send by private conveyance, or pay the postage."[20]

Nor was there often a need for editors to speak *directly* of the business of magazine publication with the readers. Subscription rates and information about sales agents were most often posted under the name of the publisher-printer, not the editor, on the front or back pages. But because magazines had not yet discovered the potential of advertising to cover the costs of publication, they were inordinately dependent on direct sales and subscriptions to stay afloat; and if subscribers were delinquent in their payments, editors periodically felt compelled to beseech readers directly for prompt payment—sometimes in amusing detail, as when Caroline Gilman (in the same notice cited above) appeals to subscribers of the *Rose-Bud*, "It is requested that Subscribers will remit their Subscription for the present year by January 1st. Where it is practicable, private conveyance, vessels, or the gratuitous agency of post masters, would be preferable, to save postage. To justify this notice, our friends will remember the small price of subscription."[21] The point here is that, in this era of unfavorable postal regulations for magazines, dependence upon subscriptions, and chronically delinquent payments, it was routine for editors to dun their readers for payment; but for lady editors to do so was to expose the transgressive nature of their real work and to violate Sarah Hale's injunction to "keep our women and children from the contagion [of money-making] as long as possible."

More often, however, the discourse with which the lady editor spoke to her readers about the *business* of magazine publication was indirect, insinuated between the lines of more high-minded or literary matters. Antebellum magazines in general, but especially those edited by women, tended to emphasize (or affect) noncommercial aspirations: the role they hoped to play in the project of universal education, in building informed and virtuous citizens of the republic, or, at the very least, in cultivating the tastes of an emerging middle class. It was therefore natural for lady editors to represent themselves to their readers as embodying a public extension of conventional women's roles—self-deprecating, service-oriented, and moral. But the underlying commercial dimensions of their enterprise invariably revealed themselves, and here the language through which they exercise their role becomes particularly complex.

In her "Introduction" to the inaugural issue of the *Ladies' Magazine* in January 1828, for example, Sarah Hale begins by declaiming, "To prove the advantages of a general diffusion of literature, among all classes and both sexes, happily for me, no arguments are necessary. Throughout our country the truth of the proposition is felt, its utility acknowledged; and the result of the experiment of universal instruction is considered as involving within its practicability and influence of the perfection of our social happiness, the perpetuity of our dearest privileges." She goes on to announce that the special mission of this periodical is women's education, "not that they may usurp the station or encroach on the prerogative of the man; but that each individual may lend her aid to perfect the moral and intellectual character of those within her sphere." But in her opening paragraph, Hale concedes that "These publications, depending, as they necessarily must, on the patronage of individuals for support, cannot always succeed, even when meriting success." It is therefore not surprising that Hale ultimately turns to *men*, who hold the purse strings and upon whose patronage she therefore depends, to launch an elaborate sales pitch. "The gentlemen are respectfully invited to examine [the magazine's] contents. If they find nothing which promises advantage to their own minds, yet they will not surely withhold their support, if convinced of the utility of the plan, and that it is calculated to please and instruct those nearest and dearest to them." The "gentlemen" are then solicited in each of their possible roles in relation to women: If, as a *husband*, he must leave his wife at home while he earns a living in the public sphere, he "should rejoice that he has it in his power to afford her the means of agreeably beguiling the interval of his absence." As a *father* he can "bestow on his children a memento of his affection, which shall be a source of improvement to the objects of his fond solicitude—will he not give his name as a patron of this work? . . . The *brother*," she writes, who is about to venture out into the world, "will he not gladly embrace the opportunity to offer the Magazine to those dear and tender relatives whose hearts are anxious for his prosperity?" And finally, "the *lover*" "will present [to his beloved] his subscription for the Ladies' Magazine; and the sweet smile with which his gift is received, will recur, like a dream of light, to his memory, while reflecting that the soft eyes of his charmer are, for *his* sake, often employed on its pure pages, while her fancy, and taste, and mind, are improving by its scenes, characters, and sentiments."[22]

Hale overtly presents her magazine in terms of a social vision, but she exposes the fact that "women's sphere" is not only a social ideology but also a market niche. Given the ideology of separate spheres, her role as lady editor is necessarily ambivalent, and her rhetoric is revealingly double-voiced: the sentimentality and high moral tone of the lady-as-educator vie with the shrewd, knowing appeals of editor-as-salesperson. That is, while we saw in Kirkland's correspondence an example of the radical bifurcation of commercial and genteel discourses, Hale's introduction exemplifies an alternative linguistic response to the split identity of the lady editor: to generate a double-voiced rhetoric that attempts to incorporate both discourses simultaneously. Ultimately, the two roles are perhaps irreconcilable. Hale cannot promote a version of female education that remains "compatible with the cheerful discharge of [woman's] domestic duties, and that delicacy of feeling, and love of retirement, which nature so obviously imposes on the sex,"[23] and at the same time step forward to hawk subscriptions to the magazine, without both voices teetering on the verge of mere parody.

Moreover, while she projects a predominantly (though not exclusively) female *readership* for the magazine, Hale knows she needs to promote her product to *men*, who control the money and are therefore the *primary* consumers. The magazine, in other words, is represented as a *gift* commodity, whose value to men, as the actual purchasers, is in their presenting it to women, who, as readers, are its *secondary* consumers. Rhetorically, the editor must therefore find a way of appealing to both primary and secondary consumers. The ideology of separate spheres itself thus complicates not only the rhetoric of the lady editor, but the implied audience as well. Hale's appeal to male readers and buyers here would therefore seem to complicate Patricia Okker's claim that Hale's magazine created a "separate . . . public sphere for women" in which the editor wrote as a "woman writing to other women" (40, 60, passim).[24] In *Domesticity with a Difference*, Nicole Tonkovich takes the contrary position, that Hale, "in all her writing, in fact addresses a reader whose gender is male" (34). But this too seems like an over-simplification. My point regarding the double-voiced rhetoric of the lady editor and the complex audience of the magazine as gift commodity is that, while the ideology of separate spheres is always operative, the magazine does not have either an exclusively male or female audience, but is, of necessity, continually navigating across gender lines.[25]

Like Hale's "Introduction" to the *Ladies' Magazine*, Ann Stephens's opening "Address" in the inaugural issue of her *Portland Magazine* also employs hyperbolic rhetoric to express her social and moral altruism while simultaneously insinuating the financial considerations that underlie the publishing venture. Stephens begins, "Noah, when sending out the dove upon the waste of waters, could not have felt more anxiety for its safe return with the green leaf of promise in its bill, than is experienced for the success of the specimen number of the *Portland Magazine*."[26] On one level, the biblical allusion here conveys the high moral or spiritual design of her undertaking—suggesting, by association, both the piety of the editor herself and the moral propriety and ambitions of the magazine's designs on the public. But the stakes in the success of the *Portland Magazine* are not, after all, commensurate, either in kind or degree, with those of Noah's venture. While we might regard Stephens's rhetorical amplification, or auxesis, as a manifestation of her mawkish earnestness and sincerity, the passage also allows for a slyer, more ironically humorous and self-conscious reading. The multiple meanings of the word "bill" make it particularly tempting to extract from Stephens's opening remark a play on words that exposes the double-voiced role of the lady editor: If Noah was anxious for the "safe return" of the dove "with the green leaf of promise in its bill," the editor sends forth the *leaves* of her magazine, anxious for the promise of a *safe return* on her investment in the form of *green bills*. Read yet another way, it is the "bill of sale," or subscription, which promises a return of "green leaves" of money.

Stephens does seem quite capable of such disingenuous irony, for she goes on to describe her ambitions for the magazine in such a way as to recast her very *un*-ladylike preference for professional and public labor over private and domestic work precisely in terms of the feminine virtues of self-sacrifice, moral service, and duty: "The editor is fully aware of all that can be said in opposition to the present undertaking." The "opposition" she has in mind here, however, is *not*, as we might have expected, to a *lady* assuming the responsibilities of editor (objectionable because they constitute a commercial, public, self-serving, and thus "unwomanly" violation of her proper sphere). Rather, it is the "editor" as businesswoman, not the *lady*, who can imagine "opposition" to her undertaking based on the presupposed criteria of practical, business values: the editorship will require too much selfless (i.e., unremunerative) labor from her, and so will not provide a sufficient material return on her investment. And to *this* imagined objection she replies that, *like a good woman*, she will nevertheless do her duty and make that sacrifice:

> She knows that days and nights of application and anxiety will be but a small part of the task she has imposed upon herself. With no hopes of fame or personal distinction does she step into the field of literature. Well she knows that what could be attained through the medium of a magazine would be far outbalanced by the sacrifice of private ease and personal comfort; yet knowing this, she still undertakes the task, certain that her object is good, and feeling resolved to do her duty to her subscribers so far as her powers will admit.[27]

Not to go forth with this undertaking would be to succumb to the temptation of "private ease and comfort"; she will sacrifice herself and do her "duty"—though her duty is not that of a woman, to home, husband or child, but that of an editor, to "her subscribers." Stephens appropriates the *rhetoric* of domesticity here—the language of self-less labor, personal sacrifice, and higher duty—in order to subvert the underlying *ideology* of separate spheres, and so to justify her actual renunciation of the private and domestic for the public and professional.

A concluding example of the lady editor's double-voiced rhetoric is again provided by Ann Stephens, this time in a brief sketch entitled "Visiting Cards," which appeared in the January 1835 issue of the *Portland Magazine*. The speaker in this piece is looking through old visiting cards left at her home; the cards evoke memories of their owners, whom the speaker goes on to recall and describe in a series of succinct character sketches. The premise itself—that calling cards of visitors to her home draw forth rich and deep associations from the sensitive and cultivated soul of the speaker—marks the speaker emphatically as a genteel lady. The same aesthetics of association governed the accounts of tourist excursions *into the world* to encounter famous landscapes, or monuments, or places, in the sketches and travelogues of the day (by both men and women), but here the speaker remains pointedly in place in the domestic sphere. The calling cards are the tangible emblems of the gentility that her recollections corroborate, while her entrenchment in the private sphere remains inviolate.

Of the last card she takes up she writes, "My heart aches as I look upon it, for it is a relic of the dead, of one whose inheritance of genius was too much for his vigor. Ambition—literary ambition, cost him his life." She first describes its owner's appearance and character in stereotypically romantic terms ("I never saw a handsomer mouth and chin than his—there was something so very chaste and spiritual in the expression; but his eyes were too bright and large.... His forehead was white and very high"). Then she continues,

> In his twenty-third year the fire of his genius was turned upon his heart in disappointment, and he died.
> I have said he was ambitious. He had just engaged in his first literary enterprise, a *monthly magazine*. The first number came out, written almost entirely by himself, full of promise and beauty. Critics lauded, the world approved, *but few subscribed*. The publisher became discouraged, would not consent to risk money in the establishment of the work, and it never reached its second number. This was a death-blow to poor J.... He had ascended one step on the ladder of fame, had been hurled back with a sudden violence; and his spirit was crushed in the fall. I saw him two months after the failure of his work, and in a low but very sweet voice, he told me he should not live many days.... Why did this card present itself? I was sad enough without it. I will close this box, I can look no further.[28]

The sensitive, romantic spirit *as magazine editor* is crushed between the indifference of an obtuse public who would not subscribe and the crass materialism of a miserly publisher who would not risk underwriting the venture. Significantly, the piece is signed, not "Mrs. Ann Stephens," but "ED[ITOR]." In doing so, Stephens establishes an identification between herself and the tragic would-be editor of her sketch, even as that character is a *doubly* masked alter-ego. For beneath the mask of a *man* too sensitive to endure the world of business (an inversion of gender roles) is in fact a *businesswoman* whose implicit but inescapable message to her readers is, "you have it in your power to avert precisely this tragedy that so moves you: If you are moved, or elevated, or entertained by these tales, you must *buy* them."

The construction of the "lady editor" is a fundamentally conflicted role in antebellum America. Within the ideology of separate spheres, the authority of the "lady" and of the "editor" are not only distinct but at some point mutually exclusive. Yet however precarious, unstable, and contradictory such a masquerade was, it was also—for a brief period, in the decades before the Civil War—eagerly exploited (by publishers and by the editors themselves) and consumed (by readers). The work and the language of the lady editors expose the fault lines in the ideology of separate spheres. They suggest both that the separate spheres were in fact less separate, more permeable than they were represented as being, and also that the very real force that this ideology exerted on the culture resulted in the ironies and tensions of the bifurcated and double-voiced rhetoric of our "lady editors."

Notes

1. Compare this to the similar literary rendition in *Little Women*, when Jo March first enters the editorial office of the "Weekly Volcano": Dressed in her very best, Jo also climbs "dark and dirty stairs to find herself in a disorderly room, a cloud of cigar smoke, and the presence of three gentlemen sitting with their heels rather higher than their hats, which articles of dress none of them took the trouble to remove on her appearance" (426). Jo March models her sensation fiction on that of "Mrs. S.L.A.N.G. Northbury"—an obvious play on the actual Mrs. E.D.E.N. Southworth—but Louisa Alcott modeled this scene, at least, on Fanny Fern's novel, written thirteen years earlier.

2. The theme of hypocrisy versus sincerity, and the consequent concern with masquerade, in nineteenth-century America are brilliantly explored by Karen Halttunen in *Confidence Men and Painted Women*. Literary masquerading by women writers is insightfully explored by Nicole Tonkovich in *Domesticity with a Difference*.

3. [Sarah Josepha Hale], *Ladies' Magazine* 3.1 (January 1830): 42–43. This remark is from Hale's review of Lydia Maria Child's *The Frugal Housewife*, in which Hale's praise is tempered by her concern that Child is too overt in addressing financial considerations. For Hale, the chief value of this book, "by the author of Hobomok," is "not so much for the system of economy recommended, as for the example the author has exhibited. She is a lady of the first literary attainments, and yet shows herself acquainted with housekeeping in its most minute and closely calculated details. Here then is proof that learning, imagination, genius, do not unfit a lady for domestic usefulness" (42).

4. On the earliest American magazine fashion plates, see Bertha Monica Stearns, "Early Philadelphia Magazines for Ladies."

5. In the text accompanying the fashion plate in the September 1831 issue, Hale confessed, "There is no part of our duty as editor of a ladies' Journal, which we feel so reluctant to perform, as to quote, or exhibit the fashions of dress." As Lawrence Martin has pointed out, Hale valiantly tried to use her editorial text as a counterforce to the fashion plates, critiquing their frivolity and their servile deference to European (i.e., decadent and antirepublican) values, and so making of the fashion plate "a moral cartoon" (55).

6. On Hale's attitude toward fashion and fashion plates, see, in addition to Martin's still valuable essay, cited above, Nicole Tonkovich, *Domesticity with a Difference*, especially 72–74; and Isabelle Lehuu, "Sentimental Figures." On the history of Hale's and Godey's magazines, see Frank Luther Mott, *A History of American Magazines, 1741–1850*, 580–94.

7. Caroline Kirkland to William Cullen Bryant, 15 May 1847, Bryant-Godwin Collection, New York Public Library; transcribed in Audrey Joyce Roberts, "The Letters of Caroline M. Kirkland" (Ph.D. dissertation, University of Wisconsin, Madison), 1976, 120–21.

8. Caroline Kirkland to Rev. Henry Bellows, 21 June 1847; in Roberts, "Letters," 122. Bellows was the editor of the *Christian Enquirer*, which Kirkland was also helping edit, in place of her recently deceased husband, who had been its assistant editor. Bellows remained a close friend of Kirkland's to the end of her life.

9. Caroline Kirkland to Evert Duyckinck, June 1847; in Roberts, "Letters," 123–24.

10. Caroline Kirkland to Henry and Eliza Bellows, 6 August 1847; in Roberts, "Letters," 131.

11. Mrs. [Caroline M.] Kirkland, "Reading for Amusement," 23. An earlier and shorter version of this essay was published in *Sartain's Union Magazine* 6.3 (March 1850): 192–96,

which, not surprisingly, did not include this passage. Kirkland remained a contributing editor to *Sartain's* after Israel Post sold the *Union* in 1849 to John Sartain, who moved the magazine from New York to Philadelphia and hired John S. Hart as principal editor.

12. Caroline Kirkland to William Cullen Bryant, 15 May 1847; in Roberts, "Letters," 121.

13. Caroline Kirkland to William Cullen Bryant, 24 August 1847; in Roberts, "Letters," 136.

14. Caroline Kirkland to Bayard Taylor, 16 November 1847; in Roberts, "Letters," 145.

15. Caroline Kirkland to Henry Wadsworth Longfellow, 22 September 1847; in Roberts, "Letters," 139. It is perhaps worth noting that Kirkland eventually succeeded in getting contributions from her friends Bryant, Bayard Taylor, and Evert Duyckinck, but failed with Longfellow, who was then under an exclusive contract with *Graham's*.

16. Caroline Kirkland to Eliza Bellows, 8 July 1847; in Roberts, "Letters," 126–27.

17. As Kirkland described them, one was "the daughter of two of our first and haughtiest families," but her "pale face and swollen eyelids and agitated manner refer . . . to the character and conduct of her husband"; another was one of Kirkland's former schoolmates, younger than she "but brought by continued misfortune into the condition of a broken down old woman—looking sixty at least [Kirkland was forty-six at the time]—and trying to support a husband who is completely broken in spirit and hopeless"; and the third was "a well-bred woman, the widow of a British officer—left with a large family and no other earthly dependence than a pension of $400 pr annum" (Ibid).

18. Caroline Kirkland to Bayard Taylor, 6 April 1848; in Roberts, "Letters," 271.

19. Quoted in Algernon Tassin, *The Magazine in America*, 107.

20. *The Rose-Bud, or Youth's Gazette* 1.11 (10 November 1832): 43.

21. Ibid.

22. [Sarah Josepha Hale], "Introduction," *Ladies' Magazine* 1.1 (January 1828): 1–3. In "The Genesis of Godey's Ladies' Book," Lawrence Martin calls this introduction "a masterpiece of diplomatic urging to come buy a new product" (48).

23. Ibid, 2.

24. A similar reading is offered by Amy Beth Aronsen, who argues that, "Although it may appear that the *Ladies' Magazine* is meant to serve patriarchal fathers, brothers, and husbands, her ulterior motives are clear from the start," and that Hale "undercuts male authority by speaking to them from within a 'feminine' context" (3, 4).

25. In this regard it is also noteworthy that Sarah Hale's encyclopedic work *Woman's Record* was "Inscribed to the Men of America; who show, in their laws and customs, respecting WOMEN, ideas more just and feelings more noble than were ever evinced by men of any other nation: may "WOMAN'S RECORD" meet the approval of the sons of our great republic; the world will then know the Daughters are Worthy of Honour" (v).

26. Ann S. Stephen, "Address," *The Portland Magazine* 1.1 (1 October 1834): 1–2.

27. Ibid.

28. "ED." [Ann S. Stephens], "Visiting Cards," *The Portland Magazine* 1.5 (2 February 1835): 129–31.

Works Cited

Alcott, Louisa May. *Little Women*. New York: Modern Library, 1983.

Aronsen, Amy Beth. "Domesticity and Women's Collective Agency: Contribution and Collaboration in America's First Successful Women's Magazine." *American Periodicals* 11 (2001): 1–23.

Coultrap-McQuin, Susan. *Doing Literary Business: American Women Writers in the Nineteenth Century*. Chapel Hill: University of North Carolina Press, 1990.

Douglas, Ann. *The Feminization of American Culture*. New York: Knopf, 1977.

Entrikin, Isabelle Webb. *Sarah Josepha Hale and* Godey's Lady's Book. Lancaster, Pa.: Lancaster Press, 1946.

Fern, Fanny. *Ruth Hall and Other Writings*, ed. Joyce W. Warren. New Brunswick: Rutgers University Press, 1986.
Fuller, Margaret. *The Letters of Margaret Fuller*, ed. Robert N. Hudspeth, 6 volumes. Ithaca, N.Y.: Cornell University Press, 1983–1994.
[Gilman, Caroline.] "Charleston." *The Rose-Bud, or Youth's Gazette* 1.1 (10 November 1832): 43.
[Hale, Sarah J.] "Introduction." *Ladies' Magazine* 1.1 (January, 1828): 1–3.
Hale, Sarah J. *Woman's Record; or, Sketches of All Distinguished Women, From "The Beginning" Till* A.D. *1850*. New York: Harper, 1853.
Halttunen, Karen. *Confidence Men and Painted Women: A Study of Middle-Class Culture in America, 1830–1870*. New Haven, Conn.: Yale University Press, 1982.
Kelley, Mary. *Private Woman, Public Stage: Literary Domesticity in Nineteenth-Century America*. New York: Oxford University Press, 1984.
Kirkland, Mrs. [Caroline M.] "Reading for Amusement." In *A Book for the Home Circle; or, Familiar Thoughts on Various Topics, Literary, Moral, and Social. A Companion for The Evening Book*. New York: Charles Scribner, 1853.
Lehuu, Isabelle. "Sentimental Figures: Reading *Godey's Lady's Book* in Antebellum America." In *The Culture of Sentiment: Race, Gender and Sentimentality in Nineteenth-century America*, ed. Shirley Samuels. New York: Oxford University Press, 1992.
Martin, Lawrence."The Genesis of Godey's Lady's Book," *New England Quarterly* 1.1 (1928): 41–70.
Mott, Frank Luther. *A History of American Magazines, 1741–1850*. New York: Appleton, 1930.
Okker, Patricia. *Our Sister Editors: Sarah J. Hale and the Tradition of Nineteenth-Century American Women Editors*. Athens, Ga.: University of Georgia Press, 1995.
Roberts, Audrey Joyce. "The Letters of Caroline M. Kirkland," Ph.D. dissertation, University of Wisconsin, Madison, 1976.
Stearns, Bertha Monica. "Early Philadelphia Magazines for Ladies." *Pennsylvania Magazine of History and Biography* 64 (1940): 479–91.
Stephens, Ann S. "Address." *The Portland Magazine* 1.1 (1 October, 1834): 1–2.
[Stephens, Ann S.] "Visiting Cards." *The Portland Magazine* 1.5 (2 February, 1835): 129–31.
Tassin, Algernon. *The Magazine in America*. New York: Dodd, Mead, 1916.
Tonkovich, Nicole. *Domesticity with a Difference: The Nonfiction of Catherine Beecher, Sarah J. Hale, Fanny Fern, and Margaret Fuller*. Jackson: University of Mississippi Press, 1997.
Weathersby, Robert W., II. *"The Ladies' Companion,"* in *American Literary Magazines*, ed. Edward E. Chielens. New York: Greenwood Press, 1986. 196–99.

"Introduction"
Ladies' Magazine, January 1828

To prove the advantages of a general diffusion of literature, among all classes and both sexes, happily for me, no arguments are necessary. Throughout our country the truth of the proposition is felt, its utility acknowledged; and the result of the experiment of universal instruction is considered as involving within its practicability and influence the perfection of our social happiness, and the perpetuity of our dearest privileges. It is this public enthusiasm in the cause of education which encourages the numerous aspirants for fame, or profit, to send forth their periodicals in every form that fancy can devise to attract, and under every name ingenuity can discover to allure. These publications, depending, as they necessarily must, on the patronage of individuals for support, cannot always succeed, even when meriting success; they doubtless sometimes fail in consequence of the indolence or inability of those who conduct them. But if the motives, which prompted the undertaking, be pure and praise-worthy, a failure should not be considered as disgraceful.

In this age of innovation, perhaps no experiment will have an influence more important on the character and happiness of our society, than the granting to females the advantages of a systematic and thorough education. The honor of this triumph, in favor of intellect over long established prejudices, belongs to the men of America. They appear willing to risk the hazard of proving, experimentally, whether that degree of literature which only can qualify woman to become a rational companion, an instructive as well as an agreeable friend, be compatible with the cheerful discharge of her domestic duties, and that delicacy of feeling, and love of retirement, which nature so obviously imposes on the sex. To make the plan as completely successful as its most sanguine advocates can desire, it is only necessary that the ladies should be fully sensible of the importance of the privileges now accorded them; not that they may usurp the station, or encroach on the prerogative of the man; but that each individual may lend her aid to perfect the moral and intellectual character of those within her sphere. It is that mothers may be competent to the task of instructing their children, training them from infancy to the contemplation and love of all that is great and good, and the practice of piety and virtue. Then the sons of the republic will become polished pillars in the temple of our national glory, and the daughters bright gems to adorn it.

Every effort, therefore, to accelerate the progress of the mental improvement, is certainly deserving of attention from a people who acknowledge no honorary distinctions, save those acquired by superior personal merit, or talent, or virtue. And while offering the *Ladies' Maga-*

zine to public notice, and soliciting patronage, the editor flatters herself she shall, at least, receive the good wishes of the community in her behalf.

This magazine, although ostensibly designed for the ladies, is not intended to be exclusively devoted to female literature. The gentlemen are respectfully invited to examine its contents. If they find nothing which promises advantage to their own minds, yet they will not surely withhold their support, if convinced of the utility of the plan, and that it is calculated to please and instruct those nearest and dearest to them.

Will not the husband, while compelled by the duties of his vocation to leave the partner of his fortunes in a solitary home, rejoice that he has it in his power to afford her the means of agreeably beguiling the interval of his absence? He may rest assured, that nothing found on the pages of this publication, shall cause her to be less assiduous in preparing for his reception, or less sincere in welcoming his return.

The father, wishing to bestow on his children a memento of his affection, which shall be a source of improvement to the objects of his fond solicitude—will not he give his name as a patron of this work? where nothing shall be found to weaken parental authority, or foster that fervor of the imagination, which, when undisciplined by reading and reflection, often hurries youth, of either sex, into those follies and extravagances that disturb family concord, and destroy domestic felicity.

The brother, about to "set out on his stormy career," will not he gladly embrace the opportunity to offer the Magazine to those dear and tender relatives whose hearts are anxious for his prosperity? He may, though far separated from the household band, feel confident, that the ties of kindred affection will be sacredly cherished, by the examples exhibited in this work.

The lover, ay, the favored lover—on him we confidently depend for support. He will no longer, when bidding adieu to the "lady of his love," request her to gaze on that inconstant thing, the moon, so often obscured by clouds, and then remember her vows. He will present her his subscription for the Ladies Magazine; and the sweet smile with which the gift is received, will recur, like a dream of light, to his memory, while reflecting that the soft eyes of his charmer are, for *his sake*, often employed on its pure pages, while her fancy, and taste, and mind, are improving by its scenes, characters, and sentiments.

The Editor does not ask this patronage, nor offer these pledges, depending on her own resources to merit the one, or redeem the other. But she is confident, those friends, who have so generously interested themselves in her favor, will continue their assistance; and their names, were she at liberty to reveal them, would at once satisfy the public, that the work will be deserving the rank it has assumed; that of a miscellany, which, although devoted to general literature, is more expressly designed to mark the progress of female improvement, and cherish the effusions of female intellect.

The present number will better exhibit the plan intended to be followed in the choice and arrangement of the matter, than a labored paragraph on the subject. However, it may not be amiss to observe, that the work will be national—be American;—and well written communications, whether poems, letters, sketches, tales, or essays, descriptive of American scenery, character, and manners, will be most welcome to its pages.

Perhaps it may be thought quite unnecessary to add, that competition, even were it *possible*, with any established literary journal, is neither wished nor intended. The conductors of those publications which have already acquired a reputation, and are enjoying the reward of their labors, will not surely, frown upon this attempt because it is unprecedented, or endeavor to perplex the task of one already trembling for the issue of an enterprise in which she has reluctantly engaged. She would now hardly dare proceed, did not the hope sometimes whisper—

—"Our doubts are traitors,
And make us lose the good we oft might win,
By fearing to attempt."

Subtle Subversion:
Mary Louise Booth and *Harper's Bazar* (1867–1889)

PAULA BERNAT BENNETT

IN 1867, the powerful New York publishing firm Harper and Brothers launched its third periodical venture, *Harper's Bazar*, inviting thirty-six-year-old Mary Louise Booth to guide the innovative high-fashion magazine in its formative stages. Given the nature of the newly created editor's position, Harper's choice of Booth might seem an odd one. Not only was Booth not a woman of wealth and fashion herself but her father, the manager of a night-watchman service, was at best lower middle class and contributed little to his daughter's support. As an apprentice-journalist, Booth had spent her days working low-paying jobs, reading and writing at night. At the time of her appointment to the *Bazar*, translating had become her principal means of support, and the texts she translated were not those likely to appeal to the elite audience Harpers had in mind. "[B]eginning with a *Marble-Workers' Manual* . . . in 1856," *Britannica Online* records, Booth "translated some 40 volumes from French, including works of Pascal and Victor Cousin. . . . In a week of almost ceaseless labor in 1861, she produced a translation of Count Agénor de Gasparin's *The Uprising of a Great People: The United States in 1861*."[1] Booth followed up Gasparin's *Uprising* with his *America Before Europe* (1862), Edouard Laboulaye's *Paris in America* (1863), Augustin Cochin's *The Results of Slavery* and *The Results of Emancipation* (both 1863), and Henri Martin's three-volume *History of France* (1864–66). Such was the life experience and résumé earning Mary Booth her new and no doubt coveted position as editor of New York City's and the nation's first full-blown high fashion magazine.

Yet odd as the fit between Booth's résumé and the *Bazar*'s high fashion profile might seem, what she made of the periodical, in the end, could not have better reflected who and what Mary Booth was. Booth's contribution to the *Bazar* (and to the concept of the U.S. high fashion magazine) went well beyond the organization of the magazine's fashion component, the details of which she left to a fashion editor. Far more important was her handling of the *Bazar*'s general content: its choice of essays, fiction, poetry, and illustrations. Booth was a shrewd businesswoman, and this was undoubtedly one of the reasons that the Harper brothers hired her, but, like all superior editors, she was also a woman with vision, who brought her own personal sense of mission to the magazine. Succinctly, this essay will argue that Booth, whose commitment to the women's rights movement was steadfast throughout her adulthood, recognized the potential in the high fashion magazine's generic position as trend-setter—its futuristic orientation—and exploited it from the start, using it as a cover for her advocacy of social and, in particular, gender reform.

In fashion, as Booth pointed out in the *Bazar*'s mission statement, "newness" is of the essence ("Our Bazar"). What women who could afford this year's European styles wanted was to have them immediately, not next year, which was the best that earlier women's magazines such as *Godey's* and *Peterson's* had done. But what of this year's values? this year's ways of living or thinking? Were not the myriad choices women made in such matters determined to a great extent by the same forces that generated changes in the way they dressed and, where the "cutting edge" was concerned, did this not place these other choices under the rubric of "fashion" also? For Booth, as to a greater or lesser extent for all her successors, the high fashion magazine—one of industrialized society's more inimitable by-products—had of necessity to serve a dual purpose. Selling clothing, on the one hand, it sold cultural modernity—under Booth, specifically gender modernity—on the other, indexing shifts in clothing preferences to shifts in female subjectivity and to shifts in the ways in which upper- and upper-middle-class women, in particular, chose to live their lives.

In using her editorial position to influence her readers' decisions on how they should live, not just what they should wear, Booth, at least in principle, was doing nothing new. Possibly because bourgeois women's formal education lagged so far behind that of men, editors of women's magazines had long touted the instructional as well as the pleasurable as part of their package, even as the *Bazar*'s subtitle—"*A Repository of Fashion, Pleasure, and Instruction*"—reads,[2] and its female subscribership consciously went to the magazines for both. "Who is there could ask a loftier monument," Harriet Spofford enthused in her 1889 memorial to Booth in the *Bazar*, "than she has made for herself in twenty-one years of work that has entered half a million families, and helped to mould a whole generation in gentleness, intelligence, and virtue." This was what a proper nineteenth-century ladies' magazine editor was supposed to do: produce the gentle, intelligent, and virtuous "true woman." Where Booth diverged—rather more than Spofford may have realized or chose to admit—was in the specific direction that the *Bazar*'s instructional activities took or, put another way, the kind of woman the magazine sought to produce.

Both publicly and privately, Mary Booth insisted that the *Bazar* was a "family magazine." Indeed, she warned Thomas Wentworth Higginson, whom she garnered in the 1880s to write a column on gender issues, that discussions of suffrage and the like were off-limits: "'It has always been thought inexpedient to advocate woman suffrage . . . either explicitly or implicitly. It has been a cardinal principle with the *Bazar*, as a home journal . . . to abstain from the discussion of vexed questions of religion, politics, and kindred topics'" (qtd. in Beasley 71). Officially speaking, this was the *Bazar*'s policy from its mission statement on and Booth never publicly wavered from it (see, for example, "Our Bazar" and Wingate 259). Years before coming to the *Bazar*, Booth told Susan B. Anthony that her refusal to advocate women's rights openly was strategic, however, and should not be read as an unwillingness to aid the cause she called the "polar star" of her life: "If it were possible I would do this directly, but the fashion of the times has made me a dependent. . . . If I succeed [in becoming independent], count on me. All that I can do, I will, to rescue my sex from the fetters which have chafed me so bitterly . . . but if I speak at present I forfeit all claims on my home forever" (as qtd. in Harper 146).

Booth never achieved the independence that "the fashion of the times" denied her, though her very use of the term "fashion" in this context suggests that she recognized early on how much a matter of social "style" gender restrictions were. She served as secretary for a number of women's rights conventions; she was a delegate to the New York State Teachers' Association, where she supported Anthony's demands for equal education for African American children and equal pay for teachers; she was a member of the New York Anti-Slavery Society; she formed an association for the intellectual and social improvement of women ["Alpha"]; and she translated texts which both Lincoln and Charles Sumner, the senatorial spearhead for abolition, viewed as significant contributions to the war effort. (According to Spofford, Sumner considered Booth's translation of Gasparin's *Uprising* "worth a whole phalanx in the cause of human freedom" [232].) However, as Booth's near total absence from histories of the women's rights movement testifies, this highly political and highly influential woman also knew how to bend and when to conceal, staying within prescribed limits or, at least, making it appear as if she did, even as "the fashion of the times" demanded.

If Booth found this strategy frustrating, as her comment to Anthony suggests she did, in the end, it garnered her an editorial power and freedom she could not have had in any other way. When asked by Charles Wingate in an 1875 interview "What features, in your view, constitute the essentials of a complete journal, devoted to the field which the *Bazar* covers?" Booth responded, "'the *Bazar* itself, which represents my idea, as far as I have been able to carry it out'" (*Views* 256). Since few editors ever completely fulfill their "idea," Booth's comment could be read as pro forma apology; but at a deeper level, she spoke the truth. Before coming to the *Bazar*, Booth, in one last bid for autonomy, had tried—and failed—to get funding for her own women's rights periodical (Zakrzewka 106). If only because of the tie-in with Harper and Brothers—a publishing house that prided itself on its "family values"—the *Bazar* could never be that journal. Booth remained, as she would for the rest of her career, "dependent."

This does not mean Booth sold out, however. On the contrary, and ironically, because the *Bazar* was what it was—a fashion magazine—it gave its editor the opportunity of a lifetime, enabling Mary Booth to reach a female audience far greater than any independent feminist journal of the period achieved.[3] This audience consisted, moreover, primarily of women who, because of their class privilege, were best positioned to take full advantage of such feminist reforms as the magazine favored. With the fashion magazine's modernizing social orientation as her cover, Booth used her editorial privilege to seed the *Bazar* with articles, poems, illustrations, and fiction critiquing traditional gender and class values and advocating a woman's right to substantive education, meaningful work, and a decent wage. Most crucial for me here, Booth contributed directly to the *Bazar*'s feminist thematics through the convention of the anonymous editorial essay. In these essays, all of which are unsigned, she provided her readership with explicit coverage of a wide range of issues vital to women—from labor-saving devices that didn't save labor to the raft of new job opportunities opening up for women at every level. Learned, sophisticated, prescient, and (not infrequently) caustic, these essays are the beating heart of the *Bazar*'s feminism, indelibly marking the magazine with Mary Booth's values and concerns. But precisely because the essays are unsigned, before turning to them, it would be best to say more about Mary Booth and, generally, about the magazine she created.

Mary Louise Booth (1831–1889)

Nothing points more surely to Booth's desire *not* to call attention to herself than the tiny number of contemporary biographies dedicated to her, except, perhaps, the wide divergence in the "facts" the biographies themselves record. According to Spofford's eulogistic obituary in the *Bazar*, Booth fit the mold of one of the nineteenth-century's favorite female types: the woman of precocious literary genius, e.g., Lydia Huntley Sigourney, Elizabeth Oakes-Smith, Margaret Fuller, and the Davidson sisters. Casting a veil of romance over Booth's lower-middle-class origins, Spofford describes Booth's paternal British ancestors as "kinsm[e]n" to nobility while her mother, we are told, descended from "old French émigrés"—giving Booth a pedigree any editor of a high fashion magazine would die for. Of Booth's intellectual growth, Spofford is even more hyperbolic, "[o]ne might almost say that she chose a literary career in her infancy, as she had no recollection of ever learning to read either French or English, having read the Bible and Plutarch at five; at seven, Racine, at which time she began Latin, while before she was ten she was familiar with Hume and Gibbon, and was an omnivorous reader." At the completion of her education, Booth, Spofford claims, "read and spoke easily French and Italian, German and Spanish," having been supported throughout by loving and admiring parents who, "early comprehending her powers, . . . took every pains with her education."

When, shortly after Spofford's memorial appeared, Dr. Marie E. Zakrzewka, a lifelong personal friend of Booth's, used her memorial in *The Woman's Journal* to set the record straight, she told a dramatically different, if, to some, I expect, more impressive story.[4] Zakrzewka, a Polish-born émigré, had met Booth while the latter was still working nights as an (unpaid) freelance reporter. In Zakrzewka's narrative, Booth's life remains a tale of genius, but genius unromanticized, unacknowledged, and forced to bear up against great odds. "When but a little child, she picked up a stray French primer, and began to spell out and compare the French with the English words. Her interest was quickened, and she continued this self-instruction; later she acquired German in the same way. . . . She never could speak in either of these languages . . . but so thorough was her study that her translations were of the highest character." Nor, according to Zakrzewka, did Booth's parents support her. On the contrary, her father "felt almost ashamed of [her] choice of a career [i.e., journalism], and whenever we spent an evening in her father's house, it was understood between us that I should never speak of her work" (106). Booth's father wanted her to get married—or, failing that, to become a teacher, the only career he thought fit for a woman; and, as she told Anthony, it was his fetters she struggled against throughout her career.

Yet if in the light of Zakrzewka's memorial, Spofford's narrative seems more myth than reality, testifying mostly to how little Booth shared of herself with others (she told Wingate flatly she disliked autobiography [258]), still, like Zakrzewka's version, it helps make clear why Harper and Brothers' selection of her to head up the *Bazar* was an inspired choice. Most obviously, whatever the means by which Booth acquired French and German, her knowledge of these languages, together with her extensive business experience with Europeans, ideally positioned her to conduct the very sort of overseas relationships crucial to the *Bazar*'s initial success (see "Our Bazar"). Booth's career as translator had, moreover, steeped her in European high culture so that, though not socially advantaged herself, she knew the European turf in most ways far better than her elite readership did. Where they were hungry for European-style sophistication, her awareness of European manners and mores was uncluttered by romantic illusions, giving her considerable edge.

Equally important, by the time Booth arrived at the *Bazar*, her reputation as a translator of note had given her extensive connections in the United States as well, especially among New York City's literati. Well before the *Bazar*, Booth had begun attending Alice and Phoebe Cary's famous Saturday night soirees. At these affairs, Booth mingled freely with the city's literary elite, female and male. Her relationship with Alice, whose portrait, according to Marjorie Pryse, hung in Booth's library, was particularly close. As Pryse speculates, Booth's strong bond with women like the Carys and, later, Mary Wilkins Freeman, was probably rooted, partially at least, in their mutual situation as unmarried women (143, 144). (Under Booth's tenure, poems, stories, and essays on "old maids" are legion in the *Bazar*.)[5] However, it is very likely that these women were also drawn together by the strength of their shared commitment to working-class women, a commitment in Booth's case undoubtedly reinforced by her own work history. Single, without resources, and self-taught, Booth had supported herself during her apprentice years the way so many working women did, by sewing, for two years toiling as a vest maker. This experience, which gave Booth invaluable knowledge of the garment industry's basement, also gave her, no doubt, an unforgettable dose of the life too many women led without hope of escape. Insofar as the *Bazar*, even for a nineteenth-century publication, overflows with laments for the poor seamstress, the reason probably lies here.[6] Booth knew first hand the fate confronting uneducated and unsupported women; and no less than her knowledge of Europe, her knowledge of these women's plight ubiquitously shapes the *Bazar*, her text.

Last, but not least, as a self-made, self-supporting woman, Booth also had extensive experience in being financially independent and fiscally responsible. According to Harper historian, Eugene Exman, Booth was a consummate businesswoman who had a no frills approach to her work, symbolized by her small, sparsely furnished office: two chairs, a small sofa, and a desk. Miss Booth, Exman writes, "was treated with deference and respect by the Harper partners not only because of the success of her magazine but also because she had a masculine grasp of business and the quick decisiveness of a man of affairs. And she could not be pushed around"

(124). In the nineteenth century as today, a magazine stood or fell by the determination and vision of its managing editor and by her managerial as well as editorial skills. Booth apparently had the former as well as the latter in abundance. By 1880, twelve years after its inception, the *Bazar* matched *Godey's Lady's Book*'s peak circulation, 150,000, which *Godey's* had reached in 1861 (Exman 122). In contrast, between 1850 and 1865, *Harper's New Monthly Magazine's* sales averaged 110,000 while the *Atlantic Monthly's* nineteenth-century highpoint came in 1869 with 50,000 subscribers. Most special-interest feminist magazines never went beyond a few thousand even at the height of their popularity.

Although the *Bazar*'s sales figures would eventually be eclipsed by the mass-market women's magazines coming into existence in the 1890s, such as *Ladies' Home Journal* (Zuckerman 25–42), Booth was well within her rights in telling Wingate that the *Bazar*'s first seven years represented (to that date), "the most rapid success ever known in journalism" (259). If one accepts that the *Bazar* was a feminist magazine, even if an undeclared one, then these figures mean not only that it was the nineteenth century's most widely circulated "feminist" (as opposed to "women's") journal but also that its success would remain unrivaled for the greater part of the next century as well. Let me now turn, therefore, to how Booth managed this feat even while producing a magazine whose unilateral dedication to fashion and domesticity has, to my knowledge, never been challenged before.

Mary Booth's Bazar *(1867–1889)*

In a wily double-edged comment, Booth told Wingate how the *Bazar* should be read, following absolute truth with an out-and-out lie. "It is," Booth declared, "only by looking over a volume of the paper that one can form an idea of the numerous subjects treated therein during the year. Care is taken to exclude everything of a political or sectarian nature, as well as all objectionable matter, and to make a paper which may be read aloud with pleasure and profit to the whole family" (259). If Wingate had followed Booth's advice and read a year's worth of the magazine's contents, he would have discovered that the *Bazar* did indeed treat "numerous subjects." However, contrary to its editor's assertion, the blatantly "political" and "sectarian" could be found in its pages along with, one suspects, material no True Woman would have dreamt of reading aloud in the family circle, certainly not with her husband present. In discussing the *Bazar*, I will focus on this material, taking the more conventionally "domestic" writing with which the *Bazar* is also filled (Catherine Beecher on baking bread, for example)[7] as a given not requiring further elaboration.

As noted earlier, insofar as Booth introduced feminist material into the *Bazar*, she did so under cover of the magazine's commitment to modernity—or, put another way, its commitment to changes occurring in what she once called, "the fashion of the times." Thus, to take a straightforward example, not only was the *Bazar*, to the surprise of some modern scholars, willing to illustrate women in swimwear—as, for example, in "The Bathing Hour," an engraving by Winslow Homer (see Exman 122; Beasley 70); it also discussed women's participation in a wide range of other "new athletics" as well. Tennis, boating, gymnastics, bicycling all receive attention—although on safety grounds, the magazine preferred tricycles for women ("Cycling for Women"). Displays of the clothes appropriate for such activities typically accompany discussions of the significance of the activities themselves as indices of upper- and upper-middle-class women's changing subjectivities (see, e.g., Higginson). Indeed, in many instances new styles in female subjectivity are treated in precisely the same way that clothing fashions were—in short descriptive squibs. Thus, for example, the magazine ran a series of brief word-portraits of the "new" women of the late 1880s, one of whom, "The Modern Girl," could have stepped right out of a novel by Henry James or (since James published in the *Bazar*) perhaps served him as a model:

> The Modern Girl hardly knows what she wants, whether it is the higher education, an aesthetic wardrobe, love or fame; she does not always sit at home and submit to the dictation of her elders, but teaches these same elders what is best for them; she plays tennis, . . . reads Herbert Spencer, and very often writes; she dabbles in music and talks theosophy. . . . Withal, she is restless as the wind; she does not love the quiet of home; she lives on excitement; she goes to Europe, to the springs, the mountains, the theatres, the receptions . . . , or to the *modiste*; she can always fall back on clothes as a diversion; and when everything else fails she has the nervous prostration and a trained nurse.

Along with "The Modern Girl," this same series treats "The Society Girl," "The Maiden of To-Day," "The Passée Girl," and so on.

What gives a squib like "The Modern Girl" its peculiar interest, however, is the distinctive edginess with which it approaches its topic—the description of an emergent "New Woman." (For instance, after taking a swipe at the Modern Girl's proneness to nervous prostration, the author concludes that what she really needs is a job.) This kind of edginess seems an outgrowth of the anxious concern that the *Bazar* typically displays when discussing what women were in the present or might become in the future. Indeed, I would argue that this anxiousness is the defining quality of the *Bazar*'s specifically feminist approach to female modernity, an approach whose problematizing bent reflects the two-sidedness of late-nineteenth-century bourgeois women's modernity itself. As the beneficiaries, willy-nilly, of ever-increasing social freedom, what would this new generation of upper- and upper-middle-class young ladies make of themselves?[8] Would they use their advantages to study Spencer, becoming authors and thinkers themselves, or would they use them merely to pursue more pleasures? Would they educate themselves to be contributors to society, sensitive to the needs of those less privileged than themselves—seamstresses and shop girls, for example—or would they care only for satisfying their own selfish desires? When it came to the new female modernity, these questions seem uppermost in the *Bazar*'s mind, intruding into the magazine contents regularly over the years of Booth's tenure, even to the poems and illustrations the magazine published.

For example, in April 1870, "The Wife of the Period"—a woman whose subject position and subjectivity are temporally marked by the sobriquet that identifies her as speaker—is given a voice. Far from exhibiting "gentleness, intelligence, and virtue," this woman establishes her up-to-dateness by cruelly mocking her husband's domestic expectations. He wants a True Woman "To stay at home from morn till night, / And shun the world's enjoyment, / With servants for society, / And sewing for employment." But she will have none of it. Cheerfully turning two thousand years of misogynistic literature on its head, she boasts her "frailties" instead: "A splendid creature I should be / To pass my time as *you'd* like! / A sweet domestic nondescript, / Insufferably prude-like! / No, thank you, Fred; I freely own / The frailties of a woman, / Quite unashamed because my tastes / Are social, Sir, and—human!"

A few months later, "A Sweet-Heart of the Period" gets to express similar sentiments. To her fiancé, she blithely declares: "*One* feature our engagement has, / Quite comforting and jolly: / An utter lack of sentiment, / And all such dismal folly." No victim she. No sentimentalist either. Poems such as these, caustically satirical as they are, provide a deconstructive counterpoint to the more conventional verse that the magazine also published, destabilizing the latter's ideological commitments. In these "other," nonconventional poems, women's "bad" behavior is not a matter of moral failings. Rather, it is a projection of changing class and gender values. If nothing else, such poems help undermine the apparent transparency of sentimental poetry's traditionally essentialist assumptions. Reading them, some women might just conclude that only a fool would sacrifice herself on her grandmother's domestic altar now that women actually had the opportunity to live more varied and interesting lives, the potential risk to woman's "angelic" reputation notwithstanding.

Obviously, since poems are not editorials, one cannot read too much into them about any given author's or editor's position, but what of illustrations? Over time, the *Bazar* published a number of illustrations that diverge, sometimes dramatically, from the magazine's self-proclaimed focus on domestic (family) values. In these images, old ways are critiqued and / or new forms of modernity for women are celebrated. On June 12, 1869, for example, the *Bazar* published a memorial engraving, "The Champions of Woman Suffrage," featuring flattering portraits of some of the most notorious "female politicians" the century produced, including Lucretia Mott, Susan B. Anthony, Elizabeth Cady Stanton, and Ernestine Rose (381). Lest there be any doubt, the engraving is accompanied by a descriptive squib that makes the *Bazar*'s own stance on suffrage perfectly clear. "We take pleasure in laying before our readers," the squib declares, "a group of noble and dignified portraits, comprising some of the most eminent advocates of Woman's Suffrage—a cause which at this moment is largely engrossing public attention, both here and in Europe, and continually swelling the numbers of its adherents" (379). Insofar as the writer identifies suffrage as a modern issue sweeping society at home and abroad, Booth apparently felt that it too could be legitimately treated among "the fashions of the time," its political bias (and its implied critique of traditional "family values") notwithstanding. While Booth never let the *Bazar* violate its own stated first principles quite so blatantly again, feminism's inroads into "the fashions of the time" remained, as we shall see, a persistent subject in the magazine throughout her tenure.

Other suspect illustrations include "Women and their Work in the Metropolis," a centerfold spread devoted entirely to illustrating—and celebrating—the various new jobs open to blue-collar women: silver burnishers, paper-collar makers, fur sewers, seamstresses, shoe fitters, umbrella makers, photograph mounters, and so on. Equally striking is "The Sister Slaves," a diptych comprised of "The Slave of Fashion," a parody of Hiram Powers's much-admired "Greek Slave," and "The Slave of Toil." The first image features a flirtatiously shy young woman chained to the pillar of "Fashion." The second depicts a working-class woman whose powerful and dignified face is etched in lines of pain. In "Here is a Sight for a Free-Born American!" female family members kneel in worship before a baby while his ignored older brother stands disconsolately aside; and in "The Revised Version of the New Testament," a small group of women cluster about the new Bible while an ancient pater familias holds an equally ancient leather Bible half opened in his lap. This last image, unequivocally identifies religious modernity, with women and with a democratizing approach to the Word that challenged what had once been uncontested patriarchal control.

Like the poems cited above, these and similar images create a destabilizing counterpoint to the dominant ways in which women and domesticity were constructed in Booth's period and in much of the *Bazar* itself, critiquing women's excessive confinement to dress and family duties, on the one hand, while empowering them as modern readers and thinkers, on the other. Taken together, they suggest a magazine that was not only alert to the changes that were going into the making of the modern female subject, but was also, albeit cautiously, advocating them. It is only in the *Bazar*'s unsigned editorial essays, however, that the depth and complexity of the *Bazar*'s feminist commitment fully emerge. In the final section of this article, therefore, I want to turn to these essays since it is on them that my case for the *Bazar*'s status under Booth as a self-conscious, if subversively organized, feminist magazine of relatively radical character primarily rests.

Reading Feminism Back into the Bazar

One of the truisms of periodical research noted earlier is that any given magazine stands or falls on the ability and dedication of its general editor. To succeed, the editor must have an "idea" or "vision" that he or she instantiates in the magazine's material form. "The successful editors," Zuckerman writes, speaking primarily of mass-market magazines of the 1890s, "tended to be authoritative, forceful, possessed of a vision for their journals, yet attending to the interests and preferences of readers" (44). But what was Mary Louise Booth's vision and, with respect to my point here, how feminist was it?

Whether or not Mary Booth's actual authorship of the unsigned *Bazar* essays can ever be proved, we do know that her control over the magazine's contents was complete (Beasley 71). In this sense, if in no other, she was responsible for them just as she was responsible for the *Bazar*'s publication of signed essays such as Gail Hamilton's four-part discussion of married women's property rights legislation and the contents of Higginson's late but pungent column, "Women and Men." Sandwiched between discussions of the latest fashions, gossip at home and from abroad, and advice on the handling of servants, the unsigned essays, taken in the aggregate with the squibs, poems, and illustrations already discussed, provide incontrovertible evidence that Booth had far more controversial goals for her magazine than her public statements would allow. In brief, they establish the *Bazar*'s status as a feminist magazine, Booth's many disclaimers to the contrary.

The *Bazar* was, in fact, only three months old when the first two unsigned essays on feminist topics appeared, placed one after the other in the magazine's second page editorial slot. The first article, "Business Women," compares French women's practical training to the "sentimental and ornate" education given American girls. Using as her example the formidable widow Clicquot, who upon her husband's death took over his failing winemaking business, eventually becoming a multimillionaire, the essayist compares this forceful French response to the culturally inculcated passivity of the American woman, who would leave her "bankrupt estate to the lawyers to settle," the latter "effectually . . . sinking it [and the widow] in ruin." In the second essay, "Working Together," the speaker returns to Europe for her examples, this time to prove the value of higher education for women. Pointing to the cultural contributions of writers like George Eliot and the Brontë sisters, the essayist comments, with no small amount of edge: "If it has required nineteen centuries of Christian civilization in its slow progress toward maturity to call forth this potent [female literary] agency, we may be sure that this is the best presumptive evidence of its invaluable worth." Did the essayist hope that by using European examples of women's acquisition of "agency" in business and literature, she could make feminism "chic" for fashionable American women? Possibly. Certainly, the image of Madame Clicquot literally rolling up her sleeves and going to work seems an odd one to import into a high fashion magazine otherwise.

Appealing to national pride two months later, the essayist gives the European comparison a reverse twist, suggesting that she was far less interested in what women were doing in Europe than in what they were or were not doing in the United States. In "Women and their Work," which takes a historical and social science approach, such as Booth used in her widely admired *History of the City of New York* (her only signed, single-authored text), the writer argues that, at least in some respects, American women had surged well ahead of their European counterparts "emancipati[ng themselves] . . . from household drudgery," by taking jobs in commerce, industry, and the professions. "This revolution," the essayist asserts, "though beginning later in this country, has moved with greater speed than in either France or Germany, and woman's liberty in this, as in every other social respect, is less contracted and more firmly established in the United States than in any other land." In almost excruciating detail, the article then surveys the various jobs American women now hold, together with their expected remuneration;, $2,000 to $15,000 per year for women physicians, depending on where they lived; $12 to $15 per week for forewomen and cutters in the garment industry; $7.50 per week for washerwomen and ironers; and so on. Like the illustrations of blue-collar women workers mentioned earlier, so here, the social-leveling effect of the *Bazar*'s way of treating women's work legitimates working-class women in ways distinctly at odds with the magazine's presumed elitist high fashion bias.

Jumping ahead—and over numerous other essays—in March 1870, the *Bazar* published "The Physiology of Political Women," a title that by itself should have given any conservative *Bazar* reader pause. Whether or not it did, this essay is also a particularly good example of the kind of passionate rage that the *Bazar* essayist often brought to her rebuttals of unctuous male authorities (here British) who indulged in self-serving theorizations of gender bent on returning woman to "her sphere":

> A writer in the *Pall Mall Gazette* has lately advanced the theory that it is dangerous to open a new and a most intense source of excitement to women—that they will go mad, in short, in larger numbers than they now do, if admitted into the arena of politics. *The Spectator* says in reply, that the very few women in modern history who can be shown to have taken an intense personal interest in politics have been women of unusually sane minds and healthy physiques.

Using the *Spectator*'s observation as her starting point, the *Harper's* essayist then cites a long list of well-known female historical figures who proved themselves, if nothing else, shrewd and able, as well as healthy, politicians: Catherine de Medici, Mary of Guise, Queen Elizabeth, Catherine of Russia, Madame de Pompadour, and so forth. These women all lived long and vigorous lives, the essayist asserts, demonstrating nary a taint of insanity. "Those who go mad," she opines, in a swerve that comprises one of the most powerful moments in the essays

> are governesses, whose minds are concentrated on their monotonous toil, old maids, whose affections can not find the center which would give their minds full play; women in whose brains, from want of political or other intellectual interest, religion has come to be a one idea, a monomania; and the women of vacant minds, minds which like bandboxes, might, if filled by politics or any thing else—the more solid the thing the better—keep their perfect form, but unfilled are crushed by the first blow.

The message could not be clearer: whether it be in politics or in some other arena, women need work and they need to utilize their minds. If they do not, they will indeed lose them. It is not leaving her sphere that destroys a woman; it is remaining docilely within it, with nothing to occupy her except "monotonous toil" and "religion."

Booth's statements to the contrary, the *Bazar*, at least in its unsigned essays, is as critical of mindless domesticity as it is of excessive fashionability, although it readily acknowledges women's desire for both.[9] Possibly because the *Bazar* was skeptical, unlike the later mass-market women's magazines, it is distinctly unenthusiastic about the recent technological innovations that manufacturers were beginning to pitch to women as improvements in their lot. In a brilliant essay published in August 1871, "Woman's Work," the essayist runs down various ways in which these "improvements" were actually making women's lives more rather than less difficult. The writer's arguments are sufficiently akin to those Betty Friedan and others made a century later to warrant quoting at length. Now, the writer observes, we have the sewing-machine that "weaken[s] . . . ankles and bring[s] on nameless diseases, with all the countless intricacies of tucks and bands it has originated" and "rubber wringers" which enable women to wring ten garments where once they would have wrung only one, and

> in spite of all the ameliorations of life to those who dwell in city houses—the description of which their grandmothers could only treat as a fairy tale, with the account of the gas and water and elevators and speaking-tubes and all the rest—in spite of these things and such as these a thousand new wants have arisen with them, and have become necessities, and made life not one iota less laborious now than in the good old days, "so-called."

Nor, the writer says, is she talking about the lives of wealthy women, who have servants to labor for them while they "lol[l] at their ease." Rather her concern is the plight of "the great tide" of average women, who must deal with all the new expectations without help, combining in themselves "the office of wife, mother, housekeeper, [and] servant." Contemplating their predicament, the essayist concludes:

> We confess that when we . . . know such statements to be true, and that the odalisque of the harem has hardly a more absolute bondage than such women have, we are appalled with all it intimates and threatens. And we must declare that it behooves the race, wishing to be elevated, first to elevate its women out of such serfdom—to . . . find some remedy to a state of things universally accepted as the only state at present to be had. For ourselves, we are free to say that the surest help out of the darkness which we can see is in the adoption of the Cambridge plan of associated kitchens, furnishing hot meals and clean clothes to families at cost price, and leaving the mother of the family in her own house still, and with time to consider if the life she lives is worth the price of living.

Published some twenty-seven years before Charlotte Perkins Gilman's celebrated *Women and Economics*, the *Bazar*'s "Woman's Work" marks a significant step toward Gilman's text, even while it draws on earlier thinking from Plato to Robert Owen to Brook Farm. Like Gilman's book, the essay is part of a swelling stream of socialist-feminist discourse that identified women's unremunerated labor within the home as the primary obstacle to the full development of their personal potential. If an essay identifying Western household angels with harem women on the one hand

and serfs on the other, and urging a radical reorganization of domestic life, is not political and sectarian, I am not sure what is. Yet this essay, knowledgeable, richly detailed, comprehensive, above all angry, traveled into seventy thousand plus "family homes" where no feminist journal had, in all likelihood, gone before, taking its message with it: not Spofford's "gentleness, intelligence and virtue" but righteous indignation and a vivid call for change. In subsequent essays published through the 1870s and the 1880s, the voice of the unsigned essays remains essentially unchanged, the author's goal as ever to make the strongest case she can for what in the twentieth century we called "women's liberation," thinking no one had ever put it like that before.

Pleasurable though it would be to continue quoting passages from these essays, the point, I think, is clear. One can hear the same voice in "Women and the Centennials." Published in August, 1875, this essay looks back over a time when "there were but three poor ways in which a woman could earn a respectable living—as teacher, as seamstress, as servant," in order to celebrate just how far women had now come:

> the first consequence of liberty . . . has been the slow and sometimes half-grudged opening of almost every avenue to [woman] in which her feet were able to tread. Women now have the care of parishes, and minister to minds diseased and the cure of souls as skillfully as ever their masters did. Women now are at the head of hospitals, carry on large practices, and are not scorned as consulting physicians by the most eminent; women edit successful newspapers; women are heard before the bar, are respected on Change [the stock exchange], are architects, are sculptors, are painters, are printers, are multitudinous as authors—in short, are vindicating their equal right with men to work, to live, to think, as complementary halves of the same creation.

In all its dignity and righteous outrage, this same voice can also be heard in April 1883, in "Discord in the Spheres," castigating those who, despite all the progress that women had made, continue to demand that they return to "their sphere" anyway:

> [W]omen are each as individual as men are, and being individuals, and having arrived at legal age, who is there with the moral or with any other right to utter an *ipse dixit* as to the way in which they shall walk, or fix their sphere for them other than as they choose. . . .
>
> To every created being identity is a sacred thing, and the last enormity that can be practiced is the sacrilege committed when another, without right, and usually without reason, undertakes to interfere with it, to mould it, order its outgrowth, hamper, hinder, or command it. To every woman identity is as much as it is to every man and that she should be coerced in its respect . . . is an outrage upon personality and upon the whole race, to say nothing of its being an outrage upon herself so long used to outrage.

Although Spofford claims that Booth grew more conservative with time, there is little evidence that this late conservatism affected what she chose to publish (or, as I argue, write). In the 1880s, as in the 1860s, the feminist material appearing in the *Bazar*, the vast bulk of it anonymously authored, dances, if anything, ever further on the radical edge. Viewed from the perspective of these essays, this fashion and family magazine's real concerns could not, in fact, have been more different from those that Booth's original mission statement claimed. They focused on lower-middle-class and working-class women—mill girls, shop girls, and, above all, women in the garment industry—and on families that had to make do on $500 a year (the title of a long-running series by Juliet Corson in the late 1880s) or considerably less. And they focused on those "average" women whose lives, for all their relative comforts, weren't really that much better, given their entrapment within the home. As an aspect of its commitment to these concerns, the *Bazar*, consistently and often with great passion, promoted higher education, better jobs, and decent pay for all women. The only major change I found was that after 1870, the year the Fifteenth Amendment passed, giving African American men the vote, the *Bazar*, which had ranked among the few nineteenth-century publications *not* publishing racist material, joined its sibling publication *Harper's Weekly* in publishing racist jokes. The *Bazar*'s racism never remotely matches that of the *Weekly*, but the development is deeply disheartening nonetheless and probably reflects Booth's continuing ties to Stanton, Anthony, and the suffrage movement, as the first racist cartoon it published—"Effect of the Fifteenth Amendment"—seems to suggest.

Conclusion

In sum, the profile of the *Bazar*'s editor that emerges from a study of the magazine's contents during the years of Booth's tenure is a close to perfect match with what we know of Booth herself, albeit nowhere more so than in the unsigned essays that carry the brunt of the magazine's feminist slant. The implied author of these essays is a woman of wide knowledge and sophistication, familiar with modern and ancient cultures, fiercely independent, historically informed, and socially attuned. She does not suffer fools gladly; she is not afraid to rake men, especially self-proclaimed gender experts, over the coals; she is deeply sympathetic with the travails of working women. She considers domestic labor drudgery and, when unpaid, a form of enslavement. She believes in education and social equality and wants women to take themselves as seriously as she takes them. Although it is possible that over the twenty-one years of her editorship, Mary Booth found some person or persons of genius to pen these essays anonymously, all essentially in this one voice, it is unlikely. Given that the essays most often appear in the magazine's second page editorial slot, it seems simplest to conclude that Booth wrote them herself, at least until in-depth archival research can prove the thesis wrong. Certainly content- and style-wise, Booth's signature is all over these pieces. But whether or not one accepts this last conclusion, one can say unequivocally that, insofar as these essays made a "feminist" perspective on women's needs and potentials part of elite American culture's understanding of what female modernity entailed, they made Mary Booth's *Bazar* a triumph of subversion, one long overdue for the recognition it deserves.

Notes

1. http://women.eb.com/women/articles/Booth-Mary-Louise.html (July 30, 1998). Booth was forced into the Herculean labor of translating Gasparin in a week by a publisher who, convinced that the war would be over in a few months, refused to publish it otherwise.

2. Booth took the "pleasure" component very seriously, boasting to Charles Wingate that her magazine published some of the best names in "light literature" (257). Since, along with well-known women authors like Mary Wilkins Freeman, the Cary sisters, Gail Hamilton, Rose Terry Cooke, Harriet P. Spofford, Louisa May Alcott, and Sarah Piatt, the *Bazar* published Wilkie Collins, Henry James, Lafcadio Herne, and others, her boast was no exaggeration.

3. Stanton and Anthony's *Revolution*, for example, had 3,000 subscribers in 1869, and ceased publication a few years later (Mott 392).

4. From her "little sketch," Zakrzewka observes, "the reader will learn that Miss Booth was not the favored child of circumstances, as one might judge from some obituary notices" (106). Zakrzewka's version, as Stern notes, has external evidence to support it (208). However, Spofford's biography is valuable insofar as it suggests just how mythic Booth became to those who knew her only after she achieved success. Class issues were probably involved here. Prior to becoming a security manager, Booth's father had been a teacher and school principal, and Spofford only mentions the last. Even being a school principal's daughter, however, would not have redeemed Booth in terms of class as, at best, her family would have been ranked among the genteel semipoor, hardly the most appropriate background for America's voice of high fashion.

5. For example, see "The Single Lady," "An Old Maid," "The Single Woman," "The Old Maid," and "A Neglected Career for Unmarried Women." According to Spofford, Booth shared her home with "her adopted sister," a Mrs. Wright, "whose life was one of absolute devotion to [Booth]." Significantly, no work of fiction published in the *Bazar* got better treatment under Booth than Cooke's tale of spinsterhood triumphant, "How Celia Changed Her Mind," which garnered two gorgeous full-page illustrations in the December 1, 1888, issue.

6. See, for example, "The Wedding Dress," "The Ball Dress," and "Dresses—Those Who make Them and Those Who Wear Them."

7. "How to Make the Best Family Bread with Least Time." In the early 1880s, Mrs. Julian Hawthorne contributed a column on manners and housekeeping.

8. Like many a parent, the *Bazar* felt quite free to criticize the young women of the new generation but then defended them when they were attacked by others. Thus, in "In New

Bottles" the "moralists of the *Saturday Review*" are urged to deal patiently with behavior that the *Bazar* itself castigates any number of times:

> Moralists of the *Saturday Review* school deplore the tendency of young girls to fastness and impropriety of speech. It is probable that their critics simply mistake their new sense of liberty for license. Custom and opinion have pressed so heavily on women for generations that it would not be strange if they find it a little difficult to adjust themselves to the new environment. There may be the destruction of old and beloved ideals. There may be much froth and muddy sediment before the new wine runs clear.

9. One classic comment comes in "His Sisters, His Cousins, and His Aunts," which opens, "That cage in the menagerie which contains 'The Happy Family' is usually surrounded by the largest crowd. The wonder of seeing natural enemies maintain an unbroken treaty of peace, of beholding the ravager subduing his fierceness, and the coward outliving his timidity, never palls. But, after all, it is not a more extraordinary sight, nor does it involve a more extraordinary skill in training, than the spectacle of a happy family among human animals."

Works Cited

Texts, Illustrations, and Cartoons in *Harper's Bazar*

"A Neglected Career for Unmarried Women," 4 March 1882, 130.
"A Sweetheart of the Period," 27 August 1870, 558.
"An Old Maid," 23 March 1872, 206.
"The Ball Dress," 4 September 1875, 574.
Beecher, Catherine. "How to Make the Best Family Bread with the Least Time," 14 August 1869, 522–23.
"Business Women," 8 February 1868, 226.
"Champions of Woman Suffrage," 12 June 1869, 379 and 381.
"Cycling for Women," 31 July 1886, 493.
"Discord in the Spheres," 7 April 1883, 210.
"Dresses—Those Who Make Them and Those Who Wear Them," 17 March 1877, 168 and 169.
"Effect of the Fifteenth Amendment," 4 March 1871, 144.
"Here's a Sight for a True-Born American," 13 September 1879, 596.
Higginson, Thomas Wentworth. "The New Athletics for Women," 31 July 1886, 494.
"His Sisters, His Cousins, and His Aunts," 22 July 1882, 450.
Homer, Winslow. "The Bathing Hour," 8 October 1881, 648–49.
"In New Bottles," 25 November 1882, 738.
"The Modern Girl," 13 August 1887, 562.
"Our Bazar," November 2 1867, 2.
"The Physiology of Political Women," 26 March 1870, 206.
"The Revised Version of the New Testament," 13 August 1881, 517.
"The Single Lady," 21 November 1868, 886.
"The Single Woman," 1 November 1873, 690.
"The Slave of Fashion," 20 April 1878, 256.
"The Slave of Toil," 20 April 1878, 257.
Spofford, Harriett Prescott. "Mary Louise Booth," 30 March 1889, 232.
"The Wedding Dress," 13 July 1872, 466.
"The Wife of the Period," 2 April 1870, 214.
"Woman's Work," 19 August 1871, 514.
"Women and the Centennials," 28 August 1875, 554.
"Women and Their Work," 18 April 1868, 394.

"Women and Their Work in the Metropolis," 18 August 1868, 392–93.
"Working Together," 8 February 1868, 226.

Secondary Texts

Beasley, Maurine H. "Mary L. Booth." In *American Magazine Journalists, 1850–1900. Dictionary of Literary Biography*. Detroit: Gale Research, 1989.
"Booth, Mary Louise." Britannica Online. http://women.eb.com/women/articles/Booth Mary-Louise.html (July 30, 1998).
Byers, Inzer. "Mary Louise Booth." In *American Women Writers: A Critical Reference Guide from Colonial Times to the Present*, vol. 1, ed. Lina Mainiero. New York: Frederick Ungar, 1979.
Endres, Kathleen L., and Therese L. Lueck, eds. *Women's Periodicals in the United States: Consumer Magazines*. Westport, Conn.: Greenwood Press, 1995.
Exman, Eugene. *The House of Harper: One Hundred and Fifty Years of Publishing*. New York: Harper & Row, 1967.
Harper, Ida Husted. *The Life and Work of Susan B. Anthony*. 3 vols. Indianapolis: Bowen Merrill, 1898–1908.
Mott, Frank Luther. *A History of American Magazines*. Vol. 3, *1865–1885*. Cambridge, Mass.: Harvard University Press, 1938.
Pryse, Marjorie. "Mary E. Wilkins Freeman." In *Modern American Women Writers*, ed. Elaine Showalter, et al. New York: Charles Scribners, 1991.
Stern, Madeleine B. "Booth, Mary Louise." In *Notable American Women, 1607–1950: A Biographical Dictionary*, ed. Edward T. James, et al. Cambridge, Mass.: Harvard University Press, 1971.
Wingate, Charles, ed.. *Views and Interviews on Journalism*. New York: F. B. Patterson, 1875.
Zakrzewka, Dr. Marie E. "Mary L. Booth." *Woman's Journal* (6 April 1889), 105–06.
Zuckerman, Mary Ellen. *A History of Popular Women's Magazines in the United States, 1792–1995*. Westport, Conn.: Greenwood Press, 1998.

"The Physiology of Political Women"
Harper's Bazar, 26 March 1870

A writer in the *Pall Mall Gazette* has lately advanced the theory that it is dangerous to open a new and a most intense source of excitement to women—that they will go mad, in short, in larger numbers than they now do, if admitted into the arena of politics. The *Spectator* says in reply, that the very few women in modern history who can be shown to have taken an intense personal interest in politics have been women of unusually sane minds and healthy physique. Catherine de Medicis [sic] surely took an interest in politics, and who, except the first Bourbon, ever defied her wit successfully? Her pupil, Mary of Guise—the woman whom Scotchmen will persist in talking of as if she were a Scotchwoman, whereas she was from toque to boots, in virtues and in vices, in her strong passions and her cold heart, in her brain for business and her incapacity of sympathy, Parisienne—lived and died for politics, and, to her death, was Burleigh's equal in state craft. Her rival, Elizabeth, a woman of the typical sort, vain, mean, vacillating, and given to intrigue, lived fifty years of active life, during which she subordinated every interest to politics, and died to leave behind, throughout a race like ours, the tradition of large-hearted competence. Did Anne of Austria go mad? or Adalaide of Orleans? or Louisa of Prussia, who really ruled the kingdom through that awful tempest of French invasion? or Catherine II. of Russia? Or any one of the dozen or so women whom modern history classes as rulers and politicians? Why, the Pompadour, with the Parc aux Cerfs upon her conscience, and that horrible, "unamusable," keen-sighted, heartless voluptuary perpetually upon her hands, did not go mad because mainly of the interest with which politics invested her life; as they did that of the good bourgeoise Maria Theresa, who patronized her, and governed Austria, and fought Frederick, and dismembered Poland, and suppressed the Jesuits, and after a life of fierce political warfare died a comfortable, serene old lady at sixty-three. These were empresses, or queens, or kings' mistresses? How old was Madame De Recamier? How old are the half dozen women in Paris who still keep up the tradition of the political salon? Not to mention living names, though it is a certainty that among the best balanced intellects in England are half a dozen political dames, there was Lady Palmerston, steeped in politics throughout life, and, at eighty, sanest of English womankind. We might multiply instances forever, but we do not understand even the *a priori* argument. Why should one of the noblest, most varied, and least selfish of all interests, the one which if thoroughly felt of all others most widens the intellects of average men tend to destroy the intellects of average women? Because it is an excitement? So is dress; so is intrigue; so is the social struggle; so, above and before all, is ambition outside the political circle:

yet women who feel all these do not go mad. Those who go mad are governesses, whose minds are concentrated on their monotonous toil, old maids, whose affections can not find the centre which would give their minds full play; women in whose brains, from want of political or other intellectual interest, religion has come to be a one idea, a monomania; and the women of vacant minds, minds which like bandboxes, might, if filled by politics or any thing else—the more solid the thing the better—keep their perfect form, but unfilled, are crushed by the first blow, the most trifling accident. Excitement, intimates the *Pall Mall Gazette*, is very injurious to women. Is it? Why is it not beneficial, as Michelet, a very bad authority, but a well-known one, and every doctor in every country, perpetually asserts? Of all excitement nothing is, we believe, quite equal to immense success at the opera; for the applause comes quick, and the applause gives all that is dear to all—money, position, personal worship; yet the great female singers of the world, Jenny Lind, Tietjens, Alboni, Patti, Lucca, Sessi, are certainly not among the women who create the impression of approximate insanity. Even if excitement were bad for women—a notion, we believe, to be born exclusively of the results of the one excitement our civilization promotes—the struggle against hot air, late hours, and injurious food—the struggle to buy the success of the salon at the price of physical health—that would not show that political excitement was specially bad. On the contrary, it would seem to be specially good, if only because its first condition is self-restraint, instead of *abandon*. The pursuit of politics hardly admits of the monomaniacal concentration of thought on a single object which tends to produce, or rather, as we should say, to develop, insanity; it is too varied, admits of too many interests, of too rapid an alternation of success and defeat. No doubt women who get interested in politics betray more interest in them than in any thing else, get more excited, talk more at random, flush more deeply, are more carried out of their ordinary restraints than men are; but is not that true of all pursuits, or where it is specially true, is not the cause the law which prohibits them from action? Dumb men always seem, and usually are, very fierce men, but speech would not make them insane. (898)

Discord in the Spheres
Harper's Bazar, 7 April 1883

In fact, it has ceased to be considered that home is a cage, analogous to that old iron cage in which mediaeval husbands used once to lock up refractory wives; it is a nest while a nest is needed; it is always a place of growth, or should be so, not only for the nestlings, but for all within its bounds. Those who would deny this would deny that woman is an individual, that she has either a mind or a soul, or that she is entitled to any growth. Yet perhaps the hardiest of our assailants will not deny us the possession of a soul; and having once granted that, they have granted all the rest; for in that case women are each as individual as men are, and being individuals, and having arrived at legal age, who is there with the moral or with any other right to utter an *ipse dixit* as to the way in which they shall walk, or fix their sphere for them other than as they choose to fix it for themselves?

We presume that no woman ever dreamed of denying that home was her sphere, although she may claim the right to put her own interpretation on the word "home." There is no woman who does not know that she is or would be the happier for a husband's love and the opportunity to love and rear their children with him. That there are women who are capable of having their houses well kept, their tables well served, their husbands well cared for, and their children well taught and well reared in every respect, and are yet capable of doing something more, of following what is called a career, does not signify; for there are few of them, however greatly they yearn for art, or literature, or science, who would not sacrifice all hopes of a career therein to their affections, if need were, and there are thousands of them who have done so; and all that women in the mass demand is that such sacrifice shall be made unnecessary, and that a woman may be allowed to be all she should be in a home, and all she would or could be elsewhere. . . .

To every created being identity is a sacred thing, and the last enormity that can be practiced is the sacrilege committed when another, without right, and usually without reason, undertakes to interfere with it, to mould it, order its outgrowth, hamper, hinder, or command it. To every woman identity is as much as it is to every man and that she should be coerced in its respect, or that the attempt at coercion should be made, is an outrage upon personality and upon the whole race, to say nothing of its being an outrage upon herself so long used to outrage. Neither men nor women will greatly heed such attempts, for to the credit of men in the aggregate be it said, and to that of their sense of justice, they as fully appreciate the advantage of education to women as women desire it; and we need nothing to testify to this further than the ardent endeavor which every father in the land makes to give his daughter the completest education she can have, and fit her for any career she may pursue; for we may be sure that if a father expends the resources of leisure, comfort, wealth, for his daughter, foregoing much himself for the sake of it, it is for what he thinks that daughter's good; and for it is for the good of that daughter, it stands to reason that the same thing is for the good of all other men's daughters, making merely increment or deduction to meet the differentiation of different individuals. (632)

"It has served the truth without fear and without favor": Kate Field and *Kate Field's Washington*

GARY SCHARNHORST

THOUGH she is virtually unknown today, the journalist Kate Field (1838–1896) was "one of the best-known women in America" during her life, according to her obituary in the *New York Tribune* ("Kate Field Dead"). A member of the expatriate community in Florence in the late 1850s, she essayed her friendships with the Brownings, the Trollopes, and Walter Savage Landor as the Italian correspondent of the *Boston Courier* and *New Orleans Daily Picayune* while still in her early twenties. One of the first women to contribute to the *Atlantic Monthly*, she won national renown by covering Charles Dickens's final American tour in 1867–1868 for the *New York Tribune*. She published two popular travel books, *Hap-Hazard* (1873) and *Ten Days in Spain* (1875), and she was a model for the character of Henrietta Stackpole in Henry James's novel *The Portrait of a Lady* (Scharnhorst 2001). She wrote plays, worked as an actress on the legitimate stage, and lectured on such topics as "Woman in the Lyceum," "Life in the Adirondacks," "The Intemperance of Prohibition," and "Despised Alaska" in both the United States and Europe from 1869 until virtually the end of her life. In the late 1870s she worked for Alexander Graham Bell as a publicist for the telephone, and she helped to establish the Shakespeare Memorial Theatre in Stratford-on-Avon. In the 1880s she founded and managed the Cooperative Dress Association in New York and campaigned against Mormon polygamy and for a national marriage law. As the *Chicago Times-Herald* observed at her death, "To Kate Field more than to any man or to any other woman is due the extirpation of American polygamy" ("Kate Field's Career"). She led a remarkable life, even though it has been largely lost in a biographical blindspot.

More to the point, Field long cherished the dream of editing her own magazine. As early as 1875, she wrote the poet E. C. Stedman that "If I had an 'organ,'" she would "ring" the celebration of the centennial the next year (Field to Stedman). As it happened, the last of Field's many careers was that of public intellectual and editor of her own weekly paper, *Kate Field's Washington*, first issued on January 1, 1890. As her friend and biographer Lilian Whiting allowed, "There had been nothing in Kate's entire life which had so concentrated her interest, and stimulated every gift and grace of her nature, as this enterprise of founding and conducting a national review of her own. She thought of it by day and dreamed of it by night" (467–68). Field widely publicized her editorial credo even before beginning to issue the magazine:

> I believe in Washington as the hub of a great nation.
>
> I believe that a capital of a Republic of 60,000,000 of human beings is the locality for a review knowing no sectional prejudices and loving truth better than party.
>
> I believe that "men and women are eternally equal and eternally different;" hence I believe there is a fair field in Washington for a national weekly edited by a woman.
>
> I believe in home industries; in a reduced tariff; in civil service reform; in extending our commerce; in American shipping; in strengthening our army and navy; in temperance which does not mean enforcing total abstinence on one's neighbor; in personal liberty.
>
> I believe in literature, art, science, music, and the drama as handmaids of civilization.
>
> I believe society should be the best expression of humanity.
>
> I believe in a religion of deeds.
>
> The journal edited by me will reflect my opinions. Mistakes are probable. They will be born of ignorance.
>
> From an impartial public I hope for support in the welcome guise of subscription, advertising, and suggestion.
>
> From a heretofore generous press I ask for fraternal recognition. ("Kate Field's Beliefs")

Though she had been a member of the Radical Club of Boston in the late 1860s, Field expressed no radical agenda in this credo. On the contrary: she was obliged constantly during the life of her weekly to defend her patriotism, her ameliorism, her middlebrow conservatism. Put another way, as she promised a friend an entire year before the first issue of her magazine appeared, "It will be politically independent, aim for the best society all over the country and warmly support the new states and struggling territories. It will oppose all sumptuary laws and therefore will oppose prohibition, but will treat of so many subjects as not to come under the category of an organ for any specialty. It will be *my* organ, and what I conscientiously believe, of course the paper will advocate." Echoing St. Paul's admonition in his first letter to the Corinthians, she concluded that "It will avoid vituperation and endeavor to be *temperate* in all things" (*Kate Field: Selected Letters* 201).

While she may have been an unorthodox feminist,[1] Field wrote a number of editorials favorable to the cause of woman suffrage. She predicted in March 1894, for example, that by "the beginning of 1900, every State in the Union" would have admitted "the justice of equal suffrage" and would have passed laws "placing women where they belong—on a political equality with men." "Susan B. Anthony can at last put down her traveling bag and take life comfortably," she averred the next month. "She has lived to see woman suffrage fashionable in her own State [New York], and in the city of all cities most hopelessly given over to the world, the flesh and the devil" (Field, "Equal Suffrage"; "Equal Suffrage in New York"). In addition, Field devoted many pages in her magazine to such women's issues as temperance, dress reform, and the extirpation of polygamy, as well as to other liberal causes. On the basis of her editorials against polygamy, the *Philadelphia Press* even recommended that she be appointed governor of Utah by the President (Field, "Gentile Echoes"). Field also published thirty early poems, essays, and tales by Charlotte Perkins Gilman (née Stetson), the most prominent intellectual in the American women's movement at the turn of the century. Among Gilman's contributions to *Kate Field's Washington* were such stories as "The Unexpected" (21 May 1890), "Circumstances Alter Cases" (23 July 1890), and "Society and the Philosopher" (18 February 1891), all of which Gilman subsequently reprinted after the turn of the century in her monthly magazine *The Forerunner* (Scharnhorst, *Charlotte Perkins Gilman*, 59 and passim). Indeed, Field's experience as editor and publisher of her own paper may have inspired Gilman to establish *The Forerunner* in 1909.

Though Field's weekly was not strictly a woman's magazine or a suffragist organ like the Boston *Woman's Journal*, it was conducted largely by women. In addition to Field, two of her three staff employees were graduates of Vassar College at a time when it was virtually impossible for women to find jobs in journalism. Her staff, Field proudly reported, was "filled with regularly educated journalists, who have had years of experience" (Field, "The Girl"). In contrast, as she told an interviewer early in the life of the magazine, she knew "of only three women on newspapers in Washington, and they are all society reporters; clever women they are, too" ("Women in Washington" 1890). Whatever else may be said of Field, she recognized her obligation to be an equal opportunity employer.

Each sixteen-page issue of *Kate Field's Washington* contained a fairly standard array of articles. Field always led the issue with three or four pages of editorials, political commentary, excerpts from her travel journals, or occasionally the script of a play. In late 1890 she published a series of nine ethnological essays entitled "Natives of Alaska," based on her trip to Alaska in 1887. Over the months she also printed previously unpublished letters by Robert Browning, John Ruskin, Wilkie Collins, and Mark Twain, as well as her reminiscences of such figures as Landor, Dickens, Tennyson,

George Eliot, and the Irish nationalist Sir Charles Dilke. Next was a department Field entitled "The Grapevine Telephone," an interview with a public figure ostensibly conducted by telephone. Among those featured over the years were Susan B. Anthony, Theodore Roosevelt, Charles Francis Adams, Albert Bierstadt, Clara Barton, and Gifford Pinchot. A department entitled "The Players" reviewed plays or concerts or interviewed such actors, producers, and playwrights as Clyde Fitch, Bronson Howard, Daniel Frohman, Edwin Booth, P. T. Barnum, Julian Hawthorne, Henry Irving, and Dion Boucicault. Most issues included a few poems and a final page or two of book reviews and advertisements. In addition to Gilman, occasional contributors included Albert Bigelow Paine, later Mark Twain's official biographer and literary executor, the eccentric millionaire Gaylord Wilshire, the poet Charles Warren Stoddard, and the drama critic Laurence Hutton. Gilman was paid ten dollars for at least one of her pieces (Gilman 416), though the more typical payment was five dollars per column (*Selected Letters* 221). Hutton received only a complimentary year's subscription for his first contribution (429). In truth, Field usually wrote much of the material in each issue, especially during the first couple of years, sometimes using such pseudonyms as "Everpoint" and "Straws" (pen names her father Joseph M. Field had used a half century earlier) or "Olla," short for "Ollapodrida."

From the first, the critical miscellany was a lightning rod for controversy. Susan B. Anthony publicly alleged that Field's weekly was sponsored by liquor interests, specifically California brewers and vintners, and certainly the magazine contained advertising week after week for such firms as Inglenook, Kohler and Frohling, the George Wiedemann Brewing Company, To-Kalon Wine Company, Pleasant Valley Wine Company, and Urbana Wine Company. Certainly, too, Field had been hired on a retainer by the California Viticultural Commission in 1887 to promote table wine as an alternative to hard liquor, for which she had been roundly criticized by members of the Women's Christian Temperance Union and other prohibitionists ("Miss Field's Experience"; "Mrs. Foster on Kate Field"). Stoddard later conceded that the magazine had been "backed by friendly financiers" (367), but Field disputed the implication that her editorial policy was dictated by them. As she replied to Anthony in February 1890, less than six weeks after issuing her first number,

> I heard that you had stated publicly that my paper was subsidized by liquor-dealers. I did not believe the story and have taken the first opportunity I ever had to pay you respect by giving you the place of honor in my issue of Feb. 12th (Field, "A Good Woman's Secret"). I did this half on your account, and half on account of the suffragists and prohibitionists who because I don't entirely agree with [them], either slander me basely or let me severely alone.

I can return good for evil and give anyone who is honest a fair hearing in my paper. I don't expect to get the least credit for a decent act. (*Selected Letters* 209)

Because Field also boosted Washington as the "hub of a great nation" and touted its potential for investors, such local real estate developers as John F. Waggaman, who was selling lots in Wesley Heights, also advertised in her magazine. In addition, she formed a limited partnership to publish the weekly, selling shares in the company for $100 apiece and hoping to raise a total of $24,000. As Field wrote Laurence Hutton in September 1890, "I'm always fighting for the stage & ought to be backed by rich actors but, so far, they have not materialized even as subscribers" (Field to Hutton). Or as she wrote Hugh McCulloch in April 1891, she wished to sell stock in her company to residents of Washington "as I am 'booming' this lovely town and increasing the value of their property" (Field to McCulloch). However egregious such apparent conflicts of interest, Field stoutly maintained that her weekly was dependent on neither party nor faction—and there is no evidence that she ever quashed an article or changed a word in the magazine to suit an advertiser or a stockholder.

From all indications, however, *Kate Field's Washington* survived on its sale of advertising and shares of the company because it enjoyed only modest income from subscribers and over-the-counter purchases. Hardly a month after its first issue appeared, Field wrote Anna C. Lynch Botta that the "Paper is doing very well but I want it to do better. I want the earth" (Field to Botta). A week or so later she told an interviewer that "We are paying expenses . . . and we are only seven weeks old" ("Women in Washington" 1890). Similarly, she reported to Elizabeth Cady Stanton in mid-February 1890 that "my paper . . . is just two months old and pays expenses" (Field to Stanton). She claimed in May that the weekly had six hundred subscribers (*Selected Letters* 212), but it probably never attracted more than a couple of thousand paying readers at the height of its popularity. In order to attract more subscribers (and so presumably to increase advertising revenues), Field halved the price of the paper at the end of 1890 from four dollars a year and ten cents a copy to two dollars a year and five cents a copy. The panic of 1893 and the economic depression that ensued clearly took their toll on all publishing enterprises at the time. The only complete runs of *Kate Field's Washington* extant today are the proprietary copy at the Boston Public Library and another file in the Salt Lake City Public Library, and it has never been microfilmed for public use. Part of the problem of preservation is that it was printed on cheap paper to save on production costs.

Still, the weekly exercised an influence on contemporary thought far out of proportion to its modest sales. Among those who subscribed were President Grover Cleveland, Vice-President Levi P. Morton, O. B. Frothingham, Russell A. Alger, John C. and Jessie Benton Frémont, M. M. Ballou, E. C. Stedman, Charles Dudley Warner, Richard Watson Gilder, Mary Mapes Dodge, George William Curtis, Phoebe Hearst (mother of William Randolph Hearst), David Dudley Field, and William Tecumseh Sherman (*Kate Field's Washington*, 1 January 1890; Field to Hearst; Whiting 528; *Selected Letters* 207; Field, "The Washington's Mail Bag"). Ambrose Bierce occasionally cited it in his "Prattle" column in the *San Francisco Examiner* (Bierce), and the novelist Gertrude Atherton remembered in her autobiography that it made "something of a sensation" and that she "read it with interest," too (185). Its articles were also widely copied from Maine to Alaska and in England in such papers as the Boston *Woman's Journal*, the *Springfield Republican*, the *New Orleans Daily Picayune, Minneapolis Tribune*, Brooklyn *Union, Chicago Zeitung, Portland Press, New York Tribune, St. Louis Magazine*, Salt Lake City *Daily Tribune*, and the *Anglo-American Times* (e.g., Field, "Concerning Brains," "Lawrence Barrett," "A Mormon Ruse," "The New Massachusetts"). Field bragged as late as November 1894 that "my Washington . . . is more quoted than any paper in the country" (Field to St. John). Or as she told an interviewer in September 1891,

> I am highly gratified at the way in which the baby has been received by both press and public. I am more than ever convinced that I made no mistake in claiming Washington as the hub of this nation. Eventually it will be our social, literary and artistic as well as political and scientific centre. The beauty of our Capital, its freedoms from the turmoil of commerce, the attractions which Congress of necessity presents, and last, but not least, the mildness of the climate and charm of the surrounding country make Washington unique in America. . . .
>
> For all these reasons I moved to Washington and founded what I believe you will admit is a National independent review for intelligent men and women, regardless of politics and religion. I work early and late to deserve success; so does every member of my staff, and a cleverer staff of man and women—yes, there's one man, I don't believe in separating the sexes, even in work—it would be difficult to find anywhere.
>
> I want the reading public to look upon this new review as a friend that will always have the courage to tell the truth, and will aim to do so without being stupid. ("Very Faithfully Recorded")

As Field privately insisted a month after she suspended its publication (only briefly, she thought) in the spring of 1895, "The paper has been a great success and can be more so in better times and with better business management" (Field to L. and E. Hutton).

In all, Field's campaigns for progressive causes during the run of the paper seem to have paid dividends. She published contributions by Stedman, Gilder, Dodge, Curtis, Brander Matthews, W. T. Harris, Oliver Wendell Holmes, W. D. Howells, and James Russell Lowell in support of international copyright—and such a protocol was soon adopted (Field, "International Copyright"; "A Word"; "A Victory"). She praised the exhibition of the John Brown fort at the Columbian Exposition in Chicago and, in 1894, after the close of the exposition, she raised money to return the fort to Harper's Ferry. A local resident donated five acres, and the B&O Railroad shipped the fort to West Virginia at no charge. In 1895, the fort was rebuilt some three miles from the town on a bluff overlooking the Shenandoah River (*Selected Letters* 229; Field, "An Historical Incident"). She favored free silver and civil service reform—the first a pet populist concern and the second a key plank in the Mugwump platform—and argued for the creation of a "labor bureau" or department of labor in the federal government and for expanded opportunities for Native Americans and African Americans. Each of these issues would eventually be addressed legislatively by the U.S. Congress.

Field tried, according to her lights, to explain the social causes of oppression. As early as 1864, influenced by the teachings of the radical abolitionist Wendell Phillips, she had defended the rights of freed slaves in the South (Field, "From New York"). In her weekly, she went even further in indicting racism. "White citizens," she opined, have "allowed their poor brethren to live like pigs in alleys where tenements should not be tolerated. . . . There should be an end to this great wrong, and the quickest way to end it is to establish my Labor Bureau" (Field, "Sixteen Thousand"). Field commented as early as the fall of 1890 after spring graduation at Harvard on the promising career of W. E. B. Du Bois, one of the first references to him in any national publication. To be sure, her words betray traces of racial condescension. As the "best orator of Commencement Day,"

> Du Bois pleaded for Jefferson Davis as "a great man," "a keen thinker," "a strong leader." . . . It has been left to a colored man, born in New England, to praise a mistaken but thoroughly honest man who, like Robert E. Lee of Virginia, had the courage of his convictions. The victor can always afford to be just, and no history of the civil war will be worth reading, save as fiction, until sectional prejudices are buried and the spirit of . . . Du Bois inspires its writer. (Field, "Moses")

In one of the last issues of her magazine, Field published an interview with C. H. J. Taylor, an African American who was recorder of deeds for the District of Columbia, for which she was thanked by the Reverend Walter

H. Brooks of the Nineteenth Street Baptist Church in Washington, D.C. (Field, "My Mailbag").

Not that Field was always on the side of the angels. For example, she advocated restrictive immigration laws at the height of the nativist movement at the turn of the twentieth century. She editorially opposed the admission of Utah to the Union until polygamy was completely extirpated and opposed the admission of New Mexico until more of its citizens spoke English; yet she also urged the annexation of the Republic of Hawaii by the United States. She excoriated Eugene V. Debs and the American Railways Association for their strike against the Pullman Company in the summer of 1894. On balance, however, her independent weekly was remarkably progressive.

Field's enlightened politics were most apparent in her editorializing on a pair of other issues: the development of the American West, specifically the creation of Yosemite National Park, and the reduction or elimination of the tariff on imported art. By design, *Kate Field's Washington* was "a good friend to the new states and to the territories" (*Selected Letters* 206). She touted the Western Art Association and the Western Opera Association, both headquartered in Omaha; hailed Pueblo, Colorado, as "the Pittsburgh of the West," Colorado Springs as a health resort, and Alaska as a recreational paradise; and welcomed "the coming state of Idaho" and other northern tier states (Field, "Art in the West"; "Western Opera"; "Pittsburgh of the West"; "Health and Art"; "Alaska"; "Coming State"). More to the point, as Field wrote Mary Mapes Dodge in 1890, "I'm out gunning for Yosemite and am making converts" (*Selected Letters* 206). She published in her *Washington* an open letter to Leland Stanford, U.S. senator from California, in which she appealed to him "to rescue God's noblest work from the hands of vandals"—that is, to help preserve the Yosemite under the stewardship of the national government. "Every section [of California] commands attention," she wrote, "but above all looms Yosemite Valley, unique in character and grandeur, awe-full in solemnity. It is Nature at prayer. Human beings who remain unmoved in the presence of such scenery should walk on four legs and browse on tin cans." She urged Stanford to introduce a bill in Congress "for the preservation of Yosemite Valley," contending that if it were "controlled by competent officers of the United States, no such condition of nature and man as now disgraces it could endure." When she visited the valley in 1888, "much of it was enclosed by hideous, cruel, barbed-wire fences. . . . I couldn't walk. There were no footpaths." Trees had been cut down "promiscuously, . . . leaving an army of ragged stumps that make portions of the Valley look like a brutal backwoods clearing" (Field, "Vandalism"). Robert Underwood Johnson, editor of *Century*, wrote her that her open letter to Stanford was *"admirable and will prove effective"* (Whiting 474), and indeed two days after it appeared, the *New York Times* commended Field's "vigorous protest" against the "neglect of the Yosemite.... Of the neglect there can be no doubt. All tourists have nearly the same story of discomfort and extortion to tell, though they do not tell it so vividly as Miss Field" (*New York Times*). Yosemite National Park was finally established, at least partly through her efforts, in October 1890, and Field did not hesitate to take credit for the legislation. *Kate Field's Washington* "deserves a great deal more than thanks from California" for lobbying on behalf of the park, she remarked, "but blessed are they who expect nothing, for they will not be disappointed" (Field, "A National Yosemite Park"). Or as she noted in her retrospective of her first year as editor of the weekly: "Remember that Congress has given to the world a National Yosemite Park two million acres in size, and do not forget the source of its inspiration," she admonished the readers of her *Washington* (Field, "A Year Old").

Field also campaigned indefatigably for a reduction or elimination of the tariff on imported art. Her testimony before Congress on March 27 and her editorial on free art in her *Washington* for 2 April 1890 prompted responses in such leading papers as the *Boston Traveller, Boston Courier, Boston Post, Boston Advertiser, Boston Herald, New York Commercial, New York Tribune, New York Herald,* New York *World, Hartford Times,* and *Philadelphia Public Ledger* (Field, "What They Say"). As Stedman later wrote her, "If *Kate Field's Washington* were not (as it is) the brightest weekly that comes to us, your success in reducing the art duties would have been its sufficient excuse for being" (544). The tariff was initially reduced from 30 percent to 15 percent in 1890, and it was eliminated entirely in late 1894. For her advocacy of "free art," Field received the Palm of the Academy, the highest honor the French government could award an individual for service to art ("The Academic Palm"; Field, "Decorated"). In all, as Field insisted in September 1891, in the brief life of her *Washington* it had "played a part in national politics, affected legislation, secured 15 per cent reduction on the art tariff, obtained 2,000,000 acres for the National Yosemite Park, helped Alaska and Gentile Utah, upheld the great West in its righteous endeavors to obtain proper recognition, fought the battles of real temperance against impossible prohibition, opposed all sumptuary legislation, and in fact taken what I believe to be the right side on every subject, regardless of politics" ("Broad as the Atlantic").

After issuing nearly three hundred weekly numbers over a period of slightly over five years, after contributing as many as three thousand items to its pages (some of them as brief as a single paragraph), Field suspended her paper in April 1895 for reasons of failing health. She had suffered from malaria since the summer of 1893 (so much for the health benefits of Washington) and, as she explained in the circular she sent her subscribers announcing the suspension, "An attack of grip, added to excessive work, forces me to give myself an interval of rest from the unceasing care of journalism. Without health, life is a delusion, and, as I have had no vacation for over five years, nature rebels. Unfortunately, I cannot relegate my work to another, as personal journalism demands personal presence. Self-preservation being the first law of nature, I must postpone the next issue of the 'Washington' for perhaps another year. In that time I hope by freedom of responsibility to be of more value to myself and others. Brains need to be fallow no less than soil." She went to great pains to reassure her subscribers and advertisers alike that not only did she expect to resume its publication after a year, but that the weekly had not failed for financial reasons. As she explained the day after her suspension was announced,

> Nobody knows what I have gone through within the last five years—starting as I did, only six months before the Baring failure, and from that on facing a succession of panics induced by stupid legislation. . . . The "Washington" is in good shape now to stop publication for a while. It does not owe a dollar—has not a single debt. Such subscribers as have paid in advance will receive their money back. I have paid off my office people, and got places for them—none turned out to shift for themselves. I have retained one young woman, increasing her salary to make it an object for her to stay a while, until all the business with subscribers is settled. I am not sorry to have had the experience given me by the publication of the 'Washington,' even if the suspension should not prove, as I expect, temporary. To me it has been a liberal education. To have founded it was one of the good inspirations of my life. It has served the truth without fear and without favor. If its weekly appearance gave its readers as much satisfaction as it has given me, my goal has been reached. What is more, it has taught me the value of money. I never before knew the value of money, but I know it now, and am glad of it. ("Women in Washington" 1895)

Unfortunately, Field never resumed publication of her *Washington*. She died in Hawaii while on assignment for the *Chicago Times-Herald* the following year.

At her death, Field's obituarists paid tribute to her editorial work on *Kate Field's Washington*. W. J. McGee of the Columbia Historical Society declared the weekly had been "one of the foremost American examples of personal journalism. . . .To the future historian of the national capital 'Kate Field's Washington' will be a boon, and the history of the nation cannot be written fairly without recognition of the journal and the shaping of public affairs through its influence" (5–6). According to Rounseville Wildman, editor of the *Overland Monthly*,

"Kate Field's Washington" was not a failure. It was a gigantic success. True, it died with its brilliant editor's failing health but the measures of great public import it made live, and the practical reforms it brought about make it rank high among the great journals of the past. The International Copyright Law, the reduction of the tariff on works of art, the admission of the news States of the Northwest, the civilization of Alaska, the preservation of John Brown's home, and the cause of true womanhood, true Americanism, and true temperance, all owe Kate Field much, more than the world will tax itself to remember. (126–27)

As Maurine Beasley has concluded more recently, *Kate Field's Washington* "deserves to be remembered as a pioneer attempt by a woman to edit a highly personal journal" (404). As editor of her *Washington* for over five years, Field proved to be imaginative, provocative, opinionated, brave, and influential—a fitting coda to her remarkable life and careers.

Note

1. Field staked out a position early in her career that satisfied neither suffragists nor archconservatives: she advocated woman suffrage, but not universal suffrage. Both men and women, she contended, ought to qualify for the vote by passing a literacy test. She changed her opinion only in 1893 at the behest of Susan B. Anthony. See Field's "A Talk" and "To Hear Kate Field."

Works Cited

"The Academic Palm for Kate Field," *New York Times*, 20 November 1894, 1.

Atherton, Gertrude. *Adventures of a Novelist*. New York: Liveright, 1932.

Beasley, Maurine. "Kate Field and 'Kate Field's Washington,' 1890–1895," *Records of the Columbia Historical Society* 49 (1976): 392–404.

Bierce, Ambrose. "Prattle," *San Francisco Examiner*, 7 August 1892, 6; 16 April 1893, 6; 23 April 1893, 6.

"Broad as the Atlantic," *Minneapolis Tribune*, 20 September 1891, 14.

Field, Kate. "Alaska as a Sportsman's Paradise," *Kate Field's Washington*, 20 May 1891, 320–21.

———. "Art in the West," *Kate Field's Washington*, 21 October 1891, 262–63.

———. "The Coming State of Idaho," *Kate Field's Washington*, 26 February 1890, 140–41.

———. "Concerning Brains," *Kate Field's Washington*, 8 February 1893, 83. Rept. in *Woman's Journal*, 18 February 1893, 50.

———. "Decorated by France," *Kate Field's Washington*, 21 November 1894, 321.

———. "Equal Suffrage," *Kate Field's Washington*, 20 March 1894, 194–95.

———. "Equal Suffrage in New York," *Kate Field's Washington*, 11 April 1894, 225.

———. "From New York / . . . Gross Injustice to the Negroes," *Springfield Republican*, 22 November 1864, 2.

———. "Gentile Echoes," *Kate Field's Washington*, 21 January 1891, 47–48.

———. "The Girl Who Thinks She Can Write," *Youth's Companion*, 8 September 1892, 447.

———. "A Good Woman's Secret," *Kate Field's Washington*, 12 February 1890, 108–09.

———. "Health and Art in Colorado Springs," *Kate Field's Washington*, 16 December 1891, 405.

———. "An Historical Incident," *Kate Field's Washington*, 26 September 1894, 194–95.

———. "International Copyright," *Kate Field's Washington*, 21 May 1890, 331.
———. *Kate Field: Selected Letters*, ed. Carolyn J. Moss. Carbondale and Edwardsville: Southern Illinois University Press, 1996.
———. "Kate Field's Beliefs," *New York Times*, 1 December 1889: 4.
———. "Lawrence Barrett," *Kate Field's Washington*, 25 March 1891, 183–84. Rept. in *Springfield Republican*, 29 March 1891, 6.
———. Letter to Anna C. L. Botta, 9 February 1890 (West Virginia Division of Culture and History).
———. Letter to E. C. Stedman, 4 December 1875 (Butler Library, Columbia University).
———. Letter to Elizabeth Cady Stanton, 18 February 1890 (Library of Congress).
———. Letter to Hugh McCulloch, 30 April 1891 (Lilly Library, Indiana University).
———. Letter to Laurence and Eleanor Hutton, 29 May 1895 (Manuscripts Division, Department of Rare Books and Special Collections, Princeton University Library). Published with permission of the Princeton University Library.
———. Letter to Laurence Hutton, 25 September 1890 (Manuscripts Division, Department of Rare Books and Special Collections, Princeton University Library). Published with permission of the Princeton University Library.
———. Letter to Mr. St. John, 1 November 1894 (Fales Library, New York University).
———. Letter to Phoebe Hearst, 12 July 1893 (University of Carolifornia at Berkeley).
———. "A Mormon Ruse—Beware!" *Kate Field's Washington*, 29 July 1891, 69–71. Rpt., Salt Lake City *Daily Tribune*, 2 August 1891, 9.
———. "Moses in Mississippi," *Kate Field's Washington*, 8 October 1890, 1.
———. "My Mailbag." *Kate Field's Washington*, 16 February 1895, 99–100; 9 March 1895, 148–49.
———. "A National Yosemite Park at Last!" *Kate Field's Washington*, 22 October 1890, 258–59.
———. "The New Massachusetts," *Kate Field's Washington*, 26 August 1891, 134–35. Rpt., *New Orleans Picayune*, 6 September 1891, 2.
———. "The Pittsburgh of the West," *Kate Field's Washington*, 25 November 1891, 345–46.
———. "Sixteen Thousand Needy People," *Kate Field's Washington*, 25 January 1893, 49.
———. "A Talk," in *The Congress of Women*, ed. Mary K. O. Eagle. Chicago: American Publishing, 1894.
———. "Vandalism in Yosemite Valley," *Kate Field's Washington*, 12 February 1890, 105–06.
———. "A Victory for International Copyright," *Kate Field's Washington*, 10 December 1890, 373.
———. "The Washington's Mail Bag," *Kate Field's Washington*, 8 April 1891, 231.
———. "The Western Opera Association," *Kate Field's Washington*, 17 May 1893, 305–06.
———. "What They Say About Free Art," *Kate Field's Washington*, 9 April 1890, 245–46.
———. "A Word from W. D. Howells," *Kate Field's Washington*, 11 June 1890, 378–79.
———. "A Year Old," *Kate Field's Washington*, 31 December 1890, 433.
Gilman, Charlotte Perkins. *The Diaries of Charlotte Perkins Gilman*, ed. Denise D. Knight. Charlottesville and London: University Press of Virginia, 1994.
Hutton, Laurence. "The Literary Life," *Critic* 45 (1904): 426–37.
"Kate Field Dead," *New York Tribune*, 31 May 1896, 7.
"Kate Field's Career," *Chicago Times-Herald*, 1 June 1896, 6.
Kate Field's Washington, 1 January 1890, unpaginated flyer.
McGee, W. J. "Memorial of Kate Field," *Records of the Columbia Historical Society* 1 (1897): 2–6.
"Miss Field's Experience," *New York Tribune*, 17 July 1889, 4.
"Mrs. Foster on Kate Field," *New York Tribune*, 28 July 1889, 5.
New York Times, 14 February 1890, 4.
Scharnhorst, Gary. *Charlotte Perkins Gilman: A Bibliography*. Metuchen, N.J.: Scarecrow, 1985.

———. "James and Kate Field," *Henry James Review* 22 (Spring 2001): 200–06.
Stedman, E. C. *Life and Letters of Edmund Clarence Stedman*, ed. Laura Stedman, et al. New York: Moffat, Yard, 1910.
Stoddard, Charles Warren. "Kate Field, Cosmopolite," *National Magazine* 23 (January 1906): 361–72.
"To Hear Kate Field," *Chicago Times-Herald*, 1 June 1893, 9.
"Very Faithfully Recorded," *Rochester Democrat*. Rpt. in *Kate Field's Washington*, 23 September 1891, 212.
Whiting, Lilian. *Kate Field: A Record*. Boston: Little, Brown, 1900.
Wildman, Rounseville. "The Death of Kate Field." *Overland Monthly* new series 28 (July 1896): 126–27.
"Women in Washington," *New York Star*, 2 March 1890, 10.
"Women in Washington," *New York Tribune*, 29 April 1895, 7.

"A Talk with Susan B. Anthony"
Kate Field's Washington, 9 March 1895

No one can talk to Miss Anthony without realizing her honesty. Were all reformers as unselfish and genuine, reforms would have fewer critics. It is the male and female Tartuffes who are the worst enemies of trust and justice.

It always refreshes me to meet a real person; so I bearded all sorts and conditions of women to have a talk with Miss Anthony while she helped to make the third triennial meeting of the Women's Council a downright success.

"Believe in this Council? Of course I do," replied this Nineteenth Century Sibyl to my query. "It is the grandest educator that ever was evolved for women."

"How does it affect your special cause of suffrage?"

"You have no business to ask, because you know well enough; but I suppose you want me to talk for the WASHINGTON's readers?"

"Precisely."

"Well, my dear, there are twenty organizations represented at this Council, and I feel as if I were the mother of all. I sit and actually see them grow before my very eyes. The different religious sects learn to tolerate and respect each other. Protestants admit the honesty of Catholics, and both welcome the Jewish Women's League. Yes, we've had the Hebrews with us for the first time, and nobly have they borne themselves. Not only have we broken down religious intolerance but race intolerance as well. We have received the Colored Woman's League with open arms, and I thank God for the broadening influence of association."

"Women are narrow-minded because they are too often narrow-lived. You can't expect the creature that is bounded by four walls to see the glory of the universe and admit the virtues of unknown peoples."

"Certainly not, and there's where our critics make a fatal mistake. They insist that contact with humanity will destroy womanliness. They don't know what they are talking about."

"Very few do. If people limited their remarks to their knowledge, conversation would cease."

"Now *I* didn't say that; but it's true in the main. To return to your question. All these twenty organizations realize as never before that to attain their ends they must be able to speak with authority to legislators. They realize that authority comes only with power, and that the only power recognized by law-makes is the ballot. Therefore, however these organizations may differ in other respects, they unite on suffrage, believing it to be the factor needed to accomplish their special purposes. The workingwomen of the Public Printing Office have forced conviction on many. With the adjournment of Congress many employees of this office will be discharged. The majority, if not all of those to receive their congés, will be women. Why? The officers do not hesitate to admit that employment must be reserved for men. 'We must look out for the voters,' they exclaim with brutal frankness. Having this object-lesson thrust upon them, women become converts to suffrage who never before appreciated its advantage."

"Rather than a low view to take of what should be considered as a principle, isn't it?"

"Yes, but we must accept the world as we find it and do the best we can with it."

"Agreed. That is my motto."

"Very well, then. As the majority of women do not recognize the dignity to be attained by the possession of suffrage and the principles and duties involved, they can be made to clamor for it as a means of self-defense. You can't expect women to be better than the men they've made. How many men regard suffrage from an exalted standpoint?"

"I shudder to think how few."

"Don't let us scan too closely the motives of women. It is enough that they are growing upward, not downward—forward, not backward. The primal underlying principle of human existence is the right of every human being to have his opinion counted."

"Whether it be good or bad? Then it must be the first business of a government founded on universal suffrage to make everybody intelligent, or republics will go to the dogs."

"Of course; and you'll not pull this country out of the slough until women know enough, first, to want to vote, and secondly, to vote intelligently. Thus men will be taught their duties as citizens. Is this revolutionary doctrine?"

"Not to me, but, alas! it is to many who shook hands with you at Mrs. McLean's last week."

"Well, you know I'm an optimist, and I've seen such progress lately that I have faith enough to believe—."

"That 'while the lamp holds out to burn the vilest sinner may return'? Then there's hope for the District of Columbia, where nobody votes; where there is not one atom of civic pride; where people are so ignorant as to actually fight against a Contagious Diseases Hospital; where the laws are so unjust to women as to put a premium on vice."

"What do you mean by that last statement?"

"Plainly this: As any husband of any workingwoman may claim her earnings, marriage is at a discount among the humble. Our colored population numbers 85,000, the largest of any city in the world. Colored women are almost invariably bread-winners. A prominent negro told me recently that the women of his race were averse to matrimony for the reason I have given. Outside of wedlock they can control their purses and their children. Once married, they are slaves. Isn't that a nice state of things? I hear people railing against the immorality of negroes. I should like to be shown where Congress has lifted its finger to help them to be moral. Neither by industrial schools, nor by just laws toward women, have National legislators made the District of Columbia a reputable part of the Union."

"Dear me! Another proof of the necessity of suffrage."

"True. As there is no suffrage whatever now, and as wealthy residents are in mortal terror of illiterate votes, I suggest a compromise. Congress can do what it pleases with a Territory. Let us have a restricted suffrage based on education, property and respectability, regardless of sex and color. A voter should read and write, and have some knowledge of the Constitution; a voter should pay a tax, however small; a voter should be able to give a reputable account of himself. I claim that suffrage is not a right, but should be a privilege, the reward of merit. What can be had without effort is never valued at its real worth. Will you consider the needs of the National Capital at your next National Convention?"

"We shall meet here next February. We'll see."

"What was the result of your recent convention in Atlanta?"

"A very good result for Atlanta, but to affect the Nation we must meet in Washington."

"Your head is level, Miss Anthony. Gradually people are coming around to my way of thinking. Washington is the Hub of the Nation, and whatever affects the Nation should emanate from here."

Then I bade goodbye to an honest, earnest woman who has given her life to a great cause. Abuse has not curdled the milk of human kindness flowing in her veins. Poverty has not embittered her generous soul. Susan B. Anthony with her honorable seventy-five years is more alive today than almost any woman of my acquaintance. . . .

NOTES ON CONTRIBUTORS

PAULA BERNAT BENNETT is Professor Emerita, Southern Illinois University at Carbondale. She is the editor of three books and the author of three books and numerous articles. Her latest book, *Poets in the Public Sphere: The Emancipatory Project of American Women's Poetry, 1800–1890*, focuses on women's political poetry.

JENNIFER BLANCHARD is a doctoral candidate in American Studies at the College of William and Mary. She is currently working on her dissertation on siblings in late-nineteenth-century American literature.

ANN MAUGER COLBERT is Journalism Program Coordinator at Indiana University Purdue University at Fort Wayne (IPFW). She has been a journalist and editor. Winner of several writing awards, she has been supported in her research on women's editions with grants from the Freedom Forum, the Indiana Historical Society, IPFW, and IU.

JAMES H. COX teaches Native American and American literatures at the University of Texas at Austin. He has published articles on Sherman Alexie and Thomas King and an article on Susanna Rowson, Catharine Maria Sedgwick, and Lydia Maria Child. He is currently completing a manuscript entitled "Native American Novelists and the Narration of Empire."

JACQUELINE FEAR-SEGAL lectures in American history at the University of East Anglia, Norwich, England, specializing in Native American history. She is currently finishing a study of Indians' schools, "White Man's Club: Schools and the Struggle of Indian Acculturation."

STEVEN FINK is Associate Professor of English at the Ohio State University, specializing in American literature. He is the author of *Prophet in the Marketplace: Thoreau's Development as a Professional Writer*, coeditor (with Susan Williams) of a collection of essays, *Reciprocal Influences: Literary Production, Distribution, and Consumption in America*, and coeditor of the journal *American Periodicals*.

LINDA FROST is an Associate Professor of English at the University of Alabama at Birmingham. Her essays on early and nineteenth-century American writing and culture have appeared in a range of journals and anthologies, and she is the author of a manuscript entitled "Blinding

Whiteness: Race and Nation-Building in American Weeklies, Miscellanies, and Story Papers, 1850–1877," forthcoming from University of Minnesota Press (2004). President of the Research Society for American Periodicals, she is editor-in-chief of the women's literary journal *PMS poemmemoirstory*.

ELLEN GRUBER GARVEY is an Associate Professor at New Jersey City University, where she teaches English and Women's Studies. She is the author of *Adman in the Parlor: Magazines and the Gendering of Consumer Culture, 1880s to 1910s*, which won the Society for the History of Authorship, Reading, and Publishing's annual prize for the best book on the history of the book. Her current project is a book about scrapbooks in which readers saved materials from periodicals.

SHARON M. HARRIS is the Lorraine Sherley Professor in Literature at TCU. She is the author or editor of several books, including *Rebecca Harding Davis: Writing Cultural Autobiography*, *Early Women's Historical Narratives*, *American Women Writers to 1800*, and *Rebecca Harding Davis and American Realism*. She is an editor of *Legacy: A Journal of American Women Writers* and founding president of the Society for the Study of American Women Writers. She has forthcoming a monograph on eighteenth-century women's narratives of race, class, and the law and is working on a study of women physicians in nineteenth-century U.S. culture.

CAROLYN KARCHER is the author of *Shadow over the Promised Land: Slavery, Race, and Violence in Melville's America* and *The First Woman of the Republic: A Cultural Biography of Lydia Maria Child*, as well as the editor of *A Lydia Maria Child Reader*, Child's *Hobomok and Other Writings on Indians* and *An Appeal in Favor of That Class of Americans Called Africans*, and Catharine Maria Sedgwick's *Hope Leslie*. She is currently working on an anthology-cum-critical-study of nineteenth-century American women journalists.

KATHARINE RODIER is an Associate Professor at Marshall University, where she directs the graduate program in English. She is coeditor of *American Women Prose Writers, 1820–1870*. In addition, she is an editorial consultant for *Legacy: A Journal of American Women Writers*.

GARY SCHARNHORST is Professor of English at the University of New Mexico. He edits the journal *American Literary Realism* and the research annual *American Literary Scholarship* in alternating years. He is also general editor of the American Realism and Naturalism series published by the University of Alabama Press. He is writing a biography of Kate Field.

LUCILLE M. SCHULTZ is Professor of English at the University of Cincinnati, where she teaches writing and studies the history of writing instruction. Her 1999 book, *The Young Composers: Composition's Beginnings in Nineteenth-Century Schools*, won the Nancy Dasher Award in 2000; her forthcoming book from Southern Illinois University Press (with Jean Ferguson Carr and Stephen L. Carr) is entitled *Archives of Instruction: Rhetorics, Readers, and Composition Books*.

HANNA WALLINGER is Associate Professor of American Studies at the University of Salzburg, Austria. She has published essays on Alice Walker, Paule Marshall, Gloria Naylor, Anna Julia Cooper, W. E. B. Du Bois, Pauline Hopkins, Dorothy Parker, and others in her main field of interest, African American Studies and Women's Studies. She is currently completing a book-length study of the life and literature of the African American writer and journalist Pauline E. Hopkins.

INDEX

abolitionist movement, 83, 99, 100, 106, 227. *See also* slavery
Adams, Charles Francis, 251
Adams, Katherine, 6
Adams, Samuel, 5
adultery, 108
"Advertisement, An" (Alcott), 110–13
advertising, xxx, 24, 26, 213, 251; ethics and, 20, 21; gender and, 34n29; as newspapers' base of support, 28; Royal Baking Powder, 26–31; student newspapers and, 7
Advocate of Moral Reform, 80
African Americans, xxv–xxvi, xxxi, 14, 92n7, 254; *Colored American Magazine* and, 146–49; education and, 227; voting rights, 101, 102
Afro-American Press and Its Editors, The, xxxi
Agitator, The, 102, 104
Alcott, Bronson, 112
Alcott, Louisa May, 109–12, 119
Alger, Russell A., 253
Allen, Sarah (pseudonym), 148, 165
Altorf (play), 85
amateur journalists, xxxiii, 20, 31n1
"America, Home of the Red Man" (Zitkala-Ša), 188
American Anti-Slavery Society, 92n7
American Equal Rights Association (AERA), 101, 102
American Indian Magazine, The, xxix, xxxii, xxxv, 174, 185; Arthur C. Parker and, 186; confrontational voice of, xxxiv; examples of writing in, 198–201
American Indian Movement, 177
American Indian Stories (Zitkala-Ša), 173, 176
American Woman Suffrage Association (AWSA), 103, 107, 108, 115
Ames, C. H., 112
Anderson, Benedict, 133
antebellum period, xxix, xxxii, 205–19
Anthony, Susan B., xxxv, 99, 101, 102, 119, 227; as female politician, 234; *Kate Field's Washington* and, 251, 261–63; National Woman Suffrage Association and, 103
Anti-Slavery Bugle, 100
Arrow, The, 140, 141
Arusmont, Phiquepal d', 91

Atherton, Gertrude, 253
"Atlanta Exposition Address" (Washington), 150, 152
Atlantic, 13, 173, 231, 248
Attucks, Crispus, 165
audiences, xxv, xxxii, 45, 215–16, 218; dialogue with editors, 63; female readers, 212; male readers, 80
Augusta, Maud, 62, 78
authority, moral and cultural, 42, 44, 48, 128–33, 226

"Ballade of Sad Biscuits, A" (poem), 26–27
Ballou, M. M., 253
Barber, J. Max, 163, 164
Barnard, Henry, 4
Barnum, P. T., 73n6, 251
Barrows, Mabel Hay, 3
Barton, Clara, 251
Beadle dime novels, 41, 57n3
Beasley, Maurine, 258
Beatty, Thomas Bayard, 6
Beecher, Catherine, 231
Beecher, Henry Ward, 109, 116
Bell, Alexander Graham, 248
Bennett, Paula Bernat, xxxii
Bentham, Jeremy, 129, 130, 131
"Better" (Larcom), 109
Bierce, Ambrose, 253
Bierstadt, Albert, 251
Big Foot (Lakota leader), 175
Billings, Josh, 109
Bishop, Robert, 116
black nationalism, 80, 164
blacks. *See* African Americans
Blackwell, Alice Stone, 101, 113–14, 118
Blackwell, Antoinette Brown, 103, 105
Blackwell, Elizabeth, 104
Blackwell, Emily, 104, 105
Blackwell, Henry Brown, 99, 100, 104; affair with Abby Hutchinson Patton, 104, 114, 116; shares of *Woman's Journal*, 105
Blaine, James G., 116
Blake, Lillie Devereux, xxx
Blanchard, Jennifer, xxvii, xxviii
Bleyer, Willard, 5
Bliss, Lucy, 108
Bloomer, Amelia, 207

269

Blue Estuaries, The: Poems 1923–1968 (Bogan), 14
Blumin, Stuart, 14
Bly, Nellie, 21
Body of This Death (Bogan), 14
Bogan, Louise, 14
Bonheur, Rosa, 107
Bonnin, Capt. Raymond T., 177, 186, 191
Bonnin, Gertrude Simmons. *See* Zitkala-Ša (Red Bird)
Booth, Edwin, 251
Booth, Mary Louise, xxix, xxxii–xxxiii, 225–41; feminism and, 235–40; life of, 228–31; tenure as editor of *Harper's Bazar*, 231–35
Boston, 43, 45, 46, 159, 163
Boston Advocate, xxxi
Boston Courier, 248, 256
Boston Latin School, 5
Botta, Anna C. Lynch, 252
Boucicault, Dion, 251
boys, 9, 12, 19
Braithwaite, William, 148
Brave, Ben, 186
"Bride's Triumph, A," 26
Brodhead, Richard, 147
Brontë sisters, 236
Brook Farm, 238
Brooks, Rev. Walter H., 254–55
Brooks, Van Wyck, 43
Brown, Abbie F., xxxiii, 3, 8, 11–13, 17n7; editorial persona and, xxviii; writing by, 19
Brown, John, 254, 258
Brown, Lt. Leroy, 123
Brown, William Wells, 151–52
Browning, Elizabeth Barrett, 109
Browning, Robert, 250
Bruce, John Edward, 159
Bryant, William Cullen, 209, 210, 211
Buchanan, James, 55
Buell, Lawrence, 43, 53
Bureau of Indian Affairs (B.I.A.), 139, 175, 179, 182, 184, 192; democratic principles and, 187; Indian employees of, 185; paternalism of, 188
Burgess, Marianna, xxviii, xxix, 123–126, 133–141
business, as masculine domain, 51, 208
"Business Women" (*Harper's Bazar* essay), 235–36
Butler, Benjamin, 116
Byron, Lady, xxx, 114

capital punishment, 89, 92
capitalism, 82
Carby, Hazel, 148
Carlisle Indian Industrial School, xxix, xxxiv, 123–24, 173; closing of (1918), 174, 187; *Indian Helper* published at, 125–37; student insubordination at, 138–41; Zitkala-Ša at, 175
Carroll, Lewis, 3, 11, 15
Carter, Robert, 70, 73n6
Cary, Alice, 109, 230
Cary, Mary Ann, 80
Cary, Phoebe, 230
Catherine de Medici, 237, 244
Catherine II (empress of Russia), 237, 244
Catholicism, 87, 173, 175, 261
Catt, Carrie Chapman, 60, 70, 71
censorship, 11, 17n6
Centennial Exposition (Philadelphia, 1876), 25
Central Interscholastic Press Association, 6
Changing Woman (Navajo deity), 187
Cheney, Ednah Dow, 112
Cherokee tribe, xxxi, 63
Child, Lydia Maria, 45, 80, 92, 207
children, 45, 108; books for, 11; compared to literary pursuits, 47; education of, 83, 90; race and class issues and, 14
"Chipeta, Widow of Chief Ouray, With a Word About a Deal in Blankets" (Zitkala-Ša), 181–82
Choat, J. R., 128
Christianity, 96, 130, 139, 191
"Christmas Letter From Zitkala-Ša, A," 181
churches, 31, 100
Cincinnati Tribune, 23, 24
circulation, xv, 162, 231
"Circumstances Alter Cases" (Gilman), 250
civil rights, 162
Civil War, 5, 13, 14, 24, 101, 107
civilization, 131, 149, 176–78, 180
Cleveland Gazette (newspaper), xxxi
Cleveland, Grover, 116, 118, 253
Cleveland Plain Dealer, 22–23
Clicquot, Madame (widow), 236
Colbert, Ann Mauger, xxvi, xxix
Collier, John, 192–93
Collins, Wilkie, 250
Colored American League, 153, 154, 156, 158
Colored American Magazine, xxv–xxvi, xxvii, 146–49, 153, 155; announcements in, xxxiv–xxxv, 170–72; audience for, xxxii; emergence of (1900), xxxi

Colored Co-operative Publishing Company, 147, 170
Colored Woman's League, 261
Comenius, John Amos, 4
Commercial Gazette, 24
Composition Writing: A Practical Guide (Davis), 6
Conflicting Paths: Growing Up in America (Graff), 5
conservatism, xxv, xxxi, 91, 99, 240
Constitution, amendments to, 118, 121
Constitution, of United States, 263
Contending Forces (Hopkins), 147, 148, 157, 161
"Converting Fanny" (Hopkins), 165
Cook-Lynn, Elizabeth, 177
Coolidge, Rev. Sherman, 198
Cooper, Anna Julia, 151
Coppin, Fanny J., 151
"Coronation of Chief Powhatan Retold" (Zitkala-Ša), 189, 200–201
Corson, Juliet, 240
Coultrap-McQuin, Susan, 206, 207
courts, reform of, 89
Cox, James, xxix
Crazy Horse, 175
crime and punishment, 89
cultural exchange, 49
cultural guidance, 42, 48
Curtis, George William, 253, 254
Custer, Gen. George Armstrong, 175, 182

"Dangerous Frolic, The" (Stephens), 50
"Dark Races of the Twentieth Century, The" (Hopkins), 163, 164
Dark Summer (Bogan), 14
"Daughter, The" (Stephens), 46
Davidson, Cathy N., 72–73n2
Davidson sisters, 228
Davis, Rebecca Harding, 109
Davis, W. W., 6
Day, Maurice, 11
Debs, Eugene V., 255
Deloria, Ella, 178, 195n12
democracy, 89, 188, 189, 198–99, 200
Democratic Party, 90, 102, 116
Demortie, Mark René, 165
Dial, The, 207
"Diamond Necklace, The" (Stephens), 50
Dickens, Charles, 55, 248, 250
Dickinson, Emily, 118
Dietz, Angel DeCora, 188
Dilke, Sir Charles, 251

"Discord in the Spheres" (*Harper's Bazar* essay), 239, 246–47
divorce, 61, 108
Dodge, Mary Mapes, 15, 253, 254, 255
domestic violence, xxx, 61, 69
domesticity, xxxiv, 45, 51, 61, 237; domestic role, 205; rhetoric of, 217
Domesticity with a Difference (Tonkovich), 216
Douglas, Ann, xxvi, 206
Douglass, Frederick, 151
Dow, James B., 209
Du Bois, W. E. B., 150, 163, 164, 254
Dupree, William, 153, 154, 156, 159, 170
Duyckinck, Evert, 209

Eadle Keahtah Toh (*The Morning Star*), 123, 141nn3–4
Eastern State Penitentiary, 129–30
Eastman, Charles Alexander, 174, 183, 186, 190
Easy Exercises in Composition (Frost), 4–5
Eckhardt, Celia Morris, 81
economic issues, 89, 102, 108
editorials, xxxiii–xxxiv, 63; in *American Indian Magazine*, 179–80; in *Free Enquirer*, 87–88, 96–98; in *Harper's Bazar*, 228, 235; in *The Jabberwock*, 8; in *Woman's Journal*, 108
editors: apprentice, xxvi; business side of publishing and, 208–19, 230–31; career, xxxii–xxxiii; controversies and, 114; as cultural authorities, xxviii–xxix, 42; editorship as bridge, xxvi–xxxii; "editresses," 25; obstacles faced by, 229; readers' letters to, xxxiv–xxxv, 61, 62, 64–69; as voice of power, 127–29; women's experience as, 36–38
education, xxvii, 4, 108, 214; African Americans and, 150–51, 152, 159, 160, 227; Native Americans and, 175, 178; race and class issues in, 14; state-funded boarding schools, 90–91; U.S. Indian policy and, 123–41
egalitarianism, xxxi, 90
eight-hour workday, 102
electoral system, 89
Eliot, George, 236, 251
Elizabeth I (queen of England), 237, 244
Elliott, R. S., 146
Elliott, Robert Browne, 152
Ely, Annie, 134
Embury, Emma, 213

Emerson, Ralph Waldo, 4, 110, 112
Emporia Gazette, 30
English language, 135, 138
"Enlightenment thinking," 4
Ethiopianism, 164, 171
Eugenie, Empress, 76
Everybody's Magazine, 173
Exman, Eugene, 230
"Explanatory Notes" (Wright), 83–84

family/fireside culture, 65, 69, 89, 99, 231
"Famous Men of the Negro Race" (Hopkins), 148–49, 153, 165
Fanny Wright: Rebel in America (Eckhardt), 81
fashion, xxv, xxxii, 60, 208; in *Harper's Bazar*, 226; opposition to, 209; promoted by male publishers, 210
Fear-Segal, Jacqueline, xxviii
femininity, 46, 53, 205, 210
feminism, xxvi, 71, 109, 146; *Harper's Bazar* and, 228, 232, 234–40; historians, 81; masked, 24; socialism and, 238; special-interest feminist magazines, 231
Fern, Fanny, 205
Fettered for Life (Blake), xxx
fiction, 45, 58
Field, David Dudley, 253
Field, Kate, xxxiii, xxxv, 248–58
Fifteenth Amendment, 101, 107, 240
Fink, Steven, xxix, xxxii
Fisk University, 146, 154
Fitch, Clyde, 251
Follin, Miriam Florence. *See* Leslie, Miriam Frank
Forerunner, The, 250
Fortune, Harper S., 147
Foster, Stephen, 100
Fourth Estate (trade publication), 23, 28, 29
Frank Leslie's Chimney Corner, 60, 64, 66, 69, 75–79
Frank Leslie's Illustrated Newspaper, 61, 62
Frank Leslie's Lady's Gazette Fashion, 73
Frank Leslie's Lady's Journal, 61
Frank Leslie's Lady's Magazine, 61
Frank Leslie's Popular Monthly, 62
Frazier, Margaret, 186, 198
Frederick Douglass's Paper, 80
Free Enquirer, xxv, xxx, 80–92, 86; confrontational voice of, xxxiv; editorial, 96–98
free love, 83, 102–3, 108
Freeman, Mary Wilkins, 230
Frémont, John C. and Jessie Benton, 253

Frentz, Edward, 11
Freund, John C., 154, 156–60
Friedan, Betty, 238
Frohman, Daniel, 251
"From a True Woman to New Woman" (Kitch), 27–28
Frost, John, 4–5
Frost, Linda, xxvii
Frothingham, O. B., 253
Frugal Housewife, The (Child), 219n3
Fuller, Margaret, xxvii, xxxiii, 80, 91, 206–7, 228
fund-raising, 21, 22, 25–26, 31, 103

Gage, Matilda Joslyn, 119
Garfield, James, 62
Garnet, Henry Highland, 165
Garrison, William Lloyd, 104, 106, 121, 160
Garvey, Ellen Gruber, xxv, xxx, 27
Gemme, Paola, 45
gender, xxxiii, 91, 226; gaze of authority and, 130; gender roles, 68, 218; white male voice of authority, 137
Gentleman from Indiana, The (Tarkington), 20
"Gentleman Publisher," 206, 207
Ghost Dance, 175, 184
Gilder, Jeannette L., 21
Gilder, Richard Watson, 253
Gilman, Caroline Howard, 207, 213
Gilman, Charlotte Perkins, 238, 250
Gilman, Elizabeth, xxxiii
Gilmer, Elizabeth M., 22, 32n12, 36–38
Girls' Latin School (Boston), 3, 6, 9, 13, 14–15, 16n1
Godey, Louis A., 208, 209, 212
Godey's Lady's Book, xxxii, 24, 49, 54, 207; circulation of, 231; fashion in, 208, 226; market priorities and, 213
"Going to School" (Brown), 12, 19
Golden Era weekly, 63
Goldsby, Gardner, 163
Goldsmith, Barbara, 102, 104
Goodale, Elaine, 186
Graff, Harvey J., 5
Graham's magazine, 41, 54
"Grapevine Telephone, The" (Field), 251
Great War. *See* World War I
Greeley, Horace, 101
Greenwood, Grace, xxxiii
Griffith, Sally Foreman, 30
Grimes, Rev. Leonard Andrew, 165
Grimké, Sarah and Angelina, 91–92

Gruber, Frederick, 6
Guardian (Boston newspaper), 146

Hafen, P. Jane, 176, 177
Hagar's Daughter: A Story of Southern Caste Prejudice (serial novel), 148, 158
Haiti, 83, 85, 91, 165
Hale, Edward Everett, 112
Hale, Sarah Josepha, xxv, xxxiv, 24, 41, 207; antifashion principles, 209, 219n5; on domesticity and authorship, 45; as founding editor of *Ladies' Magazine*, 80; on market forces, 208, 213, 214–15; market value as "lady editor," 212; separate-spheres ideology and, 215–16
Hall, Ruth, 212
Hamilton, Gail, xxxiii, 235
Hancock, John, 5
Hanson, William F., 177
Hantock, H. Irving, 11
Hap-Hazard (Field), 248
Harlan, Louis R., 150
Harper's Bazar, xxv, xxxii, xxxiii, 13, 117, 240–41; essays from, 244–47; feminism in, 235–40; as first high-fashion magazine, 225–28; Mary Booth's tenure as editor, 231–35
Harper's Magazine, 173
Harper's New Monthly Magazine, 231
Harper's Weekly, 240
Harris, W. T., 254
Harte, Bret, 109
Harvard Crimson, 6
Hawthorne, Julian, 251
Hay, John, 55
Hearst, Phoebe, 253
Hearst, William Randolph, 21, 26, 28, 253
Hertzberg, Hazel, 178, 185, 186
Hickock, Wild Bill, 21
Higginson, Thomas Wentworth, 104, 106, 108, 116–18, 227, 235
High School Course in English, The, 5–6
Hispanic Americans, 14
History of the City of New York (Booth), 236
History of Woman Suffrage (Stanton et al.), 81, 91, 99, 119
Hoagland, Joseph C., 28, 33n25
Holmes, Oliver Wendell, 254
Home Mission Monthly, The, 188
Hopkins, Pauline, xxvii, xxviii, xxxi–xxxii, 146, 157, 165–66; correspondence with Trotter, 154–55, 158–59; criticism of Booker T. Washington, 151–53, 161; editorial talents, xxxiv; as journalist, 148–49; literary career, 147–48; political activism, xxxiii
Hough, Walter, 191
Howard, Bronson, 251
Howe, Julia Ward, 24, 104, 106, 112, 114
Howells, W. D., 254
Hubbard, Henry Vincent, 13
Hubbard, Theodora Kimball, 13
Humboldt, Alexander von, 55
Hussey, Cornelia, 117
Hutton, Laurence, 251, 252
Hyde, Grant Milnor, 6

identity, xxix, xxxiii, 239, 246; assimilation and, 135; editorial authority and, 131–33; language and, 68, 70; names, 78; Native American children and, 127–28; race and, 153; split identity of "lady editor," 210, 215
"imagined community," 133, 140
immigrants, 63, 255
"In School Days" (Whittier), 109
Independent, 101
Indian boarding schools, 175, 176
"Indian Gifts to Civilized Man" (Zitkala-Ša), 187
Indian Helper, The, xxxiv, 123–41, 144–45
"Indian Mother's Song, The" (Longfellow), 47
Indian Sentinel, 187
Indianapolis Sentinel, 20, 21
"Indian's Awakening, The" (Zitkala-Ša), 182–83
infanticide, 108
Irving, Henry, 251
Italy, 91, 96

Jabberwock, The, xxvi, xxvii, xxxiii, 3–4, 14–16; founding and editing of, 7–14; history of student writing and, 4–6; writings from, 15–16, 19
Jackson, Helen Hunt, 109, 118
James, Henry, 232, 248
James I (king of England), 189, 200
Jefferson, Thomas, 83
Jeffersonian weekly, 42
Jennings, Robert, 87
Jewish Women's League, 261
Johnson, Abby Arthur, 148
Johnson, Robert Underwood, 255–56
Johnson, Ronald Maberry, 148
Johnson, Walter Alexander, 147

Jordan, Elizabeth, 22, 32n11
Jo's Boy's (Alcott), 109
journalism, 6, 80; African American, 148–49; appeal to reason in, 85; fundraising and, 21; historians of, 27, 30
"Journalism in the High School" (Hyde), 6
Juergens, George, 28
Juvenile Miscellany (Child, ed.), 80, 207
juvenilia, 7, 17n5

Kaestle, Carl, 14
Kate Field's Washington, xxxv, 248–58, 261–63
Kelley, Abby, 92, 100
Kelley, Mary, 205–6
Kennedy, Charles, 22, 23
Kerr, Andrea, 102, 104
Kirkland, Caroline, 207, 209–12, 215
Kitch, Carolyn, 27
Knightstown Sun (Indiana newspaper), 27
knowledge, power and, 129, 141n14
Kowacura, Stiya, 136

labor struggles, 108
Ladies' Companion, The, 41, 54, 55, 212
"Ladies' Conversazione" (column), 60–72
Ladies' Home Journal, The, 27, 71, 231
Ladies' Magazine, 41, 45–46, 58, 207; founding of, 80; Hale as editor of, 208; inaugural issue (1828), 214–15, 222–24; ownership changes, 209
lady, role of, 211–12, 215
Lady Byron Vindicated (Stowe), 114
Lafayette, Marquis de, 83
Lakota language, 123
Landor, Walter Savage, 248, 250
Landscape Architecture (journal), 13
Langston, John Mercer, 152
language, 68, 70
Larcom, Lucy, 109
Laurie, Ann (pseudonym), 25–26
Lawless, Greg, 6
Lawrence, Emma, 113
"Laws in Relation to the Property Rights of Married Women in Massachusetts" (Stone), 112
Lectures on Knowledge (Wright), 87–88
Leslie, Frank, 60, 62, 73n6
Leslie, Miriam Frank, xxvii, xxxiv, 60–72
"Letter to the Chiefs and Headmen of the Tribes" (Zitkala-Ša), 189–90
letter writing, in nineteenth century, 5
liberalism, 86, 112

librarians, 13
Life magazine, 13
Lincoln, Abraham, 55, 61, 227
Lind, Jenny, 245
literary careers, xxvi, 147–48
Literary Journal (student newspaper), 5
literature, 22, 55, 185, 194n8, 210
Livermore, Mary, 102–3, 104, 114
Locke, John, 4
Longfellow, Henry Wadsworth, 47, 53, 211
Louisa May Alcott: From Blood and Thunder to Hearth and Home (Stern), 109
love stories, 210
Lowell, James Russell, 254
Lyons, Mary, 100

Madison, James, 83
magazines, xxv, 214; commerce and, 27, 213–14; feminist, 231; as gift commodity, 215–16; high fashion, 225, 226, 229
Malaeska (Stephens), 41, 54
male personas, of women editors, xxviii, 62–63, 68–70, 125–28, 134–35
Man Without a Country, The (Hale), 112
Manifest Manners (Vizenor), 177
Mann, Horace, 4
Mann, Mary Peabody, 112
marriage, 31n2, 61, 62, 108, 248; criticism of, 81, 84, 88–89; fidelity in, 99; readers' comments on, 66; Stone's views on, 115–16
Martin, Lawrence, 219n5
"Mary Derwent" (Stephens), 54
Mary of Guise, 237, 244
masculine domains, 51
masculinity, 135
masquerade, xxvi, 206
Massachusetts Anti-Slavery Society (MASS), 100
Mather, Cotton, 5
Matthews, Brander, 254
May, Samuel Joseph, 112
McClure, S. S., 31n3
McClure's magazine, 30
McCulloch, Hugh, 252
McGee, W. J., 257
McKenzie, Fayette A., 178
men: editorial appeal to, 214–15; "gentleman publisher," 206; male authority, 80, 210; male readers, 68–69; politicians and woman's suffrage, 116; as primary consumers of women's magazines,

215–16; representation of, 66; *Woman's Journal* and, 105
"Men of Vision" (Hopkins), 164, 165
Mercer, Capt. William A., 140
Meriam Report (1928), 175
middle-class culture, 65, 66
"Miggles: Episode on a California Stage Ride" (Harte), 109
Mill, John Stuart, 109
Millville School (Pennsylvania), 133
Milwaukee Journal, 26, 29–30
Miner, Harriet, 108
Mrs. Stephens' New Monthly, 54
Mitchell, Maria, 108
"Modern Girl," 232
modernity, 226, 232, 234, 241
Monroe, James, 83
Montezuma, Carlos, 174, 179, 183, 191
Montgomery, Maud, 20–21, 26
Monument (periodical), 24
Moore, Fred R., 154, 161–63, 165
moral guidance, 42, 51
Mormonism, 175, 248
Morton, Levi P., 253
motherhood, 46–47, 53
Mott, Lucretia, 92, 234
Moulton, Louise Chandler, 109
Mount Holyoke Female Seminary, 99–100
"Muffled Knocker, The" (Sigourney), 47
Mugwumps, 116, 254
Mussey, Mabel Hay Barrows, 7, 11, 17n6
"My Heart and I" (E. B. Browning), 109
"My Natal Bowers" (Stephens), 44

Nashoba plantation (Tennessee), 83–84, 85, 91
Nashville American (newspaper), 29, 36–38
Nation, The, 3, 11
National Anti-Slavery Standard, 207
National Council of American Indians, 192
National Endowment for the Arts, 14
National Negro Business League, 161
National Union Catalogue, 13
National Woman Suffrage Association (NWSA), 103, 107, 108
Native American Church, 174, 175
Native Americans, xxix, xxxi, 254; armed conflict with U.S. government, 175; assimilation and, 135, 173, 174, 176, 178–81; Carlisle School and, 123–41; Christianity and, 130–31, 139; educational opportunities and, 14; ethnocentric representations of, xxxiv; issues in Native studies, 173–74;

Native intellectuals, 174–76, 193; spiritual practices of, 190–91; U.S. citizenship and, 123, 175, 178, 184, 190, 199; in World War I, 188, 198
"Natives of Alaska" (Field), 250
nativist movement, 255
Neal, John, 43–44, 47, 53, 55
New Century (newspaper), 25
New England, 42, 48
New England Woman Suffrage Association (NEWSA), 103, 109, 121
New Era Magazine, 164–65
New Harmony colony, 83
New-Harmony Gazette, 80, 84–86, 86, 93n15
New Orleans Daily Picayune, 248, 253
New Orleans States (newspaper), 23
"New Woman," 31, 107, 232
New York Anti-Slavery Society, 227
New York City, 53, 54–55, 86, 159, 162–63, 225
New-York Commercial Advertiser, 89
New York Correspondent (newspaper), 85
New York Herald, 61, 256
New York Mercury (weekly), 63
"New York Subway, The" (Hopkins), 163
New York Tribune, 80, 101, 248, 253, 256
New York World (newspaper), 28
New Yorker, The, 14
newspapers, xxv, 92; Progressivist politics and, 30; "society pages," 25; student, 3; women's editions, 20–34, 32n11
Nineteenth Amendment, 118
normal schools, 14
"November Afternoon, A" (Davis), 109

Oakes-Smith, Elizabeth, 228
Oberlin Collegiate Institute, 99
Of One Blood. Or, The Hidden Self (Hopkins serial novel), 148
"Of One Blood" (Hopkins), 171
ohunkakan, 173, 193n1
Okker, Patricia, 24, 45, 62, 63, 216
"Oklahoma's Poor Rich Indians" (Zitkala-Ša, co-author), 192
Old Indian Legends (Zitkala-Ša), 173, 176, 188, 193n1
Olmsted, Frederick Law, Sr. and Jr., 13
"Only a Piece of Ice" (Brown), 12
Orange Chronicle (N.J. newspaper), 29
Osgood, Frances, 213
Oskison, John M., 179, 198
"Our Office" (Stone), 112–13, 121–22

Overland Monthly, 257
Owen, Robert Dale, 80–81, 82, 86, 87, 238; critique of marriage, 88; New Harmony and, 83; Working Men's Party and, 90
"Owls, The" (Wright), 87, 98

Packard, Clarissa, 49
Paine, Albert Bigelow, 251
panopticon, 129
Parker, Arthur C., 178–81, 183, 184; editorial conflicts with Zitkala-Ša, 193; ousted as editor of *American Indian Magazine*, 186; pan-Indian efforts and, 187
"Passing Wish, A" (Cary), 109
Passion Flower, 49
patriarchy, 135, 220n24, 234
Patton, Abby Hutchinson, 104, 114, 116
Pawnee Manual Labor School, 133
Peabody, Elizabeth Palmer, 112, 206
Peacock, David, 61
Pearl (Boston journal), 48, 49
Pearson, Edmund, 55
periodicals, xxv, xxvii, 64
Pestalozzi, Johann Heinrich, 4
Peterson, Charles J., 54, 56
Peterson's Magazine, xxxii, 41, 54, 226
peyote, 173, 175, 181–82, 184
Philadelphia Press, 250
philanthropy, 20, 21
Phillips, Wendell, 254
"Physiology of Political Women, The" (*Harper's Bazar* essay), 237, 244–45
Pinchot, Gifford, 251
Plessy v. Ferguson, 150
Pocahontas, 189, 200
Poe, Edgar Allan, 55, 213
poetry, 14, 44, 45, 58
"Polish Boy, The" (Stephens), 44
politics, 29, 237, 244–45, 255
polygamy, 248, 250, 255
Pompadour, Madame de, 237, 244
Porter, Maria S., 112, 119
Portland Advertiser (newspaper), 41, 45
Portland Magazine, xxvii, xxxiv, 41–59, 207; business side of publishing and, 216–18; as counterpart to *Ladies' Magazine*, 46; decline of, 52; inaugural issue (1834), 58–59, 216; reader submissions to, 49–50
Portland, Maine, 43, 46, 47, 53, 56
Portland Sketchbook anthology, 53–54
Portrait of a Lady, The (James), 248
Post, Israel, 209, 212
postal regulations, 214

Powhatan, xxxiv, 189, 200–201
Pratt, Capt. Richard Henry, 127, 134, 139–40, 145, 183; campaign against peyote, 173, 188; Carlisle School's mission and, 123
Pratt, Mason, 123
Pray, Isaac C., Jr., 48, 49
presidential elections, 116–17
Primer of Facts, A (Hopkins), 164, 165
private sphere, 61, 66
Private Women, Public Stage (Kelley), 206
professionalization, xxvi, 206
Progressivism, 30
property rights, 235
Protestantism, 87, 97, 261
Provincial Freeman, 80
Pryse, Marjorie, 230
pseudonyms, 136, 148
public citizen, role of, 7, 10
public opinion, xxx, 9–10
public schools, 5, 14
public sphere, 66–67, 72, 211, 212, 215, 216. See also separate-spheres ideology
publicity, 101
Publishers' Row, 60
publishing industry, xxix–xxx, xxxii, 208–19
Pueblo Indians, 136–37, 192
Puerto Rico, 165
Pulitzer, Joseph, 28
Purvis, William, 108

Quakers, 129, 133, 134
Quarterly Journal of the Society of American Indians, 174, 181

race issues, xxx, xxxi, 71, 81, 146; audience and, xxxiv–xxxv; definition of races, 149; journalism and, 158; paradox of, 164; race-mixing, 83–84; suffrage and, 101; U.S. Indian policy, 123, 127, 179–81. See also African Americans; Native Americans; whites
racism, xxviii, xxxiv, 102, 240
Radcliffe Quarterly, 13
Radical Club of Boston, 249
reader submissions, 49–50
rebellion, hidden, 138
Recollections of a Housekeeper (Packard), 49
Reconstruction period, 101, 148, 171
Red Man, The (Carlisle School publication), 139, 140
"Red Man's America, The" (Zitkala-Ša), 182

"Regret" (Thaxter), 109
religion, 81, 82, 86–87, 96–98, 234
Repository of Religion and Literature and of Science and the Arts, xxxi
Republican Party, 116, 192
reservation system, Native Americans and, 175, 185
Revolution, The (newspaper), 101, 102, 107
revolutions, European, 91
Rhodes, Wilma R., 199
Rinehart, Mary Roberts (Running Eagle), 191
Rodier, Katharine, xxx
Rolfe, John, 189
"Romance and Reality" (Stephens), 44
romanticism, 4, 218
Roosevelt, Franklin D., 192
Roosevelt, Theodore, 150, 158, 160, 251
Rose, Ernestine, 234
Rose-Bud magazine, 207, 213
Rousseau, Jean Jacques, 4
Royal Baking Powder, 26–27, 28–31, 33nn25–26
Ruskin, John, 250
Ruth Hall (Fern), 205–6

St. Mark's School (Southborough, Mass.), 5
St. Nicholas magazine, 15, 17n7
Sams, Myrta Eddleman, xxxi
San Francisco Examiner, 21, 25–26, 32n5, 253
Sand, George, 108
sanitary fair newspapers, 24–25
Sarett, Lew, 191
Schultz, Lucille M., xxvi
science, 55
Scott, James C., 138
Scribblers (writers' group), 11
Sedgwick, Catharine Maria, 206
segregation, 150, 153
Seneca Falls conference, 92
sentimental discourse, 64
separate-spheres ideology, xxxii, 66, 72–73n2, 99, 206; audience (readers) and, 215–16; commercial imperatives and, 210; protection of women and, 211; role of lady and, 212, 215, 218–19; subversion of, 217; women editors and, 207
Shadrach, J. Shirley (pseudonym), 148, 166n4
Sherman, William Tecumseh, 253
Sherwood, Helen (fictional character), 20, 21

Shirley, Anne (fictional character), 20, 21, 26
Sigourney, Lydia, 47, 213, 228
Silko, Leslie Marmon, 137
Simmons, Gertrude. *See* Zitkala-Ša (Red Bird)
Simmons, Roscoe Conkling, 161–62
Sitting Bull, 175, 186, 194n3
slavery, xxix, xxx, 83, 85, 148. *See also* abolitionist movement
Sleeping Fury (Bogan), 14
Sloan, Thomas, 191, 192
Smith, Jeanne, 176
Smith, John, 189, 200–201
Smith-Rosenberg, Carroll, 134
Snowdon, William, 212–13
social class, xxx, xxxi, 82, 88, 91, 241n4; "Boston's Smart Set," 147; fashion and, 226; middle-class family values, 65, 66; student writing and, 5
social reform, 129, 131
socialism, 82
"Society and the Philosopher" (Gilman), 250
Society of American Indians (S.A.I.), 173, 177, 181, 184–86, 193; conferences, 190, 191, 198; Native intellectuals in, 174; official beginning of (1911), 178
"society pages," 25
Soga, A. Kirkland, 171–72
South Africa, xxxiv–xxxv, 171–72
Southern Rose magazine, 207
Spectator, The, 237, 244
Spofford, Harriet, 226, 227, 228, 229, 240
Springfield Republican (newspaper), 24
Springfield Union (newspaper), 24
Squier, Ephraim George, 61
Standing Bear, Luther, 177–78
Stanford, Leland, 255
Stanton, Elizabeth Cady, 81, 99, 101, 119; criticism of *Woman's Journal*, 108; as "female politician," 234; *Kate Field's Washington* and, 252; National Woman Suffrage Association and, 103; *The Revolution* and, 101–2
Stedman, E. C., 248, 253, 254, 256
Stephens, Ann S., xxvii, xxviii, 207; as authority, 42, 44, 48, 50; on business side of publishing, 216–18; early life, 42–43; editorials and, xxxiv; life after *Portland Magazine*, 53–56; motherhood theme and, 46–47, 53; in New York, 54–56; *Portland Magazine* editorship, 41–59, 216

Stephens, Edward, 43, 54, 55
stereotypes, 27–28, 205
Stern, Madeleine B., 70, 72n1, 109
Stiya: A Carlisle Indian Girl at Home ("Embe"), 136–37
Stoddard, Charles Warren, 251
Stone, Lucy, xxix, xxx, 92; critics of, 114–16; letters and memoirs of, 119; *Woman's Journal* and, 99–122, 113
"Story of a Peach Tree" ("Man-in-the-Bandstand"), 144–45
"Story of an Old Young Man" (Moulton), 109
Stowe, Harriet Beecher, 45, 114
student newspapers, 3
subscriptions, 213–14
suffrage, xxx, 67, 101, 116; African American men and, 150, 162, 240; fashion magazines and, 227; "female politicians" and, 234; Leslie Bureau of Suffrage Education, 71–72; news items about, 109; Nineteenth Amendment (1920), 118; state laws and, 249–50; women of color and, 165
Sumner, Charles, 227
Sun Dance Opera, The (Hanson and Zitkala-Ša), 177
Supreme Court decisions, 150
surveillance, 129, 130
Susag, Dorothea, 176
Sweet, Winifred, 25
Swisshelm, Jane, 92

Tarbell, Ida, 31
Tarkington, Booth, 20–21, 31–32n3
Tarkington, Haute, 21, 31–32n3
Tate, Claudia, 148
Taylor, Bayard, 211, 212
Taylor, C. H. J., 254
teachers, 64–65, 133–34
technology, 237–38
Ten Days in Spain (Field), 248
Tennyson, Alfred, Lord, 250
Terhune, Mary Virginia, 206
Terrell, Judge Robert, 151
Thackeray, William M., 55
Thaxter, Celia, 109
Thompson, E. P., 138
Through the Looking Glass (Carroll), 3, 15–16
Tilton, Elizabeth, 116
Tilton, Theodore, 101, 103, 116
Tilton-Beecher scandal, xxx, 115–16
"To My Mother" (Stephens), 46

Tompkins, Jane, 42
Tonkovich, Nicole, 216
"Topsy Templeton" (Hopkins), 164
Toussaint L'Ouverture, 151
trade publications, 23–24, 28
"Tradesman's Daughter, The" (Stephens), 42
Train, George F., 102
Treadwell, Viola, 66, 67
Tribal Secrets: Recovering American Indian Intellectual Traditions (Warrior), 174
Trotter, William Monroe, 146, 154, 158
True Womanhood, ideal of, 45, 65, 107, 233
Tsinah, Lucy, 136
Tuskegee Institute (Alabama), 149–50, 158; Booker T. Washington and, 152
Twain, Mark, 9, 250
Twin Territories: The Indian Magazine of Oklahoma, xxxi

Uncle Sam's Boys Smash the Germans (Hantock), 11
Uncle Zeb and His Friends (Frentz), 11
"Unexpected, The" (Gilman), 250
Union Magazine, 207, 209, 211, 212
Unitarians, 112
United States: Indian policy, 127, 132–33; reform movements in, 80, 82; slavery in, 83; transience in, 63
Up from Slavery (Washington), 150
utopianism, 80, 82, 83, 86

Views of Society and Manners in America (Wright), 82
Vindex, The (student newspaper), 5
"Visiting Cards" (Stephens), 217–18
Vizenor, Gerald, 177–78
Voice of the Negro, The, 162–64
voyeurism, 128, 130

Waggaman, John F., 252
Wallace, Walter W., 147, 153, 164
Warner, Charles Dudley, 253
Warner, Susan, 206
Warrick-Fuller, Meta, 164
Warrior, Robert Allen, 174
Washington Bee (newspaper), xxxi
Washington, Booker T., 146, 147, 154; *Colored American Magazine* and, 155, 156–65, 159–61; Tuskegee Institute and, 149–50, 152
Washington, Margaret Murray, 161
Watkins, Jesse W., 147, 153, 162, 170

"Wealth and Money" series (Wright), 91
Weaver, Jace, 185
"Welding of the Link, The" (Goldsby), 163
Wells-Barnett, Ida B., 31, 151
West, William O., 153, 170
Wheeler-Howard/Indian Reorganization Act (1934), 176, 194n6
Whig Party, 90
Whipple, Charles K., 109
White, William Allen, 30, 33n24
whites, xxxiv, 14, 150, 154–60, 162. *See also* race issues
Whiting, Lilian, 249
Whittier, John Greenleaf, 109
Wild West shows, 175, 177, 194–95n10
Wilde, Oscar, 62
Wilde, Willie, 62
Wildman, Rounseville, 257–58
Willard, William, 192
Willis, Nathaniel Parker, 53
Wilshire, Gaylord, 251
Wilson, Butler R., 158
Wilson, Edith Bolling Galt, 189, 195n19, 200
Wilson, Woodrow, 189
Wingate, Charles, 227, 229, 231
Winona: A Tale of Negro Life in the South and Southwest (serial novel), 148
Winterbotham, Ann Sophia. *See* Stephens, Ann S.
Winterbotham, John, 43
Wissler, Clark, 191
Wollstonecraft, Mary, 81
Womack, Craig, 176, 177
Woman Citizen (weekly), 72
"woman question," 101
Woman's Era, xxxi
Woman's Journal, The, xxix, 99, 105–19, 229, 253; controversial topics in, xxx; "Our Office," xxxiv, 121–22
Woman's Suffrage Tracts, 109
"Woman's Work" (*Harper's Bazar* essay), 238–39
women: African American, 163, 262–63; assertiveness versus modesty, xxxiv; changing subjectivities of, 232; of cultural elite, 42; education of, 214, 226; European compared with American, 236; "fallen," 80; female politicians, 237, 244; feminine homogeneity, 64; innocence of, 71; jobs and pay of, 236; lesbian relationships, 133–34; literary aspirations of, 22, 45; male authority challenged by, 80; as mothers, 46–47; Native American, 175, 182, 188; private sphere ideology and, 61; productive work and, 65; property rights, 235; public speaking by, 86; in public sphere, 66–67, 72; roles in society, xxv; self-effacing rhetoric and, 50; social progress and, 81; subjectivities of, 233; white middle-class, 61, 101; working-class, 230, 234, 236–37, 240; writing and domestic duties, 45
Women and Economics (Gilman), 238
"Women and Men" (Higginson), 235
"Women and the Centennials" (*Harper's Bazar* essay), 239
"Women and Their Work" (*Harper's Bazar* essay), 236–37
"Women of Genius" (Stephens), 55
women's colleges, 133
women's history, 119
women's rights, xxix, xxx, xxxii, 226, 227–28
Woodhull & Claflin's Weekly, xxx, 114
Woodhull, Victoria, 115–16
Working Men's Party, 89–90, 91
"Working Together" (*Harper's Bazar* essay), 236
World War I, 15, 180, 186–87, 189, 198
Wounded Knee massacre, 174, 175
Wright, Frances, xxv, xxviii, xxx–xxxi, xxxiii, 80–92

Yankee weekly, 44
Yellow Robe, Chauncey, 177
Yosemite National Park, 255–56
Young, Rose, 72

Zakrzewka, Marie E., 229
Zboray, Ronald, 63
Zitkala-Ša (Red Bird), xxix, xxxi; *American Indian Magazine* and, 173–95, 178–92; at Carlisle Indian School, 133, 175; confrontational voice of, xxxiv; diasporic role of, xxxii; as lobbyist for Indian cause, 192–93; opposition to peyote, 173, 181–82, 184; reader audience and, xxxii; U.S. Indian policy and, 176–78
"Zitkala-Ša: Sentimentality and Sovereignty" (Hafen), 176
Zuckerman, Mary Ellen, 235